# Studies in Contemporary Economics

Niklaus Blattner · Hans Genberg
Alexander Swoboda (Eds.)

# Banking in Switzerland

With 36 Figures and 40 Tables

Physica-Verlag
A Springer-Verlag Company

Professor Dr. Niklaus Blattner
Labour and Industrial Economics Research Unit (LIU)
Missionsstr. 64 A
CH-4055 Basel, Switzerland

Professor Dr. Hans Genberg
International Centre for Monetary and Banking Studies (ICMB)
11 A Avenue de la Paix
CH-1211 Geneva 21, Switzerland

Professor Dr. Alexander Swoboda
Graduate Institute of International Studies (IUHEI)
132 Rue de Lausanne
CH-1211 Geneva 21, Switzerland

ISBN 978-3-7908-0735-6 ISBN 978-3-642-51516-3 (eBook)
DOI 10.1007/978-3-642-51516-3

Die Deutsche Bibliothek - CIP-Einheitsaufnahme
Banking in Switzerland : with 40 tables / Niklaus Blattner ... (Eds.). -
Heidelberg : Physica-Verl., 1993
(Studies in contemporary economics)

NE: Blattner, Niklaus [Hrsg.]



88/7130-543210 - Printed on acid-free paper

## Preface

**Oliver Landmann**

Nobody needs to be convinced of the importance of banking for the Swiss economy. The financial sector grew well above average in the past decade and now accounts for almost 10 % of GDP. Compared to the economy-wide average, it creates more than double as much value added per employee and it is a major contributor to Swiss export revenues. But this is no cause for complacency. The industry is subject to rapid change as the competitive climate has become rougher nationally and internationally. Major structural weaknesses have come to the surface which raise serious questions about the extent of the required structural adjustments.

Thus, banking was an ideal candidate for a major case study in the framework of the National Research Programme No. 28 which is devoted to Switzerland's external economic challenges. The programme was commissioned by the Swiss government and is carried out by the Swiss National Science Foundation. The research project on the financial sector was directed by Professors Niklaus Blattner, Hans Genberg and Alexander Swoboda who assembled a team of research economists from the Graduate Institute of International Studies, the International Centre for Monetary and Banking Studies (both at Geneva) and the Labour and Industrial Economics Research Unit at the University of Basel. This joint research effort has yielded an impressive crop of descriptive data, analytical insights and policy-oriented conclusions. First presented at two research conferences in 1991 and 1992, this material is now collected in two books of which the present volume is the second. The first was Competitiveness in Banking, edited by the same authors.

The two volumes cover a broad range of issues, but they are nevertheless held together by the unifying analytical approach of industrial economics. They shed much light on the determinants of the performance of banks, market shares, trade in financial services and locational decisions. Also, they reveal an amazing variation in performance and a substantial potential for efficiency gains on the firm-level. Interestingly, the financial sector seems to be split by much the same dichotomy that an earlier NFP 28 study highlighted for the Swiss economy as a whole (Borner et al. 1990):

An efficient and fiercely competitive sector, engaged in global competition, coexists with (and supports) a bloated and much less efficient domestic sector which is largely shielded from foreign competition. However, the banks may be well ahead of the rest of the economy in streamlining their traditionally 'non-tradeable' activities, i.e. essentially their retail banking operations. The main driving force is the increasing competitive pressure, in particular from abroad, and the concomitant erosion of market segmentation and local monopoly power (see Genberg et al. 1992). The restructuring process has already caused some turmoil and pain in the industry, and it is far from over. Sooner or later, other hitherto sheltered sectors of the Swiss economy will have to undergo similar restructuring.

A number of conclusions with respect to the role of competitive strategies and public policies emerge from this research. They are succinctly summarized in Part V of the present volume. As the editors point out in their introduction, though, it should be borne in mind that all the results are based on a research methodology which has not been extensively applied to the banking sector before. More work along these lines is clearly desirable, especially as a richer data base becomes available with the passing of time. Whatever further insights such future work will bring, the twin volumes of Competitiveness in Banking and Banking in Switzerland represent a major step forward in bringing industrial economics to bear on financial sector issues.

**Literature**

Borner, S., Brunetti, A., and Straubhaar, Th. (1990), Schweiz AG - vom Sonderfall zum Sanierungsfall?, NZZ-Verlag, Zurich.

Genberg, H., Helbling, Th., and Neftci, S. (1992), "Monopoly Power in Swiss Financial Markets", in: Blattner, N., Genberg, H., Swoboda, A. (eds.), Competitiveness in Banking, Physica-Verlag, Heidelberg.

## Table of Contents

# Introduction

**Niklaus Blattner, Hans Genberg, Alexander Swoboda**

The present volume on **Banking in Switzerland** contains papers produced in the framework of a research project carrying the title 'The Swiss Financial Sector at the Turn of the Century'[1]. As such they complement and follow up on those that were published in **Competitiveness in Banking** last year (Physica-Verlag, Studies in Contemporary Economics, 1992).

Compared with the earlier one, the present volume shows three specific characteristics: First, the analysis of micro data stands in the centre of many of the investigations. As the issue of 'competitiveness' is closely linked to the performance, the costs, and the efficiency of the production of financial services by individual banking firms, it was natural to extend our research in this direction. Second, since we identified 'attractiveness' as the core notion when discussing the competitiveness of international financial centres, we decided to search for a more detailed explanation of the presence of foreign financial institutions in Switzerland. Third, in many ways results pointed to the importance of the off-balance sheet business when explaining the banks' performance. Hence, we found it useful to incorporate the effects of foreign competition on the Swiss stock markets into our research. There is no question that the understanding of the attractiveness of a financial centre like Switzerland, characterised by universal banking, would be grossly incomplete without a study of the efficiency of its stock markets.

The papers and comments related to these topics are presented in Parts I - III of the volume which in addition contains a study on the rôle of Swiss banks in the international bond market (Part IV) and by a paper which attempts to synthesise the findings from the entire research project (Part V). We now turn to a brief description of the content of these parts.

---

1 The papers were presented at a conference which was held in Geneva in May 1992. They were subsequently revised in light of remarks made by the conference participants. This is also the procedure followed for the formal comments which are included in the volume.

**Part I: Performance, Costs and Efficiency of Banking in Switzerland**, contains three papers. Matthias Wirth from the Swiss Bankers Association (SBA) discusses the conceptual problems in measuring the performance of individual banks, and applies different indicators to the empirical description of the banks' performance in the period of 1987 - 1991. The second paper is devoted to an explanation of the performance of banks over the same period. This study was carried out by Urs Haegler and Matthias Jeger, who, at the time of the project, were members of the Labour and Industrial Economics Research Unit (LIU) at the University of Basel. The third paper was written by George Sheldon from the LIU, together with Urs Haegler, and consists of an application of modern production economics (Data Envelopment Analysis, DEA) to the data of almost the totality of banks incorporated in Switzerland. Here, the aim was the identification of economies of scale and scope and of cost and allocative inefficiencies in Swiss banking. The papers in Part I are particularly influenced by the paradigm of industrial economics and show clearly its merits for the analysis of the financial services industry.

**Part II: The Attractiveness of Switzerland for Foreign Banks**, contains a paper by Thomas Helbling from the International Centre for Monetary and Banking Studies (ICMB) and the Graduate Institute for International Studies in Geneva. He extends work presented in the previous volume with the aim to provide an explanation of the presence of foreign financial intermediaries in Switzerland. This is especially welcome because foreign banks and finance companies count among the most dynamic elements in the Swiss financial centre.

**Part III: The Swiss Stock Markets**, contains the second contribution by Thomas Helbling. Here he discusses theoretically and empirically the effects of foreign competition on the efficiency of Swiss stock markets. This is a topic of great practical relevance, since these markets everywhere are increasingly facing tremendous pressure from international competition.

In **Part IV: The International Market for Bank Deposits and Bonds**, Ulrich Camen from the ICMB offers a sequel to his contribution in the volume on 'Competitiveness in Banking'. There he studied the evolution of the share of Swiss banks in the international market for non-bank deposits. This time he focuses his analysis on the international bond markets.

In **Part V: The Swiss Financial Sector at the Turn of the Century**, the volume is concluded with a paper which summarises the entire research project on 'The Swiss Financial Sector at the Turn of the Century', and which proposes some policy considerations. This paper was written by Niklaus Blattner from the LIU, and by Hans Genberg and Alexander Swoboda, both from the ICMB.

Together with those contained in 'Competitiveness in Banking', the papers included here represent an extensive investigation of the Swiss Financial Sector. Topics such as the attractiveness of financial centres, the performance of banks, the performance of securities markets, and the evaluation of the impact of regulation have been investigated in detail, and significant conclusions have been established in each case. At the level of methodology, the studies show that the application of theoretical and empirical techniques of industrial economics to banking, stock trading, and to international capital markets is both feasible and fruitful.

The fact that this volume is presented under the heading of **'Banking in Switzerland'** does not mean that it is of relevance for a Swiss audience only. Not only is Switzerland an interesting and important case in and of itself, but the problems encountered and the solutions found in our work might also prove stimulating for those concentrating their efforts on the study of other international financial centres.

We finally again wish to extend our thanks to the Swiss National Science Foundation, which contributed the required financial means, and to Professor Oliver Landmann, the executive director of the National Research Programme No. 28, who continued to support us intellectually and pratically throughout the project.

# Part I: Performance, Costs and Efficiency of Banking in Switzerland

**Measuring the Performance of Banks: Conceptual Problems and Results for Switzerland (1987 - 1991)**

**Matthias Wirth**

## 1. Introduction

In a market economy the continued success of an enterprise hinges on its performance. Measuring performance is therefore a matter of central concern to both management and investors (market for corporate control). Consequently analysts are also interested in performance. The approach followed in studies of industrial economic organization involves a theoretical elucidation of performance and its empirical verification.

The present article has been written from the analytical viewpoint. Its aim was an analysis of various performance indicators and their application to the data of banks in Switzerland for the period 1987 - 1990. This will in the first place set the scene for the subsequent attempts to explain performance in terms of industrial economics (Haegler, Jeger, 1992). Secondly, the appraisals will permit former ad hoc comparisons of performance to be extended over time and also to cover various banks and banking groups in a manner not previously available for Switzerland.

In this study, we are interested in performance in terms of the ability of a firm to maximise the value of the outputs over the inputs it uses. To asses performance profitability ratios are mostly used, especially return on equity (ROE) and return on assets (ROA). Central to another concept is the notion of all the incomes generated in the banking process - what is called the value added. In comparing banking institutions the notion of value added per employee can be used.

Recently there has been a further development in the measurement of performance: the added value concept, as it is called. This defines the performance of firm by the gain accruing to the economy as a whole from the input of the production factors in the business in question. The concept has hitherto been applied to industrial and commercial firms but not to financial enterprises such as banks and insurance companies.

In this paper we shall proceed as follows: After a short discussion of the given data, various approaches to the measurement of performance which are commonplaces in the literature will be described and applied to the Swiss banks. After a critical assessment of the traditional indicators we shall turn our attention to the added-value concept. We shall discuss the possibilities of applying it to the banking sector and determine the results for banks in Switzerland. We shall compare the various indicators and attempt to use the results obtained as a basis for general statements on the performance of banks in Switzerland.

## 2. Data

The Swiss banking system embraces at about 600 banks and financial institutions. The Swiss National Bank (SNB) divides them into eight groups. In the publication "Das schweizerische Bankwesen im Jahre..." the SNB publishes detailed annual figures on the individual banking groups but not on the individual institutions.

The data utilized in this paper refer to the individual data of the institutions in the groups comprising Cantonal banks, Big banks, Regional and Savings banks and Other banks supplied by the Swiss National Bank. Omission is made of the groups Credit Co-operatives and Raiffeisen banks (for which data is available only on the two federations but not on the individual institutions), finance companies, branches of foreign banks and private bank. The latter are omitted because their data are not generally accessible. **Table 1** in the appendix lists the number of institutes divided into banking groups and for the years 1987 to 1991. These are published annual figures, specifically details of the balance sheet and the profit and loss account (presented so as to comply with the requirements of the Banking law) and also data on staff size for the years 1987 to 1991.

## 3. Traditional ratios for the measurement of performance

### 3.1. Return on equity, return on assets and productivity

Performance is usually measured by reference to profitability ratios. This means that an enterprise is successful if the ratio of the profit to the amount of capital employed (total capital or balance sheet total, or equity capital) is as high as possible. In other words: the performance of a bank is measured by the income remaining after deduction of all expenditures except indemnification for the equity capital at the institution's disposal. In the market economy return on capital has the function of guiding the allocation of resources (Blattner, Maurer and Weber, 1987).

Profit can also be defined in other terms: profit before deduction of value adjustments and income tax (net income), profit before tax, cash flow and profit after tax are some commonly used definitions.

Since not all banks in Switzerland are on an equal tax footing (Cantonal banks) 'profit before tax' is more appropriate than 'profit after tax' for comparing banks.

Profitability ratios can be determined for Swiss banks on the basis of the available data as follows:

**Return on assets, ROA**

$$\text{ROA} = \frac{\text{Net profit (- Net loss) + Income taxes}}{\text{Balance sheet total}}$$

**Return on equity, ROE**

$$\text{ROE} = \frac{\text{Net profit (- Net loss) + Income taxes}}{\text{Equity}}$$

Equity = Capital
+ Reserves

To complement these ratios, and more particularly to assess performance in terms of the overall economy, firstly of a sector and then of individual undertakings, we quite commonly use the concept of value added and, based thereon, productivity (cf. Swiss Federal office of statistics, 1987 and 1988, for the concept of value added accountancy for Switzerland, also Beier, 1990, for the application of the concept in banking).

The value added represents, on the one hand, the output of an enterprise less expenditure on goods and services purchased from other firms and consumed in creating the product. On the other hand it can be defined as the sum total of the incomes generated in the firm's production process (profit, wages, rents, leasing charges, taxes). A distinction must be made between gross value added and net value added.

The value added of the banks can be defined as follows:

| | | |
|---|---|---|
| **Gross value added** | = | **Net interest income** |
| | + | **Non-interest income (net)** |
| | - | **Purchased inputs** |

| | | |
|---|---|---|
| **Net value added** | = | **Gross value added** |
| | - | **Depreciations and provisions** |

Using the value added concept, the measurement of performance is not therefore restricted to profit, i.e. to the incomes of the investors (distributed profit) and to the incomes retained within the enterprise (retained profit). The criterion for measuring the performance of a firm is provided by all the incomes accruing in the production of goods and services.

This approach, hitherto used mainly for assessing the performance of economic sectors within the economy as a whole, is transferred to the level of the individual business in the hope of eliminating some of the existing weaknesses of measuring performance on the basis of profitability indicators, one of these being the marked volatility of these criterions.

To compare various firms the value added concept is generally used in the form of the ratio 'value added per employee', which is designated productivity. The indicator 'value added over staff expenses' is also used.

Annual value added data on firms is not available in Switzerland. Using the profit and loss account available, it is possible to produce for the banks in Switzerland a ratio which can be defined roughly as labour productivity. For a more precise measurement, however, it would be necessary to have more detailed data on expenses for rents and leasing charges (contained under the expense item 'business and office expenses').

**Productivity (PROD)**

$$\text{PROD} = \frac{\text{Gross value added}}{\text{Number of employees}}$$

Gross value added = Net interest income
+ Commission income net
+ Net income from trading in foreign exchange and precious metals
+ Net income from securities
+ Miscellaneous
- Business and office expenses

Income from permanent participations is to be regarded as part of the value added of the profit-distributing firm and cannot be counted a second time as a component of the value added of the receiving bank.

### 3.2. Results

By way of illustration the values for the ratios ROE, ROA and PROD and the year 1990 are listed in **Table** 2. The table is restricted to those 50 banks which have shown the absolute highest profits for this year.

There are sometimes notably different results in the ranking order for the three performance measures. Difference of up to 38 places in the ranking of institutions occur in the total of 50 institutions (cf. Nordfinanz Bank Zurich and Banque des Dépots).

**Tables** 3 and **4** show the ROA and ROE values for the same 50 institutions for 1987 to 1991, always with the ranking orders. It is notable that, whichever of the two ratios is used, the ranking order remains the same over the period of time with some exceptions.

## 4. Problems of Measurement

### 4.1. Data problems

There are no data free from problems. This is a point that must be borne in mind in all empirical work. The data problems discussed below afflict all performance concepts without distinction.

Both the balance sheet and the profit and loss account can be distorted by the existence or the setting up of undisclosed reserves and need not therefore reflect the actual assets or the annual profits (or losses).

The new regulations on the setting up and writing back of undisclosed reserves issued so as to be effective for the annual statement of accounts for 1990 should, however, enhance the value of the data. The most important points in the new regulations are that it is categorically forbidden to set up undisclosed reserves by cutting back earnings and that the writing back of undisclosed reserves to any significant extent must be published.

The measurement of performance on the basis of a year may, moreover, be affected by special events. For example the TDB American Express Bank in 1989 took Fr. 465 million out of reserves for distribution. Hence the very favourable results shown by the performance ratios of this institution in 1989 were not a reflection of its success but rather of the extraordinary payouts. This latter problem can be alleviated by using the results of several years in measuring the performance of banks.

Data problems will be mitigated insofar as this study is confined to banks. It may be assumed that their accounting and publishing practices are comparatively uniform. More serious difficulties would no doubt be encountered on comparing banks with other undertakings.

## 4.2. Comparison of the performance of enterprises

To compare two firms the vigour of their performance is assessed. In the case of the performance ratios mentioned a one-dimensional quantity is always used for this purpose, such as the balance-sheet total for the ROA, equity capital for the ROE, and the number of employees or staff expenses for the PROD.

Problems arise when the result, the performance of an enterprise has to be related to other variables which are not contained in the denominator of the ratio. Differences between undertakings, as will be shown below by reference to the ROA ratio, may be due simply to the failure to take account of a relevant variable.

Unlike, say, the American set-up, the Swiss banking system is an universal bank system. The banks need not specialize in a particular line of business but may in principle carry on banking business in all its forms. However, not all banks avail themselves of these facilities to the same extent.

The 'Big banks', whose gross incomes derive about equally from on-balance sheet business (Net interest income, income from securities and participations and income from bills and money market papers) and from off-balance sheet business (commissions, income from transactions in foreign exchange and precious metals, other earnings), are true all-purpose banks. But by their side there are also banks specializing in one field or another. For instance, the institutes also figuring in **Table 2**, Banque de l'Etat de Fribourg and Crédit Foncier Vaudois, derived about 90 % of their income for 1990 from interest difference business whereas the earnings of the CBI-TDB Union Bancaire P., the Bank J. Vontobel & Co. AG and J.P. Morgan (Suisse) SA came from non-credit business to the extent of almost 90 %.

Differences in income structures give rise to problems affecting the measurement and assessment of performance on the basis of the ratio 'return on assets' ROA. A relation can be established between the balance-sheet total and the income deriving therefrom (interest received or interest paid). However, incomes from the non-interest business, which are contained in the profit, are not reflected in the balance sheet total. Banks transacting predominantly non-interest business have a higher 'indicator induced' value for the ratio ROA than those mainly active in balance-sheet business. The use of the ratio ROA to assess the performance of banks with different income structures can thus lead to misinterpretations.

The problems incurred by failure of the ROA ratio to allow adequately for off-balance sheet business cause trouble not only in cross comparisons. Likewise, if the income structure is in a process of change, only qualified use of the ratio ROA is possible for the analysis of performance trends over a period of time.

There is another problem in Switzerland which is due to the fact that not all banks have the same minimum requirements in respect of equity capital. The Swiss Federal Law on Banks and Savings Banks (BL) and the Banking Ordinance (BO) contain special provisions for:

- Cantonal banks whose total liabilities are secured by the respective cantons (Art. 5 para 2 BL, Art. 11 para 3 BO, Art. 13 para 3 lit. b BO);
- 'Commune' institutions where there is a documented guarantee cover amount (Art. 11 para 1 lit. c BO);
- Cooperative societies whose members are obligated to pay up further capital when called (Art. 11 para 1 lit. b BO);
- Private bankers who do not publicly solicit customer deposits' (Art. 4 para 4 BL, Art. 5 para 2 BL).

Finally, under Art. 2 of the Order concerning foreign banks in Switzerland, the branches of foreign banks are not subject to the rules on capital resources stated in BL Art. 4 para 1.

Moreover, secondary advances and loans together with hidden reserves may, within certain limits, be reckoned by the bank to be part of the statutory equity capital (with the exception of cantonal banks whose total liabilities are guaranteed by the canton). Legal requirements as to equity capital may therefore be fulfilled through a variety of channels. The amount of the reported equity capital (capital and open reserves) represents one possibility and also, which is not unimportant, stands in relation to other possibilities.

ROE is therefore not determined solely by the 'success' of the bank but also by the legal requirements relating to the equity capital basis and the policy adopted by the institution with regard to it.

## 5. Added value as alternative

### 5.1. Basic features

In two recent articles an alternative approach to the measurement of corporate performance was discussed and the results published for industrial and commercial enterprises (cf. Davis and Kay, 1990, Davis, Flanders and Star, 1991).

The starting point is an analysis of the weaknesses of traditional performance ratios for comparing enterprises in different sectors of the economy. Performance ratios such as profit-turnover ratio, return on assets, return on equity, value added per unit of staff expense, etc. are capable of exhibiting certain aspects of an enterprise's performance. But none of them can produce a satisfactory picture of the quality of the firm's performance. The fact that firms present a reassuring picture when measured by certain ratios is sometimes due not to their overall company result but rather, for example, to peculiar features of the firm or the sector in which it operates or even to the ratio itself. Varying capital intensities in particular can be disturbing factors.

It is a common practice to attempt to deal with these problems by using a combination of ratios. But the necessary weighting of the indicators employed raises additional questions which are no less problematical.

The starting point of the new approach, like a number of other concepts, is the corporate profit (cf. **Figure 1**). The profit of a firm is the difference between receipts and expenses (merchandise, material, staff, depreciation).

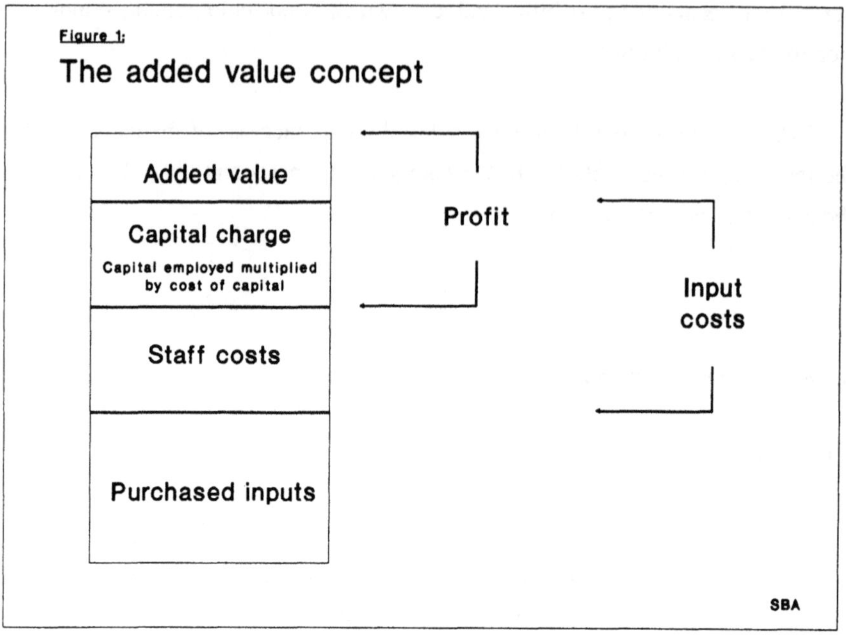
Figure 1:
The added value concept
Added value
Capital charge
Capital employed multiplied by cost of capital
Staff costs
Purchased inputs
Profit
Input costs
SBA

The actual succes of a firm, and hence its performance, is, according to the 'added value concept', reflected only by that part of the corporate profit remaining after the additional deduction of the costs of the capital employed. The capital employed by the firm, represents an input, like, say, labour. The costs of the capital employed (i.e. the capital charge) are therefore deductible from the corporate profit, like the staff costs. The result is described as the pure profit or economic rent or 'added value' of the enterprise.

On the assumption that all inputs are evaluated at prices that could have been achieved if the inputs had been put to alternative uses, added value represents the additional value that accrues to the national economy as a whole from the existence of the firm, i.e. as a result of inputs being utilized in this particular firm. Or expressed in other terms: The performance of a firm is to be measured by the loss that would be incurred for the economy if the firm in question were to be dissolved and its production factors (labour, capital) put to use elsewhere in the economy.

A firm achieves a positive added value if it has a lead over its competitors. This may be due to a variety of factors such as its capacity for innovation or the reputation of a firm or of its products or services. Firms may also have a competitive edge in the infrastructure, in logistics, or in sales channels. A competitive lead may also be established by a monopolistic or monopoly-like position of the firm. What is true of all criteria relating to the performance of individual businesses is also true of the added value criteria: High figures do not necessarily mean high efficiency in the economic sense.

With the added value concept, in contrast to profitability ratios and productivity, a firm's performance is not attributed to one specific input factor; instead explicit account is taken of the interplay of all the input factors in a firm. The added value concept does for the measurement of a firm's specific performance what the concept of the total factor productivity does for the measurement of the overall productivity of the economy.

## 5.2. Ascertainment of added value and setting up of performance ratios

To determine the added value of a firm we need information on the profit of the firm, the capital employed and the earnings that might have been achieved if the capital had been used otherwise, i.e. the opportunity costs of capital). Added value is therefore equivalent to the difference between the corporate profit and the opportunity costs of the capital employed (product of capital employed and cost of capital).

The definition given to the capital input is not of ultimate importance. What is much more important is that corporate profit and the definition of capital chosen should coincide.

If the total capital of a firm (operating and financial assets, balance sheet total) is defined as the capital employed, this corresponds to a corporate profit including interest received but before deduction of interest paid. If, on the other hand, the operating assets are the quantity taken for the capital employed, income from the financial assets drops out on the receipts side, given the corresponding definition of profit. Interest paid is not included on the expenditure side. If equity is defined as the capital empoyed, this is equivalent to a corporate profit taking into account interest received (on the income side) and interest paid (on the expenditure side).

Like other input factors the capital employed has to be evaluated at current costs, i.e. at replacement and not historical costs.

As an indicator of the opportunity costs of capital a nominal long-term rate of interest (return on Federal bonds) is proposed. Thus a risk-free investment is regarded as an alternative use. We shall revert to this point below. The long-term rate of interest is to be preferred to a short one, since the capital invested in a firm cannot be so rapidly reinvested as, say, a money market investment. A nominal rate of interest is therefore to be preferred because it would be difficult to determine the real interest for alternative uses and because all the other data are anyhow also of a nominal character.

The added value of a firm can thus be determined by the following formula:

**Added value (AV)**

| | | |
|---|---|---|
| **AV** | = | **Profit - Opportunity costs of capital** |
| Profit | = | Corporate profit (in accordance with the definition given to the capital input) |
| Opportunity costs of capital | = | Capital employed x Cost of capital |
| Cost of capital | = | Return on Federal bonds |

To compare firms of different sizes the added value must be relativist. The value added of the firm would be the most suitable. Relativization is frequently easier to achieve by combining staff and capital costs (input costs) or sales.

Performance ratios for comparing firms can be obtained as follows:

**Added value over input costs (AV/IC)**

$$\textbf{AV/IC} = \frac{\textbf{Added value}}{\textbf{Input costs}}$$

| | | |
|---|---|---|
| Added value | = | Profit - Opportunity costs of capital |
| Input costs | = | Staff costs + Opportunity costs of capital |

**Added value over sales (AV/SALES)**

$$\text{AV/SALES} = \frac{\text{Added value}}{\text{Sales}}$$

Application of the added value concept gives rise to a number of problems, some of them being identical with those already encountered with other performance concepts (cf. also Section 4).

A point to be mentioned in connection with the available data is that the actual values for the revenue and expenditure items, and hence for the profit, can be distorted by the setting up and writing back of undisclosed reserves. The results for a single year can also be affected by extraordinary factors.

To determine the income that could be earned by alternative uses of the capital employed in a specific firm, the capital must be valued at current costs (replacement costs). The financial assets of a firm, however, as a rule figure in the balance sheets as historical costs.

The alternative use is not the only criterion for determining how high the opportunity costs of a firm's capital are. The business risk is also a potent factor. Capital invested via the firm in business ventures with an element of risk must yield a higher return than funds invested without any risk at all. Failure to take proper account of business risks in determining the opportunity costs of the capital (e.g. by an increase in the interest rate) causes the added value to augment with the risk. Levels of added value determined in this way may thus reflect not only a competitive lead (cf. section 5.1) but also the risk specific to the business. This is a common problem and also occurs in connection with ROA and ROE.

The result of assigning values to expenditures at prices that could have been obtained by alternative uses is that the added value of a firm flows into the profit undiminished. In practice, however, firms may pass part of the added value on to employees, customers or suppliers by rewarding their services at levels above the market rate or charging prices below the market rate for their own products.

## 6. Added value in the banking sector

### 6.1. Survey

Until May, 1992, the added value concept has not been applied to financial institutions such as banks, insurance companies or pension funds. In this section we shall first take a look at the application of the concept in the banking sector. We shall go on to work out added value ratios for Swiss banks. We shall then investigate how sensitively the results react to changes in the assumptions. Finally, we take stock of other research in this area and, furthermore, compare the various indicators for measuring performance based on accounting data with indicators supplied by the market.

### 6.2. Putting the concept into operation

To determine the added value of banks we have to work out, just as with other firms, the capital employed, the profit corresponding to it according to concept, and the indicator of the opportunity costs of capital.

**Figure** 2 shows a simplified version of the balance sheet and profit and loss account of a bank. Two definitions can in principle be applied to the capital employed: on the one hand the total capital of a bank (total assets, balance sheet total), and on the other, the equity. The profits consist in the case of the total capital concept of the sum of the net profit and interest paid, and in the case of the equity concept exclusively of the net profit.

The formula for obtaining the added value of banks is therefore:

| | | |
|---|---|---|
| **Added value** | = | **Profit - Opportunity costs of capital** |
| | = | **Profit - (Capital employed x Costs of capital)** |

| | | |
|---|---|---|
| Cost of capital | = | Return on Federal bonds |

Figure 2:

**Added value in the banking sector: Capital employed and profit**

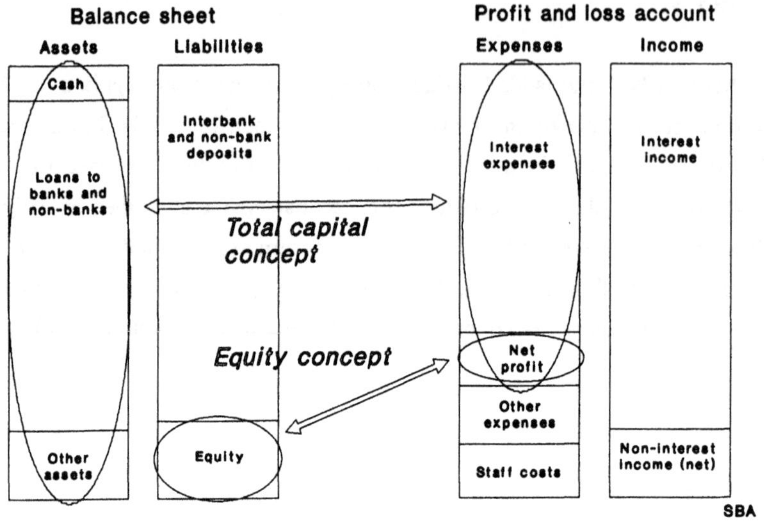

**Total capital concept**

| | | |
|---|---|---|
| Capital employed | = | Cash |
| | + | Loans to banks and non-banks |
| | + | Other assets |
| | = | Balance sheet total |
| Profit | = | Interest income |
| | + | Non-interest income (net) |
| | - | Staff costs |
| | - | Other expenses |
| Profit | = | Net profit |
| | + | Interest expenses |

**Equity concept**

| | | |
|---|---|---|
| Capital employed | = | Equity (Capital and reserves) |
| Profit | = | Interest income |
| | - | Interest expenses |
| | + | Non-interest income (net) |
| | - | Staff costs |
| | - | Other expenses |
| | = | Net profit |

We will now examine the suitability of the total capital concept for studying the performance of banks by taking a simple example as an illustration:

Two virtually identical banking institutions A and B have a balance sheet total of Sfr. 1 billion and an equity capital of Sfr. 100 million. In both banks annual staff costs come to Sfr. 5 million and office expenses Sfr. 10 million. The interest margin, i.e. the net interest income (interest income less interest expenses) as a percentage of the balance sheet total, stands at 1 % and is at the same level in both cases. The sole difference is in the amount of interest income and interest expenses. In bank A the interest income is Sfr. 60 million and the interest expenses Sfr. 50 million, whereas in bank B the corresponding figures are Sfr. 70 million (income) and Sfr. 60 million (expenses). Non-interest income is in each case Sfr. 20 million. The return on Federal bonds (indicator for opportunity costs of capital) would be 7 %. The net profit is the same in both cases, viz. Sfr. 15 million.

On the basis of the total capital concept, the added values for the two banks are as follows:

| | Bank A | Bank B |
|---|---|---|
| Net profits (million Sfr.) | 15 | 15 |
| + Interest expenses (million Sfr.) | + 50 | + 60 |
| - Balance sheet total x Cost of capital (million Sfr.) | - 70 | - 70 |
| **= Added value (million Sfr.)** | - 5 | 5 |

The comparatively better performance of bank B is due solely to the fact that interest income accounted for a higher proportion of the balance sheet total (in per cent) than in bank A. If in bank B interest expenses had been the same amount as interest income (Sfr. 70 million) and the net profit had been correspondingly less (Sfr. + 5 million), the performance of bank B measured by the added value using the total capital concept would have remained unchanged. In the total capital concept the drop in profits is offset by the higher interest expenses.

However, for a bank operating in the on-balance sheet business it is not really material what interest income (gross) is earned but rather what net sum remains after interest expenses have been deducted. In view of the bank's special function as a financial intermediary there is a close link between liabilities and the credits granted. The result of a bank in the balance sheet business depends on the management of the assets and liabilities side of the balance sheet. Accordingly, the alternative earnings of the total capital (total assets, balance-sheet total) may be regarded as predetermined by the activities of the bank as a financial intermediary. The added value concept using the total capital concept as a basis is therefore not suitable for analysing the performance of banks.

For comparing banks of different sizes the levels of added value determined must be relativist. In the following exposition we shall in particular use the costs of the inputs (i.e. input costs) as the reference figure.

For the reasons already stated (cf. Section 3) the profit before tax should be regarded as the corporate profit. With the data of the SNB as a basis, the following added value ratio can be obtained for the Swiss banking sector:

**Added value over input costs (AV/IC) (Equity concept)**

$$\text{AV/IC} = \frac{\text{Added value}}{\text{Input costs}}$$

Added value (AV) = Net profit (- Net loss)
+ Income taxes
- Equity x Interest rate

Interest rate = Return on Federal bonds (averaged year)

Input costs (IC) = Expenses for bank directors and staff
+ Contributions to staff welfare funds
+ Equity x Interest rate

The general problems encountered in determining performance ratios for banks has already been discussed below (cf. sections 4 and 5.2). The results have again been computed on the basis of published data. Another point to note is that end-of-year data have been used for the equity capital instead of average annual values.

## 6.3. Results

### 6.3.1. Institutions with the absolute highest profits

In **Table 5** are listed the added value ratios for 1987 - 1991 on the same lines as in **Tables 2 - 4** for the 50 banks which showed the absolute highest profits for 1990.

There are marked differences between the institutions with regard to the AV/IC values obtained. In each of the four years there were banks with negative values and also those with a value in excess of 80 %.

There was no substantial change in ranking order from year to year. Banks which were up at the front in 1987 were also to be found there in 1990. One very marked change in the ranking order was due to extraordinary circumstances (e.g. CBI-TDP Union Bancaire Privée).

In 1990 and 1991 virtually all institutions showed a distinctly lower value for the ratio AV/IC, which was due to the increased opportunity costs of capital following the trend in interest rates. Furthermore, differences in ranking order were larger between 1989 and 1991 than in the previous years.

### 6.3.2. All banks

**Figure** 3 shows the AV/IC results for all institutions in the groups Cantonal, Regional, Big and Other banks (all banks) for 1987 to 1991 in the form of cumulative frequency functions. For each AV/IC value it is possible to pick out the share of all institutions which was above or below this value. **Figure 4** also contains the relative frequencies in various AV/IC classes for 1987 and 1990 in the form of histograms.

The steady displacement to the left of the cumulative frequency functions in **Figure** 3, taken overall, point to a deterioration of the banks' performance. In 1987 and 1988 just over 50 % of all institution showed an AV/IC value of at least 25 %. In 1990 and 1991 it was still just on 20 %. During the same period the percentage of institutions with a negative AV/IC value increased almost threefold (from 13.3 % for 1987 to 36.9 % for 1990, 35.7 % for 1991).

**Figure 3:**

**Added value over input costs AV/IC (cumulative frequency functions for all banks, 1987-1991)**

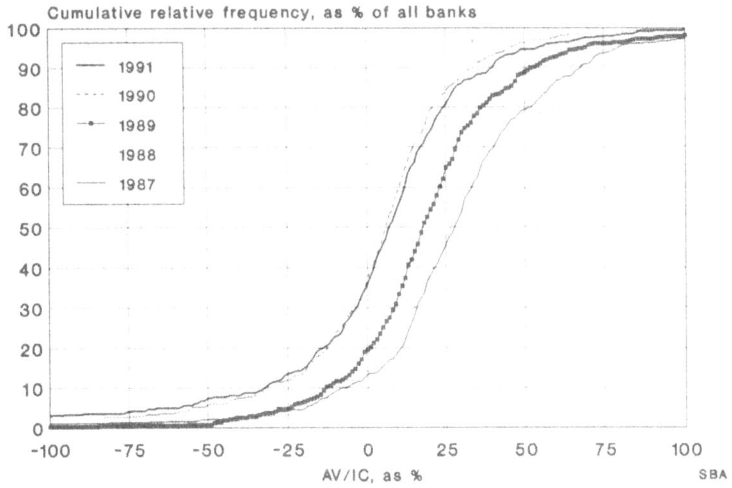


**Figure 4:**

**Added value over input costs AV/IC (histograms for all banks, 1987 and 1990)**

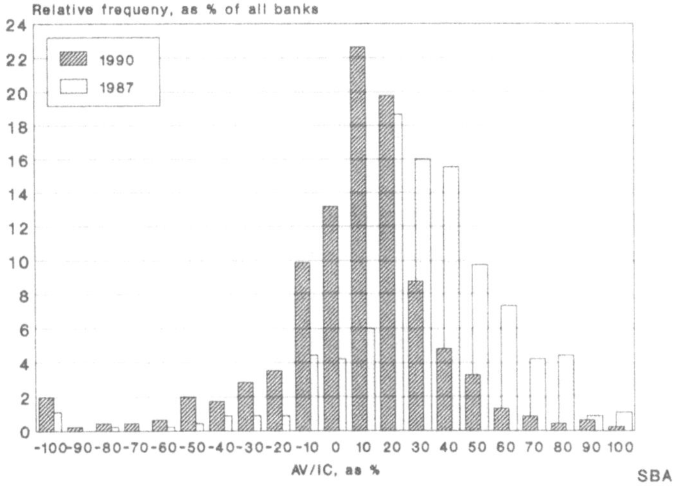

### 6.3.3 On-balance-sheet banks versus off-balance-sheet banks

**Figure** 5 shows the cumulative frequency functions for the AV/IC values and the year 1990 of two groups of approximately the same size comprising banks which are described as balance-sheet and off-balance-sheet banks. Allocation to one group or the other depended on the proportion of non-credit business earnings (commission balance, income from foreign exchange and precious metals and other revenue) in the gross income.

At both intersections points of the cumulative frequency functions the shares accounted for by the two groups of banks are always the same. 30 % of the balance-sheet banks and about 45 % of the off-balance sheet banks show a negative AV/IC. On the other hand. there are about 20 % of the institutions engaged in the off-balance-sheet business that exhibit an AV/IC value of more than 25 %. In the balance-sheet banks, by contrast, it is 'only' 10 %.

### 6.3.4 Relationship between AV/IC and ROE

Even firms showing a positive net profit in the relevant financial year have negative values when their performance is measured by the added value concept in contrast to the return on investment approach.

There is a close link between AV/IC and ROE. If the return on a bank's equity capital is at precisely the same level as the rate of interest employed in the added value concept, the bank achieves neither a positive nor a negative added value. A positive (negative) added value is achieved if the ROE is above (below) the rate of interest used. **Figure 6** highlights the relationship between the two ratios.

The relationship between the ratios AV/IC and ROE would be even closer than it is if it were not for the fact that in the added value concept a quantity is incorporated that is specific to the institution, namely staff expenses, in addition to net profit and equity. This enables additional distinctions to be made. Two institutions, both having the same values for net profit and for equity capital, will also be found to have equal values on application of the ratio ROE and they will rank as equally efficient in terms of this concept of performance. If, however, one of them has higher staff costs than

**Figure 5:**

**Added value over input costs AV/IC (cumulative frequency functions for on-balance sheet and off-balance sheet banks, 1990)**

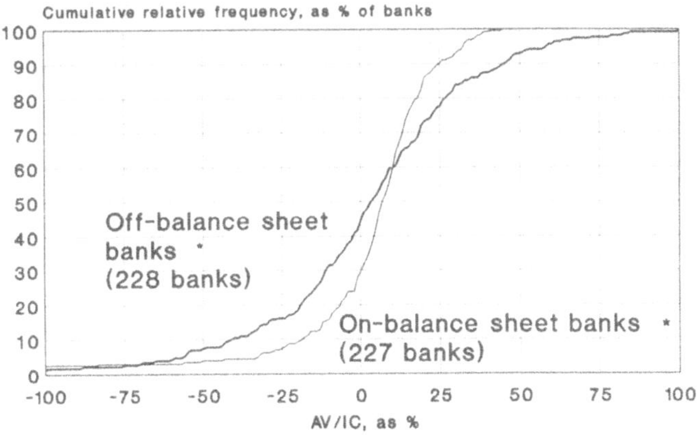


* On-balance sheet banks: Non-interest income as % of gross income < 32,9 %
Off-balance sheet banks: Non-interest income as % of gross income > 32,9 %

SBA

**Figure 6:**

**AV/IC and ROE (all banks, 1990)**

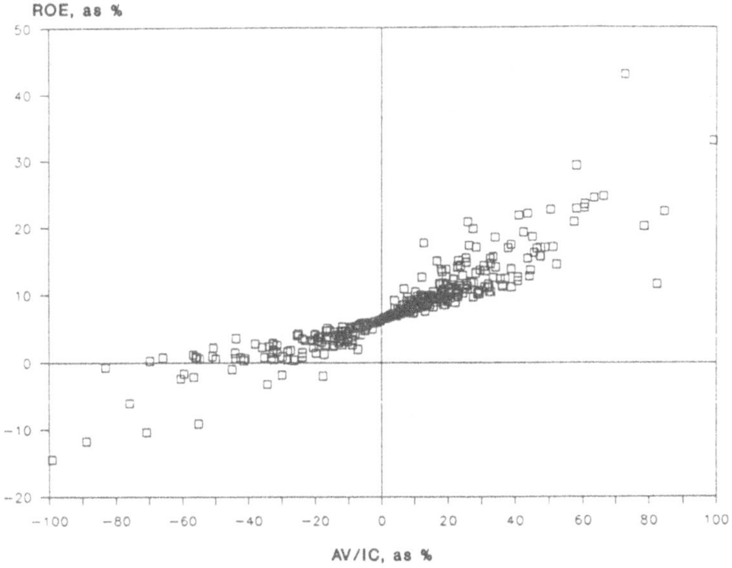


SBA

the other, this will be reflected in a comparatively low value for the ratio AV/IC but not in the case of ROE.

**Figure** 7 clearly shows that banks differ with regard to the opportunity costs of capital and to the staff costs. Thus in 10 % all banks the opportunity costs of capital were higher than the staff costs. On the other hand, there was virtually the same number of institutions whose staff costs were more than four times the opportunity costs of capital.

## 6.4. Sensitivity of the results to changes in the assumptions

We shall now look into the question whether and to what extent the AV/IC results react to changes in the assumptions. We shall do this by comparing the ranking order based on the original AV/IC results for all banks in 1990 with ranking orders based on altered added value ratios and calculate the coefficients of rank correlation. The added value ratios are described in **Table 6** and the results shown.

The coefficients of rank correlation obtained warrant the conclusion that changes in the assumptions have only minor effects on the ranking order of the banks.

In **Figures 8 and 9** the original ranking orders for the 50 banks with the absolute highest profits are compared for illustrative purposes by using the added value ratios AV/IC (8.4 %) and AV/gross income respectively.

## 6.5. Another application of the added value concept to banks

In August, 1992, a research team from London published a study on the application of the added value concept to financial institutions (cf. Gouzouli et al. 1992). They used the following formule and applied it on a group of 25 large European retail banks:

$$\textbf{Added value to inputs (AV/I)} \quad = \quad \frac{\textbf{Added value}}{\textbf{Inputs}}$$

Figure 7:

**Ratio of staff costs and opportunity costs of capital (cumulative frequency function for all banks, 1990)**

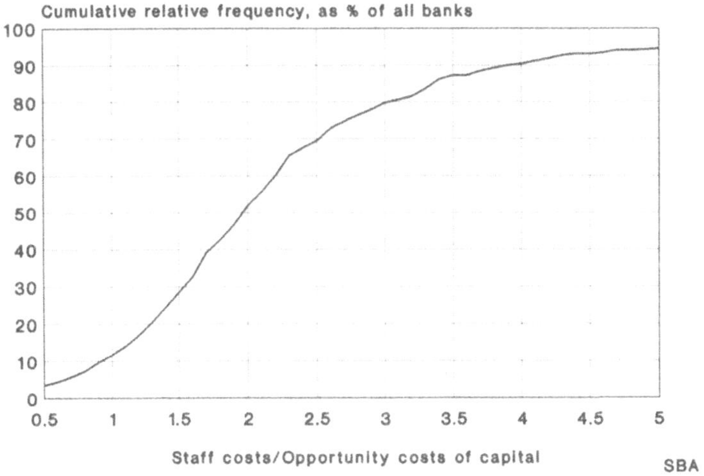

**Figure 8:**

**Sensitivity of added value results:**
**AV/IC (6,4 %) versus AV/IC (8,4 %) 1990**

**(Ranking orders of the 50 banks with the absolute highest profits 1990)**

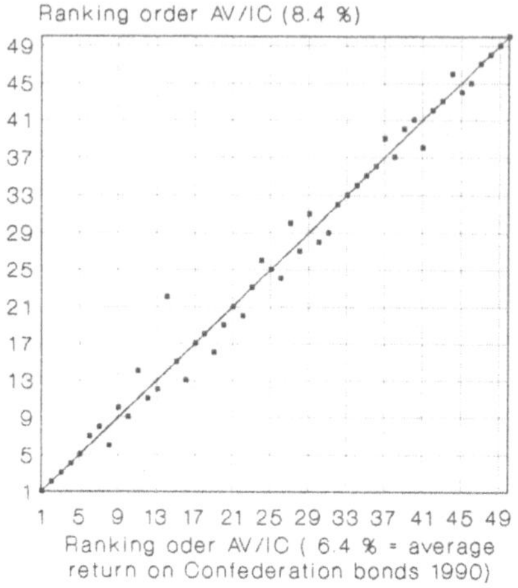


SBA

**Figure 9:**

**Sensitivity of added value results:**
**AV/IC versus AV/gross income 1990**

**(Ranking orders of the 50 banks with the absolute highest profits 1990)**

SBA

| | | |
|---|---|---|
| Added value | = | Profits before tax and after bad debts, minority interests and extraordinary items +/- reserve changes - costs of equity including premium |
| Cost of equity including premium | = | Long term bond yield for the relevant country and year + ten percentage points (risk premium) |
| Inputs | = | All operating costs + cost of equity including premium |

**Table 7** shows the results of an application of both concepts to a group of Cantonal banks and the Big banks for the year 1991. A correlation coefficient of 0.95 indicates a strong relation between AV/IC and AV/I. As a consequence of the inclusion of the risk premium, AV/I-results are substantally lower than the AV/IC-values for Swiss banks. Using the added value concept of the London based research team, 28 of the 30 banks had a negative ratio for 1991. Highly capitalized financial institutions like the Swiss banks are "punished" by the risk premium to a large extent. Since the risk premium is more or less arbitrarily fixed at the level of 10 percentage points, the benefits of the modified results are open to doubt.

### 6.6. ROA, ROE and AV/IC versus price-earnings ratio

The purpose of this section is a comparison of performance indicators based on accounting data (balance sheets and income statements) with indicators supplied by the market. In Switzerland, shares of only few but larger banks are listed on a stock exchange. **Table 8** gives figures for the total market capitalization of 30 banks in Switzerland.

The market capitalization of a firm corresponds to the value of its equity at a given point in time. Assuming efficient capital markets, a firm's equity value is equivalent to the present value of expected future profits. Taking the profit of a firm in a given period as an indicator of its succes, the price-earnings ratio (P/E) defined as market capitalization divided by (current) profit can be seen as a performance indicator: A firm which performs badly compared with its competitors will ceteris paribus have a higher P/E and vice-versa. In reality, P/Es in a cross-sectional sample can also differ because of differences concerning other things (e.g. differences in risk, growth opportunities and future profits).

P/E is typically calculated by dividing the market capitalization of a firm by the sum of the earnings (profits) of the previous year (cf. Ibbotson, 1992). Data on market capitalization at the end of 1991 were not available for the banks in question. Therefore, our results (cf. Table 7) are based on firms' equity value for mid 1991. In analogy to ROA, ROE and AV/IC, the price-earnings ratio PES91 is based on profit before tax. In contrast to this, PE91 is calculated on profit after tax. For comparison of ROA, ROE and AV/IC with price-earnings ratios, correlation coefficients were calculated and are shown in **Table 9**.

The correlation coefficients obtained show a slightly stronger relationship between the price-earnings ratio and AV/IC than between P/E and ROE (results do not change if values for market capitalization of mid 1992 or average values of 1991 and 1992 enter the calculation). This result is surprising in so far as P/E and ROE both contain the same figure (profit before or after tax) in the nominator (ROE) or in the denominator (P/E). **Figure 10** highlights the relationshsip between the two ratios PES91 and AV/IC.

In this context, however, important questions remain unanswered, e.g.: Is P/E a priori a better performance indicator, because it is supplied by the market? Is the relationship between AV/IC and P/E "really" stronger? Might changes in concept (cf. Section 6.5.) affect results? Etc.

Figure 10:

**PES91 and AV/IC (30 banks, 1991)**

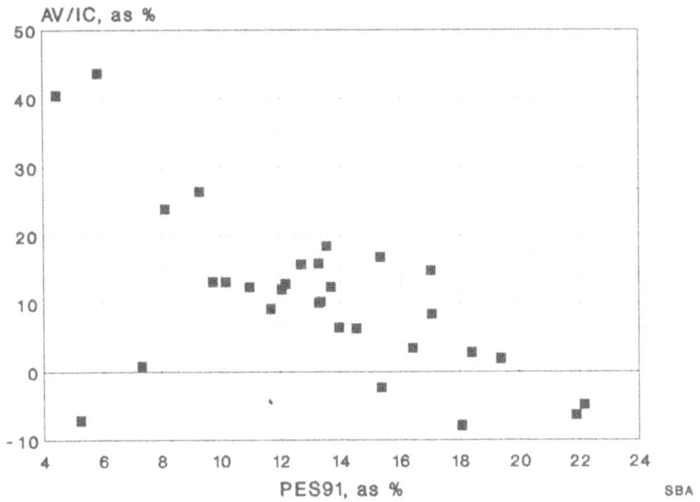

## 7. Summary and conclusions

The various concepts for measuring and analysing the performance of banks on accounting data used in this study have been focused on quite disparate aspects. In the case of the profitability indicators (ROA, ROE) the performance is measured in terms of the corporate profit remaining after expenses have been deducted. For assessing the performance of a bank, and also for comparing enterprises, the return obtainable per unit of capital is taken as a basis. The concept is thus particularly helpful in answering questions on the efficiency of the capital invested. With the value added approach the total earning power is at the focus of interest. Performance is measured by the incomes generated during the undertaking's performance, i.e. by the total of net profit, wages and salaries, rents, leasing charges, taxes, etc. The ratio PROD is therefore a reflection of the income which a bank as a whole can generate per employee. If the added value approach is followed, a bank is above average in its performance and competitive ability if, after all the input factors in the enterprise have been indemnified in a manner in line with market principles, an added value, as it is called, results. This concept affords a more comprehensive answer to the question of how efficient the total factor input is than is possible with the other indicators.

It is not an easy task to measure and compare the performance of banks. The available data give only an approximately correct picture of financial assets and the year's results. Undisclosed reserves set up in the past can result in an undervaluation in the published figures for the year (balance sheet, profit and loss account) of assets and hence also of the equity capital and the actual corporate profits. Conversely, the unreported writing back of reserves leads to an overvaluation of profits. The measurement of performance is thus distorted to a matching degree. And in the final analysis all performance concepts are affected.

ROA is a ratio in common use. It is easy to work out values for individual banks. However, as inadequate consideration is given to off-balance sheet business, ROA has some serious disadvantages for comparing the performance of Swiss banks. Parameters based on the value added concept are, because of the wide survey taken, less liable to major fluctuations than the other ratios used in this study. The level of value added per employee (PROD) is especially dependent on the capital intensity of a bank's performance. If the ROE approach is followed, more allowance is made for the off-balance-sheet business than in the ROA concept. As there are differences regarding equity requirements and also the policy pursued in equity matters (undisclosed reserves, overfilling), ROE can produce a distorted picture of performance. Different equity capital intensities (measured by the ratio between opportunity costs of equity capital and staff costs) can also produce differences in the ROE values. The added value approach takes account of the different intensities of capital and reserves by using an inclusive quantity in the denominator. Yet even this concept is unable to rule out all the structural factors that might influence performance.

There is no comparison based on the added value concept between the performance of banks and that of other firms in different sectors of the economy. The added value studies referred to (cf. Davis and Kay, 1990 and Davis, Flanders and Star, 1991) calculate ratios on the basis of the total capital concept whereas in this study results are based on the equity concept. A comparison would therefore present difficulties.

Nor is there a profound comparison of the various indicators for measuring performance based on accounting data with indicators supplied by the market. The comparison undertaken in this study represents a first and incomplete attempt. The results indicate a slightly stronger relation between the price-earnings ratio and AV/IC than between P/E and ROE.

A ratio for the measurement of the performance of banks and other enterprises has an edge over others if it reacts with maximum neutrality to structural differences between banks. Disturbing factors may the variable importance of off-balance-sheet business, different rules concerning the equity base and different intensities of equity capital. Any deviations might also be the result of different risks. Compared with the other concepts, the added value concept offers certain advantages. But it is impossible to exclude all structural vulnerabilities. It is therefore important, in a further phase, to find out to what the differences in performance values are due. This might bring to light other structural influences. The study of Haegler and Jeger (1993) is devoted to this question.

**Literature**

Beier, J. (1990), "Wertschöpfung, Einkommensverteilung und Finanzierung der Banken", in: Die Bank, 3, Köln.

Blattner, N., Maurer, M. and Weber, M. (1987), Voraussetzungen der schweizerischen Wettbewerbsfähigkeit, Berne.

Davis, E., and Kay, J. (1990), "Assessing Corporate Performance", in: Business Strategy Review, Summer, London.

Davis, E., Flanders, S., and Star, J. (1991), "Who are the World's most Successful Companies?", in: Business Strategy Review, Summer, London.

Federal office of statistics (1987), "Eidgenössische Betriebszählung 1985", press release, Berne.

Federal office of statistics (1988), "Produktionskonto der Schweiz 1985: Provisorische Resultate", press release, Berne.

Gouzouli, C., Spence, M., Star, J., and Davis, E. (1992), "Measuring the Performance of Banks", First Consulting Ltd, London Business School, and The Institute for Fiscal Studies, London.

Haegler, U., and Jeger, M. (1993), "Explaining the Performance of Swiss Banks from 1987 to 1990", in this volume.

Ibbotson, R.G. (1992), "Price-Earnings Ratios", in: The New Palgrave, Dictionnary of Money & Finance, New York.

Swiss National Bank (several years), Das schweizerische Bankwesen im Jahre ..., Zurich.

## Appendix: Tables

### Tables

Table 1:
Banking groups / number of institutes 1987-1991

| Banking group | BG | Number of institutes | | | | |
|---|---|---|---|---|---|---|
| | | 1987 | 1988 | 1989 | 1990 | 1991 |
| Cantonal Banks | 10 | 29 | 29 | 29 | 29 | 28 |
| Big Banks | 25 | 5 | 5 | 5 | 4 | 4 |
| Regional and Savings Banks | 20 | 214 | 213 | 210 | 204 | 189 |
| Other Banks | 30-65 | 202 | 205 | 209 | 218 | 222 |
| Commercial banks | 30 | 27 | 26 | 25 | 25 | 24 |
| Stock broking, securities-trading and portfolio-management institutions | 35 | 49 | 48 | 51 | 51 | 54 |
| Personal-loan, hire-purchase and consumer finance banks | 40 | 11 | 11 | 11 | 11 | 10 |
| Other types | 45 | 4 | 4 | 4 | 5 | 4 |
| Foreign-controlled banks | 65 | 111 | 116 | 118 | 126 | 130 |
| Total (all banks) | | 450 | 452 | 453 | 455 | 443 |

Remarks:

- BG Number of banking group

SBA

Table 2:
50 banks with the absolute highest profits 1990 / ratios for measuring performance

| Institute | BG | Location | Net profit (million Sfr.) 1990 | ROE (as %) 1990 | ROA (as %) 1990 | PROD (1000 Sfr.) 1990 | ROE (ranking orders) 1990 | ROA (ranking orders) 1990 | PROD (ranking orders) 1990 |
|---|---|---|---|---|---|---|---|---|---|
| Schweizerische Bankgesellschaft | 25 | Zurich | 780 | 7.8 | 0.56 | 169 | 33 | 26 | 32 |
| Schweizerischer Bankverein | 25 | Basel | 697 | 9.2 | 0.54 | 167 | 25 | 27 | 35 |
| Schweizerische Kreditanstalt | 25 | Zurich | 470 | 8.4 | 0.52 | 144 | 32 | 28 | 41 |
| Schweizerische Volksbank | 25 | Berne | 111 | 6.6 | 0.32 | 128 | 40 | 37 | 46 |
| Zürcher Kantonalbank | 10 | Zurich | 89 | 5.3 | 0.20 | 114 | 49 | 50 | 49 |
| CBI-TDB Union Bancaire Privée | 35 | Geneva | 70 | 10.9 | 0.93 | 255 | 21 | 18 | 13 |
| BSI-Banca della Svizzera Italiana | 30 | Lugano | 58 | 10.1 | 0.81 | 169 | 22 | 20 | 33 |
| Banque Cantonale Vaudoise | 10 | Lausanne | 57 | 9.0 | 0.58 | 179 | 28 | 25 | 27 |
| Banque Paribas (Suisse) SA | 65 | Geneva | 51 | 9.1 | 0.87 | 218 | 26 | 19 | 19 |
| Banca del Gottardo | 65 | Lugano | 42 | 8.7 | 0.75 | 186 | 30 | 22 | 25 |
| Bank Julius Bär & Co AG | 30 | Zurich | 35 | 13.9 | 1.18 | 181 | 12 | 17 | 26 |
| Kantonalbank von Bern | 10 | Berne | 34 | 8.9 | 0.32 | 118 | 29 | 38 | 48 |
| Luzerner Kantonalbank | 10 | Luzern | 32 | 5.4 | 0.27 | 122 | 48 | 46 | 47 |
| St.Gallische Kantonalbank | 10 | St.Gallen | 32 | 6.0 | 0.24 | 112 | 43 | 49 | 50 |
| BDL Banco di Lugano | 30 | Lugano | 31 | 12.7 | 1.57 | 234 | 14 | 15 | 16 |
| Bank J. Vontobel & Co AG | 35 | Zurich | 30 | 17.2 | 3.08 | 230 | 6 | 6 | 17 |
| Basellandschaftliche Kantonalbank | 10 | Liestal | 30 | 8.6 | 0.35 | 224 | 31 | 35 | 18 |
| Neue Aargauer Bank 1) | 20 | Aarau | 29 | 9.0 | 0.47 | 139 | 27 | 31 | 43 |
| Crédit Foncier Vaudois | 10 | Lausanne | 27 | 11.3 | 0.48 | 304 | 20 | 30 | 7 |
| Discount Bank & Trust Co | 65 | Geneva | 25 | 10.0 | 0.68 | 168 | 23 | 24 | 34 |
| Thurgauer Kantonalbank | 10 | Weinfelden | 25 | 6.4 | 0.29 | 171 | 42 | 43 | 31 |
| Rothschild Bank AG | 65 | Zurich | 24 | 17.1 | 2.47 | 383 | 7 | 9 | 2 |
| Banque hypoth. du Canton de Genève | 10 | Geneva | 23 | 7.4 | 0.34 | 174 | 35 | 36 | 29 |
| Bank Cantrade AG | 35 | Zurich | 23 | 18.7 | 2.31 | 348 | 4 | 11 | 3 |
| GZB Genossenschaftl. Zentralbank | 30 | Basel | 23 | 7.3 | 0.41 | 150 | 36 | 33 | 38 |
| Guyerzeller Bank AG | 65 | Zurich | 22 | 15.8 | 7.89 | 343 | 10 | 1 | 4 |
| Graubündner Kantonalbank | 10 | Chur | 22 | 7.1 | 0.30 | 149 | 37 | 41 | 39 |
| Banque Procrédit SA | 40 | Fribourg | 22 | 20.3 | 2.46 | 276 | 3 | 10 | 10 |
| Dreyfus Söhne & Cie | 35 | Basel | 22 | 11.7 | 5.05 | 338 | 16 | 2 | 5 |
| Caisse d'Epargne Genève | 10 | Geneva | 21 | 7.6 | 0.39 | 146 | 34 | 34 | 40 |
| Basler Kantonalbank | 10 | Basel | 20 | 6.8 | 0.31 | 153 | 39 | 40 | 37 |
| Banque Vaudoise de Crédit | 20 | Lausanne | 19 | 16.3 | 0.79 | 175 | 9 | 21 | 28 |
| Banque Privée Rothschild | 35 | Geneva | 18 | 11.7 | 1.57 | 195 | 18 | 14 | 24 |
| Aargauische Kantonalbank | 10 | Aarau | 18 | 6.5 | 0.29 | 136 | 41 | 44 | 44 |
| Migros Bank | 30 | Zurich | 17 | 5.6 | 0.31 | 141 | 45 | 39 | 42 |
| Banque de l'Etat de Fribourg | 10 | Fribourg | 17 | 11.6 | 0.30 | 203 | 19 | 42 | 23 |
| Algemene Bank Nederland | 65 | Zurich | 17 | 13.3 | 1.85 | 243 | 13 | 13 | 14 |
| Crédit Lyonnais (Suisse) SA | 65 | Geneva | 17 | 5.9 | 0.72 | 211 | 44 | 23 | 20 |
| Bankers Trust AG | 65 | Zurich | 16 | 33.1 | 3.71 | 416 | 1 | 5 | 1 |
| Banca del cantone Ticino | 10 | Bellinzona | 16 | 11.7 | 0.42 | 154 | 17 | 32 | 36 |
| Banque Cantonale d.Valais | 10 | Sion | 15 | 7.1 | 0.28 | 171 | 38 | 45 | 30 |
| Solothurner Kantonalbank | 10 | Solothurn | 14 | 5.4 | 0.26 | 128 | 47 | 48 | 45 |
| Hypothekarkasse des Kantons Bern | 10 | Berne | 14 | 9.8 | 0.26 | 271 | 24 | 47 | 11 |
| Nordfinanz Bank Zürich | 65 | Zurich | 14 | 5.4 | 0.49 | 284 | 46 | 29 | 8 |
| Banque Bruxelles Lambert | 65 | Lausanne | 14 | 12.4 | 1.21 | 240 | 15 | 16 | 15 |
| J.P. Morgan (Suisse) SA | 65 | Geneva | 14 | 17.5 | 3.98 | 313 | 5 | 4 | 6 |
| Bank Leumi le-Israel | 65 | Zurich | 13 | 17.1 | 2.65 | 284 | 8 | 8 | 9 |
| Clariden Bank | 35 | Zurich | 13 | 29.4 | 3.04 | 207 | 2 | 7 | 22 |
| Ferrier Lullin & Cie SA | 35 | Geneva | 13 | 15.1 | 4.32 | 210 | 11 | 3 | 21 |
| Banque de Dépôts | 30 | Geneva | 12 | 4.8 | 2.08 | 255 | 50 | 12 | 12 |

Remarks:

- BG Number of banking group (cf. table 1)
- 1) The 1987 and 1988 data for "Neue Aargauer Bank" resulted from the addition of the results from "Aargauische Hypotheken- & Handelsbank" and "Allgemeine Aargauische Ersparniskasse"

SBA

Table 3:

50 banks with the absolute highest profits 1990 / ROA values and ranking orders 1987-1991

| Institute | BG | Location | Net profit (million Sfr.) 1990 | ROA (as %) 1991 | 1990 | 1989 | 1988 | 1987 | (Ranking orders) 1991 | 1990 | 1989 | 1988 | 1987 |
|---|---|---|---|---|---|---|---|---|---|---|---|---|---|
| Schweizerische Bankgesellschaft | 25 | Zurich | 780 | 0.66 | 0.56 | 0.69 | 0.66 | 0.68 | 25 | 26 | 24 | 24 | 25 |
| Schweizerischer Bankverein | 25 | Basel | 697 | 0.55 | 0.54 | 0.62 | 0.61 | 0.63 | 28 | 27 | 26 | 26 | 27 |
| Schweizerische Kreditanstalt | 25 | Zurich | 470 | 0.71 | 0.52 | 0.80 | 0.69 | 0.70 | 23 | 28 | 23 | 23 | 23 |
| Schweizerische Volksbank | 25 | Berne | 111 | 0.19 | 0.32 | 0.45 | 0.45 | 0.47 | 47 | 37 | 33 | 32 | 30 |
| Zürcher Kantonalbank | 10 | Zurich | 89 | 0.21 | 0.20 | 0.23 | 0.24 | 0.23 | 46 | 50 | 50 | 49 | 50 |
| CBI-TDB Union Bancaire Privée | 35 | Geneva | 70 | 1.11 | 0.93 | 8.47 | 0.96 | 1.49 | 17 | 18 | 1 | 19 | 17 |
| BSI-Banca della Svizzera Italiana | 30 | Lugano | 58 | 0.75 | 0.81 | 0.82 | 0.78 | 0.91 | 21 | 20 | 22 | 22 | 22 |
| Banque Cantonale Vaudoise | 10 | Lausanne | 57 | 0.56 | 0.58 | 0.68 | 0.62 | 0.65 | 27 | 25 | 25 | 25 | 26 |
| Banque Paribas (Suisse) SA | 65 | Geneva | 51 | 0.49 | 0.87 | 1.46 | 1.42 | 1.57 | 30 | 19 | 17 | 15 | 16 |
| Banca del Gottardo | 65 | Lugano | 42 | 0.79 | 0.75 | 0.91 | 0.92 | 1.01 | 19 | 22 | 20 | 21 | 21 |
| Bank Julius Bär & Co AG | 30 | Zurich | 35 | 1.26 | 1.18 | 1.40 | 1.39 | 1.65 | 16 | 17 | 18 | 16 | 14 |
| Berner Kantonalbank / KB von Bern | 10 | Berne | 34 | 0.07 | 0.32 | 0.35 | 0.37 | 0.39 | 48 | 38 | 37 | 36 | 36 |
| Luzerner Kantonalbank | 10 | Luzern | 32 | 0.25 | 0.27 | 0.28 | 0.29 | 0.29 | 44 | 46 | 47 | 44 | 46 |
| St.Gallische Kantonalbank | 10 | St.Gallen | 32 | 0.25 | 0.24 | 0.28 | 0.26 | 0.26 | 43 | 49 | 49 | 48 | 49 |
| BDL Banco di Lugano | 30 | Lugano | 31 | 1.06 | 1.57 | 1.60 | 1.35 | 1.46 | 18 | 15 | 16 | 17 | 18 |
| Bank J. Vontobel & Co AG | 35 | Zurich | 30 | 1.97 | 3.08 | 3.86 | 3.52 | 3.38 | 11 | 6 | 7 | 8 | 8 |
| Basellandschaftliche Kantonalbank | 10 | Liestal | 30 | 0.33 | 0.35 | 0.36 | 0.34 | 0.35 | 34 | 35 | 36 | 38 | 40 |
| Neue Aargauer Bank 1) | 20 | Aarau | 29 | 0.48 | 0.47 | 0.47 | 0.46 | 0.47 | 31 | 31 | 32 | 31 | 31 |
| Crédit Foncier Vaudois | 10 | Lausanne | 27 | 0.52 | 0.48 | 0.51 | 0.48 | 0.49 | 29 | 30 | 30 | 29 | 29 |
| Discount Bank & Trust Co | 65 | Geneva | 25 | 0.70 | 0.68 | 0.88 | 0.93 | 1.11 | 24 | 24 | 21 | 20 | 20 |
| Thurgauer Kantonalbank | 10 | Weinfelden | 25 | 0.30 | 0.29 | 0.29 | 0.26 | 0.28 | 38 | 43 | 46 | 47 | 48 |
| Rothschild Bank AG | 65 | Zurich | 24 | 2.38 | 2.47 | 2.75 | 2.14 | 2.66 | 9 | 9 | 11 | 12 | 11 |
| Banque hypoth. du Canton de Genève | 10 | Geneva | 23 | 0.25 | 0.34 | 0.34 | 0.31 | 0.29 | 42 | 36 | 38 | 42 | 45 |
| Bank Cantrade AG | 35 | Zurich | 23 | 2.82 | 2.31 | 3.17 | 2.96 | 3.21 | 8 | 11 | 8 | 9 | 9 |
| GZB Genossenschaftl. Zentralbank | 30 | Basel | 23 | 0.44 | 0.41 | 0.39 | 0.44 | 0.44 | 33 | 33 | 35 | 33 | 32 |
| Guyerzeller Bank AG | 65 | Zurich | 22 | 11.23 | 7.89 | 7.01 | 5.79 | 7.38 | 1 | 1 | 3 | 2 | 1 |
| Graubündner Kantonalbank | 10 | Chur | 22 | 0.30 | 0.30 | 0.31 | 0.33 | 0.35 | 37 | 41 | 43 | 39 | 41 |
| Banque Procrédit SA | 40 | Fribourg | 22 | 1.77 | 2.46 | 3.07 | 3.99 | 4.25 | 13 | 10 | 10 | 5 | 6 |
| Dreyfus Söhne & Cie | 35 | Basel | 22 | 5.55 | 5.05 | 4.62 | 4.83 | 4.37 | 2 | 2 | 6 | 4 | 5 |
| Caisse d'Epargne Genève | 10 | Geneva | 21 | 0.22 | 0.39 | 0.50 | 0.47 | 0.42 | 45 | 34 | 31 | 30 | 34 |
| Basler Kantonalbank | 10 | Basel | 20 | 0.29 | 0.31 | 0.32 | 0.32 | 0.31 | 39 | 40 | 40 | 41 | 43 |
| Banque Vaudoise de Crédit | 20 | Lausanne | 19 | 0.75 | 0.79 | 0.55 | 0.57 | 0.54 | 20 | 21 | 29 | 28 | 28 |
| Banque Privée Rothschild | 35 | Geneva | 18 | 1.80 | 1.57 | 2.32 | 2.21 | 2.71 | 12 | 14 | 13 | 10 | 10 |
| Aargauische Kantonalbank | 10 | Aarau | 18 | 0.28 | 0.29 | 0.30 | 0.30 | 0.30 | 40 | 44 | 45 | 43 | 44 |
| Migros Bank | 30 | Zurich | 17 | 0.31 | 0.31 | 0.30 | 0.28 | 0.39 | 35 | 39 | 44 | 46 | 37 |
| Banque de l'Etat de Fribourg | 10 | Fribourg | 17 | 0.31 | 0.30 | 0.31 | 0.32 | 0.33 | 36 | 42 | 41 | 40 | 42 |
| ABN AMRO / Algemene Bank Nederland | 65 | Zurich | 17 | 1.75 | 1.85 | 1.85 | 1.94 | 2.21 | 14 | 13 | 15 | 13 | 12 |
| Crédit Lyonnais (Suisse) SA | 65 | Geneva | 17 | 0.73 | 0.72 | 0.59 | 0.07 | 0.41 | 22 | 23 | 28 | 50 | 35 |
| Bankers Trust AG | 65 | Zurich | 16 | 3.71 | 3.71 | 4.75 | 3.81 | 3.58 | 4 | 5 | 5 | 6 | 7 |
| Banca del cantone Ticino | 10 | Bellinzona | 16 | 0.45 | 0.42 | 0.41 | 0.39 | 0.43 | 32 | 32 | 34 | 34 | 33 |
| Banque Cantonale d.Valais | 10 | Sion | 15 | 0.26 | 0.28 | 0.28 | 0.28 | 0.29 | 41 | 45 | 48 | 45 | 47 |
| Solothurner Kantonalbank | 10 | Solothurn | 14 | 0.00 | 0.26 | 0.31 | 0.39 | 0.36 | 49 | 48 | 42 | 35 | 38 |
| Hypothekarkasse des Kantons Bern | 10 | Berne | 14 | NV | 0.26 | 0.33 | 0.35 | 0.35 | NA | 47 | 39 | 37 | 39 |
| Nordfinanz Bank Zürich | 65 | Zurich | 14 | 0.57 | 0.49 | 0.60 | 0.59 | 0.68 | 26 | 29 | 27 | 27 | 24 |
| Banque Bruxelles Lambert | 65 | Lausanne | 14 | 1.59 | 1.21 | 1.06 | 0.98 | 1.18 | 15 | 16 | 19 | 18 | 19 |
| J.P. Morgan (Suisse) SA | 65 | Geneva | 14 | 3.68 | 3.98 | 5.88 | 5.06 | 6.22 | 5 | 4 | 4 | 3 | 2 |
| Bank Leumi le-Israel | 65 | Zurich | 13 | 3.64 | 2.65 | 2.54 | 2.14 | 2.01 | 6 | 8 | 12 | 11 | 13 |
| Clariden Bank | 35 | Zurich | 13 | 3.35 | 3.04 | 3.09 | 3.67 | 4.51 | 7 | 7 | 9 | 7 | 4 |
| Ferrier Lullin & Cie SA | 35 | Geneva | 13 | 4.39 | 4.32 | 7.29 | 6.56 | 5.50 | 3 | 3 | 2 | 1 | 3 |
| Banque de Dépôts | 30 | Geneva | 12 | 2.22 | 2.08 | 1.95 | 1.60 | 1.58 | 10 | 12 | 14 | 14 | 15 |

Remarks:

- NA Data not available
- BG Number of banking group (cf. table 1)
- 1) The 1987 and 1988 data for "Neue Aargauer Bank" resulted from the addition of the results from "Aargauische Hypotheken- & Handelsbank" and "Allgemeine Aargauische Ersparniskasse"

SBA

Table 4:
50 banks with the absolute highest profits 1990 / ROE values and ranking orders 1987-1991

| Institute | BG | Location | Net profit (million Sfr.) 1990 | ROE (as %) 1991 | 1990 | 1989 | 1988 | 1987 | (Ranking orders) 1991 | 1990 | 1989 | 1988 | 1987 |
|---|---|---|---|---|---|---|---|---|---|---|---|---|---|
| Schweizerische Bankgesellschaft | 25 | Zurich | 780 | 9.5 | 7.8 | 9.6 | 10.9 | 11.2 | 25 | 33 | 32 | 25 | 25 |
| Schweizerischer Bankverein | 25 | Basel | 697 | 9.2 | 9.2 | 10.5 | 10.3 | 10.5 | 28 | 25 | 28 | 29 | 26 |
| Schweizerische Kreditanstalt | 25 | Zurich | 470 | 11.5 | 8.4 | 12.4 | 10.9 | 11.3 | 20 | 32 | 19 | 24 | 24 |
| Schweizerische Volksbank | 25 | Berne | 111 | 4.0 | 6.6 | 8.0 | 8.0 | 8.1 | 47 | 40 | 37 | 33 | 34 |
| Zürcher Kantonalbank | 10 | Zurich | 89 | 5.6 | 5.3 | 6.1 | 6.2 | 6.3 | 42 | 49 | 45 | 45 | 43 |
| CBI-TDB Union Bancaire Privée | 35 | Geneva | 70 | 15.4 | 10.9 | 159.9 | 10.6 | 14.5 | 9 | 21 | 1 | 26 | 14 |
| BSI-Banca della Svizzera Italiana | 30 | Lugano | 58 | 9.8 | 10.1 | 10.3 | 10.4 | 10.3 | 22 | 22 | 29 | 28 | 29 |
| Banque Cantonale Vaudoise | 10 | Lausanne | 57 | 9.3 | 9.0 | 12.1 | 11.4 | 11.6 | 26 | 28 | 20 | 22 | 22 |
| Banque Paribas (Suisse) SA | 65 | Geneva | 51 | 5.3 | 9.1 | 15.1 | 14.8 | 15.1 | 43 | 26 | 14 | 11 | 13 |
| Banca del Gottardo | 65 | Lugano | 42 | 9.7 | 8.7 | 10.1 | 9.6 | 10.3 | 23 | 30 | 30 | 32 | 28 |
| Bank Julius Bär & Co AG | 30 | Zurich | 35 | 14.5 | 13.9 | 16.4 | 16.8 | 19.7 | 11 | 12 | 12 | 10 | 10 |
| Berner Kantonalbank / KB von Bern | 10 | Berne | 34 | 2.1 | 8.9 | 9.7 | 9.8 | 9.9 | 48 | 29 | 31 | 31 | 31 |
| Luzerner Kantonalbank | 10 | Luzern | 32 | 5.3 | 5.4 | 6.0 | 6.1 | 5.8 | 44 | 48 | 47 | 46 | 45 |
| St.Gallische Kantonalbank | 10 | St.Gallen | 32 | 6.7 | 6.0 | 6.3 | 6.4 | 5.7 | 36 | 43 | 44 | 43 | 47 |
| BDL Banco di Lugano | 30 | Lugano | 31 | 9.2 | 12.7 | 12.9 | 12.1 | 13.9 | 27 | 14 | 16 | 17 | 16 |
| Bank J. Vontobel & Co AG | 35 | Zurich | 30 | 8.7 | 17.2 | 27.7 | 25.9 | 29.1 | 30 | 6 | 6 | 7 | 6 |
| Basellandschaftliche Kantonalbank | 10 | Liestal | 30 | 8.8 | 8.6 | 8.1 | 7.2 | 7.1 | 29 | 31 | 36 | 41 | 40 |
| Neue Aargauer Bank 1) | 20 | Aarau | 29 | 9.6 | 9.0 | 10.6 | 9.9 | 9.7 | 24 | 27 | 27 | 30 | 32 |
| Crédit Foncier Vaudois | 10 | Lausanne | 27 | 12.8 | 11.3 | 11.6 | 10.4 | 10.5 | 16 | 20 | 23 | 27 | 27 |
| Discount Bank & Trust Co | 65 | Geneva | 25 | 10.4 | 10.0 | 12.8 | 13.0 | 14.0 | 21 | 23 | 17 | 15 | 15 |
| Thurgauer Kantonalbank | 10 | Weinfelden | 25 | 6.4 | 6.4 | 6.5 | 5.5 | 5.8 | 38 | 42 | 43 | 47 | 46 |
| Rothschild Bank AG | 65 | Zurich | 24 | 16.0 | 17.1 | 20.5 | 18.7 | 21.3 | 7 | 7 | 10 | 9 | 9 |
| Banque hypoth. du Canton de Genève | 10 | Geneva | 23 | 5.6 | 7.4 | 8.4 | 7.5 | 5.6 | 41 | 35 | 34 | 37 | 48 |
| Bank Cantrade AG | 35 | Zurich | 23 | 22.2 | 18.7 | 27.6 | 28.8 | 32.1 | 3 | 4 | 7 | 5 | 5 |
| GZB Genossenschaftl. Zentralbank | 30 | Basel | 23 | 8.1 | 7.3 | 7.4 | 7.3 | 7.2 | 31 | 36 | 38 | 40 | 39 |
| Guyerzeller Bank AG | 65 | Zurich | 22 | 20.7 | 15.8 | 24.5 | 19.6 | 27.6 | 5 | 10 | 9 | 8 | 8 |
| Graubündner Kantonalbank | 10 | Chur | 22 | 7.5 | 7.1 | 7.0 | 7.3 | 7.3 | 32 | 37 | 40 | 39 | 37 |
| Banque Procrédit SA | 40 | Fribourg | 22 | 13.5 | 20.3 | 25.5 | 31.4 | 34.1 | 12 | 3 | 8 | 3 | 3 |
| Dreyfus Söhne & Cie | 35 | Basel | 22 | 12.3 | 11.7 | 12.8 | 12.2 | 13.6 | 18 | 16 | 18 | 16 | 17 |
| Caisse d'Epargne Genève | 10 | Geneva | 21 | 4.6 | 7.6 | 8.8 | 7.9 | 8.1 | 46 | 34 | 33 | 34 | 35 |
| Basler Kantonalbank | 10 | Basel | 20 | 6.9 | 6.8 | 6.8 | 6.6 | 6.4 | 34 | 39 | 42 | 42 | 42 |
| Banque Vaudoise de Crédit | 20 | Lausanne | 19 | 15.3 | 16.3 | 10.7 | 11.5 | 9.9 | 10 | 9 | 26 | 21 | 30 |
| Banque Privée Rothschild | 35 | Geneva | 18 | 12.8 | 11.7 | 16.4 | 14.7 | 17.3 | 15 | 18 | 11 | 12 | 11 |
| Aargauische Kantonalbank | 10 | Aarau | 18 | 6.7 | 6.5 | 6.8 | 6.4 | 6.2 | 35 | 41 | 41 | 44 | 44 |
| Migros Bank | 30 | Zurich | 17 | 5.7 | 5.6 | 5.3 | 5.2 | 7.2 | 40 | 45 | 48 | 48 | 38 |
| Banque de l'Etat de Fribourg | 10 | Fribourg | 17 | 11.5 | 11.6 | 11.8 | 12.0 | 12.3 | 19 | 19 | 21 | 18 | 18 |
| ABN AMRO / Algemene Bank Nederland | 65 | Zurich | 17 | 12.9 | 13.3 | 13.9 | 13.4 | 15.6 | 14 | 13 | 15 | 13 | 12 |
| Crédit Lyonnais (Suisse) SA | 65 | Geneva | 17 | 6.6 | 5.9 | 4.8 | 0.6 | 2.7 | 37 | 44 | 50 | 50 | 50 |
| Bankers Trust AG | 65 | Zurich | 16 | 26.9 | 33.1 | 43.8 | 29.5 | 28.1 | 1 | 1 | 3 | 4 | 7 |
| Banca del cantone Ticino | 10 | Bellinzona | 16 | 12.6 | 11.7 | 11.4 | 11.3 | 12.3 | 17 | 17 | 24 | 23 | 19 |
| Banque Cantonale d.Valais | 10 | Sion | 15 | 6.9 | 7.1 | 8.2 | 7.8 | 7.7 | 33 | 38 | 35 | 35 | 36 |
| Solothurner Kantonalbank | 10 | Solothurn | 14 | 0.0 | 5.4 | 6.1 | 7.6 | 6.9 | 49 | 47 | 46 | 36 | 41 |
| Hypothekarkasse des Kantons Bern | 10 | Berne | 14 | NA | 9.8 | 11.6 | 11.7 | 11.5 | NA | 24 | 22 | 19 | 23 |
| Nordfinanz Bank Zürich | 65 | Zurich | 14 | 6.1 | 5.4 | 7.1 | 7.3 | 8.2 | 39 | 46 | 39 | 38 | 33 |
| Banque Bruxelles Lambert | 65 | Lausanne | 14 | 13.2 | 12.4 | 10.9 | 11.6 | 11.6 | 13 | 15 | 25 | 20 | 21 |
| J.P. Morgan (Suisse) SA | 65 | Geneva | 14 | 21.1 | 17.5 | 53.3 | 36.1 | 49.4 | 4 | 5 | 2 | 1 | 1 |
| Bank Leumi le-Israel | 65 | Zurich | 13 | 19.6 | 17.1 | 15.3 | 13.3 | 11.8 | 6 | 8 | 13 | 14 | 20 |
| Clariden Bank | 35 | Zurich | 13 | 25.7 | 29.4 | 33.9 | 33.2 | 37.7 | 2 | 2 | 4 | 2 | 2 |
| Ferrier Lullin & Cie SA | 35 | Geneva | 13 | 15.6 | 15.1 | 28.2 | 26.3 | 33.7 | 8 | 11 | 5 | 6 | 4 |
| Banque de Dépôts | 30 | Geneva | 12 | 5.0 | 4.8 | 4.8 | 3.9 | 3.9 | 45 | 50 | 49 | 49 | 49 |

Remarks:
- NA Data not available
- BG Number of banking group (cf. table 1)
- 1) The 1987 and 1988 data for "Neue Aargauer Bank" resulted from the addition of the results from "Aargauische Hypotheken- & Handelsbank" and "Allgemeine Aargauische Ersparniskasse"

SBA

Table 5:
50 banks with the absolute highest profits 1990 / AV/IC values and ranking orders 1987-1991

| Institute | BG | Location | Net profit (million Sfr.) 1990 | AV/IC (equity concept) (as %) 1991 | 1990 | 1989 | 1988 | 1987 | (Ranking orders) 1991 | 1990 | 1989 | 1988 | 1987 |
|---|---|---|---|---|---|---|---|---|---|---|---|---|---|
| Schweizerische Bankgesellschaft | 25 | Zurich | 780 | 15.4 | 6.8 | 23.3 | 33.6 | 35.6 | 24 | 33 | 29 | 26 | 26 |
| Schweizerischer Bankverein | 25 | Basel | 697 | 11.7 | 11.9 | 24.8 | 33.7 | 36.7 | 29 | 25 | 26 | 25 | 24 |
| Schweizerische Kreditanstalt | 25 | Zurich | 470 | 21.1 | 8.5 | 33.3 | 34.5 | 35.7 | 20 | 32 | 20 | 23 | 25 |
| Schweizerische Volksbank | 25 | Berne | 111 | -6.8 | 0.6 | 10.4 | 15.0 | 16.0 | 45 | 41 | 39 | 42 | 41 |
| Zürcher Kantonalbank | 10 | Zurich | 89 | -2.6 | -4.4 | 4.4 | 9.6 | 9.7 | 40 | 45 | 47 | 47 | 47 |
| CBI-TDB Union Bancaire Privée | 35 | Geneva | 70 | 40.4 | 18.9 | 590.5 | 43.6 | 71.7 | 10 | 21 | 1 | 17 | 11 |
| BSI-Banca della Svizzera Italiana | 30 | Lugano | 58 | 11.8 | 11.9 | 18.4 | 25.9 | 27.4 | 28 | 26 | 32 | 32 | 32 |
| Banque Cantonale Vaudoise | 10 | Lausanne | 57 | 12.5 | 11.0 | 27.7 | 32.4 | 32.9 | 26 | 30 | 24 | 27 | 27 |
| Banque Paribas (Suisse) SA | 65 | Geneva | 51 | -4.8 | 13.0 | 47.2 | 55.3 | 56.8 | 43 | 24 | 14 | 11 | 14 |
| Banca del Gottardo | 65 | Lugano | 42 | 16.5 | 11.7 | 28.9 | 37.0 | 41.0 | 23 | 27 | 23 | 21 | 21 |
| Bank Julius Bär & Co AG | 30 | Zurich | 35 | 21.8 | 19.4 | 29.3 | 33.9 | 41.1 | 17 | 19 | 21 | 24 | 20 |
| Berner Kantonalbank / KB von Bern | 10 | Berne | 34 | -16.5 | 9.0 | 17.8 | 24.0 | 25.0 | 48 | 31 | 33 | 33 | 33 |
| Luzerner Kantonalbank | 10 | Luzern | 32 | -5.1 | -5.6 | 5.1 | 12.9 | 11.6 | 44 | 48 | 46 | 45 | 45 |
| St.Gallische Kantonalbank | 10 | St.Gallen | 32 | 2.1 | -1.8 | 6.9 | 13.8 | 10.2 | 35 | 43 | 44 | 43 | 46 |
| BDL Banco di Lugano | 30 | Lugano | 31 | 18.7 | 40.9 | 56.7 | 64.8 | 79.3 | 21 | 9 | 11 | 8 | 7 |
| Bank J. Vontobel & Co AG | 35 | Zurich | 30 | 6.7 | 28.5 | 53.2 | 53.6 | 58.5 | 31 | 12 | 12 | 12 | 13 |
| Basellandschaftliche Kantonalbank | 10 | Liestal | 30 | 12.2 | 11.2 | 16.7 | 19.4 | 18.8 | 27 | 29 | 35 | 37 | 39 |
| Neue Aargauer Bank 1) | 20 | Aarau | 29 | 14.5 | 11.6 | 23.9 | 28.8 | 27.8 | 25 | 28 | 27 | 29 | 31 |
| Crédit Foncier Vaudois | 10 | Lausanne | 27 | 40.4 | 30.9 | 45.6 | 50.2 | 50.9 | 9 | 11 | 15 | 13 | 17 |
| Discount Bank & Trust Co | 65 | Geneva | 25 | 18.5 | 15.1 | 36.3 | 48.4 | 59.9 | 22 | 23 | 19 | 15 | 12 |
| Thurgauer Kantonalbank | 10 | Weinfelden | 25 | 0.9 | 0.0 | 8.8 | 10.3 | 12.3 | 38 | 42 | 43 | 46 | 44 |
| Rothschild Bank AG | 65 | Zurich | 24 | 53.7 | 49.0 | 71.5 | 69.1 | 77.1 | 6 | 4 | 6 | 7 | 9 |
| Banque hypoth. du Canton de Genève | 10 | Geneva | 23 | -3.0 | 5.2 | 16.6 | 20.1 | 9.6 | 42 | 35 | 36 | 36 | 48 |
| Bank Cantrade AG | 35 | Zurich | 23 | 58.6 | 45.2 | 91.1 | 106.2 | 115.1 | 4 | 8 | 5 | 3 | 3 |
| GZB Genossenschaftl. Zentralbank | 30 | Basel | 23 | 8.9 | 4.5 | 12.1 | 19.1 | 19.3 | 30 | 36 | 38 | 38 | 35 |
| Guyerzeller Bank AG | 65 | Zurich | 22 | 60.9 | 47.5 | 69.7 | 57.2 | 77.2 | 3 | 6 | 7 | 10 | 8 |
| Graubündner Kantonalbank | 10 | Chur | 22 | 5.5 | 3.2 | 9.9 | 18.5 | 19.3 | 32 | 37 | 40 | 39 | 36 |
| Banque Procrédit SA | 40 | Fribourg | 22 | 38.5 | 78.6 | 124.5 | 181.9 | 194.7 | 11 | 2 | 4 | 1 | 1 |
| Dreyfus Söhne & Cie | 35 | Basel | 22 | 28.7 | 25.5 | 37.1 | 43.2 | 47.6 | 12 | 15 | 18 | 19 | 18 |
| Caisse d'Epargne Genève | 10 | Geneva | 21 | -7.6 | 5.4 | 19.0 | 21.9 | 19.5 | 46 | 34 | 31 | 35 | 34 |
| Basler Kantonalbank | 10 | Basel | 20 | 2.8 | 1.9 | 9.0 | 15.8 | 15.8 | 33 | 39 | 41 | 41 | 42 |
| Banque Vaudoise de Crédit | 20 | Lausanne | 19 | 43.3 | 45.7 | 27.2 | 37.2 | 30.0 | 8 | 7 | 25 | 20 | 29 |
| Banque Privée Rothschild | 35 | Geneva | 18 | 25.4 | 19.4 | 43.6 | 43.5 | 53.8 | 13 | 20 | 16 | 18 | 16 |
| Aargauische Kantonalbank | 10 | Aarau | 18 | 2.0 | 0.7 | 8.8 | 13.6 | 12.7 | 37 | 40 | 42 | 44 | 43 |
| Migros Bank | 30 | Zurich | 17 | -2.8 | -4.4 | 1.0 | 7.2 | 19.2 | 41 | 46 | 48 | 48 | 37 |
| Banque de l'Etat de Fribourg | 10 | Fribourg | 17 | 21.5 | 21.2 | 29.1 | 36.6 | 37.7 | 18 | 18 | 22 | 22 | 23 |
| ABN AMRO / Algemene Bank Nederland | 65 | Zurich | 17 | 25.1 | 28.3 | 38.1 | 43.7 | 54.9 | 14 | 13 | 17 | 16 | 15 |
| Crédit Lyonnais (Suisse) SA | 65 | Geneva | 17 | 2.0 | -3.3 | -3.0 | -23.4 | -9.4 | 36 | 44 | 49 | 50 | 50 |
| Bankers Trust AG | 65 | Zurich | 16 | 85.9 | 99.1 | 163.2 | 128.2 | 111.7 | 1 | 1 | 2 | 2 | 4 |
| Banca del cantone Ticino | 10 | Bellinzona | 16 | 21.3 | 17.8 | 23.5 | 28.0 | 31.4 | 19 | 22 | 28 | 31 | 28 |
| Banque Cantonale d.Valais | 10 | Sion | 15 | 2.7 | 2.9 | 12.9 | 17.3 | 16.7 | 34 | 38 | 37 | 40 | 40 |
| Solothurner Kantonalbank | 10 | Solothurn | 14 | -31.8 | -5.1 | 5.8 | 22.1 | 19.0 | 49 | 47 | 45 | 34 | 38 |
| Hypothekarkasse des Kantons Bern | 10 | Berne | 14 | NV | 27.6 | 58.6 | 82.0 | 81.8 | NA | 14 | 10 | 5 | 5 |
| Nordfinanz Bank Zürich | 65 | Zurich | 14 | -0.7 | -7.6 | 17.1 | 30.6 | 40.3 | 39 | 49 | 34 | 28 | 22 |
| Banque Bruxelles Lambert | 65 | Lausanne | 14 | 24.9 | 21.6 | 23.1 | 28.7 | 29.2 | 15 | 17 | 30 | 30 | 30 |
| J.P. Morgan (Suisse) SA | 65 | Geneva | 14 | 49.0 | 38.8 | 129.2 | 82.2 | 118.3 | 7 | 10 | 3 | 4 | 2 |
| Bank Leumi le-Israel | 65 | Zurich | 13 | 66.2 | 47.6 | 51.8 | 49.1 | 43.0 | 2 | 5 | 13 | 14 | 19 |
| Clariden Bank | 35 | Zurich | 13 | 54.8 | 58.1 | 69.1 | 73.4 | 79.8 | 5 | 3 | 8 | 6 | 6 |
| Ferrier Lullin & Cie SA | 35 | Geneva | 13 | 24.8 | 23.1 | 63.1 | 60.2 | 76.8 | 16 | 16 | 9 | 9 | 10 |
| Banque de Dépôts | 30 | Geneva | 12 | -11.6 | -15.5 | -3.5 | -1.0 | -1.3 | 47 | 50 | 50 | 49 | 49 |

Remarks:
- NA Data not available
- BG Number of banking group (cf. table 1)
- 1) The 1987 and 1988 data for "Neue Aargauer Bank" resulted from the addition of the results from "Aargauische Hypotheken- & Handelsbank" and "Allgemeine Aargauische Ersparniskasse"

SBA

Table 6:
Sensitivity of added value results 1990 to changes in the assumptions

| Added value ratios | Coefficients of rank correlation AV/IC (6,4 %) |
|---|---|
| 1 AV/IC (6,4 %) | 1.00 |
| 2 AV/IC (1,4 %) | 0.80 |
| 3 AV/IC (4,4 %) | 0.98 |
| 4 AV/IC (8,4 %) | 0.99 |
| 5 AV/IC (11,4 %) | 0.95 |
| 6 AV/gross income | 0.99 |
| 7 AV/value added | 0.98 |

Remarks:

- The AV/IC results 1990 (added value ratio 1) are based on the average annual return on Confederation bonds (6,4 %).
- The added value ratios 2, 3, 4 and 5 are based on different costs of capital (indicators of opportunity costs of capital).
- The added value ratios 6 and 7 use gross income and value added (cf. section 3.1) in the denominator instead of input costs.

SBA

Table 7:
30 Cantonal and Big banks / added value concepts in comparison 1991

| Institution | Location | BG | AV/IC (%) | AV/IC (rank) | AV/I (%) | AV/I (rank) |
|---|---|---|---|---|---|---|
| Aargauische Kantonalbank | Aarau | 10 | 2.0 | 20 | -20.2 | 21 |
| Appenzell-Ausserrhoden KB | Herisau | 10 | -17.5 | 29 | -39.1 | 29 |
| Appenzell-Innerrhod. KB | Appenzell | 10 | 7.8 | 16 | -17.4 | 16 |
| Banca del cantone Ticino | Bellinzona | 10 | 21.3 | 3 | -1.4 | 3 |
| Banque Cantonale du Jura | Porrentruy | 10 | 6.1 | 17 | -19.6 | 20 |
| Banque Cantonale d.Valais | Sion | 10 | 2.7 | 19 | -16.7 | 15 |
| Banque Cantonale Vaudoise | Lausanne | 10 | 12.5 | 9 | -9.2 | 6 |
| Banque de l'Etat de Frib. | Fribourg | 10 | 21.5 | 2 | 4.5 | 1 |
| Basellandschaftliche KB | Liestal | 10 | 12.2 | 10 | -12.0 | 11 |
| B.cantonale neuchâteloise | Neuchâtel | 10 | 8.1 | 15 | -18.9 | 19 |
| B.hyp.du canton de Genève | Genève | 10 | -3.0 | 25 | -23.9 | 27 |
| Caisse d'Epargne Genève | Genève | 10 | -7.6 | 28 | -22.7 | 25 |
| Crédit Foncier Vaudois | Lausanne | 10 | 40.4 | 1 | 2.8 | 2 |
| Glarner Kantonalbank | Glarus | 10 | 14.1 | 6 | -10.5 | 9 |
| Graubündner Kantonalbank | Chur | 10 | 5.5 | 18 | -17.7 | 17 |
| Kantonalbank Schwyz | Schwyz | 10 | 12.5 | 8 | -10.3 | 8 |
| Luzerner Kantonalbank | Luzern | 10 | -5.1 | 26 | -28.8 | 28 |
| Nidwaldner Kantonalbank | Stans | 10 | 1.1 | 23 | -20.3 | 22 |
| Obwaldner Kantonalbank | Sarnen | 10 | 9.7 | 13 | -15.2 | 14 |
| Schaffhauser Kantonalbank | Schaffhausen | 10 | 10.3 | 12 | -14.2 | 12 |
| Solothurner Kantonalbank | Solothurn | 10 | -31.8 | 30 | -45.7 | 30 |
| St.Gallische Kantonalbank | St.Gallen | 10 | 2.1 | 21 | -23.5 | 26 |
| Thurgauer Kantonalbank | Weinfelden | 10 | 0.9 | 22 | -18.0 | 18 |
| Urner Kantonalbank | Altdorf | 10 | 12.7 | 7 | -14.6 | 13 |
| Zürcher Kantonalbank | Zürich | 10 | -2.6 | 24 | -21.5 | 23 |
| Zuger Kantonalbank | Zug | 10 | 9.7 | 14 | -11.6 | 10 |
| Schweizerische Volksbank | Bern | 25 | -6.8 | 27 | -22.2 | 24 |
| Schweiz. Bankgesellschaft | Zürich | 25 | 15.4 | 5 | -9.7 | 7 |
| Schweiz. Bankverein | Basel | 25 | 11.7 | 11 | -8.1 | 5 |
| Schweiz. Kreditanstalt | Zürich | 25 | 21.1 | 4 | -3.5 | 4 |

AV/IC = [Profits before tax - Opportunity costs of capital] / [Staff costs + Opportunity costs of capital]

AV/I = [Profits before tax +/- Reserve changes - Cost of equity including premium] / [Staff costs + Office expenses + Cost of capital including premium]

Reserve changes = Reserves at the end of 1991 - Reserves at the end of 1990

Cost of equity including premium = Equity (at the end of 1991) x [Return on federel bonds + 10 percentage points]

SBA

Table 8:
30 banks listed on stock exchange / ROA, ROE and AV/IC versus P/Es 1991

| | Equity end of 1991 (million Sfr.) | Market capitalization mid of 1991 (million Sfr.) | Market capitalization mid of 1992 (million Sfr.) | Profit before tax 1991 (million Sfr.) | ROA 1991 (as %) | ROE 1991 (as %) | AVIC 1991 (as %) | PES91 | PE91 |
|---|---|---|---|---|---|---|---|---|---|
| Banca del Gottardo | 598 | 884 | 880 | 58 | 0.79 | 9.70 | 16.51 | 15 | 19 |
| Bank Langenthal | 82 | 81 | 73 | 7 | 0.56 | 9.02 | 11.95 | 11 | 14 |
| Banque Cantonale du Jura | 64 | 67 | 68 | 5 | 0.26 | 7.59 | 6.13 | 14 | 18 |
| Banque Cantonale Vaudoise | 815 | 760 | 781 | 75 | 0.56 | 9.26 | 12.48 | 10 | 12 |
| Banque Vaudoise de Crédit | 168 | 147 | 131 | 26 | 0.75 | 15.27 | 43.33 | 6 | 7 |
| Basellandschaftliche KB | 351 | 374 | 366 | 31 | 0.33 | 8.79 | 12.22 | 12 | 12 |
| Basler Kantonalbank | 318 | 357 | 354 | 22 | 0.29 | 6.87 | 2.84 | 16 | 17 |
| BSI-B.della Svizzera Ita. | 758 | 1013 | 920 | 74 | 0.75 | 9.76 | 11.76 | 14 | 17 |
| B.hyp.du canton de Genève | 322 | 276 | 236 | 18 | 0.25 | 5.62 | -3.00 | 15 | 15 |
| B.Linthgebiet-Sarganserl. | 119 | 147 | 151 | 8 | 0.27 | 6.78 | 2.44 | 18 | 21 |
| Caisse d'Epargne Genève | 331 | 78 | 78 | 15 | 0.22 | 4.56 | -7.65 | 5 | 7 |
| Crédit Foncier Vaudois | 418 | 233 | 230 | 53 | 0.52 | 12.78 | 40.42 | 4 | 8 |
| EKN Bank in Nidwalden | 70 | 63 | 66 | 4 | 0.38 | 5.05 | -8.42 | 18 | 23 |
| Ersparniskasse Aarwangen | 81 | 37 | 35 | 5 | 0.27 | 6.32 | 0.57 | 7 | 10 |
| Gewerbebank Baden | 114 | 119 | 109 | 9 | 0.54 | 7.92 | 9.98 | 13 | 17 |
| Gewerbekasse in Bern | 87 | 93 | 85 | 10 | 0.49 | 11.60 | 26.11 | 9 | 14 |
| Graubündner Kantonalbank | 317 | 344 | 387 | 24 | 0.30 | 7.47 | 5.53 | 15 | 15 |
| GZB Genossensch.Zentralb. | 397 | 373 | 340 | 32 | 0.44 | 8.07 | 8.93 | 12 | 15 |
| Hypothekarbank Lenzburg | 99 | 88 | 86 | 11 | 0.49 | 10.95 | 23.48 | 8 | 11 |
| Luzerner Kantonalbank | 634 | 738 | 752 | 33 | 0.25 | 5.27 | -5.12 | 22 | 22 |
| Luzerner Landbank AG | 80 | 105 | 100 | 8 | 0.45 | 9.69 | 18.04 | 14 | 18 |
| Neue Aargauer Bank | 441 | 718 | 576 | 42 | 0.48 | 9.59 | 14.45 | 17 | 22 |
| Regiobank beider Basel | 83 | 105 | 104 | 5 | 0.31 | 6.56 | 1.57 | 19 | 25 |
| Schweizerische Volksbank | 2200 | 1936 | 1156 | 89 | 0.19 | 4.04 | -6.76 | 22 | 28 |
| Schweiz. Bankgesellschaft | 13866 | 17483 | 17955 | 1323 | 0.66 | 9.54 | 15.40 | 13 | 18 |
| Schweiz. Bankverein | 10099 | 11042 | 9332 | 925 | 0.55 | 9.16 | 11.73 | 12 | 15 |
| Solothurner Handelsbank | 89 | 77 | 69 | 8 | 0.41 | 8.95 | 12.74 | 10 | 12 |
| Spar-u. Leihkasse in Bern | 115 | 131 | 136 | 10 | 0.47 | 9.02 | 15.30 | 13 | 15 |
| St. Gallische Creditanst. | 58 | 78 | 77 | 5 | 0.39 | 7.98 | 8.03 | 17 | 22 |
| Zuger Kantonalbank | 177 | 213 | 195 | 16 | 0.25 | 9.03 | 9.68 | 13 | 14 |
| Average | | | | | 0.43 | 8.41 | 10.36 | 13 | 16 |

Remarks:

| | |
|---|---|
| Equity: | Capital and reserves |
| Market capitalization: | Market value on June 3, 1991, and May 15, 1992<br>(Equity (share, certificate, cooperative and endowment capital)<br>valued at market prices less reserved shares valued at market prices;<br>Dividend-bearing capital valued at market prices) |
| ROA, ROE, AVIC: | Indicators based on profit before tax and end-year data |
| PES91: | Market capitalization (1991) / Profit before tax (1991) |
| PE91: | Market capitalization (1991) / Profit after tax (1991) |

Sources:

Finanz und Wirtschaft, Aktienführer '91 und '92, Zurich, 1991 and 1992
(for elucidation of market capitalization).

SBA

Table 9:
30 banks listed on stock exchange / relation between ROA, ROE, AV/IC and P/Es 1991

(Correlation coefficients)

| | ROA | ROE | AV/IC | PES91 | PE91 |
|---|---|---|---|---|---|
| ROA | 1.000 | 0.732 | 0.676 | -0.335 | -0.218 |
| ROE | 0.732 | 1.000 | 0.981 | -0.582 | -0.505 |
| AVIC | 0.676 | 0.981 | 1.000 | -0.603 | -0.514 |
| PES91 | -0.335 | -0.582 | -0.603 | 1.000 | 0.946 |
| PE91 | -0.218 | -0.505 | -0.514 | 0.946 | 1.000 |

SBA

**Comment on**

**Matthias Wirth: "Measuring the Performance of Banks: Conceptual Problems and Results for Switzerland (1987 - 1991)"**

**Klaus Spremann**

1. Many attempts have been undertaken to identify 'successful companies'. Usually they are ranked, for the particular year, according to criteria such as size, output, profit. So far, however, no such assessments were published for Swiss banks. Matthias Wirth fills this gap. He presents performance indicators for some 50 banks in Switzerland. His work is original and deserves consideration.

Wirth bases his study on accounting figures and ranks banks according to indices like return on equity (ROE), return on assets (ROA), and added value over input costs (AV/IC).

2. In addition, Wirth addresses some of the conceptual problems related to measuring performance. He says a few words on the difficulties arising from off-balance sheet business and he comments on the problems related to hidden reserves. His aim is to interpret accounting figures more reliably in order to calculate the indices selected.

Wirth never specifies which of the indicators he actually prefers. Diagrams show that the choice is not important for the final ranking of the firms. The reason is that in Wirth's sample of banks indices like ROE and AV/IC, though different in nature and by definition, are highly correlated. The reader may discover from **Figure 6** that ROE and AV/IC yield almost the same ranking of banks. **Figure 9** tells the same for AV/IC versus added value over gross income. Finally, the sensitivity of the ranking order to changes in the underlying assumptions is analyzed. **Figure 8** indicates that the ranking order remains almost unchanged if the rate of interest (average return on Confederation bonds) is assumed to be 2 % higher. All this underlines the robustness of the ranking order produced by Matthias Wirth.

3. Academic tradition, however, requires that a discussant has not only words of praise. Remember the old and true saying "you get what you measure". The reader

might try to figure out which banks ought to work particularly hard to improve their performance. The author does not attempt to give an explicit answer to this crucial type of question. Unfortunately, there are substantial differences in what the study identifies as performance and what theory supposes the goal of firms to be.

To see these differences, start from the model of a perfectly competitive economy. The basic assumption is that under such conditions all aspects of economic value are adequately reflected in market prices. In fact, general equilibrium reflects the preferences of all individuals. Theory implies that the ultimate goal of everybody and the purpose of every economic activity is to create market value. Performance is just another word for creating market value.

In the real world, this leads to the need to identify the markets that correctly evaluate economic activities. In Wirth's analysis, the markets chosen are those for commodities, outputs and inputs. This is completely correct for single activities and simple production processes, which create market value as long as the value of outputs exceeds the costs of inputs.

4. But the market of commodities is only of little help to assess the performance of corporations. Although the performance definition of 'creating market value' is correct also for whole firms, the market that values whole firms is that for corporate control. The performance of a bank can therefore be equated with its value to the shareholders.

Although the market for corporate control appears to work well for major corporations in Switzerland, such as Ciba, Nestlé, UBS, it is not a liquid and perfectly organized market for the medium-sized or even the smaller banks. Remember that some of the banks ranked in the study (Cantonal banks) are publicly owned, and the freedom of management is consequently restricted. This difficulty is usually overcome by simulation. If one estimates the value of such a firm, one imitates the assessment methods and the reasoning that theory supposes to guide agents in a well-working market for corporate control.

In view of the by now broad literature on the shareholder value, the value of a corporation is understood as the discounted value of free cash flow. The forecasting of cash flow presupposes a business plan. This plan also defines the payouts related to investments. This allows for the transformation of total cash flow into free cash flow. Discounting requires the determination of the cost of capital, which heavily depends on the risk of the bank.

5. Although this 'discounted-free-cash-flow-concept' must be refined to cope with the special structure of banks, the essential ingredients are the business plan, its implications for cash flow prospects, and risks. In simple words a bank performed well during last year if the management was able to enhance prospects and to control risk.

No argument of that kind can be found in Wirth's paper. UBS, to give an example, takes place 33 in his ranking (ROE for 1990). No word about the fact that UBS has the lowest leverage and therefore the lowest risk, apparently of all banks in the world, that UBS is reorganizing to define five global regions with decentralized management, and that UBS introduced a most promising strategy called 'marketing 2000'. These are indicators for a superior performance of UBS. In fact, share prices reflected this outstanding performance.

6. Apart from the business plan, cash flow prospects, and risk, there is another issue related to the performance of banks. In all countries the banking system is regulated. Regulation in any industry intends to increase the product quality. This is also the reason why authorities impose restrictions an banks, insurance companies, as well as on the suppliers of health care. Quality in our context means the security of the banking system, in particular the liquidity of banks and the security of customers' deposits. So the regulation of banks, if not indispensable, undoubtedly has merits.

Regulation has two effects on profits, value creation, and performance, however. First, there is obviously a cost to follow the rules imposed by regulators in terms of deviation from market optimality (Wirth mentions the minimum requirements of equity). In addition, regulation hinders competition. Weaker competition means less incentives to improve the efficiency of production and internal organization. For both reasons, costs are higher in a regulated industry. Today's higher costs in the banking industry have many names such as capital requirements, excess capacity or overbanking, other costs refer to the fact that risks are not identified and managed properly in every bank. All this has a negative effect on performance.

The second effect of regulation is that markets are more protected. There are usually fewer entries by potential competitors into the banking industry. Consequently, a regulated industry can charge higher prices. This helps to improve the performance of the single bank (though it might be detrimental to the welfare of society as a whole).

Hence, there are three main reasons why the performance of banks could differ from that of other businesses: Costs of regulation, lesser efficiency in protected industry, and higher product prices. It is not clear whether the performance of banks should be higher or lower than the performance of firms operating in more competitive environments. Analyzing the performance of banks requires to pay attention to the implications of regulation on cash flow prospects and on risk. No attempt in this direction is undertaken in the present study.

7. To conclude, the good news is that Matthias Wirth presented a very readable study in a new field - measuring the performance of Swiss banks. The bad news: His ranking order is not sufficiently rooted in the theory of corporate value, risk, cost of capital, and of regulated markets. The paper relies too much on accounting figures, and not enough weight is given to the concept of performance which reflects the market value of a corporation.

**Comment on**

**Matthias Wirth: "Measuring the Performance of Banks: Conceptual Problems and Results for Switzerland (1987 - 1991)"**

**Beat C. Philipp**

Matthias Wirth's paper examines the performance of a very broadly defined and as such heterogeneous group of banks in historical perspective, that is, over the period 1987 to 1991. The measures used are the traditional profitability ratios: return on equity, return on assets as well as a productivity measure. In addition to this, value added is also used as an alternative measure of bank performance. The result is set a of rankings which vary according to the criterion and period selected and which, despite the inevitable reservations mentioned by the author, provide an interesting and informative analysis of the banking sector.

I should like now to focus on a number of aspects in the paper that I consider important for a discussion of the banks and to present some - partially critical - ideas which I feel are of relevance to the subject.

Certainly there are never any data without problems - in this I could not agree more with the author. It is my personal feeling from everyday experience, however, that the data problem is particularly pronounced in the banking sector, especially when I compare my difficulties with those confronting my fellow analysts in other sectors of industry. The assumption on which this study is necessarily based - that of relatively uniform accounting and reporting standards among the sample banks - is in reality non-existent. In actual fact there are significant differences in accounting practices, especially when it comes to "depreciation, write-downs and provisions" - an expense item which has gained enormously in importance not least as a result of the current economic environment. In addition to this, there is some doubt whether the directives issued by the Federal Banking Commission for the 1990 accounts regarding the creation and release of hidden reserves really increased the transparency of accounts in the period concerned, as the author assumes. On the contrary, it must be assumed that this change in regulatory practice had rather the opposite effect in the year in which it was implemented.

Let me demonstrate this point in somewhat greater detail since it is an interesting example of how changes in the regulatory area, although beneficial to reporting transparency over the long term, in this particular case are likely to produce the opposite effect at their time of introduction. The Banking Commission circular gave banks the freedom to decide whether to allocate their assets to current or fixed assets, such reclassification to be made retroactively to 1st January 1990 at the market value on that date. The only condition attached was that an internal record should be kept of how the assets were allocated, which could not be altered later. Fixed assets are defined to include not only real estate, furniture and equipment and long-term equity participations but also securities and precious metal holdings. In principle, fixed assets may not be valued above their historic cost but adjustments to their value may be made where "appropriate to the circumstances". Value adjustments are considered "appropriate" if there is a market-related reduction in the value of assets, although fixed-interest investments (bonds, notes) need not be written down if they are funded by liabilities with matching maturities. This last stipulation is the decisive point. The banks' securities holdings consist for the most part of equity capital which is invested in fixed-interest paper. This means that they are by definition funded by matching liabilities. At the beginning of 1990 fixed-interest investments as a percentage of total securities holdings at UBS were about 83%, at SBC 75% and at Credit Suisse 71%. The possibility of reclassifying these securities as fixed assets obviated the need to mark them to market in the 1990 accounts. In the case of equities, value adjustments are based on the difference between market value and historic cost. It is worth noting, however, that large quantities of equities have often been held over a period of several years and have thus already been written down. In conclusion we can say that the possibility afforded by the Banking Commission's 1990 directive of reallocating securities and precious metal holdings retroactively from current to fixed assets made it possible for the banks to deal with their securities losses without charging them to income. Moreover, it should not be forgotten that 1990 was a year in which securities performance was more than disappointing for the banks due to the outbreak of the Gulf crisis. It is also certain that the extent to which this possibility of avoiding charging securities losses to income was utilized varied considerably from bank to bank.

Another point which relates to the general problem of data is the question of which definition of equity is to be used in calculating return on equity and all the other indicators which contain this variable. It is obvious that a study such as the one presented today must rely on published data. In the case of many banks, however, there is a difference between the published equity figure and the bank's real level of equity. This was clearly visible in UBS's transfer of taxed hidden reserves to published reserves in 1989. The effect on the bank's ROE was naturally negative. Apart from the problem of different capital adequacy requirements for the various groups of banks we also have the additional difficulty that the degree to which individual banks meet their capital adequacy requirements varies from bank to bank. One of the big three Swiss banks, for instance, has an equity level which is continually around the legal minimum, whereas the biggest of the three is consistently in excess of this minimum. Both aspects are dealt with by Matthias Wirth in his paper and they seem to me of great importance in assessing the meaningfulness of return on equity comparisons. One possible solution in my opinion would be to compute all return on equity ratios for the banks using the legal capital adequacy minimum. This makes sense because there is in practice a close connection between the corporate form and the balance sheet structure of a bank as deteriminants of its minimum capital requirements on the one hand and its corresponding earnings possibilities on the other. Fortunately there are an increasing number of banks who state in their annual reports by how much published equity exceeds the minimum requirements. The accuracy of return on equity as an indicator of performance could also be further improved if gross income, instead of net profit before tax, is set in relation to equity (gross return on equity). This would at least reduce the data problem since the directives on the creation and release of hidden reserves mentioned above no longer permit the formerly common practice of netting off expenses against income positions.

As far as the problems relating to return on assets as a performance indicator are concerned I have nothing to add to Matthias Wirth's remarks, the more so as the volume of the banks' off-balance-sheet business is increasing all the time given the current boom in derivatives.

With regard to the productivity approach to performance measurement based on gross added value per employee I shall confine my remarks to the question of whether it would not make more sense to use net added value. In interest-earning operations income is inconceivable without the corresponding need for loan loss provisions.

The added value approach has not found much application up till now at least in the area of financial analysis, which from my point of view makes it all the more interesting. However, in calculating added value using the formula corporate profit less the opportunity costs of capital employed we are naturally confronted with the same data problems as with return on equity. Modifying this definition of added value by using input costs, being the sum of personnel expense, business and office expense plus opportunity costs of capital, undoubtedly makes sense.

In his comparison of the total capital concept with the equity concept Matthias Wirth demonstrates with a simple example the absurdity of the total capital concept for the banking industry. It is obvious that the banks' function as financial intermediaries must exclude any other but a net interest approach.

It is also interesting to note that the value added approach incorporates a market interest rate component (in this case the government bond yield as a risk-free alternative return on investment) - an element which is missing in the return on equity measure. In practice, however, ROE ratios for individual banks or groups of banks are regularly compared to a risk-free or low-risk long-term rate of interest. Shareholders would see little sense in giving their capital to a company which over a longer period of time generated a rate of return on capital employed which was below the long-term risk-free interest rate. When setting medium and long-term ROE targets bank managements are increasingly choosing to formulate them in terms of a risk premium over the government bond yield, an approach which in my opinion makes a lot of sense.

These ideas also follow on from the connection cited by Matthias Wirth between added value/input costs and return on equity. It is clear that added value, defined as corporate profit minus opportunity costs of capital employed, is zero if the government bond yield is equal to the return on equity and that it can only be positive if ROE is higher than the benchmark interest rate.

In his measurement of the performance of all the banks over the period 1987 to 1991 using the criterion added value over input costs the author notes a steady movement in the cumulative frequency functions over time, which indicates a deterioration in the banks' performance. A rough analysis of returns on equity for the same period indicates the same phenomenon.

I agree to a very large extent with the author's summary and conclusions. The various performance indicators for banks available today, based as they are on the published financial statements, display obvious weaknesses which render them unsatisfactory. Nor is the broader approach of the added-value-over-input-costs concept very well suited to providing a measure which can be applied universally to all industries because for the banks as well as for the insurances the equity capital concept is probably the only suitable approach, whereas for the manufacturing sector probably the total capital concept is more suited. Performance comparisons between sectors are therefore not very meaningful.

## Explaining the Performance of Swiss Banks from 1987 to 1990

**Urs Haegler, Matthias Jeger**

### 1. Introduction

In the 1980s the Swiss financial sector began to experience the effects of more intense competition induced by the rapid changes of the regulatory and economic environment. Little doubt exists that this process has not yet come to an end and - in the light of an ongoing financial integration - will continue throughout the Nineties. Switzerland is probably only at the beginning of a longer phase of accelerated structural change in banking.

Despite this, comparatively little empirical research has been done on the structure of the Swiss banking sector.[1] Among the most prominent reasons for this modest state of research are the heterogeneity of Swiss banks, resulting from the universal banking system, and the scarceness of firm data due to the weak accounting requirements faced by Swiss financial institutions.

In contrast, there is a vast body of literature on the structure of the U.S. banking system,[2] presumably not least of all because there the bank groups are more homogeneous, and it is easier to separate the firms geographically. Gilbert (1984) divides the studies for the U.S. into two groups, cost studies and market structure studies. The first group is concerned with the banks' cost efficiency and the extent of scale and scope economies in the banking industry. Hermann and Maurer (1991) as well as Sheldon (1992) have provided first papers of this type for the Swiss banks. The studies in the second group - within which also the present paper may be settled - can be seen as a straightforward extension of the market-structure approach since they deal with the profitability differentials among banks. To put it more precisely, they examine the structure-performance hypothesis which states that there is a positive relationship between bank performance and market concentration. Among the

---

1 For a recent example of a descriptive study see Bossard et al. (1992).

2 See Rhoades (1977,1982) as well as Gilbert (1984) for surveys on earlier studies.

numerous studies that test the structure-performance relationship and frequently find it to be significant, we mention the works by Graddy and Kyle (1979) and, on an international level, Short (1979). There has not yet been any corresponding research for the Swiss financial sector.

The present study is of interest for bank regulators as well as for the banks themselves. As far as regulation is concerned the problem of market power influence is one of the central issues. In order to provide guidance for competition policy and antitrust legislation, which seems to have become increasingly important for the Swiss banking sector recently, it is necessary to examine the relationship between performance and market structure. The well-known structure-performance paradigm assumes that profitability is influenced by market structure.

Due to the eventual existence of economies of scale and of diversification, it is equally important to address questions concerning the effects of size and of the degree of specialization, either on more "traditional" banking services or on non-balance sheet services, the latter playing an important role in the Swiss banking system. The implicit danger of a banking sector becoming more and more concentrated might motivate policy makers to increase regulation.

Another potential source of profitability differentials are deviations from efficiency. If inefficiency were important, policy measures to be taken would tend in the opposite direction: more competition, i.e. less regulation.

The second target group of this study are the banks themselves. In their strategic planning they will inevitably be confronted with questions of optimal size or degree of specialization. We hope to provide some insights here. Our results might be of equal interest with respect to the contribution of the different bank activities, as reflected in the balance sheet structures, to the profitability of Swiss banks.

Regarding methodology, an extended version of the statistical cost accounting approach seems appropriate for these problems because it considers industrial organization and balance sheet variables at the same time. The extended versions of the statistical cost accounting models are a combination of two major methodological approaches in the banking literature. The first and - from a theoretical point of view - basic part is formed by the traditional statistical cost accounting model drawing on

Hester and Zoellner (1966), which focuses on the relationship between bank profitability and balance sheet structure. The second part consists of a collection of further potential factors - in our case of the industrial organization type - to explain the variation in bank performance. Extended versions of the statistical cost accounting model have already been utilized in previous studies (see, for example, Kwast and Rose, 1982).

The above approach enables us also to compare three profitability measures within a structure performance framework. We utilize two, more traditional and well-known measures of bank performance: the Return on Assets (ROA) and the Return on Equity (ROE). In addition, and following Wirth (1992), we make use of a relatively new measure, Added Value divided by Input Costs (AV/IC) which will be defined below. This indicator draws on the work of Davis and Kay (1990). More recent studies have acknowledged the importance of taking more than one performance measure into consideration.[3]

The paper is organized as follows. The second section gives some information on the data and the sample. In section three and four we introduce the model to be estimated and the variables used in the specifications. Section five presents and comments on the estimation results. The last section contains a summary and some preliminary conclusions.

## 2. Data and Sample

The data we use are drawn from individual firm balance sheets and income statements as well as from employment figures of 473 to 477 Swiss banks for the years 1987 to 1990 as reported to the Swiss National Bank [4]. Thus the underlying database allows a multi-period performance analysis of the banks located in Switzerland. Not included are private banks and financial institutions that do not accept deposits from the public at large.

---

3 See, e.g., Arshadi and Lawrence (1987). However, they use canonical correlation analysis which differs substantially from the multiple regression approach we have chosen.

4 These are the data that are presented in an aggregate form by the Swiss National Bank in its statistical yearbook ("Das schweizerische Bankwesen im Jahre 19..").

However, what is subsequently named "full sample" does not cover all the banks. A few foreign banks' affiliates had to be left out for lack of positive equity in Switzerland, a fact that prevents the calculation of the ROE measure. For reasons of comparability we also excluded the same banks from all other estimations. Furthermore, we omitted the observations of those few banks that did not exist in all periods. After these eliminations our full sample provides 4 × 445 observations.

We estimated our model using the full sample and then using two separate groups of subsamples. The criterion for constructing the first group of subsamples is the share of off-balance sheet income to total income. The first subsample contains the 223 institutions with the highest shares, the other one contains the 222 banks with the lowest shares. With respect to the validity of the performance measures it is interesting to note that the difference between the average ROA of these two subgroups is statistically significant at the 5 percent level while the difference in average AV/IC is not. These subsample estimations serve the purpose of finding differentials in the return structures due to the degree of specialization.

The second group of subsamples contains, on the one hand, the banks that were members of one of the three stock exchanges Basle, Geneva and Zurich in at least three of the four periods considered, and, on the other hand, the rest of the banks that are not stock exchange members. This separation is supposed to capture eventual profitability differentials due to advantages in pricing enjoyed only by stock exchange member banks ("courtage").

## 3. Model

As mentioned in the introduction the starting-point of our analysis is a variation of the traditional statistical cost accounting model (see, e.g., Hester and Zoellner, 1966, or Hester and Pierce, 1975). This model starts from a revenue equation for I banks and T periods with f assets and g liabilities each, described by

$$V = Av_A + Lv_L + \varepsilon \tag{3.1}$$

where V is a (IT×1)-vector that denotes the banks' revenues, A and L are (IT×f)-and (IT×g)-matrices of the banks' assets and liabilities, respectively, $v_A$ and $v_L$ are (f×1)- and (g×1)-coefficient vectors representing the gross rates of return on the corresponding assets and liabilities, and $\varepsilon$ is a (IT×1)-vector of normal error terms with an expected value of zero and a variance which is not necessarily homoscedastic (see end of this section).[5]

Analogously, one can write the cost equation as

$$W = Ac_A + Lc_L + \eta \tag{3.2}$$

with W as the costs, $c_A$ and $c_L$ as the rates of cost vectors, and $\eta$ as the error term.

Subtracting (3.2) from (3.1) yields the profit equation

$$Y = Ar + Ls + \delta \tag{3.3}$$

where $Y \equiv V\text{-}W$, $r \equiv v_A - c_A$, $s \equiv v_L - c_L$, and $\delta \equiv \varepsilon - \eta$. Since we want to explain profitability, i.e. a rate, we divide (3.3.) by some scalar deflator D[6] assigned to the corresponding bank. Thus, defining $\mu := \delta/D$, we arrive at the linear stochastic relationship

$$\frac{Y}{D} = \frac{A}{D}r + \frac{L}{D}s + \mu \tag{3.4}$$

The coefficients r and s can be interpreted as the net average returns (net average costs) of the corresponding assets (liabilities).[7] The deflator always corresponds to the divisor used to calculate the rate of the profitability measure appearing on the left-hand side of (3.4).

---

5 Note that, unlike Hester and Zoellner (1966), we have not included intercepts in the revenue and cost equations. Since these equations are not directly estimated, this involves no loss in generality, as will be seen in the course of development of the final model.

6 Y corresponds to profits in the ROA and ROE cases and to Added Value in the AV/IC case. D denotes total assets in the ROA equation, equity in the ROE case, and Input Costs as defined below in the AV/IC equation.

7 That means that the coefficients are "corrected" for the the average operating costs assigned to the provision of each item by the model.

In a next step, we extend this model by a deflated off-balance sheet income variable, K, with coefficient $\alpha$, as well as a matrix Z of industrial organization and other control variables, with the corresponding coefficient vector $\beta$. Thus, the model becomes

$$\frac{Y}{D} = \frac{A}{D}r + \frac{L}{D}s + \frac{K}{D}\alpha + Z\beta + \mu \tag{3.5}$$

The inclusion of the matrix Z is necessary because the initial statistical cost accounting model (3.3) presupposes that all banks face identical net returns on different assets and liabilities. However, because of individual market demand and supply conditions including market structure, the returns and costs of assets and liabilities as well as off-balance sheet activities may vary across the banks. Therefore, the additional variables are required to control for banks' deviations from net average returns.[8]

Considering equation (3.2) we recognize that, due to the balance sheet identity, we are not allowed to include all assets and liabilities as explanatory variables. Particularly when deflating by total assets (as in the ROA estimations), one has to omit one item on either side of the balance sheet in order to avoid linear dependence within the model. Now, the question arises as to how this procedure will affect the interpretation of the coefficients.

---

[8] We omitted one additional variable, the inverse of total assets, which is often included by other authors to control for size differences, and the coefficient of which is supposed to measure income and cost flows unrelated to balance sheet items. There are several reasons for this. First, since we do not always use total assets as the deflator we have corresponding variables in the ROE and AV/IC estimation that do not necessarily proxy the inverse of size. Second, the most important off-balance sheet income flows are introduced separately into the equations through K. Moreover, the interpretation of the coefficent as a measure of returns to scale in on-balance-sheet activities, as suggested by various authors (e.g., Kwast and Rose, 1982), involves strong assumptions. Not only is it necessary that the average costs for off-balance sheet activities are constant, but in the case of decreasing returns to scale we would have to measure coefficients that reflect situations where the prices for these services are lower than average costs. This would mean that providing these services would cause losses to the firm.

Let f be the number of assets and g the number of liabilities again. The equation

$$\frac{Y}{A} = \sum_{m=1}^{f} r_m \frac{A_m}{A} + \sum_{n=1}^{g} s_n \frac{L_n}{A} + \frac{K}{A}\alpha + Z\beta + \mu \qquad (3.6)$$

with *total assets* A as its deflator can be expressed as

$$\frac{Y}{A} = C + \sum_{m=1}^{f-1} R_m \frac{A_m}{A} + \sum_{n=1}^{g-1} S_n \frac{L_n}{A} + \frac{K}{A}\alpha + Z\beta + \mu \qquad (3.7)$$

with $C \equiv (r_f - s_g)$ as the constant, $R_m \equiv (r_m - r_f)$ and $S_n \equiv (s_n - s_g)$, since by definition $A_f/A \equiv 1 - \sum_{m=1}^{f-1} A_m/A$ and $L_g/A \equiv 1 - \sum_{n=1}^{g-1} L_n/A$.

Some problems arise when the deflator is not total assets, i.e. $D \neq A$, but rather equity or Input Costs, as in the equations for ROE and AV/IC, respectively. The above identities are not valid in these cases since any asset (liability) is not a linear combination of 1 minus the other assets (liabilities). Thus, we cannot simply leave out one item on either side.

We circumvent this problem by multiplying the corresponding equations with (equity/total assets) in the ROE estimation, and with (input costs/total assets) in the AV/IC estimation which yields

$$\frac{Y}{D}\frac{D}{A} = \sum_{m=1}^{f} r_m \frac{A_m}{D}\frac{D}{A} + \sum_{n=1}^{g} s_n \frac{L_n}{D}\frac{D}{A} + \frac{K}{D}\frac{D}{A}\alpha + Z\frac{D}{A}\beta + \mu \qquad (3.8)$$

where D is either equity or input costs.

The "accounting part" of these transformed models are then identical to the ROA equation (3.6) and can be converted into (3.7), but all other (industrial and control) variables, summarized in Z, differ for the three measures by the transforming variable. Thus, we end up with a kind of a weighted least squares approach in the

ROE and AV/IC cases. Proceeding in this manner has the advantage that the meaning of all coefficients stay the same across all three measures, i.e. equations estimated. However, statements can only be made about the influence of the balance structure on ROA, while the estimations do not provide any information on its effect on ROE and AV/IC.

Furthermore, a single constant in the model above, in principle, requires by implication that firms perform equally well as long as they exhibit identical values for the right-hand variables. Similarly, a particular bank would exhibit a constant performance as long as its right-hand variables stayed constant over time. In the light of the numerous individual differences not captured by the explanatory variables and the ever changing macroeconomic environment, these implications are not satisfactory.

In order to eliminate these shortcomings we have to allow for firm- and time-specific constants, $C_i$ and $C_t$ respectively, so-called fixed effects:

$$\frac{Y}{A} = C + C_i + C_t + \sum_{m=1}^{f-1} R_m \frac{A_m}{A} + \sum_{n=1}^{g-1} S_n \frac{L_n}{A} + \frac{K}{A}\alpha + Z\beta + \mu \qquad (3.9)$$

With this specification we would have to estimate, along with the other coefficients, I+T fixed effects. With I=445 and T=4 this would result in 449 fixed effects. Since their primary purpose is to avoid biases in the other parameter estimated and their values are of no further interest, it is not necessary to estimate all of them explicitly. One way to reduce the number of estimated fixed effects is to measure the variables in deviations from their respective time-specific means, a procedure that yields

$$Y - \overline{Y} = (C_i - \overline{C}_i) + \sum_{m=1}^{f-1} R_m \left[\frac{A_m}{A} - \overline{\frac{A_m}{A}}\right] + \sum_{n=1}^{g-1} S_n \left[\frac{L_n}{A} - \overline{\frac{L_n}{A}}\right] + \left[\frac{K}{A} - \overline{\frac{K}{A}}\right]\alpha$$
$$+ \ (Z - \overline{Z})\beta + (\mu - \overline{\mu}) \qquad (3.10)$$

where a "–" over a variable denotes a period-specific mean. Equation (3.10) is the specification of the model used in our different estimations.

To estimate the models, we basically apply ordinary least squares regressions. However, as is widely known, cross-sectional data are usually very susceptible to heteroscedasticity. While parameter estimates are still unbiased in such cases, the application of ordinary least squares techniques in the presence of heteroscedasticity leads to inconsistent estimates of the covariance matrix[9]

$$\sigma^2 (X'X)^{-1} X'\Psi X (X'X)^{-1} \tag{3.11}$$

where $\sigma^2\Psi$ is the error covariance matrix and X is the design matrix. As a result, invalid inferences will be drawn when testing statistical hypotheses.

A test for heteroscedastic disturbances in a linear regression model is proposed by Breusch and Pagan (1979). These authors consider the model

$$y_t = x_t\beta + \mu_t \qquad (t = 1,\ldots,N) \tag{3.12}$$

where $\mu_t \sim N(0, \sigma^2\Psi)$ and $\sigma^2\Psi$ is given by the functional relationship $\sigma^2\Psi = f(z_t'\alpha)$ (with the first element of $z_t'$ being unity) which is sufficiently general to include a wide range of heteroscedastic constellations.

Breusch and Pagan show that half of the explained sum of squares in a regression of $\frac{\hat{\mu}_t^2}{\sum(\hat{\mu}_t^2)/N}$ upon $z_t$ where $\hat{\mu}_t^2$ and $\sum(\hat{\mu}_t^2)/N$ are the estimated square residuals and their variance, respectively, corresponds to the Lagrangian multiplier statistic for testing $H_0$:$a_2 = \ldots = a_m = 0$ (homoscedastic disturbances), which is asymptotically Chi-square-distributed with (m-1) degrees of freedom when the null hypothesis is true.

If one finds evidence for the violation of the heteroscedasticity assumption, which was the case in all our specifications, one can improve estimations by making use of models that generate the differing error variances. But, since there are no particular indications concerning the structure of heteroscedasticity, it is not clear how to weight the observations in order to create a specific heteroscedastic formulation. Thus, we retain the OLS parameter estimates which are inefficient but still consistent. However, we apply a consistent covariance matrix estimator in those cases where it is

---

9 See, e.g., Judge et al. (1985), p. 329.

suggested by the Breusch-Pagan test results. Whenever OLS is used, every test of the coefficient vector should be based on the covariance matrix (3.11). But since $\Psi$ is unknown, one has to find an estimate for this expression.

White (1980) suggests a consistent covariance estimator that does not depend on the form of the model. He demonstrates that the covariance matrix estimator

$$(X'X)^{-1} \sum (\hat{\mu}_t) \; x_t' x_t \; (X'X)^{-1} \tag{3.13}$$

asymptotically approaches the expression (3.11). This is an adequate basis to draw inferences when testing statistical hypotheses.

## 4. Variables

As already mentioned, we use three profitability measures as left hand variables: return on assets (ROA), return on equity (ROE) and added value by input costs (AV/IC). In this study ROA is defined as net profit plus taxes divided by total assets, and ROE is defined by net profits plus taxes divided by equity. With these two measures at least two problems arise.[10] First, the accounting profit cannot, a priori, be set equal to economic rents. For example, as far as ROE is concerned, capital-intensive banks tend to realize lower ROE values than more labour-intensive firms. Second, these indicators have the disadvantage of measuring the performance of a firm with respect to one factor only although it uses a multitude of inputs. An alternative indicator of performance is Added value over input costs, which is supposed to measure an enterprise's economic rents, i.e. performance, more appropriately. Added value in our context and following Wirth (1992) is given by net profits plus taxes minus capital charges. Capital charges are calculated by multiplying equity (supposed to approximate the tangible assets tied to the banking firm) with a long-term interest rate (opportunity costs), in our case, the yearly average return on federal bonds. Since physical assets are rather specific and can be reinvested only after quite a long phase of transition (if at all), it is recommendable to use long-term

---

10 See Davis and Kay (1990) and Wirth (1992) for more on this subject.

interest rates. Input costs consist of the expenses for labour and capital, i.e. operating costs related to personnel plus capital charge.[11]

Taxes were included in order to avoid distortions induced by different tax requirements for the various bank groups. Especially the Cantonal banks carry lower tax burdens, if any, than the rest of the financial institutions.

The explanatory variables are summarized in **Table 1**. On the asset side we omitted "buildings and other assets" and on the liability side excluded "other liabilities and equity" (except for AV/IC where we included the "equity" part of this item because it is fundamental for the construction of this indicator). The advantage of these "deletings" lies with the fact that some of the "softer" items of the balance sheet do not impair our estimations.

The first group of variables contains balance sheet variables and off-balance sheet activity variables. Some expectations with respect to the signs of the coefficients (net returns and average costs) are possible even without recurring to an explicit theoretical model. So, one could expect a tendency for asset coefficients to be positive and liability coefficients to be negative. Unfortunately, we are not in a position to formulate stronger hypotheses since, as can be seen in equation (3.7), the coefficients $(r_m-r_f)$ for $m=1,\ldots,f-1$ and $(s_n-s_g)$ for $n=1,\ldots,g-1$ do not reflect the gross rates of return (or the costs) of each item. As far as the asset side is concerned there are two forces that drive coefficients towards the zero level. First and implicit in $r_m$, there are the operating costs that are related to item i by the model regression, and second, the net return $r_f$ of the omitted asset is subtracted from $r_m$. On the liability side, the situation is somewhat different. There, only the second of these effects counteracts the negativity of a liability's gross cost while the first works in a negative direction.

[11] Of course, some other problems are not evitable even when applying AV/IC, e.g. reliability of accounting data (extraordinary items, hidden reserves etc.) or validity of the valuation of the operating capital.

**Table 1: List of Variables**

| | |
|---|---|
| Dependent variables | |
| AV/IC | Added value over input cost |
| ROE | Return on equity |
| ROA | Return on assets |
| Balance sheet items and profit and loss account variables (divided by the appropriate deflator) | |
| LIQ | Cash and less-than-three-months bank debitor items |
| MM | Bills of exchange, rescriptions, treasury bills and all other bank debitor items |
| LOANS | Commercial loans excluding mortgage-backed loans |
| MORT | Mortgages and real estate-backed loans |
| SEC | Securities |
| BACR | Interbank credits |
| DEP | All other demand, time, and savings deposits |
| LTC | Bonds, mortgage bonds |
| EQU | Equity, reserves |
| OBS | Off-balance sheet income |
| Industrial and other control variables | |
| LNEMPL | Natural logarithm of employment |
| MSHI | Market share index |
| RISK | Risk variable |
| EFF | Radial input efficiency |
| FOR | Share of foreign business in total business |

Not even for the OBS coefficient we can predict a positive sign without hesitation, although this variable is taken directly from the profit and loss account, which means its the price is already included and does not have to be estimated. Thus, the estimated coefficient of OBS is the price-(average)cost margin associated with this kind of business. If these services could be provided costlessly one would expect a coefficient of one, but positive costs drive the latter towards zero.

However, these shortcomings should not be overemphasized since when one compares the two subsamples it is the coefficient differentials between the two groups that are crucial.

As mentioned above, we introduce a set of industrial organization and other variables to control for deviations from the average returns (costs). Following the classic study of Bain (1951), empirical examination of the basic structuralist hypothesis has involved looking for a systematic association between average industry profits and levels of industry concentration. The basic notion is that the fewer the firms, or the more the leading few dominate, the easier will be tacit or overt collusion on prices. However, to the extent that average industry profits are dominated by the profits of large firms and to the extent that such firms are large and profitable due to their superior efficiency (reflected in lower average costs), the observed correlation between concentration and industry average profitability may well be due solely to this superior efficiency; this point was initially made by Demsetz (1973). These efficiency differentials are reflected in market share differentials. We therefore introduce a market share variable, whose influence on profitability is expected to be positive.[12] Unfortunately, in the present study we failed to incorporate a measure of concentration.[13] Since market shares and concentration are not independent, positive parameter estimates of the market share variable can not be solely attributed to Ricardian efficiency rents but might also reflect monopoly power.

---

12 However, in recent studies a combination of inter- and intraindustry analysis relating market share as well as industry concentration to firm profitability has emerged (see, among others, Sheperd, 1972, Kwoka and Ravenscraft, 1986). Through the inclusion of both variables the market power hypothesis (with the concentration measure) as well as the superior efficiency hypothesis (with the market share variable) can be tested (see Harris, 1988a).

13 Originally, we intended to incorporate also a weighted Herfindahl index into the equations in order to capture the effects of concentration on profits. Unfortunately, the index showed a high positive correlation with the balance sheet variables. Thus, to avoid multicollinearity we had to restrain from including this variable.

By the preceeding argument, such a relationship may be hypothesized:

$$\frac{Y_{in}}{D_{in}} = f(m_{in}) = \beta_n m_{in} \qquad n=1,\dots,N \qquad (4.1)$$

where $Y_{in}/D_{in}$ is firm's i performance (measured either by ROA, ROE or AV/IC) in market n. The coefficient $\beta_n$ is the estimated influence of market share on performance in market n which is assumed to be the same for all firms in a market and is expected to be positive.

Because our left hand variables are measures of overall bank profitability, relationship (4.1) cannot be tested for the individual markets. But equation (4.1) can be multiplied by the internal share of a firm's total business in market n, $D_{in}/D_i$, to obtain:

$$\frac{Y_{in}}{D_{in}} \frac{D_{in}}{D_i} = \beta_n \frac{D_{in}}{D_i} m_{in} \qquad (4.2)$$

where $\Sigma_n D_{in} / D_i = 1$.

Summing (4.2) over all markets yields:

$$\frac{Y_i}{D_i} = \sum_{n=1}^{7} \beta_n \frac{D_{in}}{D_i} m_{in} \qquad (4.3)$$

The left hand side of (4.3) is the observable overall firm performance.

In empirical testing, a weighted market share for each market and each firm can be constructed. We actually tried to estimate the $\beta$ of seven different markets, using the estimated revenues in each market as proxies for the missing weights ($D_{in}/D_i$, n=1,..,7). The volumes of the seven markets (money market, loans, mortgages, securities, deposits, long term capital, off-balance sheet business) are approximated by summing up all amounts of the respective items across all banks in our sample. Unfortunately, we did not find any possibility to segment further the activity of the bank, e.g. geographically or according to other criteria, which also could have helped to control for activity differences between banks. There is no information available publicly with respect to such dimensions. Unlike e.g. the U.S. banks, Swiss banks are virtually free to do their business in any region they want.

We actually failed in estimating the market power effect in each market ($\beta_n$), because the weighted market share variables proved to be highly collinear. If $\beta$ is assumed to be the same for all markets, the overall performance becomes a function of a firm's weighted average market share.[14] The introduced weighted average market share index (MSHI) is defined as follows: $MSHI = \Sigma_n D_{in}/D_i \cdot m_{in}$. Thus, in such a specification the coefficient on MSHI measures a kind of average market power exercised by the firms under consideration.

Harris (1988a,1988b) shows within a model assuming homogeneous production functions that scale economies measured by the function coefficient (see Ferguson, 1971) are expected to influence negatively the performance of a firm. He argues and finds empirical evidence for it , that optimal margins decline as prices are cut to realize scale economies, ceteris paribus. The concentration effect associated with economies of scale goes into the opposite direction, since higher scale economies imply higher market shares and more concentration which imply higher margins.

As might be expected, estimates of the function coefficient for economies of scale are not available for the banks operating in Switzerland. In the literature, the effects of scale economies are usually proxied by some measure of plant/firm size within an industry (see Weiss, 1963 or Sawyer, 1971). Because such data are not available for research purposes we cannot incorporate a similar variable in our equations. However, we can consider individual firm size itself an admittedly weak proxy for the firm specific function coefficient. We measure the firm size by taking the natural log of the total employment (LNEMPL) of a bank. This assumption implies that the greater the size of a bank the more the bank experiences increasing returns to scale. However, in empirical testing a collinearity problem between the size and the market share variable might arise.

In the literature, the absolute firm size is also associated with many of the market power advantages often mentioned with reference to conglomerate size. In particular,

---

[14] A weighting procedure for multi-market firms is also suggested by Mueller (1986).

a corporation's ability to win profitable favors from government might closely correlate with absolute size. On the other hand, larger firms might suffer from greater internal control problems and bureaucratic inefficiencies (X-inefficiency). If we assume that the positive effects of firm size, either due to economies of scale or to market power are completely captured by the market share variable the expected sign of size alone in terms of LNEMPL would be negative. It is true that empirical work so far has uncovered more often than not negative coefficients (see, for example, Jacquemin and Lichtbuer, 1973).

The technical efficiency variable EFF is included to control for variations in performance stemming from deviations from the productive efficiency frontier. A bank that does not operate on the "best practice" frontier is expected to exhibit a relatively lower profitability, since it could improve by using inputs less wastefully. Thus, a non-negative sign for EFF is expected. A significantly positive sign means that some of the variation in the left hand variable can be explained by some banks' deviations from productive input efficiency while an insignificant sign shows that technical efficiency does not appear to be a major problem. The latter phenomenon could be interpreted as an indication that there is some room for niche strategies within the banking industry such that the competitive pressure is rather weak from this point of view. EFF corresponds to bank i's parameter $\theta_i$ that solves the linear programming problem

$$
\begin{aligned}
& \min \theta_i \\
& \text{s.t.} \quad q_i \leq \lambda Q \\
& \qquad \theta_i n_i \geq \lambda N \\
& \qquad \sum_j \lambda_j = 1 \\
& \qquad \lambda_j \in \mathbf{R}_+ \qquad \forall\, j = 1,\ldots,I \\
& \qquad \theta_i \in (0,1]
\end{aligned}
\tag{4.4}
$$

where $q_i$ is the vector of outputs produced by i and Q the matrix of all outputs of all banks; $n_i$ is the vector of inputs utilized by i and N a matrix of all inputs of all banks. Finally, $\lambda$ denotes a $(1 \times I)$-vector of intensity factors. The constraint $\sum_j \lambda_j = 1$

ensures that variable returns to scale are presupposed such that the data envelopment corresponds to the smallest possible convex hull.

This method is known in the literature as the non-parametric frontier approach to the measurement of productive (input) efficiency. The interested reader may consult Färe, Grosskopf, Lovell (1985) for more details and Sheldon, Haegler (1992) for an application to Swiss bank data. Similar estimations were utilized in this paper.

There are two types of risk measures most frequently used in the empirical literature: one based on the covariance of a firm's returns with those of other firms, another based on the variance (standard deviation) of its returns. The covariance-type risk measure is the appropriate one in a world in which capital owners hold diversified portfolios of assets (see any finance text book). The standard deviation of the return on a single asset is the appropriate measure of risk when only one asset is held. Because the time series of bank returns consists of only four observations (1987-1990), traditional risk measures cannot be calculated. But we can calculate a so called cross-section risk measure, which is based on the standard deviation of the rates of return in the various fields of activities in which the banks are engaged (see Irsch, 1988).

The RISK variable was constructed as follows. We sorted the full sample in each year according to the levels of off-balance sheet activities and partitioned it in fourteen risk classes. Then every bank was assigned the standard deviation of the corresponding performance indicatore within the risk class to which the institute belongs. Assuming that the profits of firms that run a higher risk contain a risk premium we expect the sign of the RISK coefficient to be positive. Of course, in interpreting the empirical results one must keep in mind that the risk measure used is of the variance type and not time related. So our approach might only pick up the risk differences faced by banks.

Finally, FOR was introduced to control for the foreign activities of Swiss banks. These activities have long used to be exceptionally high in Switzerland. Since the risks involved in this kind of activity are usually somewhat higher and different in nature than the ones in the domestic business it appeared worthwhile to examine the influence of the foreign activity on bank profitability.

# 5. Regression Results

## 5.1. Description of Dependent Variables

To increase the understanding of the different performance indicators, we begin the empirical discussion descriptively (see **Table 2**). Complete time series from 1987-1990 of the three left hand variables are available for a total of 445 firms (see chapter 2). Because of some missing data on the independent variables side, from the 1780

**Table 2: Descriptive Statistics of Left Hand Variables**

| Variable | ROA | ROE | AV/IC |
|---|---|---|---|
| Mean | 0.010 | 0.117 | 0.207 |
| Median | 0.005 | 0.082 | 0.189 |
| Std.dev. | 0.020 | 1.176 | 0.895 |
| Skew. | 1.920 | 38.440 | 9.950 |
| Min. | -0.234 | -6.696 | -13.110 |
| Max. | 0.215 | 48.050 | 25.450 |

FAI

observations thus obtained there remain 1742 observations for the empirical analysis. The sample mean of ROA (a little bit more than 1%) is the smallest among the three profitability indicators because its large deflator. The respective means for ROE and AV/IC are 11.6% and 20.7%. The distribution of all three indicators are slightly positively skewed, with the median exceeding the mean. The positive skewness (38.44) is most obvious for the ROE measure. This result may be partly due to the observed maximum ROE-value of 48 which is about eight times larger (in absolute terms) than the corresponding minimum value of -6.6. Not surprisingly, also the standard deviation of ROE is larger than that of AV/IC and especially that of ROA. The reason can be found in the extremley low equity base of some banks. In some cases ROE can be driven up to exotic values even if the (absolute) gains or losses of these firms are quite moderate.

## 5.2. Results for the Full Sample Estimates

We estimated equations with and without fixed effects for all three profitability measures. The general two factor fixed effects model has an overall constant as well as a "group" effect for each firm and a "time" effect for each period. The problem of multicollinearity - the time and group dummy variables both sum to one - is avoided by implicitly imposing the restrictions

$$\sum_{i=1}^{I} C_i = 0 \, ; \quad \sum_{t=1}^{T} C_t = 0 \tag{5.1}$$

Thus the sign of the coefficient of the time dummies indicate whether the overall firm performance is positively or negatively influenced by the time effects.

Using the model of equation (3.10) and the variables of **Table 1,** ordinary least squares regressions were run for the pooled sample of the 445 banks (1742 observations). The standard errors of the coefficients are derived from White's consistent estimator of the covariance matrix (see above). Estimated coefficients for the added value on input costs (AV/IC), return on assets (ROA) and return on equity (ROE) regressions are given in **Table 3**. To see whether the group effects have an influence on the parameter estimates, the model was also estimated without group effects (see **Table 4**).

We start by summarising the results with respect to coefficient levels for the AV/IC regressions. Coefficients may be interpreted as rates of return net of operating expenses, extraordinary gains and losses, but gross of taxes. With respect to all assets the signs are positive and in three out of five cases they are significant at the 5%-level. To the extent that the rate of return on the excluded asset is greater than zero, the estimated asset coefficients should be below the net rate of return on those assets. This can be seen from equation (3.7). The asset coefficients are measured relative to the rate of return on the excluded asset, so the estimated coefficients are driven down towards zero. The estimated (net) rates of returns are lower for the more liquid assets with 5.6% (LIQ) and 6.3% (MM), but higher for all other assets, ranging from 6.6% (LOANS) to 6.8% and 7.6% (SEC and MORT, respectively). The significant positive return on mortgages may be surprising if one considers the political pressure on mortgage interest rates faced by banks in Switzerland. Actually, the estimated return is even the highest among the asset items.

**Table 3: Results for Two Way Fixed Effects Models**

| | AV/IC | | ROE | | ROA | |
|---|---|---|---|---|---|---|
| Variable | Coefficient | t-ratio | Coefficient | t-ratio | Coefficient | t-ratio |
| DUM87 | 0.000 | 1.11 | 0.000 | 0.46 | 0.001 | 0.94 |
| DUM88 | 0.002 | 3.70* | 0.001 | 1.89* | 0.001 | 1.88* |
| DUM89 | 0.000 | 0.36 | 0.000 | 0.99 | 0.000 | 0.41 |
| DUM90 | -0.002 | -4.55* | -0.001 | -2.68* | -0.002 | -2.20* |
| LNEMPL | -0.071 | -3.27* | 0.006 | 0.68 | 0.008 | 0.92 |
| MSHI | 7.418 | 1.19 | 2.438 | 1.23 | 0.290 | 0.63 |
| EFF | 0.095 | 1.22 | 0.011 | 0.66 | 0.001 | 0.26 |
| RISK | 0.008 | 0.20 | -0.003 | -0.80 | 0.007 | 0.27 |
| FOR | -0.003 | -0.42 | -0.004 | -0.48 | -0.005 | -0.73 |
| OBS | 0.478 | 7.12* | 0.387 | 5.50* | 0.375 | 4.74* |
| LIQ | 0.056 | 1.34 | 0.068 | 1.60 | 0.073 | 1.66* |
| MM | 0.063 | 1.52 | 0.075 | 1.79* | 0.077 | 1.84* |
| LOANS | 0.066 | 1.73* | 0.077 | 1.97* | 0.082 | 2.01* |
| MORT | 0.076 | 1.74* | 0.086 | 1.92* | 0.090 | 1.98* |
| SEC | 0.068 | 1.72* | 0.085 | 2.08* | 0.088 | 2.10* |
| BACR | 0.037 | 1.12 | 0.036 | 0.95 | 0.016 | 0.51 |
| DEP | -0.007 | -0.27 | -0.003 | -0.15 | -0.019 | -0.67 |
| LTC | 0.006 | 0.22 | 0.006 | 0.27 | -0.012 | -0.42 |
| EQU | -0.012 | -0.51 | | | | |
| Obs. | 1742 | | 1742 | | 1742 | |
| adj. $R^2$ | 0.29 | | 0.20 | | 0.21 | |

Note: * significant at the 5% level (one-tailed test) FAI

The negative coefficients of the liabilities are expected because of interest costs. Estimated coefficients are positive (BACR, LTC) as well as negative (DEP, EQU). However, the estimated coefficients are not significant. Here again, to the extent that the rate of return on the omitted liability is negative, the coefficients of the other liability items are driven up towards or beyond zero. This may be an explanation of the positive (but insignificant) and insignificant negative coefficient estimates. In addition, the positive parameter estimates are quite small in absolute value and much more smaller than the estimated returns of the asset items. Contrary to ROE and ROA, the cost of equity capital is explicitly deducted from the net return of AV/IC. Therefore, EQU is included in the AV/IC regression and its estimated net cost is 1.2%. The estimated cost of deposits is higher than the cost of short and long term credits. This surprising result is perhaps due to the high cost in serving the deposit accounts. However, the estimated cost of the liability items are not significant.

Over all, measured against prior expectations, the signs and levels of significance of the asset and liability coefficients appear acceptable.

The coefficient of OBS measures the price-cost-margin of the off-balance sheet activities of a bank. This coefficient gives an estimate of the ratio between the off-balance sheet income net and gross of operating costs. As expected, the return on off-balance sheet activities is positive and the estimated coefficient is highly significant.

The significant coefficients of some structural and other control variables indicate that the banks experience income flows unrelated to the portfolio mix. Also, the positive (but insignificant) parameter of MSHI suggests that the market share is directly related to the added value of a bank. Several studies of the industrial sector have found a systematic positive relationship between the market shares of individual firms and their profit performance[15]. A similar relationship was found for banking already by Rhoades (1982). The result suggests that, in addition to accounting for portfolio and liability differences, estimations should control for market share also in the case of banks. In spite of measurement problems, at least some information needed for the purpose of the underlying specification appears to have been captured by our market share variable. The same is true for the other structural variable introduced in the equation. Possible scale and/or X-inefficiency effects, as far as they can be proxied by a bank's employment figure, seem to have a negative influence on

---

[15] Some of these studies are mentioned in Geroski (1988).

the net income of a bank. The coefficient of LNEMPL is, as expected, negative, and significant.

Also a higher technical efficiency seems to generate firm specific rents. The coefficient of EFF is positive, but not significant. Maybe the parameter value is biased downwards because of the high (negative) correlation between LNEMPL and EFF of -0.68. In addition, this last result can be interpreted as a strong indication of large X-inefficiencies experienced by large banks.

The time effects variables for each year of the observation period, which in part should also capture the effects of macroeconomic conditions, are significant for 1988 and 1990. The coefficients indicate that Swiss banks enjoyed, ceteris paribus, extraordinary gains in 1988 but suffered reduced earnings in 1990. This result is not surprising given the income statement of the last few years.

The remaining variables do not seem to have any major influence on a bank's income stream. The coefficient of the ratio of foreign assets to total assets (FOR) has a negative but not significant sign. However, also from a theoretical point of view the expected sign of this variable is ambiguous.

Contrary to the FOR variable, the expected sign of the overall firm risk variable - the standard deviation of the respective profitability measure within the corresponding risk group in each year - is positive, indicating a premium due to greater market risk. Although the coefficient of RISK is positive, it is not significant. Maybe this result is caused by the crude approach in measuring risk . Note that the study of Kwast and Rose (1982) showed high-profit banks to have (statistically significant) lower risk exposure, on average, than the low profit banks in the U.S..

The coefficients of the ROE and ROA regressions may be interpreted in the same way to those of AV/IC. In addition, because in the ROE and ROA specifications the dependent variable as well as the asset, liability, dummy and OBS variables are even identical, one would expect very similar absolute parameter values for these variables. Thus, not surprisingly, the ranking of the estimated returns is the same for all three performance measures, and in the case of ROE and ROA, very similar in absolute value. As mentioned before, in the ROE and ROA regressions equity is omitted since the cost of equity is not directly reflected by net earnings in the case of these performance indicators.

**Table 4: Models with and without Fixed Effects (AV/IC)**

| | Model with fixed effects | | Model without fixed effects | | | |
|---|---|---|---|---|---|---|
| Variable | Coefficient | St.err. | Coefficient | St.err. | Dev. | t-ratio |
| DUM87 | 0.000 | 0.000 | 0.064 | 0.021 | | |
| DUM88 | 0.002 | 0.000 | 0.065 | 0.021 | | |
| DUM89 | 0.000 | 0.000 | 0.064 | 0.021 | | |
| DUM90 | -0.002 | 0.000 | 0.060 | 0.021 | | |
| LNEMPL | -0.071 | 0.022 | -0.039 | 0.015 | -0.033 | -1.224 |
| MSHI | 7.418 | 6.218 | 3.585 | 1.160 | 3.832 | 0.606 |
| EFF | 0.095 | 0.078 | 0.029 | 0.084 | 0.066 | 0.576 |
| RISK | 0.008 | 0.040 | -0.081 | 0.063 | 0.089 | 1.197 |
| FOR | -0.003 | 0.008 | -0.003 | 0.003 | 0.000 | -0.020 |
| OBS | 0.478 | 0.067 | 0.361 | 0.062 | 0.117 | 1.282 |
| LIQ | 0.056 | 0.042 | 0.011 | 0.021 | 0.045 | 0.956 |
| MM | 0.063 | 0.042 | 0.019 | 0.021 | 0.044 | 0.947 |
| LOANS | 0.066 | 0.038 | 0.003 | 0.023 | 0.063 | 1.403 |
| MORT | 0.076 | 0.044 | 0.014 | 0.023 | 0.062 | 1.255 |
| SEC | 0.068 | 0.040 | 0.011 | 0.024 | 0.057 | 1.228 |
| BACR | 0.037 | 0.033 | -0.065 | 0.017 | 0.102 | 2.732* |
| DEP | -0.007 | 0.027 | -0.077 | 0.012 | 0.070 | 2.371* |
| LTC | 0.006 | 0.026 | -0.075 | 0.013 | 0.080 | 2.767* |
| EQU | -0.012 | 0.023 | -0.096 | 0.013 | 0.084 | 3.174* |
| Obs. | 1742 | | 1742 | | | |
| $R^2$ | 0.29 | | 0.54 | | | |

Note: * significant at the 5% level (one-tailed test) FAI

The greatest differences, as expected, are found in the coefficients of the structural variables. The coefficient of MSHI both in the ROA as well as in the ROE regressions is still positive. The coefficient of LNEMPL even changes its sign and becomes also positive. In the ROE and ROA specifications the influence of absolute size (measured by LNEMPL) cannot be separated from relative size (measured by MSHI). Thus in our case, AV/IC appears more appropriate in testing structure performance relationships. Because of that and of the generally higher $R^2$-values, only the results with respect to this profitability measure are discussed further on.

The results for the other control variables are also quite the same for AV/IC, ROE and ROA. Even if the sign differs sometimes the coefficient at least becomes not significant. Finally, the adjusted $R^2$ ranging from 0.20 to 0.29 are quite high given that the variables are defined as absolute deviations from their respective sample means (see equation 3.10).

Interesting conclusions emerge from the results of the two factor fixed effects model compared with a specification where the firm effects are not included in the equation (see **Table 4**). The significant differences of some parameter estimates indicate that the coefficients are biased when leaving out the group dummies. Therefore, at least in this case, the two factor fixed effects design is necessary to ensure unbiased parameter estimates.

### 5.3. Comparison of Subsamples

To see whether the estimated coefficients are the same for all banks the model was also estimated for different subsamples. The first subsample (50% of all banks in each subsample) contains the banks mainly engaged in off-balance sheet activities (high OBS) and the second contains the banks with a high share in traditional (commercial) banking (low OBS). The results are reported in **Table 5**. The group which is more engaged in off-balance sheet activities does better with respect to the difference in the OBS coefficient which is highly significant. The estimated negative (and significant) OBS coefficient of subsample 2 indicates that the more traditional banks may even suffer losses from this kind of business. Although the off-balance sheet activities seem to be very profitable (as can be seen by the higher overall profitability

**Table 5: Comparison of Subsamples (AV/IC)**

| | Subsample 1[a] Coefficient | t-ratio | Subsample 2[b] Coefficient | t-ratio | Difference | t-ratio |
|---|---|---|---|---|---|---|
| DUM87 | 0.000 | 0.69 | -0.002 | -2.28* | 0.002 | 2.096* |
| DUM88 | 0.002 | 3.96* | 0.000 | -0.44 | 0.002 | 3.570* |
| DUM89 | 0.001 | 1.87* | 0.001 | 2.01* | 0.000 | 0.414 |
| DUM90 | -0.003 | -3.90* | 0.001 | 1.48 | -0.004 | -3.902* |
| LNEMPL | -0.046 | -2.17* | -0.550 | -3.17* | 0.504 | 2.879* |
| MSHI | 4.892 | 0.94 | 170.920 | 1.88* | -166.028 | -1.819* |
| EFF | 0.083 | 1.12 | 0.361 | 0.78 | -0.278 | -0.591 |
| RISK | -0.033 | -0.64 | 0.097 | 2.28* | -0.131 | -1.949* |
| FOR | -0.007 | -1.12 | 0.006 | 0.39 | -0.013 | -0.749 |
| OBS | 0.481 | 7.11* | -1.234 | -2.38* | 1.714 | 3.278* |
| LIQ | 0.039 | 1.46 | 0.257 | 1.53 | -0.219 | -1.282 |
| MM | 0.049 | 1.68* | 0.155 | 1.25 | -0.106 | -0.833 |
| LOANS | 0.052 | 1.89* | 0.177 | 1.42 | -0.125 | -0.980 |
| MORT | 0.058 | 1.92* | 0.174 | 1.36 | -0.115 | -0.875 |
| SEC | 0.056 | 1.87* | 0.215 | 1.46 | -0.159 | -1.054 |
| BACR | 0.033 | 0.92 | 0.087 | 1.15 | -0.054 | -0.648 |
| DEP | 0.012 | 0.48 | -0.111 | -1.82* | 0.123 | 1.866* |
| LTC | 0.019 | 0.70 | -0.114 | -1.84* | 0.133 | 1.970* |
| EQU | -0.019 | -0.80 | 0.142 | 1.89* | -0.162 | -2.045* |
| Obs. | 866 | | 876 | | | |
| adj. $R^2$ | 0.36 | | 0.49 | | | |

Notes: * significant at the 5% level (one-tailed test) FAI

[a] High OBS banks

[b] Low OBS Banks

of the corresponding banks), not all banks can gain from this field of activity equally. This result might suggest that a certain specialisation is necessary to successfully compete with other banks in a market. That a certain level of activity is necessary in order to run profitable off-balance sheet operations can be seen from the positive coefficient of OBS in the full sample estimates. On the other hand, the high absolute parameter value of OBS in subsample 2 may be a little irritating; also the standard error of this coefficient is also high in absolute terms, and the off-balance sheet business constitutes only a minor fraction of the overall activities of these banks. Because the asset and liability coefficients are measured relative to the rate of returns to the excluded items the estimated coefficients of the two subsamples are not fully comparable. The results indicate that while the estimated returns (costs) of the low OBS banks are higher in absolute value they are nevertheless not always statistically significant. But again the conformity of the regression coefficients to prior expectations is satisfactory.

The coefficients of MSHI and LNEMPL are of the same sign in both subsamples, although the banks in subsample 2 seem to be more able to exploit profitably higher levels of market shares. These banks also suffer more from possible scale effects, whereas the overall technical efficiency again seems to play a minor role.

Any differences in the coefficients of the annual variables between the high OBS and low OBS banks are due to the different portfolio mix, as can be seen from the opposite signs of some dummy variables. Actually, the subsamples are differently affected by the time effects. These results suggest that the macroeconomic factors are affecting differently the earnings of the two bank groups across years. It also predicts a weak relationship between the activities of the two subsamples.

Finally, the RISK variable is positive only in subsample 2, as expected, suggesting that the higher profitability contains some risk premia.

To shed more light on the off-balance sheet activities the banks in subsample 1 who are stock exchange members are analyzed in isolation (see **Table 6**). Although the results are similar to those of the whole subsample 1 in **Table 5**, the stock exchange member banks are among themselves even more homogenous as can be seen from the extraordinarily high $R^2$-value of 0.68.

**Table 6: Stock Member Banks Compared to the Rest (AV/IC)**

| | stock member banks | | non-member banks | | | |
|---|---|---|---|---|---|---|
| | Coefficient | t-ratio | Coefficient | t-ratio | Difference | t-ratio |
| DUM87 | 0.001 | 0.49 | 0.000 | 0.92 | 0.000 | 0.14 |
| DUM88 | 0.002 | 3.12* | 0.002 | 3.17* | 0.000 | 0.08 |
| DUM89 | 0.000 | -0.29 | 0.000 | 0.79 | 0.000 | -0.51 |
| DUM90 | -0.002 | -1.48 | -0.002 | -4.22* | 0.000 | 0.11 |
| LNEMPL | -0.171 | -4.90* | -0.069 | -2.78* | -0.102 | -2.37* |
| MSHI | 6.952 | 1.27 | 79.295 | 1.85* | -72.343 | -1.67* |
| EFF | -0.092 | -0.69 | 0.096 | 1.18 | -0.188 | -1.21 |
| RISK | -0.016 | -0.34 | 0.009 | 0.21 | -0.025 | -0.39 |
| FOR | 0.007 | 0.48 | -0.005 | -0.55 | 0.012 | 0.69 |
| OBS | 0.585 | 5.39* | 0.429 | 5.79* | 0.155 | 1.18 |
| LIQ | -0.027 | -1.43 | 0.064 | 1.33 | -0.091 | -1.76* |
| MM | 0.004 | 0.15 | 0.070 | 1.46 | -0.066 | -1.24 |
| LOANS | 0.012 | 0.40 | 0.072 | 1.63 | -0.060 | -1.15 |
| MORT | 0.013 | 0.48 | 0.081 | 1.61 | -0.068 | -1.18 |
| SEC | 0.015 | 0.58 | 0.072 | 1.54 | -0.056 | -1.05 |
| BACR | -0.064 | -1.57 | 0.048 | 1.32 | -0.112 | -2.05* |
| DEP | -0.114 | -2.50* | 0.004 | 0.12 | -0.117 | -2.13* |
| LTC | -0.121 | -2.27* | 0.015 | 0.49 | -0.136 | -2.22* |
| EQU | -0.043 | -0.66 | -0.001 | -0.03 | -0.043 | -0.61 |
| Obs. | 148 | | 1594 | | | |
| adj. $R^2$ | 0.68 | | 0.25 | | | |

Notes: * significant at the 5% level (one-tailed test) FAI

The most striking difference between the samples emerges from the estimated off-balance sheet returns. The estimated off-balance sheet return (price-cost-margin) of the stock exchange members is 0.58, which is much higher than the 0.43 of the non-member banks and still higher than the 0.48 of the whole subsample 1. In addition, the estimated returns (costs) of the balance sheet items are lower (higher) for the stock exchange members compared to the non-members. For some liability items, the differences are even significant. Once again the higher returns of specializing in either balance sheet or non-balance sheet activities are confirmed. Furthermore, because of the significantly higher profitability of stock exchange members compared to all other banks, access to the Swiss stock exchanges permits extra returns. Also for this group, the structural factors are, with the exception of absolute size, not so important. The coefficient of EFF becomes even negative suggesting that the rents captured by these firms are due to general market conditions rather than cost advantages. In contrast, for the rest of the banks in our sample the structural variables are always of the right sign and, in the cases of LNEMPL and MSHI, they are even significant. Again, the coefficient of EFF is positive but insignificant. Also in traditional banking, other factors as for example market power seem to be more important for success than innovative cost cutting.

## 6. Summary and Conclusions

The paper tried to provide some answers to questions of market power influence, scale economies and profit differentials due to specialization in traditional banking or off-balance sheet activities, respectively. A variation of the statistical cost accounting model was applied and estimated in a two-way fixed effects approach. A further aim of the study was to compare three profitability measures and their performance as left-hand variables in a structure-performance framework. The results with respect to the three profitability indicators are similar although the various effects of the right-hand variables are best reflected in AV/IC, which has not been analyzed in banking thus far.

A relationship between market structure and performance is found in our study, as was the case in other investigations on the subject. However, policy makers have to be careful when choosing the banks that are supposed to belong to the target group of regulatory actions. Market power effects reflected in high market shares are most obvious in traditional banking, whereas in off-balance sheet activities other factors seem to be responsible for success. On the other hand, the high rents of the stock exchange member banks suggest supporting a policy that facilitates entry into the market of this banking group. In all equations the coefficients of the size variables point to some evidence of economies of scale.

The differing impact of the market share in the subsamples analyzed, together with the relative unimportance of being technically efficient, also confirms the existence of protected segments in the Swiss financial sector. Actually, apart from possible X-inefficiencies, serving the customers in a technically efficient way seems to be only one and a relatively unimportant factor of competitiveness in Swiss banking. Exploiting market niches and market power in price-setting as well as choosing the right portfolio mix might be more decisive factors in competing against other firms in the industry. The ability to differentiate banking services provides viability for a variety of market participants, despite possible cost disadvantages of some firms. Welfare losses caused by inefficient producers may thus be, at least partially, compensated for by increased consumer surpluses due to heterogeneous product supply. This conclusion also implies that the banking system incorporates quite heterogeneous agents.

As expected the asset coefficient estimates are always positive and the ones for the liability coefficients mostly negative. In terms of overall performance the results indicate, unsurprisingly, that 1990 was not very successful for banks.

Banks with a high proportion of off-balance sheet activities do not come off well in traditional banking, relative to those institutions specialized in this field. In contrast, they perform clearly better in the non-balance sheet business while the traditional banks fare quite poorly there. Thus, for bank managers it is important to see that there is a strong tendency for positive effects of specialization within the banking sector. It is also better to grow relative to the market, at least in some segments, than in absolute size.

Somewhat surprisingly, no significant effects of the proportion of the foreign activities and of cross-sectional risk could be shown. However, this might be due to the relatively crude way in which these aspects were captured by the variables in the model.

A promising task for future research is to identify and analyze the market segments more thoroughly. The separation in stock exchange member banks and non-member banks is only a first, though important, step in this direction.

**Literature**


Arshadi, N. and Lawrence E.C. (1987), "An Empirical Investigation of New Bank Performance", in: Journal of Banking and Finance, Vol. 11 (1987), 33-48.

Bain J. (1951), "Relation of Profit Rate to Industry Concentration: American Manufacturing 1936-1940", in: Quarterly Journal of Economics, Vol. 65, 293-324.

Bossard, A., Wirth, M., and Blattner, N. (1992), "The Swiss Banking Sector: Development and Outlook", in: Blattner, N., Genberg, H., Swoboda, A. (eds.), Competitiveness in Banking, Studies in Contemporary Economics, Physica-Verlag, Heidelberg.

Breusch, T.S., and Pagan, A.R. (1979), "A Simple Test for Heteroscedasticity and Random Coefficient Variation", in: Econometrica, Vol. 47, 1287-1294.

Davis, E., and Kay, J. (1990), "Assessing Corporate Performance", in: Business Strategy Review, 1-16.

Demsetz, H. (1973), "Industry Structure, Market Rivalry, and Public Policy", in: Journal of Law and Economics, Vol. 16, 1-10.

Färe, R., Grosskopf, S., and Lovell, C.A.K. (1985), The Measurement of Productive Efficiency, Kluwer-Nijhof, Boston.

Ferguson, C. (1971), The Neoclassical Theory of Production and Distribution, Cambridge University Press, Cambridge.

Geroski, P. (1988), "Competition Policy and the Structure-Performance Paradigm", in: Davies, S. et al. (eds.), Economics of Industrial Organisation, Longman, London.

Gilbert, R.A. (1984), "Bank Market Structure and Competition: A Survey", in: Journal of Money, Credit, and Banking, Vol. 16, 617-645.

Graddy, D.B., and Kyle, R. (1979), "The Simultaneity of Bank Decision-Making, Market Structure, and Bank Performance", in: Journal of Finance, Vol. 34, 1-18.

Harris, F.H. (1988a), "Testable Competing Hypotheses from Structure-Performance Theory: Efficient Structure versus Market Power", in: Journal of Industrial Economics, Vol. 36, 267-280.

Harris, F.H. (1988b), "Capital Intensity and the Firm's Cost of Capital", in: The Review of Economics and Statistics, 587-594.

Hermann, W., and Maurer, M. (1991), "Kostenvorteile im schweizerischen Universalbankensystem", in: Schweizerische Zeitschrift für Volkswirtschaft und Statistik, Bd. 127, 563-578.

Hester, D.D., and Zoellner, J.F. (1966), "The Relation between Bank Portfolios and Earnings, an Econometric Analysis", in: Review of Economic Studies, Vol. 48, 372-386.

Irsch, N. (1988), "Zum Zusammenhang von Unternehmensgrösse und Rentabilität in der Bundesrepublik Deutschland in der Mitte der 80-er Jahre", in: Jahrbuch für Nationalökonomie und Statistik, Vol. 205/6, 519-539.

Jacquemin, A., and Lichtbuer, M. (1973), "Size Structure, Stability and Performance of the Largest British and EEC Firms", in: European Economic Review, Vol. 4, 393-408.

Judge, G.G., Griffiths, W.E., Carter Hill, R., and Lee, T. (1985), The Theory and Practice of Econometrics (2nd Ed.), John Wiley and Sons, New York.

Kwast, M.L., and Rose, J.T. (1982), "Pricing, Operating Efficiency, and Profitability among Large Commercial Banks", in: Journal of Banking and Finance, Vol. 6, 233-254.

Kwoka, J. E., and Ravenscraft, D.J. (1986), "Cooperation v. Rivalry", in: Economica, 351-363.

Mueller, D. (1986), Profits in the Long Run, Cambridge University Press, Cambridge.

Rhoades, S.A. (1977), "Structure-Performance Studies in Banking: A Summary and Evaluation", in: Staff Economic Studies 92, Board of Governors of the Federal Reserve System, Washington.

Rhoades, S.A. (1982), "Structure-Performance Studies in Banking: An Updated Summary and Evaluation", in: Staff Economic Studies, 119, Board of Governors of the Federal Reserve System, Washington.

Sawyer, M. C. (1971), "Concentration in British Manufacturing", in: Oxford Economic Papers, Vol. 23, 352-83.

Sheldon, G. and Haegler, U. (1993), "Economies of Scale and Scope and Inefficiencies in Swiss Banking", in this volume.

Sheperd, W. (1972), "The Elements of Market Structure", in: Review of Economics and Statistics, Vol. 54, 25-37.

Short, B.K. (1979), "The Relation Between Commercial Bank Profit Rates and Banking Concentration in Canada, Western Europe, and Japan", in: Journal of Banking and Finance, Vol. 3, 209-219.

Weiss, L. W. (1963), "Factors in Changing Concentration", in: Review of Economics and Statistics, Vol. 45, 70-77.

White, H. (1980), "A Heteroskedasticity-Consistent Covariance Matrix Estimator and a Direct Test for Heteroskedasticity", in: Econometrica, Vol. 48, 817-838.

Wirth, M. (1993), "Measuring the Performance of Banks: Conceptual Problems and Results for Switzerland (1987 to 1991)", in this volume.

**Comment on**

**Urs Haegler, Matthias Jeger: "Explaining the Performance of Swiss Banks from 1987 to 1990"**

**Günter Franke**

The purpose of this paper is to test the structure-performance paradigm in the Swiss banking industry. This paradigm pretends a positive relationship between bank performance and market concentration. Moreover, the paper attempts to test for economies of scale and economies of scope effects in the banking industry. Finally, the test results should give the banks some advice for their strategic planning. These objectives are very ambitious, therefore I am delighted to comment on the results of the paper.

The paper is very careful in setting up its methodology. The basis test design is to regress performance measures on

- balance sheet variables,
- off-balance sheet income,
- employment as a proxy for bank size,
- the banks' market share,
- the banks' risk and
- the banks' efficiency.

The paper uses three performance measures, the Return on Assets, the Return on Equity, and a third measure which is called Added Value over Input Costs. Added Value is defined as profit before taxes minus the opportunity cost of equity which is taken as the equity times the long-term interest rate. Input Costs are defined as the operating costs related to personnel plus the opportunity cost of equity. Thus, the Added Value may be interpreted as a type of Marshallian economic profit. It is not added value in the normal sense since labor costs have been subtracted. If this Marshallian economic profit is divided by the operating costs related to personnel plus the opportunity cost of equity, then one obtains a productivity measure with essentially two production factors, labor and equity capital. The problem with this productivity measure is that two completely different factors are merged in the input costs which may lead to problems of interpreting the empirical results. Still, this performance measure makes more sense than the Return on Assets or the Return on Equity since assets and equity do not capture the growing importance of off-balance sheet transactions in the banking industry. Although some equity capital is required as a cushion for the risk of these transactions, there is only a vague relationship between equity and off-balance sheet transactions.

All these performance measures are profitability measures. It might be better to use the term profitability measures because performance measures are always based on a benchmark. Since this paper does not address any benchmark, the term profitability measure appears to be more appropriate.

The authors are very careful in discussing many aspects of the econometrics of the paper. Almost 2/3 of the paper is devoted towards this discussion. Therefore, I have strong sympathy for the econometric methodology of the paper. I have, however, quite a few reservations on the theoretical underpinnings of the paper. Although some hypotheses are mentioned vaguely in the introduction, there is no discussion of a theoretical model from which the testable hypotheses are derived. This makes it very difficult to interpret the regression results. This will be explained in the following.

The paper regresses profitability on the items of the asset side and of the liability side of the balance sheet. Considering the Return on Assets, the paper is careful to eliminate one position of the asset side and one position of the liability side because these positions necessarily add up to total assets. The question, however, is, why one would regress profitability on the items of the asset side and of the liability side? Such a regression starts from the hypotheses that banks' profitability is composed additively of the profitabilities of these positions. This is a strange perspective of banks since the asset side and the liability side are closely intertwined. Disregarding off-balance sheet transactions, the main banking product is intermediation, i. e. taking deposits and lending. In other words, there is a strong economies of scope effect which cannot be captured by running a regression on the items of the asset side and of the liability side as if these items were independent. The approach is similar to an analysis of the profitability of automobile production where the profitability is considered as being additively composed of the profitabilities of the various departments of the manufacturing firm.

The regression coefficients of the paper are, in addition, somehow obscured by the fact that they do not measure the profitability of some item of the balance sheet, but the profitability of this item minus the profitabilities of the eliminated items. This has been made very clear in the paper. But this differential profitability has two undesirable properties:

- It makes it very difficult to predict the sign of the regression coefficient since one has no clear idea of the profitabilities of the eliminated items.

- There is some reason to assume that the differential profitability coefficients are driven towards zero so that significance tests may be biased towards insignificance.

These problems are confirmed by **Table** 3. The items of the asset side of the balance sheet have positive coefficients, but also interbank credits and bonds which belong to the liability side. It is difficult to interpret these coefficients.

Moreover, as the authors point out, mortgage business has the highest profitability. This is a strange result since Swiss banks loose money on mortgages as compared to investments in money market instruments in the observation period. A superficial interpretation of these numbers would tell the banker to invest money in mortgages with an interest rate of say 7.5% instead of money market instruments with say 9%.

Another question concerns the employment variable as a proxy for size. Although there is certainly some relation between employment and size, the employment is also strongly related to the personnel costs. If the employment variable indicates economies of scale effects, then one would expect a positive coefficient. If however, the scale effects are measured by the market share index, then higher employment indicates inefficient personnel management, so we would expect a negative coefficient. Given this ambiguity, it is hard to interpret the sign of the employment variable coefficient.

Similarly, there is a problem in interpreting the coefficient of the off-balance sheet income. In the overall sample, this coefficient is positive. This might indicate profitability of the off-balance sheet transactions. But if the personnel cost of these transactions is captured in the regression coefficient of the employment variable, then the coefficient of the off-balance sheet income would be gross profitability instead of net profitability. Therefore, a definite conclusion cannot be drawn.

A further remark concerns the risk variable of the paper. The authors sort the full sample of all banks into fourteen classes according to the levels of the off-balance sheet income. Then for each class the standard deviation of the performance measure is calculated and taken as the risk of banks belonging to this class. This means that the risk of the bank is determined by its off-balance sheet transactions and not by the other transactions. This is clearly a problem.

A final remark concerns the lessons for strategic planning of banks. Strategies are complicated bundles of bank activities involving many positions of the balance sheet and of the income statement. Given the treatment of many of these positions as if they were independent, I am rather sceptical that a bank can infer much for its strategic planning from **Table** 3. A more promising approach would be to build subgroups of banks such that banks within one subgroup follow some strategy and banks in other subgroups follow other strategies. Then there exist control groups so that a comparison of the empirical results for different groups should give much clearer answers.

The paper does some subgrouping at the end, and I find these results most interesting. First, the paper divides the banks into two subgroups, the first comprising banks with strong off-balance sheet activities. It is interesting to see that the off-balance sheet income has a positive coefficient for those banks which are highly engaged in these activities and a negative coefficient for those which are not strongly engaged. As the authors say, this could be an indication that specialization is profitable. Second, the authors divide all banks into two subgroups according to whether a bank is a member of a stock exchange or not. Again, interestingly the authors find that off-balance sheet activities are more profitable for stock exchange members. These tests based on subgroups appear much more promising than the pooled tests. Therefore, I would strongly recommend to spend much more effort on testing subgroups of banks. Of course, there is a problem in data collection because balance sheets and income statements contain only highly condensed figures.

Summarizing, the paper is certainly a pioneering paper in analysing the profitability of Swiss banks. I suggest to spend more effort on the theoretical derivation of testable hypotheses and to use more disaggregated data in order to obtain more information on the profitability of different bank strategies.

**Comment on**
**Urs Haegler, Matthias Jeger: "Explaining the Perfomance of Swiss Banks from 1987 to 1990"**

**Peter Zweifel**

This is a very nice paper, breaking new ground in analyzing the efficiency of Swiss banks. Maybe its principal finding, ",... serving the customers in a technically efficient way seems to be only one and a comparably unimportant factor of competitiveness in Swiss banking" helps to explain the paucity of such analyses to date. However, sources of comparative advantage may well change in the future. Thus, work of the type presented by the two authors constitute an important investment for coping with the future.

As usual, however, a discussant's task is not so much to highlight the achievements of a contribution but to point to possible weaknesses. On this score, there seem to be three points worth mentioning, viz., (1) theoretical underpinnings, (2) econometric specification, and (3) impacts of banking regulation. These points are now discussed in turn.

## 1. Theoretical considerations

The authors base their analysis on an accounting model linking total profitability to the specific profitabilities of different assets and liabilities as well as a number of bank and market characteristics. In my view, it would have been preferable to use an explicit optimization model of the type developed e.g. by Baltensperger and Milde (1987) or by Müller (1985). Such a formulation would have permitted to state more specific predictions regarding signs of certain coefficients and to point to possible interaction effects, i.e. between rates of returns and risks. Such interactions are also introduced by regulation, a point that will be addressed below.

An explicit portfolio model with the probability of insolvency included would also ensure that an appropriate indicator of performance is chosen. As a matter of fact, if present value maximization is accepted as the one objective defining both the efficiency frontier and the preference field, the performance indicator AV/IC is not appropriate. The ratio of added value (AV) to input cost (IC) does not rise monotonically with present value maximization because farming out certain services may well contribute to expected profit while lowering added value relative to input cost. Moreover, it is far from clear that the non-stochastic efficiency frontier defined in equation (4.4) of the paper is comparable with an efficiency frontier relevant for portfolio optimization, where a measure of return volatility explicitly enters the picture. In the light of this argument, it does not come as a surprise that the corresponding regressor EFF fails to make a significant contribution in any of the regressions shown in **Tables 3 - 6**.

## 2. Econometric Specifications

Here, my concern is with the construction of the risk measure. The authors state: "Because the time series of bank returns consists of only four observations (1987-1990), traditional risk measures cannot be calculated." They then go on saying that a so-called cross-section risk measure can still be calculated. However, they do not proceed at all as one would expect. What one might do in this situation is to construct the variance of a bank's total return by using market returns received on the different assets and payable on the different liabilities, weighting them with the individual bank's share of these items in its balance sheet. The authors decided to construct risk classes instead, using a procedure that seems to rely on the amount off-balance sheet activities. Apparently they are led by the belief that those activities are inherently more risky than those included in the balance sheet.

In their statistical inference, authors start out by treating all banks on an equal footing and testing for differences among subsamples. While this strategy is basically the appropriate one, their definition of subgroups leaves to be desired. In particular, the amount of off-balance sheet activities is itself a decision variable and should not be used like an exogenous regressor, as it is used when basing a classification on it. Admittedly, the amount of these activities can be viewed as predetermined in a given year; however, observations covering four years are pooled in these regressions, and within this amount of time, banks certainly are able to adjust if such adjustment serves their objectives.

Especially for establishing the link with banking regulation, it would have been preferable to divide the sample among institutional lines. Of course, a great deal of overlap can be expected among those banks having much off-balance sheet business and cantonal banks and purely commercial banks.

Finally, a few interaction terms would have suggested themselves. In particular, the introduction of the Swiss Interbank Clearing System (SIC) in 1987 should have permitted at least some banks to use their LIQ position as well as their MM position more profitably. According to this argument, the relationship between the regressors LIQ and MM and profitability depends on whether the observation pertains to the time before or after the introduction of SIC. Hence, LIQ and MM might have been multiplied by a time dummy indicating the change introduced by SIC.

### 3. Regulatory Impacts

At least as far as regulation proposed by the Swiss National Bank is concerned, all commercial banks of Switzerland seem to be subject to the same regulation. However, most cantonal banks are required to conform to more stringent restrictions in their asset allocation in return for special treatment by their cantonal governments. For this reason, cantonal banks should be distinguished from the others.

But even for the remaining banks, regulatory impact can be tested for, albeit indirectly. Here, one might borrow from an idea developed by Finsinger (1983 a, b) in his analysis of the German insurance industry. German insurance companies are also subject to uniform regulation, a fact that seemed to preclude testing for regulatory impacts. Yet, Finsinger argued that mutual and public insurers have objectives different from profit-oriented ones and that regulation affects most profoundly the efforts towards cost control undertaken by for-profit firms. In likewise manner, it might be argued that mutual banks (i.e. of the Raiffeisen type) have objectives that differ from large commercial banks, which in turn may be more governed by managerial objectives than the smaller private banks whose stocks are still held by founders' families.

The differential effect of regulation may be schematically illustrated with the help of **Figure** 1. For simplicity, the difference in orientation is taken to refer to the marginal rate of substitution between expected return and variance of return. For exam-

# Fig. 1: The efficient frontier of banks and the effect of solvency regulation

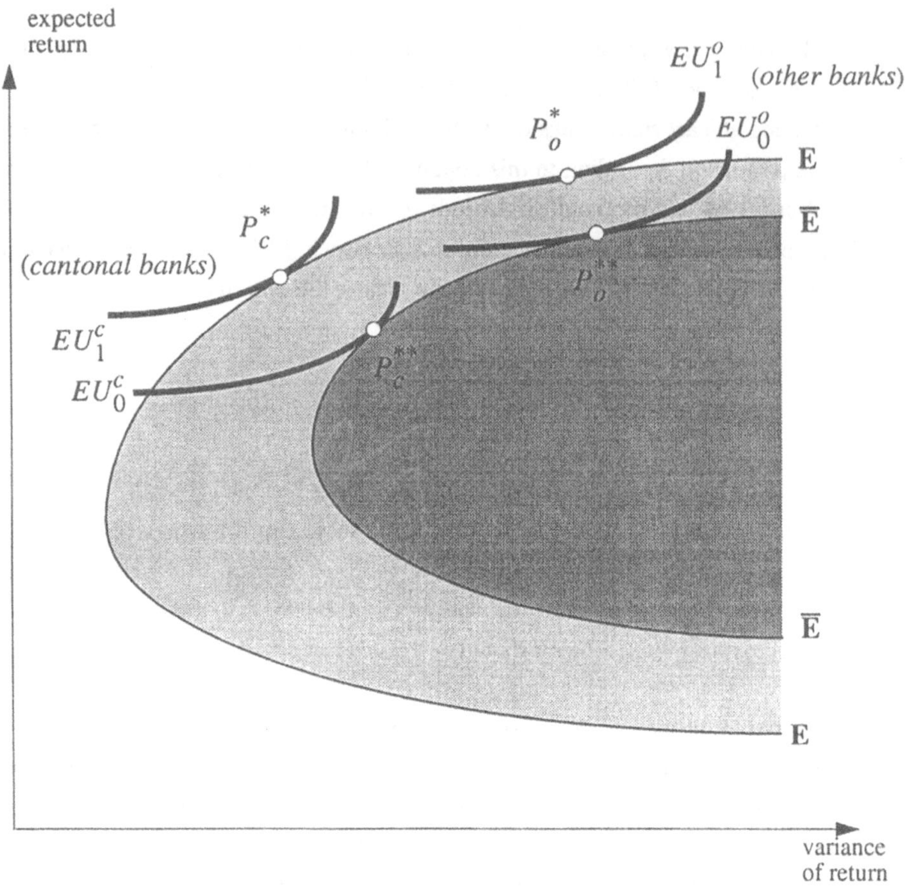

ple, cantonal banks may be predicted to pursue a policy much more characterized by risk aversion than the others, resulting in flatter indifference curves. Regulatory measures, on the other hand, tend to push the efficient frontier EE down to EE, because some very profitable and risky asset allocations are not possible any more. At the same time, solvency requirements typically force banks to hold a certain amount of reserves in domestic currency, preventing them from fully hedging against domestic inflation and generally excluding some negatively correlated assets. Therefore, the shape of the efficiency frontier is also affected by regulation, usually in the way of increasing (positive) correlation between returns.

Depending on the preference field, regulation has a different impact in terms of profitability and/or risk for cantonal banks as compared to the rest. As **Figure 1** shows, it is conceivable that solvency regulations induce cantonal banks to make up for their lower returns by increasing their risk exposure to a comparably greater degree than their commercial competitors. It is this type of conditional implication that might serve to distinguish more clearly between inefficiencies deriving from the internal workings of the banks and inefficiencies imposed on them by regulations. In the future, being able to distinguish between these two sources of inefficiency will be of utmost importance, and this paper certainly lays the groundwork for making this distinction.

**Literature**

Baltensperger, E. and Milde H. (1987), Theorie des Bankverhaltens, Studies in Contemporary Economics, Springer, Berlin.

Finsinger, J. (1983a), Versicherungsmärkte, Campus, Berlin.

Finsinger, J. (1983b), The Performance of Property / Liability Insurance Firms under the German Regulatory System, in: Journal of Theoretical and Institutional Economics, 139, 473-489.

Müller, A. (1985), Einfluss der Risikoeinschätzung, der Zinsstruktur und der Fristigkeit der Geldpolitik auf die Bankbilanz, Haag und Herchen, Frankfurt.

**Economies of Scale and Scope and Inefficiencies in Swiss Banking**

**George Sheldon, Urs Haegler**

## 1. Introduction

Signs of change in Swiss banking have been mounting in recent years. 1990 saw the abolishment of the fee-fixing agreements covering securities dealing, which had stifled competition in the domestic market for the past half-century. In October 1991 the Spar- und Leihkasse Thun collapsed under the strain of mortgage loans gone sour in the wake of rising interest rates, shocking those accustomed to thinking that Swiss banks never fail. And in 1992 Moody's downgraded the debt of Crédit Suisse and the Swiss Bank Corporation. The failure of the Spar- und Leihkasse Thun was especially unsettling. Not only the common acronym but also the similar cause of the collapse conjured up thoughts of the S&Ls in the US.

Not unlike in the US, the size distribution of banks in Switzerland is heavily skewed with a multitude of small, relatively specialized firms co-existing alongside a tiny group of giant universal banks that control over half the assets in the industry and employ a similar proportion of its workers. Given this size distribution, the question naturally arises as to whether the market structure of the Swiss banking industry is competitively viable. Can small, specialized banks expect to survive; or will large universal banks come to fully dominate the industry?

In addressing questions pertaining to future market structures, economics traditionally turns an eye to the cost structure of an industry (cf. Panzar, 1989). According to this approach, the market structure that is the most cost effective is the one that endures under free competition.[1] The concept of a natural monopoly is a case in point. The following paper holds to this tradition. It focuses on the cost variation among

---

[1] Faulhaber (1975) has shown, however, that cost efficient market structures need not be sustainable in open competition.

banks in Switzerland in an attempt to ascertain how the structure of the Swiss banking sector will develop in the future.

Essentially, cost variation across firms emanates from two sources: inefficient operation and unexploited economies of scale and scope. Inefficiencies arise when firms fail to produce on their cost frontier. Economies of scale and scope, on the other hand, result from the shape of the cost frontier and confer cost advantages either on small specialized firms or on large diversified ones. We study both sources of cost variation among banks. In line with Ferrier (1988) and Ferrier/Lovell (1990), we employ both parametric and non-parametric frontier analysis[2] in the hope of obtaining more robust results. Our data are taken from the annual balance sheets and income statements of the greater majority of banks that were operating in Switzerland at some time between 1987 and 1990.[3] In defining outputs and inputs, we employ what Humphrey (1985) terms the intermediation approach and view loans and investments as outputs, and deposits and primary factors of production as inputs.

Other work along these lines in Switzerland consists of three studies. Hermann and Maurer (1991) estimate a translog cost function employing the same data source used here but confining their analysis to 1989. They differentiate between two outputs (income from commercial banking and from investment banking, respectively). However, they ignore factor price effects and inefficiency. Their results point to limited economies of scale and scope in Swiss banking. Sheldon (1992) applies parametric and non-parametric frontier methods to the sample used in this paper but does not consider allocative efficiency and confines his study to the 381 largest banks. His findings suggest that inefficiencies dominate unexploited economies of scale and scope, a result consistent with recent evidence drawn from US research (cf. Berger/ Humphrey, 1991). Finally in a follow-up study to this paper, Sheldon (1993) investigates the changes in efficiency and total factor productivity in Swiss banking from 1987 to 1991.

The following study considers only cost, or supply-side advantages and thus ignores any demand or revenue benefits. Bank profitability and its sources, including

---

2 A recent issue of the Journal of Econometrics (cf. Lewin and Lovell, 1990) gives a good overview of these methods.

3 The data were provided by the Swiss National Bank with the permission of the banks involved. We wish to thank these institutions for their kind support.

the influence of inefficiency on profits, are the subject of a paper by Haegler and Jeger (1993).

Our paper unfolds as follows. We present our method of analysis in section 2. Section 3 describes the sample. Section 4 contains our results. In section 5 we summarize our findings and draw conclusions.

## 2. Measurement Concepts

### 2.1. Cost Efficiency

In the following, efficiency pertains to cost efficiency, i.e., to production on a cost frontier, or on the locus of minimum-cost factor combinations for given output levels. Production off the cost frontier, i.e., cost inefficiency, is broken down into two components: technical inefficiency and allocative inefficiency. Technical inefficiency is said to exist when production occurs inside the production frontier, and allocative inefficiency, when production takes place on the production frontier, yet off the cost frontier. **Figure 1**, which is adapted from Ferrier (1988, 111), depicts these concepts and their associated measures. The efficiency measures stem from Farrell (1957).

**Figure 1** presents the standard isoquant diagram for two inputs $x_1$ and $x_2$ and a single output y. The slope of the isocost curve ww' reflects given relative factor prices. Point A represents the input quantities that a given bank employs to produce at output level $y_0$, and the isoquant QQ' gives the input quantities actually required by the given technology for production at that level.

A bank at point A obviously provides its services inefficiently. It could either increase production using the same quantity of inputs or decrease inputs holding output constant.[4] Then too it could choose enumerable ways of doing so. In the following we consider only input reduction and then only proportional input contraction along the ray OA.[5]

---

4 Only under the assumption of constant returns to scale is the relative improvement in efficiency in both cases necessarily equal.

5 Färe et al. (1985) discuss other possible measures.

**Figure 1: Measures of Cost Efficiency**

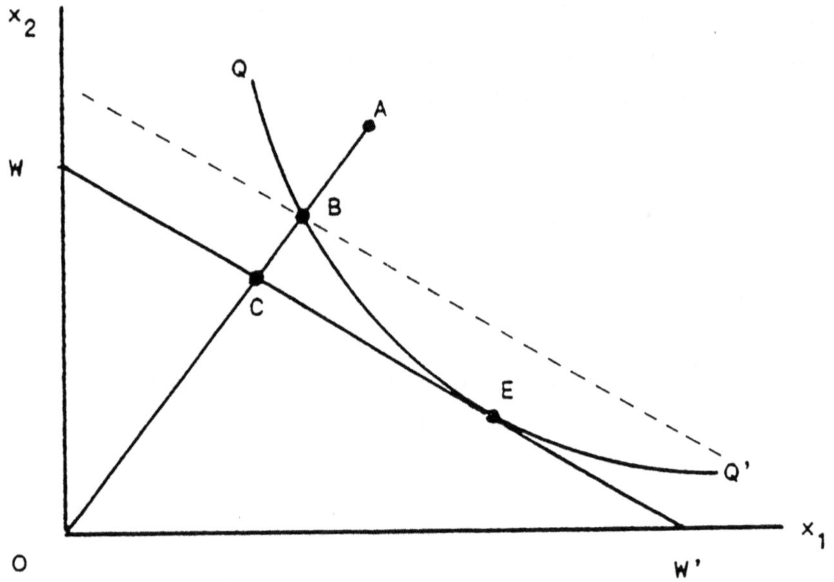


At point B, bank production is technically efficient since any further reduction of input usage would lower output. The ratio OB:OA thus corresponds to the fraction of observed input usage that the given technology demands for production at level $y_0$. This ratio serves as our measure of technical efficiency. Its value varies over the range (0, 1]. The fraction 1 - OB:OA represents the cost savings that technically efficient production would bring; and OA:OB - 1 gives the relative degree to which observed costs exceed technically efficient costs.

In point B service production is technically efficient, yet not fully cost efficient. By substituting factor $x_2$ for factor $x_1$ up to point E (the minimum-cost factor combination for given factor prices), the bank could reduce operating costs still further. This is seen by observing that production costs in point B correspond to the dashed isocost curve, which lies to the right of the isocost curve ww' that represents cost at point E. The ratio OC:OB thus corresponds to the fraction of the costs at B that the bank would incur if it produced at E. Accordingly, 1 - OC:OB gives the relative cost savings factor substitution provides; and OB:OC - 1, the relative degree of excess cost due to allocative inefficiency. The ratio OC:OB acts as our measure of allocative inefficiency.

At point E the firm would be fully cost efficient. Hence, the ratio OC:OA corresponds to the degree of cost efficiency of the bank in A. This ratio serves as our measure of overall cost efficiency. From Figure 1 it should be clear that:

$$OC:OA = (OB:OA)\,(OC:OB)\,.$$

Note that unlike the measure of technical efficiency, the measures of allocative and overall cost efficiency depend on relative factor prices.

## 2.2. Economies of Scale and Scope

Economies of scale and scope pertain to the shape of a firm's expansion path, which, in **Figure 1**, can be thought of as emanating from the origin O and passing through point E. The corresponding cost curve represents the cost frontier of the firm.

Prior to the late 80s, most bank cost studies appearing in the literature implicitly assumed cost efficiency and concentrated solely on measuring scale and, more recently, scope economies. The same holds true for the study by Hermann and Maurer (1991) for Switzerland. Ignoring inefficiency has a drawback, however. It runs the risk of confounding the effects of inefficiency with those arising from economies of scale and scope and, hence, of drawing incorrect policy conclusions. Inefficiencies are a sign of insufficient competition and thus lend support to decreasing market regulation, whereas economies pose a threat to competition and consequently provide an argument for increasing regulation.

Economies of scale could arise in banking for various reasons, foremost perhaps, because large-scale production supports specialization and the division of labor. Another possibilty unique to banking is the greater ability of big banks, thanks to their larger clientele, to pool risks. As a consequence, big banks should attract larger deposit accounts and offer larger loans than small banks (cf. Baltensperger, 1972). Since the costs of servicing accounts as a rule do not increase proportionately with account size, unit operating costs should decline with bank size.

Not only the scale of production, but also its composition could influence costs. Such so-called economies of scope refer to the cost advantages that the production of a wide range of products and services may impart to firms. Economies of scope could emerge in banking for several reasons (cf. Berger et al., 1987). For one, if fixed or quasi-fixed factors (e.g., mainframe computers) are underutilized, expanding output mix could provide an opportunity to spread fixed costs over more products. Furthermore, some inputs may have the property of a public good in the sense that they can be reused without increasing costs. For example, information acquired from providing commercial banking services could be costlessly reused for investment banking purposes, a possibility closed to US banks but open to the universal banks characteristic to Europe.

In the presence of scope economies, increasing returns to scale are neither a necessary nor a sufficient condition for a natural monopoly (cf. Panzar, 1989). In this context, not economies of scale, but subadditivity of costs is the appropriate concept to measure individual cost advantage. Essentially, subadditivity rests on a cost comparison. It is said to exist if the costs C of jointly producing any given output vector y are less than the costs of producing any additive combination of elements of the vector separately, i.e.:

$$C( \Sigma_m y_m) < \Sigma_m C(y_m), \quad m = 1, \ldots, M$$

If an industry cost function is subadditive over the relevant range of output levels, the industry is said to be a natural monopoly, i.e., a single firm could produce all relevant output vectors more cheaply than two or more firms. In the single-output case, increasing returns imply subadditivity, but not vice versa.

The concept of cost subadditivity is difficult to implement empirically because testing for it requires comparing costs over the entire range of relevant output levels. To overcome this problem, we follow the lead of Berger et al. (1987) and restrict our analysis to comparing the costs of representative banks in adjacent size classes, the thought being that potential competition is more likely to emerge from banks of similar size.

We employ four cost measures to investigate the presence of scale and scope economies. These measures describe how costs change across a multi-dimensional output plane, with each measure viewing the hyperplane from a different perspective. The measures indicate whether a representative bank of a given size class has a cost advantage over a combination of smaller banks. If not, then we conclude - in line with Berger et al. (1987) - that the larger bank is not competitively viable since a combination of smaller banks could drive the larger bank from a competitive market.

We make use of **Figure 2**, adapted from Berger et al. (1987, 505), to depict the four cost measures. The diagram presents a two-dimensional output space for products $y_1$ and $y_2$. Production costs can be pictured as lying above the output plane. Points A and B represent the mean output vectors of banks ("representative banks") in adjacent size classes. We define all four measures with respect to output bundle B.

We turn first to the so-called ray scale elasticity (RSCE), a multi-product extension of the elasticity of cost with respect to output for the single-output firm and defined as follows:

$$RSCE_B = \Sigma_m \; \partial \ln C(y^B) / \partial \ln y_m{}^B , \quad m = 1, 2$$

**Figure 2: Measures of Scale and Scope Economies**

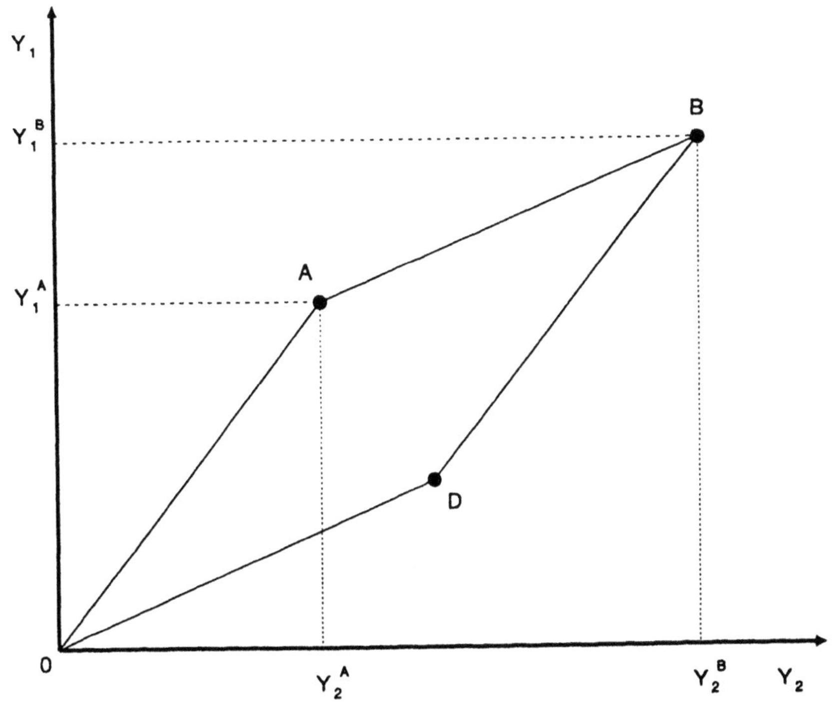

RSCE measures the relative change in cost in response to a proportional change in all outputs. With respect to point B it gives the elasticity of cost on the ray OB. The reciprocal of RSCE corresponds to the elasticity of scale. Thus, returns to scale are increasing, constant or decreasing as RSCE is less than, equal to, or less than unity. In turn, ray average costs are decreasing, constant, or increasing as RSCE - 1 is negative, zero or positive. If average costs are increasing then combinations of smaller banks with identical output mixes have a cost advantage over larger banks with this output mix. From a cost standpoint, the larger bank is not competitively viable.

Berger et al. (1987) criticize RSCE on the grounds that existing banks seldom have identical product mixes. As a consequence, RSCE may give a false impression of the actual cost competitiveness of a given bank. They suggest measuring cost elasticity instead, between the output bundles of representative banks in neighboring size classes, with respect to **Figure 2**, along the segment AB. The measure they propose, termed expansion path scale economies (EPSCE), is defined with respect to point B as follows:

$$EPSCE_B = \Sigma_m \, g_m \cdot \partial \ln C(y^B) \, / \, \partial \ln y_m{}^B \, ,$$

where: $g_m = [(y_m{}^B - y_m{}^A) \, / \, y_m{}^B] \, / \, [(C(y^B) - C(y^A)) \, / \, C(y^B)]$ und $m = 1, 2$

As in the case of RSCE, EPSCE $<$ 1 indicates economies of scale and EPSCE $>$ 1, diseconomies of scale. Note, though, that the measure EPSCE also captures the effects of scope economies should A and B not lie on a common ray.

Economies of scope are traditionally measured by comparing the cost of producing a bundle of outputs jointly with the sum of the costs of producing each element of the bundle separately. With respect to point B in **Figure 2**, that means comparing the cost of producing output vector $(y_1{}^B, y_2{}^B)$ with the combined cost of producing $(y_1{}^B, 0)$ and $(0, y_2{}^B)$ separately. Two problems arise in trying to implement this concept. For one, the costs associated with zero output levels are not defined in logarithmic specifications such as the widely used translog form. Secondly, since banks rarely produce just a single output, measuring scope economies in this way requires extrapolating well beyond the bounds of the sample, producing tenuous results.

To avoid these problems, we use the following scope measure adapted from a measure developed by Kolari and Zardkoohi (1986):

$$SCOPE_B = [\Delta C_1 + \Delta C_2 - \Delta C_{1,2}] / \Delta C_{1,2} ,$$

where:

$$\Delta C_1 = C(y_1^B, y_2^A) - C(y_1^A, y_2^A)$$

$$\Delta C_2 = C(y_1^A, y_2^B) - C(y_1^A, y_2^A)$$

$$\Delta C_{1,2} = C(y_1^B, y_2^B) - C(y_1^A, y_2^A)$$

Applied to **Figure 2**, SCOPE compares the *incremental* cost associated with producing output bundle B instead of A with the sum of the incremental costs associated with producing the output bundles $(y_1^B, y_2^A)$ and $(y_1^A, y_2^B)$, respectively, instead of A. Scope economies are said to exist if SCOPE > 0, and diseconomies of scope if SCOPE < 0. If diseconomies exist then two banks at A that each increase the production of $y_1^A$ and $y_2^A$, respectively, have a cost advantage over a bank that expands its product mix along segment AB. Note that increasing output along AB is itself cost advantageous only when EPSCE < 1.

The final measure we employ, the so-called expansion path subadditivity (EPSUB) developed by Berger et al. (1987), also has the advantage of avoiding zero output levels. With respect to **Figure 2**, EPSUB is defined as:

$$EPSUB_B = [C(y_1^A, y_2^A) + C(y_1^D, y_2^D) - C(y_1^B, y_2^B)] / C(y_1^B, y_2^B)$$

EPSUB compares the cost of producing output bundles A and D by two independent multi-product banks with the cost of producing the sum of both output bundles (i.e., B) by a single bank.

If EPSUB < 0, then joint production of bundle B provides a cost disadvantage, and if EPSUB > 0 then joint production results in a cost advantage. In the latter case, a bank providing output bundle A faces a cost enducement to acquire or to merge with its "complement" producing D.

EPSUB represents a generalization of the conventional scope measure that equates A with the output vector $(y_1^B, 0)$ and B with the output vector $(0, y_2^B)$.

## 2.3. Parametric Model

As **Figure 1** suggests, in order to separate the effects of inefficiencies and economies on costs, the cost frontier must be known. In the parametric approach identification of the cost frontier is achieved by imposing a functional structure on it. We assume the cost frontier has a translog form. Furthermore, we assume that a bank's observed costs deviate from its efficient costs for either of two reasons: cost inefficiency (u) and/or stochastic shocks ($\epsilon$). These assumptions give rise to the following equation for the observed (log) total costs of bank i at time t:

$$(1)\quad \ln(w_{it}'x_{it}) = [\,\alpha_0 + \Sigma_m \alpha_m \ln y_{mit} + \tfrac{1}{2}\Sigma_m \Sigma_{m'} \alpha_{mm'} \ln y_{mit} \ln y_{m'it}$$
$$+ \Sigma_n \beta_n \ln w_{nit} + \tfrac{1}{2}\Sigma_n \Sigma_{n'} \beta_{nn'} \ln w_{nit} \ln w_{n'it}$$
$$+ \Sigma_m \Sigma_n \delta_{mn} \ln y_{mit} \ln w_{nit} + \gamma \cdot \tau_t\,] + u_i + \epsilon_{it},$$

$$i = 1, \ldots, I;\; t = 1, \ldots, T;\; m, m' = 1, \ldots, M;\; n, n' = 1, \ldots, N\,,$$

where $y_m$ represents the quantity of output m; $w_n$, the price of input n; $x_n$, the quantity of input n; $\tau$, Hicks-neutral technical change; and $\epsilon$, a normal i.i.d. random variable. Equation (1) thus subdivides the observed (log) costs of a bank into three additive components: efficient cost, appearing in square brackets; inefficient cost (u); and random noise ($\epsilon$).

Note that (1) posits that cost inefficiency is time-invariant. That has advantages. For one, it avoids having to impose an explicit distribution on inefficiency, which stochastic parametric frontier estimation otherwise requires (Bauer, 1990). In fact, inefficiency need not even be statistically independent of the regressors since centering the variables of each bank about their respective means over time eliminates the I inefficiency terms along with the constant $\alpha_0$. That leaves us with a classical linear regression model that only requires simple OLS estimation (so-called within estimator).

Substituting the parameter estimates together with the means of bank i into (1) yields an estimate of $\alpha_0+u_i$, or $\alpha_i$, a bank-specific constant or so-called fixed effect. The following expression

$$OC:OA \;=\; \exp[\min(\alpha_1, \ldots, \alpha_I) - \alpha_i]$$

then provides us with an estimate of the degree of overall cost efficiency for bank i (cf. **Figure 1**). Note that the above expression implies that only one bank is cost efficient. That bank defines the parametric cost frontier used to calculate the four measures of scale and scope economies presented in section 2.2.

The fixed-effects approach does have a drawback, however, in as much as the assumption of time-invariant inefficiency may be untenable. In this case two alternative courses of action present themselves (Bauer, 1990). Either one assumes the statistical independence of inefficiency over time, in which case panel data cease to have an advantage over cross-sectional data; or one imposes some structure on how inefficiency varies over time (Cornwall et al., 1990; Kumbhakar, 1990). Note, however, that an approach that models the variation of inefficiency over time incorrectly does not necessarily yield better results than an approach that falsely assumes time-invariant inefficiency.

The assumption of cost minimizing production and the regulatory conditions on technology, upon which the concept of a cost frontier rests, require that the cost frontier be non-negative, homogeneous of degree one in input prices, non-decreasing in factor prices and output, and concave in input prices. Homogeneity imposes the following parameter retrictions on (1):

$$\Sigma_n \beta_n = 1, \qquad \Sigma_{n'} \beta_{nn'} = 0, \quad \Sigma_n \delta_{mn} = 0\,,$$

$$n, n' = 1, \ldots, N$$

Furthermore, since the parameters $\alpha_{mm'}$ and $\beta_{nn'}$ represent cross derivatives, the corresponding (MxM) and (NxN) matrices must be symmetric. We impose the homogeneity and symmetry restrictions on (1) prior to estimation.

## 2.4. Non-Parametric Model

The non-parametric approach we employ was developed by Charnes et al. (1978) and is termed data envelopment analysis (DEA) in the literature.[6] It differs from parametric frontier analysis in that it does not impose a functional form on the cost frontier and ignores random shocks. The first dissimilarity represents a clear advantage over the parametric approach. However, the second is a drawback if the data contain much random noise. Furthermore, DEA focuses more on measuring efficiency than on quantifying economies of scale and scope.[7]

Measurement of technical efficiency within the framework of DEA consists in solving a linear programming problem. To construct a benchmark against which the efficiency of a given bank i is measured, the program searches all convex combinations of banks in the sample that use no greater quantity of inputs than the given bank and yet produce at least as much output. The set of convex combinations fulfilling this requirement represents a piecewise linear input correspondence set ("production frontier") exhibiting strong disposability of both inputs and outputs and variable returns to scale. From this set, the program selects the linear combination that minimizes the technical efficiency measure $\Theta_i$ (OB:OA in **Figure 1**), i.e., that maximizes the input contraction required for technical efficiency to hold. If it is not possible for the bank to produce its outputs with a radially smaller input vector then $\Theta_i$ equals 1, implying that bank i lies on the production frontier. This procedure is repeated for all I banks.

---

6 Seiford and Thrall (1990) provide a good overview of DEA.

7 Exceptions in bank cost studies are Ferrier et al. (1993), who present a method of measuring scope economies in banking with DEA, and Rangan et al. (1988) as well as Aly et al. (1990), who apply the concept of scale efficiency to bank data using DEA.

Formally, the linear programming problem can be stated as follows:

$$\Theta_i \text{ --------> } \min_{\Theta_i,\, \lambda_i}$$

s.t.

$$\begin{aligned} Y\lambda_i &\geq y_i \\ X\lambda_i &\leq \Theta_i x_i \\ e'\lambda_i &= 1 \\ \lambda_i &\geq 0\,, \end{aligned}$$

where:

| | | |
|---|---|---|
| $\Theta_i$ | = | measure of technical efficiency for bank i, |
| $\lambda_i$ | = | Ix1 vector of so-called intensity weights, |
| Y | = | MxI matrix of bank outputs, |
| X | = | NxI matrix of bank inputs, |
| $y_i$ | = | Mx1 vector of outputs of bank i, |
| $x_i$ | = | Nx1 vector of inputs of bank i, |
| e | = | Ix1 vector of 1s. |

The solution $\Theta_i^*$ multiplied with the input vector $x_i$ of bank i corresponds to the costs associated with point B in **Figure 1**.

The convexity constraint $e'\lambda_i = 1$ provides the basis for measuring economies of scale in DEA (cf. Grosskopf, 1986). It determines how closely the production frontier envelops the observed input-output combinations. Specified as an equality, the restriction allows for variable returns to scale, which creates the closest fit. Relaxing the convexity restriction corresponds to tightening the scale restrictions, thereby restricting the shape of the production frontier and thus loosening its fit around the data. A wider envelopment implies, in turn, that the distance of some banks to the production frontier will increase. In those cases the efficiency score drops. The scale restriction that proves to be binding for a bank determines whether the bank exhibits increasing, constant or decreasing returns to scale. For example, the condition $e'\lambda_i \leq 1$ implies non-increasing returns to scale. If this restriction is imposed then the efficiency score of those banks with increasing returns to scale will fall. The remaining banks must then exhibit either constant or decreasing returns to scale. To separate these two groups of banks, the convexity condition is dropped altogether, which implies constant returns to scale. In this case, the efficiency score of banks with decreasing returns will fall. This procedure is repeated for every bank in the sample in order to characterize the scale economies of each bank. Note that this approach identifies the presence, but not the size of increasing, constant or decreasing returns to scale.

To measure the overall cost efficiency (OC:OA in **Figure 2**) of a bank i requires solving the following linear programming problem:

$$w_i'x_i \xrightarrow[x_i,\ \lambda_i]{} \min$$

$$\text{s.t.:} \quad \begin{aligned} Y\lambda_i &\geq y_i \\ X\lambda_i &\leq x_i \\ e'\lambda_i &= 1 \\ \lambda_i &\geq 0 . \end{aligned}$$

The programming problem consists in minimizing the costs of a bank subject to given input prices and a production technology that exhibits free disposability of inputs and outputs. The solution vector $x_i^*$ gives the cost efficient input quantities for bank i. Multiplying the solution vector with the vector of given factor prices $w_i$ yields the efficient costs ($w_i'x_i^*$) of bank i, corresponding to point C in **Figure 1**. Dividing these costs by the observed costs ($w_i'x_i$), associated with point A in **Figure 1**, provides a measure of the overall cost efficiency of bank i, corresponding to OC:OA in **Figure 1**.

Inserting the estimates of OC:OA and OB:OA in

$$OC{:}OA = (OB{:}OA)\,(OC{:}OB) .$$

yields an estimate of the degree of allocative efficiency (OC:OB). A comparison of $x_i$ with $x_i^*$ indicates which factors are overutilized ($x_i > x_i^*$), underutilized ($x_i < x_i^*$), or cost-minimally employed ($x_i = x_i^*$).

In order to impose the assumption of time-invariant inefficiency, underlying the parametric model in section 2.3, we use the mean outputs, inputs, and factor prices of a bank over time.

## 3. Data

The implementation of the parametric and non-parametric measurement concepts requires data on ouputs, inputs, and factor prices. Opinions as to what constitutes the input and the output of a bank vary in the literature, however. Humphrey (1985) provides a useful classification that distinguishes between two approaches: a production approach and an intermediation approach. The production approach views the principle function of banks as servicing accounts, both deposit and loan accounts. Accordingly, output is defined as the number of accounts, and input as bank operating costs. The intermediation approach, on the other hand, emphasizes the role of the bank as an intermediary. Thus output is defined as loans and investments, both measured in money volumes, and inputs encompass both operating costs and deposits.

Which approach is appropriate depends on the issue addressed. The production approach focuses only on operational costs and is thus better suited to studies concerned with the operational efficiency of banks, whereas the intermediation approach encompasses the overall costs of a bank and hence is better suited to studies pertaining to the market viability of banks. Since we are interested in the latter issue, we apply the intermediation approach.

**Table 1: Description of the Sample** (in SFr thousands except $w_1$)

| Variable | Mean | Std. Dev. | Minimum | Maximum |
|---|---|---|---|---|
| $w_1$ | 0.04591 | 0.02947 | 0.00108 | 0.5552 |
| $w_2$ | 80.055 | 33.416 | 2.000 | 298.600 |
| $w_3$ | 48.448 | 27.095 | 2.500 | 277.200 |
| $y_1$ | 273,760 | 2,402,900 | 0.000 | 38,280,000 |
| $y_2$ | 216,740 | 1,245,600 | 0.000 | 19,480,000 |
| $y_3$ | 742,550 | 3,692,400 | 0.000 | 57,570,000 |
| $y_4$ | 551,440 | 4,206,600 | 0.000 | 65,190,000 |
| $y_5$ | 152,720 | 799,660 | 0.000 | 11,840,000 |
| $y_6$ | 27,816 | 178,620 | 0.000 | 3,070,000 |
| $y_7$ | 19,869 | 121,400 | 0.000 | 1,942,000 |
| C | 121,990 | 800,472 | 66.000 | 13,520,176 |

FAI

The sample we use consists of 477 banks, or roughly 97% of all banks that operated in Switzerland at some time in the sample period. The institutions studied encompass 4 large banks, 29 cantonal banks, 214 regional banks, 136 foreign-controlled banks, 52 investment banks, 27 trade banks, 11 consumer credit banks, and four unclassified banks.[8] We exclude private banks, branches of foreign banks and special investment firms for lack of sufficient data. **Table 1** describes the sample.

The variables are defined as follows:

Outputs

| | | |
|---|---|---|
| $y_1$ | = | unsecured loans |
| $y_2$ | = | non-real-estate-backed loans |
| $y_3$ | = | real-estate-backed loans and mortgages |
| $y_4$ | = | money market investments |
| $y_5$ | = | securities |
| $y_6$ | = | real estate investments |
| $y_7$ | = | fee income |

Inputs

| | | |
|---|---|---|
| $x_1$ | = | bank deposits |
| $x_2$ | = | total number of employees |
| $x_3$ | = | expenditures on office space and materials |

Input Prices

| | | |
|---|---|---|
| $w_1$ | = | interest on deposits / $x_1$ |
| $w_2$ | = | total labor costs / $x_2$ |
| $w_3$ | = | $x_3 / x_2$ |

Costs

$$C = x_1 \cdot w_1 + x_2 \cdot w_2 + x_3$$

A number of aspects of the data require comment. For one, most outputs, in contrast to production theory, consist of stocks. This conforms to the practice of most bank cost studies. We make an exception, however, in the case of fee income, for

8 The classification stems from the Swiss National Bank.

which a stock equivalent (e.g., fiduciary accounts) was not available. Secondly, the inputs are highly aggregated, the available data preventing a finer breakdown. As a result, the calculated prices reflect both input price variation and unobserved differences in input composition across banks. Thirdly, an input quantity for non-labor operating costs is missing. This is not uncommon in bank cost studies (Murray/White, 1983; Mester, 1987; Ferrier/Lovell, 1990). The usual procedure in such instances is to equate costs with inputs and to divide the result either by assets (Murray/White, 1983) or deposits (Mester, 1987; Ferrier/Lovell, 1990) to obtain the associated price. We find these divisors too crude and, instead, divide non-labor operating costs by labor, since the latter closely tracks non-labor operating costs.

A small number of banks do not produce all outputs. As the natural logarithm of zero is not defined, we replaced those values with SFr1 before estimating the translog cost function. A Box-Cox transformation provides an alternative means of handling the problem (Hermann/Maurer, 1991).

## 4. Results

The estimated parameters of the translog cost frontier appear in the Appendix. The estimates imply that a number of the parameters do not conform to economic theory.[9] To be economically valid, the cost frontier should, for one, be linear homogeneous in factor prices and have a symmetric Hessian matrix with respect to factor prices. The parameter estimates at least conform to these restrictions, since they were imposed from the start, yet not tested. However, the parameter estimates do not comply with economic theory in other respects. The estimates do indicate that the cost frontier is increasing in all outputs save security investments, but the own-price elasticities of factor demand do not always carry a negative sign as required. With respect to labor this is never the case, but the own-price elasticity of deposits is often, and the corresponding elasticity for office space and materials is always positive. The incorrect signs may result from the poor quality of the input price data or from multicollinearity. Yet as they stand, the estimated parameters conflict with economic theory and thus imply that the parametric cost frontier is mis-specified.

---

9 This finding is more the rule than the exception in translog cost studies. See Evans/Heckman (1984, 620), particularly footnote 9.

The estimated value of the rate of Hicks-neutral technical progress does not conform to expectations either. It implies a rate of technical *regress* of over 12 percent per annum. This counterintuitive finding is undoubtedly in part a result of not deflating the data. Apparently factor prices rose at an annual rate of at least 12 percent during the sample period, which seems far too high given that technical progress was working in the opposite direction.

**Table 2: Economies of Scale**

| Total Assets (SFr millions) | Number | Translog 1/RSCE | Non-Parametric*) IRS | CRS | DRS |
|---|---|---|---|---|---|
| < 20 | 29 | 2.991 | 0.59 | 0.41 | 0.00 |
| 20 - 160 | 157 | 2.428 | 0.59 | 0.12 | 0.29 |
| 160 - 1,200 | 200 | 2.018 | 0.09 | 0.11 | 0.80 |
| 1,200 - 9,000 | 77 | 1.807 | 0.00 | 0.10 | 0.90 |
| 9,000 - 45,000 | 11 | 1.611 | 0.00 | 0.09 | 0.91 |
| > 45,000 | 3 | 1.333 | 0.00 | 0.00 | 1.00 |
| Full Sample | 477 | 1.837 | 0.27 | 0.13 | 0.60 |

*) Relative Frequencies
IRS increasing returns to scale
CRS constant returns to scale
DRS decreasing returns to scale

FAI

We turn now to our findings on economies of scale.[10] As **Table 2** indicates, the results from parametric and non-parametric estimation conflict somewhat. Indeed, both approaches deliver results that point to the presence of increasing returns to scale. But

[10] To neutralize the effect of factor price differences, we held factor prices constant at the mean values of all banks (see **Table 1**) in calculating those measures of scale and scope economies based on the translog cost frontier.

according to the non-parametric results[11], scale economies are exhausted in the range of SFr160-1,200 million in assets, with diseconomies setting in at the same size class thus suggesting a U-shaped ray average cost curve. The results based on the parametric model, however, imply that increasing returns persist into the largest size category, i.e., that ray average costs fall throughout the observed output range. Moreover, the unexploited returns are enormous by international standards. Bank cost studies in the US rarely yield values in excess of 1.10. The non-parametric results, on the other hand, do conform more with US studies, which usually find that scale economies are exhausted in the range of $50-100 million in deposits, with diminishing returns setting in at $200-300 million in deposits (Ferrier, 1988, 196).[12] However, these US findings rest on non-frontier estimates, i.e., they ignore the possibility of inefficiency. In contrast, Ferrier (1988) and Ferrier/Lovell (1990), using frontier methods, find pervasive scale economies that persist into the class of banks with deposits in excess of $500 million. But here again the elasticity of scale is much smaller than our results, not exceeding 1.02. Hence, we place more trust in the results from non-parametric estimation.

**Table 3: Cost Elasticities (Translog)**

| Total Assets (SFr millions) | Number | RSCE | EPSCE |
|---|---|---|---|
| < 20 | 29 | 0.334 | - |
| 20 - 160 | 157 | 0.412 | 0.676 |
| 160 - 1,200 | 200 | 0.496 | 0.746 |
| 1,200 - 9,000 | 77 | 0.553 | 0.795 |
| 9,000 - 45,000 | 11 | 0.621 | 0.828 |
| > 45,000 | 3 | 0.750 | 0.830 |
| Full Sample | 477 | 0.544 | - |

FAI

[11] Note that the non-parametric approach does not provide us with a measure of the size of scale economies. The figures in **Table 2** pertaining to the non-parametric results merely give the relative number of banks with increasing, constant, or decreasing returns to scale.

[12] Since deposits make up, on average, about 70 percent of total assets in US commercial banking (Mishkin, 1989, 163), the above ranges translate into $70-140 and $285-430 million in assets, respectively.

In contrast to RSCE, the measure EPSCE does not measure the cost elasticity along a ray but rather between two banks producing the mean output vector of adjacent size classes. Hence, the measure also captures the effects of differing output mixes. According to the results for EPSCE in **Table 3**, costs again increase less than proportionately when a bank crosses over into the next higher size class. The fact that the cost increase here is greater than along a ray (RSCE) points to diseconomies of scope between the output mixes of banks in neighboring size classes.

The results for the measure SCOPE (**Table 4**) support these findings. SCOPE measures whether producing jointly the difference between the output vectors of representative banks in adjacent size classes (incremental output) increases cost less than when incremental output is produced disjointly. In calculating SCOPE, we grouped output into loans ($y_1$, $y_2$, $y_3$) and investments ($y_4$, $y_5$, $y_6$, $y_7$). According to the findings in **Table 4**, the production of the difference between the level of loans and investments of banks in neighboring size classes would increase costs between 7.4 and 26.7 percent less if one bank in the smaller size class were to produce just the difference in loan levels and another in the same class, just the difference in investments. In other words, the total cost increase would be greater if one of the smaller banks decided instead to produce the full output bundle of a bank in the next higher size class.

**Table 4: Economies of Scope (Translog)**

| Total Assets (SFr millions) | Number | SCOPE | EPSUB |
|---|---|---|---|
| 20 - 160 | 157 | -0.074 | 0.423 |
| 160 - 1,200 | 200 | -0.106 | 0.362 |
| 1,200 - 9,000 | 77 | -0.081 | 0.332 |
| 9,000 - 45,000 | 11 | -0.133 | 0.275 |
| > 45,000 | 3 | -0.267 | -0.106 |

FAI

Together, the values for EPSCE and SCOPE indicate that size does produce a cost advantage, but that banks would gain a greater cost advantage if they specialized as they grew.

EPSUB views cost from a different angle. It addresses the issue of whether breaking up a representative bank of a given size class into a representative bank of the next smaller size class and a "residual" bank would lower aggregate production costs. Our findings indicate that a break-up of this kind would in general lead to a cost increase ranging from 27 to 42 percent. Only in the largest size class would a break-up of this sort reduce costs, and then by 10.6 percent. Note, however, that due to the width of the class intervals, the "residual" bank is larger than its complement. In fact, as a rule, it is only slightly smaller than the bank that is to be broken up. Take the largest size class, for example. In that class total assets average about SFr150 billion, whereas in the next class below total assets average around SFr17 billion. Thus, the residual bank would have assets totalling SFr133 billion making it the third largest bank in Switzerland. Consequently, in **Table 4** EPSUB really addresses the question of whether a smaller bank within a given size class faces a cost enducement to acquire or merge with a representative bank of the next lower size class. The answer is "yes", except in the largest size class. In fact, the smaller the size class, the greater is the attraction to merge in the way described. This suggests that EPSUB is capturing the effects of increasing scale since they too decline with size.

**Table 5: Degree of Cost Efficiency**

| | Mittelwert | Standardabweichung | Minimalwert | Maximalwert |
|---|---|---|---|---|
| Overall | | | | |
| Translog | 0.044 | 0.091 | 0.002 | 1.000 |
| DEA | 0.560 | 0.253 | 0.029 | 1.000 |
| Technical (DEA) | 0.910 | 0.116 | 0.343 | 1.000 |
| Allocative (DEA) | 0.645 | 0.235 | 0.038 | 1.000 |

FAI

**Table 5** contains the results on cost efficiency. As the figures there indicate, both the parametric and the non-parametric approaches discover sizable variation in overall cost efficiency across banks. But there agreement virtually ends. While the results

**Figure 3: Overall Cost Efficiency (Non-parametric)**

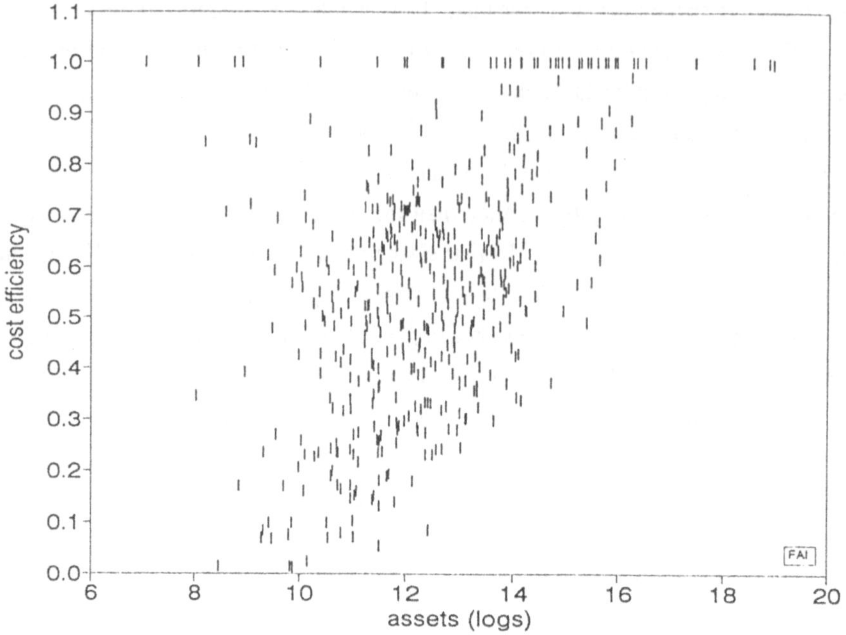


**Figure 4: Overall Cost Efficiency (Parametric)**

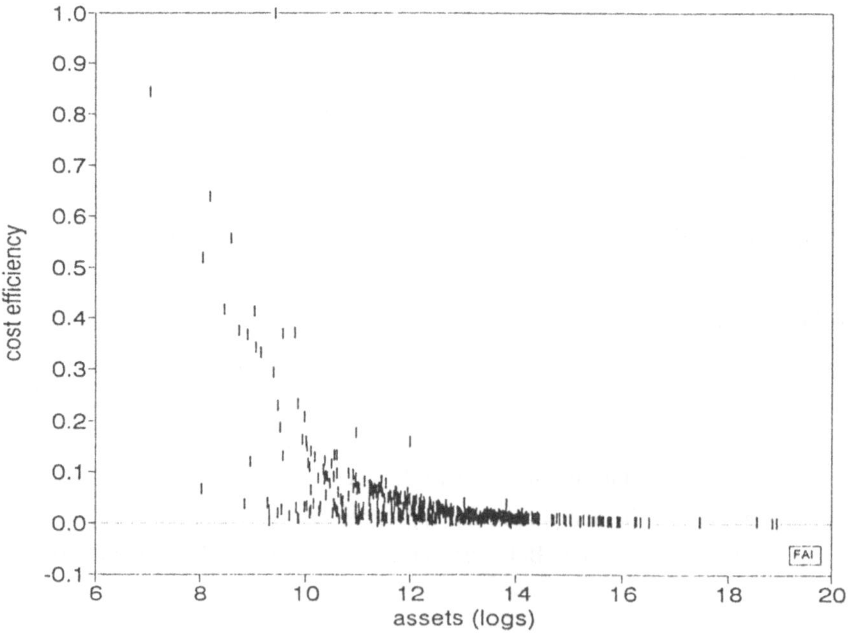

from DEA indicate that the average degree of cost efficiency is about 57 percent, parametric analysis produces an average figure of 4.4 percent. Put differently, the non-parametric results imply observed cost exceeds efficient cost on average by almost 75 percent (= $0.573^{-1} - 1$), whereas the parametric results place the figure at an astronomical 2173 percent (= $0.044^{-1} - 1$).

**Figures 3** and **4** provide a more detailed look at the cost efficiency results. Note that the horizontal scale closely follows the bank size classification in the tables. The smallest size class corresponds roughly to the interval from 6 to 10. Thereafter each interval closely matches a size class. As both figures show, the results stemming from the two approaches could not be more disparate. The efficiency scores based on the translog cost frontier are bunched between 0.0 and 0.1, while the efficiency scores yielded by DEA are rather evenly distributed across the whole range of possible values. Furthermore, the parametric approach finds a negative correlation (the Spearman correlation coefficient equals - 0.722) between size and efficiency; the non-parametric approach, a positive relationship (the Spearman correlation coefficient is 0.469). It comes then as no surprise that the Spearman correlation coefficient between the parametric and non-parametric efficiency scores is 0.01 and not significant.[13]

It is interesting to note that despite their dissimilarities the results from both approaches point to a trade off between economies of scale and cost efficiency. According to the findings from the parametric analysis, the cost advantages accruing to large banks through scale economies are offset, to a degree, by their lower cost efficiency. While the non-parametric findings suggest that the diseconomies of scale of large banks are counterbalanced somewhat by their greater cost efficiency. These countervailing effects may explain why unexploited economies of scale and inefficiencies persist.

The non-parametric approach allows a breakdown of cost efficiency into technical efficiency and allocative efficiency. These results appear in **Table 5** as well. The value obtained for technical efficiency implies that, on average, the banks in our sample could have produced the same level of output by employing 91 percent of the in-

---

[13] Ferrier and Lovell (1990, 243) also find no statistically significant relationship between parametric and non-parametric efficiency scores in a cost study of US banking.

**Figure 5: Technical Efficiency (Non-parametric)**

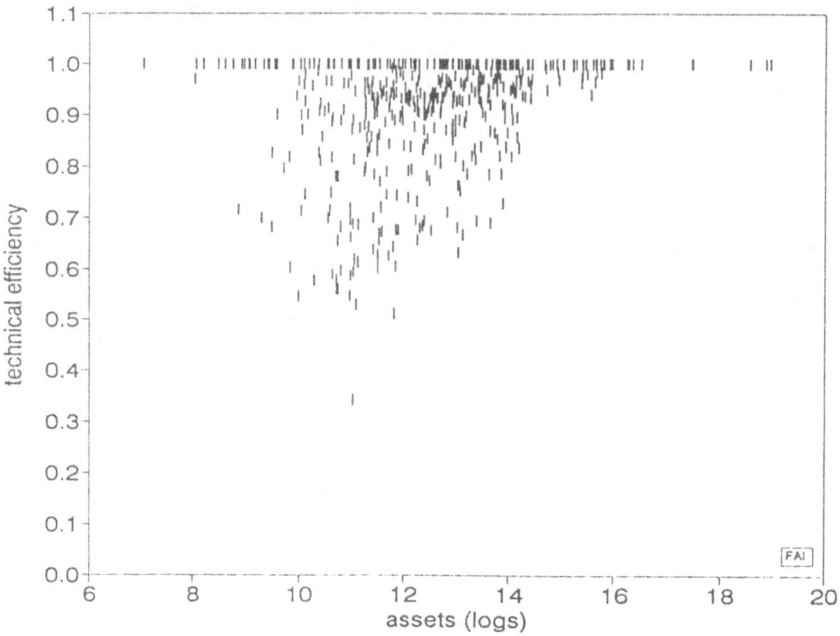


**Figure 6: Allocative Efficiency (Non-parametric)**

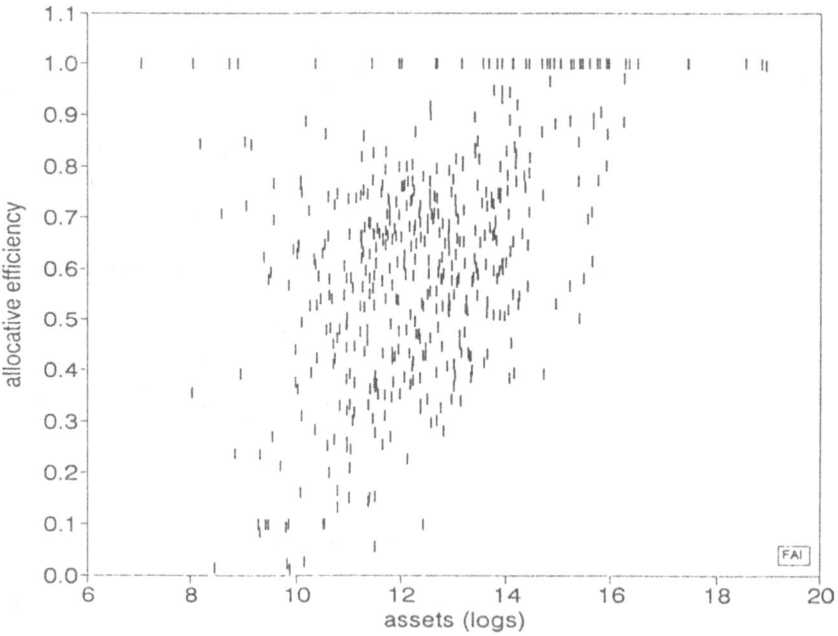

puts actually used. Allocative efficiency would have brought the greater cost savings, however. According to our findings banks could have achieved a further cost saving of 36 percent (= 1 - 0.645) had they utilized inputs in accordance to their relative prices. These results conform roughly to the findings from DEA bank cost studies in the US, except that there the relative sizes of technical and allocative efficiency are reversed.[14] The greater degree of allocative inefficiency found in our study may result from the poor quality of our factor price data, as the measure of allocative efficiency, unlike that for technical efficiency, depends on relative input prices.

**Figures 5** and **6** provide detailed views of the relationship between bank size and technical and allocative efficiency. The positive relationship they suggest is validated by the Spearman correlation coefficient. It measures 0.396 in **Figure 5** and 0.451 in **Figure 6**, and is statistically significant in both cases.

**Table 6** reveals that allocative inefficiency results from a general overutilization of labor, office space, and materials and from an underutilization of deposits. This finding stands in agreement with US results (Ferrier, 1988; Ferrier/Lovell, 1990).

**Table 6: Direction of Allocative Inefficiency (DEA)**

| Input | Over-utilization | Optimal | Under-utilization |
|---|---|---|---|
| Deposits | 0.01 | 0.11 | 0.88 |
| Labor | 0.80 | 0.11 | 0.09 |
| Office und Materials | 0.86 | 0.11 | 0.03 |

FAI

[14] The values from US studies (Ferrier, 1988; Rezvanian, 1989; Aly et al., 1990; Ferrier/Lovell, 1990) range in the case of technical efficiency from 0.63 (Ferrier) to 0.83 (Ferrier/Lovell), in the case of allocative efficiency from 0.79 (Ferrier) to 0.95 (Ferrier/Lovell), and in the case of overall efficiency from 0.54 (Ferrier) to 0.83 (Ferrier/Lovell). Surprisingly, this wide range of values apparently stems from the same sample.

## 5. Summary and Conclusions

The following picture emerges from our analysis. Economies of scale appear to be present in the Swiss banking sector. Yet whether returns are increasing throughout the sample, as the parametric results imply, or only initially increasing and thereafter decreasing, as the non-parametric results suggest, is uncertain. We find the the non-parametric results more reliable, given that the parametric cost frontier appears to be misspecified and to yield less convincing results.

Cost inefficiency seems to be a major factor underlying the cost variation among Swiss banks. The main source of inefficiency appears to be allocative inefficiency arising from the overuse of labor, capital and materials and the underutilization of deposits. However, whether efficiency decreases with size, as the parametric findings suggest, or increases with size, as the non-parametric results imply, is open to question. Here again, we find the non-parametric findings more reliable.

Be that as it may, the results of both approaches suggest that inefficiency and scale-related cost advantages tend to offset each other. This could explain why the market structure in Swiss banking is relatively stable despite the presence of (dis-)economies of scale.

Only the parametric analysis provides information on the extent of scope effects, and these results point to diseconomies of scope, suggesting that growth through specialization offers cost advantages over growing in the mold of large banks.

The potential gain to the banking industry through efficient operation appears to be large. The non-parametric estimates, which seem more reliable, suggest that cost-efficient production could lower costs in banking on average by 43 percent. Given the size of the potential profit gain to banks, the question naturally arises as to why the banks do not not exploit this opportunity.

One reason, of course, could be that this potential does not actually exist, i.e., that efficiency is falsely measured in our study. Both measurement concepts have their shortcomings, of course. DEA abstracts from data measurement error and other stochastic shocks and thus may confound random noise with inefficiency. Parametric frontier analysis, on the other hand, imposes a functional structure on the cost frontier and hence may confuse specification error with inefficiency. Furthermore, both approaches are static. What appears to be inefficiency from the viewpoint of static equilibrium may be optimal from a dynamic perspective. The assumptions of time-invariant inefficiency and a common production frontier are further model restrictions which may bias the results. Data problems exist as well. These shortcomings suggest the need of further research. Dropping restrictive assumptions; experimenting with other functional forms, different efficiency measures, and/or various subsamples; and improving the data base could bring an improvement.

As the results pertaining to scale and scope economies now stand, however, they offer scant evidence that the banking industry in Switzerland exhibits the characteristics of a natural monopoly. Hence any fear that small, more specialized banks need perish under free competition appears unfounded. Our findings do though point to sizeable cost inefficiency. Thus sharpened competition could nevertheless lead to more bank failures and takeovers.

## REFERENCES


Aly, H., Grabowski, R., Pasurka, C., Rangan, N. (1990), "Technical, Scale and Allocative Efficiencies in U.S. Banking: An Empirical Investigation," in: Review of Economics and Statistics, Vol. 72, pp. 211-218.

Baltensperger, E. (1972), "Economics of Scale, Firm Size, and Concentration in Banking," in: Journal of Money, Credit, and Banking, Vol. 4, pp. 467-488.

Bauer, P. (1990), "Recent Developments in the Econometric Estimation of Frontiers," in: Journal of Econometrics, Vol. 46, pp. 39-56.

Berger, A., Hanweck, G., Humphrey, D. (1987), "Competitive Viability in Banking. Scale, Scope, and Product Mix Economies," in: Journal of Monetary Economics, Vol. 20, pp. 501-520.

Berger, A., Humphrey, D. (1990), "The Dominance of Inefficiencies over Scale and Product Mix Economies in Banking," in: Journal of Monatary Economics, Vol. 28, pp. 117-148.

Charnes, A., Cooper, W., Rhodes, E. (1978), "Measuring the Efficiency of Decision Making Units," in: European Journal of Operational Research, Vol. 2, pp. 429-444.

Cornwall, C., Schmidt, P., Sickles, R. (1990), "Production Frontiers with Cross-Sectional and Time-Series Variation in Efficient Levels," in: Journal of Econometrics, Vol. 46, pp. 185-200.

Evans, D., Heckman, J. (1984), "A Test for Subadditivity of the Cost Function with an Application to the Bell System," in: American Economic Review, Vol. 74, pp. 615-623.

Färe, R., Grosskopf, S., Lovell, C. (1985), The Measurement of Efficiency and Production, Boston.

Farrell, M. (1957), "The Measurement of Productive Efficiency," in: Journal of the Royal Statistical Society, Series A, Vol. 120, pp. 253-281.

Faulhaber, G. (1975), "Cross-Subsidization: Pricing in Public Enterprise," in: American Economic Review, Vol. 65, pp. 966-977.

Ferrier, G. (1988), A Comparison of Alternative Analytic Techniques Available for the Study of Production Economies and Inefficiencies: An Application to the U.S. Banking Industry; PhD-Thesis, University of North Carolina, Chapel Hill (unpublished).

Ferrier, G., Grosskopf, S., Hayes, K., Yaisawarng, S. (1993), "Economies of Diversification in the Banking Industry: A Frontier Approach," in: Journal of Monetary Economics, Vol. 31 (forthcoming).

Ferrier, G., Lovell, C. (1990), "Measuring Cost Efficiency in Banking. Econometric and Linear Programming Evidence," in: Journal of Econometrics, Vol. 46, pp. 229-245.

Grosskopf, S. (1986), "The Role of the Reference Technology in Measuring Productive Efficiency," in: Economic Journal, Vol. 96, pp. 499-513.

Haegler, U., Jeger, M. (1993), "Explaining the Performance of Swiss Banks from 1987 to 1990," in this volume.

Hermann, W., Maurer, M. (1991), "Kostenvorteile im schweizerischen Universalbankensystem," in: Schweizerische Zeitschrift für Volkswirtschaft und Statistik, Vol. 127, pp. 563-578.

Humphrey, D. (1985), "Costs and Scale Economies in Bank Intermediation," in: R. Aspinwall, R. Eisenbeis (ed.), Handbook of Banking Strategy, New York, pp. 745-783.

Kolari, J., Zardkoohi, A. (1987), Bank Costs, Structure, and Performance, Lexington.

Kumbhakar, S. (1990), "Production Frontiers, Panel Data, and Time-Varying Technical Efficiency," in: Journal of Econometrics, Vol. 46, pp. 185-200.

Lewin, A., Lovell, C. (1990) (eds.), Frontier Analysis. Parametric and Nonparametric Approaches, Journal of Econometrics, Annals 1990-4, Vol. 46.

Mester, L. (1987), "A Multiproduct Cost Study of Savings and Loans," in: Journal of Finance, Vol. 42, pp. 423-445.

Mishkin, F. (1989), The Economics of Money, Banking, and Financial Markets, Glenview.

Murray, J., White, R. (1983), "Economics of Scale and Scope in Multiproduct Financial Institutions: A Study of British Columbia Credit Unions," in: Journal of Finance, Vol. 38, pp. 887-902.

Panzar, J. (1989), "Technological Determinants of Firm and Industry Structure," in: R. Schmalensee, R. Willig (eds.), Handbook of Industrial Organization, Vol. 1, pp. 3-59.

Rezvanian, R. (1989), The Effects of the Recent Deregulation on the Efficiency of the U.S. Banking Industry, PhD-Thesis, Southern Illinois University at Carbondale.

Seiford, L., Thrall, R. (1990), "Recent Developments in DEA. The Mathematical Programming Approach to Frontier Analysis," in: Journal of Econometrics, Vol. 46, pp. 7-38.

Sheldon, G. (1992), Skalenerträge, Verbundvorteile und Ineffizienz im Schweizer Bankgewerbe, paper given at Meeting of the Industrial Organization Group of the Verein für Socialpolitik, Basel, March 5-6.

Sheldon, G. (1993), Ökonometrische Untersuchungen des Kostengefälles im Schweizer Bankensektor, final report to a study commissioned by the Swiss National Bank, FAI, Basel, February 8.

## Appendix: Parameter Estimates of Translog Cost Frontier

| Variable | Parameter | Estimate | t-ratio |
|---|---|---|---|
| $\ln y_1$ | $\alpha_1$ | 0.04900 | 1.830 |
| $\ln y_2$ | $\alpha_2$ | 0.04434 | 0.959 |
| $\ln y_3$ | $\alpha_3$ | -0.06445 | -2.559 |
| $\ln y_4$ | $\alpha_4$ | 0.19842 | 2.996 |
| $\ln y_5$ | $\alpha_5$ | -0.05347 | -0.792 |
| $\ln y_6$ | $\alpha_6$ | 0.01478 | 0.819 |
| $\ln y_7$ | $\alpha_7$ | 0.28604 | 4.519 |
| $\ln y_1 \ln y_1$ | $\alpha_{11}$ | 0.00288 | 2.641 |
| $\ln y_2 \ln y_2$ | $\alpha_{22}$ | 0.00688 | 3.450 |
| $\ln y_3 \ln y_3$ | $\alpha_{33}$ | 0.00021 | 0.194 |
| $\ln y_4 \ln y_4$ | $\alpha_{44}$ | 0.00790 | 2.404 |
| $\ln y_5 \ln y_5$ | $\alpha_{55}$ | 0.00918 | 4.021 |
| $\ln y_6 \ln y_6$ | $\alpha_{66}$ | 0.00266 | 1.611 |
| $\ln y_7 \ln y_7$ | $\alpha_{77}$ | 0.02967 | 11.022 |
| $\ln y_1 \ln y_2$ | $\alpha_{12}$ | 0.00101 | 0.929 |
| $\ln y_1 \ln y_3$ | $\alpha_{13}$ | 0.00076 | 1.449 |
| $\ln y_1 \ln y_4$ | $\alpha_{14}$ | 0.00095 | 0.708 |
| $\ln y_1 \ln y_5$ | $\alpha_{15}$ | -0.00179 | -1.124 |
| $\ln y_1 \ln y_6$ | $\alpha_{16}$ | -0.00145 | -3.238 |
| $\ln y_1 \ln y_7$ | $\alpha_{17}$ | 0.00234 | 2.698 |
| $\ln y_2 \ln y_3$ | $\alpha_{23}$ | 0.00291 | 2.296 |
| $\ln y_2 \ln y_4$ | $\alpha_{24}$ | -0.01067 | -2.475 |
| $\ln y_2 \ln y_5$ | $\alpha_{25}$ | 0.00201 | 1.243 |
| $\ln y_2 \ln y_6$ | $\alpha_{26}$ | 0.00082 | 0.810 |
| $\ln y_2 \ln y_7$ | $\alpha_{27}$ | 0.00278 | 1.103 |
| $\ln y_3 \ln y_4$ | $\alpha_{34}$ | 0.00108 | 0.878 |
| $\ln y_3 \ln y_5$ | $\alpha_{35}$ | -0.00322 | -2.964 |
| $\ln y_3 \ln y_6$ | $\alpha_{36}$ | 0.00006 | 0.173 |
| $\ln y_3 \ln y_7$ | $\alpha_{37}$ | -0.00318 | -1.621 |
| $\ln y_4 \ln y_5$ | $\alpha_{45}$ | 0.00297 | 0.927 |
| $\ln y_4 \ln y_6$ | $\alpha_{46}$ | 0.00195 | 1.754 |
| $\ln y_4 \ln y_7$ | $\alpha_{47}$ | 0.00499 | 1.773 |

(cont'd.)

| | | | |
|---|---|---|---|
| $\ln y_5 \ln y_6$ | $\alpha_{56}$ | -0.00466 | -3.391 |
| $\ln y_5 \ln y_7$ | $\alpha_{57}$ | -0.00386 | -1.074 |
| $\ln y_6 \ln y_7$ | $\alpha_{67}$ | -0.00185 | -2.018 |
| $\ln w_1$ | $\beta_1$ | -0.80797 | -5.205 |
| $\ln w_2$ | $\beta_2$ | 1.09710 | 5.510 |
| $\ln w_1 \ln w_1$ | $\beta_{11}$ | -0.01369 | -0.845 |
| $\ln w_2 \ln w_2$ | $\beta_{22}$ | -0.16069 | -3.305 |
| $\ln w_1 \ln w_2$ | $\beta_{12}$ | 0.13736 | 5.438 |
| $\ln y_1 \ln w_1$ | $\delta_{11}$ | 0.00951 | 3.487 |
| $\ln y_2 \ln w_1$ | $\delta_{21}$ | -0.00226 | -0.461 |
| $\ln y_3 \ln w_1$ | $\delta_{31}$ | -0.00999 | -5.220 |
| $\ln y_4 \ln w_1$ | $\delta_{41}$ | 0.02701 | 3.501 |
| $\ln y_5 \ln w_1$ | $\delta_{51}$ | -0.00027 | -0.047 |
| $\ln y_6 \ln w_1$ | $\delta_{61}$ | -0.00433 | -2.393 |
| $\ln y_7 \ln w_1$ | $\delta_{71}$ | 0.03637 | 5.310 |
| $\ln y_1 \ln w_2$ | $\delta_{12}$ | -0.00506 | -0.985 |
| $\ln y_2 \ln w_2$ | $\delta_{22}$ | -0.05944 | -6.643 |
| $\ln y_3 \ln w_2$ | $\delta_{32}$ | 0.01439 | 3.204 |
| $\ln y_4 \ln w_2$ | $\delta_{42}$ | -0.04892 | -3.846 |
| $\ln y_5 \ln w_2$ | $\delta_{52}$ | -0.00555 | -0.505 |
| $\ln y_6 \ln w_2$ | $\delta_{62}$ | 0.00346 | 0.777 |
| $\ln y_7 \ln w_2$ | $\delta_{72}$ | -0.01791 | -1.768 |
| $\tau$ | $\gamma$ | 0.12534 | 29.832 |

| Fixed Effects | Number | Minimum | Maximum |
|---|---|---|---|
| $\alpha_i$ | 477 | 0.0433 | 6.3844 |

| | |
|---|---|
| Sample Size | 1789 |
| Adjusted $R^2$ (excluding fixed effects) | 0.9552 |

FAI

**Comment on**
**George Sheldon, Urs Haegler: "Economies of Scale and Scope and Inefficiencies in Swiss Banking"**

**Thomas Gehrig**

The paper by Sheldon and Haegler is a very welcome analysis of the cost structure of the banking industry in Switzerland. They analyze a fairly rich data set and in particular they contrast a conventional parametric production approach with a novel descriptive approach of data analysis. Interestingly the two approaches yield quite different results and so I see my role as a discussant in trying and to attempt an interpretation of the empirical findings.

1. The first question of my discussion will be devoted to the question of what did we learn. In this section I shall give another interpretation of the data, which lies between the two interpretations suggested in the paper. However, the pervasive empirical regularity seems to be some sort of inefficiency in banking.

2. Given that inefficiencies seem to play a major role in explaining the industrial structure, probably not only in banking, let me ask in the second part what the nature of such inefficiencies could be.

## 1. What did we learn?

In order to ask this question let me give you a very special example and try to interpret the empirical findings at hand of this example. Imagine a case in which the data are grouped as in **Figure** 1. Consider a single input and a single output. At small firm sizes the data suggest a frontier with sizeable economies of scale while at intermediate levels diseconomies of scale set in. So essentially the data are grouped as if they were generated by some logistic function, very much in line with the non-parametric findings on economies of scale.

The parametric approach chosen essentially attempts to fit a cubic production function to the data and then shifts this function such that no observation lies above the frontier. Now if for some reason the weight of the observations of small banks (as a group) is relatively large the turning point of the cubic production function and hence the minimum of the cost function may be achieved at very small firm sizes. Overall this would imply that the estimated production function essentially behaves as a quadratic production function for the middle and large size banks. In such an environment, as **Figure 1** suggests, given the finding that substantial economies of scale do exist for a large number of the data the frontier approach may be expected to perform quite badly when small observation errors are present. Then the low efficiency scores for large banks do not come as a surprise. Here obviously the problem arises from fitting a parametric function, which does not allow for sufficient flexibility. The translog approximation to a particular observation on the production frontier may be quite appealing, but imposing the quadratic approximation globally may nevertheless result in serious bias. This may seem ironic given that the approach is known under the heading of flexible form modelling. The problem is that the translog approximation does allow for at most one change in convexity behaviour of the underlying production frontier and that in the environment considered the interesting turning point would be expected at a firm size such that only few observations would be above this firm size. This potential explanation of the results can be checked by evaluating the firm size at the minimum of the estimated cost function.

So I agree with the authors that the non-parametric approach may be more reliable since essentially it is a descriptive approach, which allows to construct the empirical production frontier without imposing any a priori curvature restrictions. In data envelopment analysis each facet of the production frontier is constructed as a convex combination of those observations which cannot be dominated by any other convex combination. As a consequence of this approach each corner observation is efficient. So in particular the large banks providing corner observation are bound to have an efficiency score of 1 by construction. Accordingly, I should be very careful in giving the efficiency score for the large banks any deeper meaning! If the true frontier was linear the finding of decreasing returns for the large banks should be viewed as an indicator of inefficiency rather than true decreasing returns.

I guess the robust result is the finding of pervasive inefficiencies in banking. This brings me to my second question.

**Figure 1**

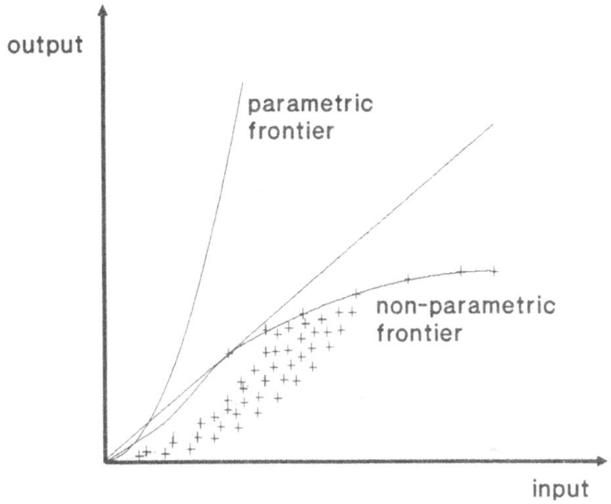
output
parametric
frontier
non-parametric
frontier
input

## 2. What do inefficiencies mean?

Starting from neoclassical production theory there is only one case in which the optimal firm size is indeterminate - the case of a linear technology. In this respect the very finding of different firms in different size classes could be an indication for either

a) linear or quite unregular production frontier (in sciing: mogles)
b) regulatory interference which prevents individual banks from achieving its optimal production mix.
c) incompetent management in most of the banks observed
d) or of strategic interaction.

If one is willing to draw policy advice from the inefficiencies observed, the question of which kind of inefficiency one is talking about seems quite important. It would be an important aspect of further work to identify the precise source of inefficiency.

The paper seems to take sympathy with suggestion c). Probably a technological explanation as in a) does not seem very plausible.

Question b) however could be partially answered in the current framework. It could be quite revealing for example to publish the efficiency scores of highly regulated banks such as the cantonal banks or savings banks for example. A high efficiency score would indicate indeed that regulation sufficiently reduces the riskiness of those banks and hence increases their profitability. This could be a convincing argument in favour of investment restrictions on banks. Of course, a low efficiency score would indicate the reverse.

Finally let me dwell somewhat on the last aspect, which is **strategic interaction.** As soon as one leaves the realm of neoclassical production theory the puzzle also looses its bite. If banking products were differentiated according to regional and product specific characteristics it is perfectly conceivable to observe an industrial structure with some banks concentrating on local markets while others maintian a large branching network. Each type of bank addresses a different type of client and clients select banks according to the type and quality of services offered alongside with the price of those services. Modern industrial economics provides a long list of reasons which might resolve the puzzle. However, whatever model is used an endogenous evolution of structure arises from the strategic interaction among the players.

Let me bring home this point more clearly at the hand of specific problems I find in the present paper:

i) One major finding is the overcapacity in offices and excessive labour costs. Now take a bank maintaining a large network of branches and compare it with a bank with only one branch. The network bank with only one branch will employ more labour and use more office space than the single unit bank to produce the same amount of loans and investments. Hence it looks less efficient. Of course, here is the fallacy. The network bank in addition to providing investment services also provides some sort of interregional matching and possibly diversification service. So it sells a bundle of different services for which it might command a higher price than the single unit bank.

Taking the **stock** approach the two banks cannot be distinguished and the network bank is bound to perform poorly since the revenue generated by its matching services is not accounted for in the data. Here the use of **flow** data would complement the information set and help to identify the value of the different services offered by different banks (in potentially different size classes).

ii) A second point addresses the so-called **intermediation** approach adopted in the paper. Both hiring and deposit decisions may be viewed as strategic variables of the individual banks as well. In this case one would like to have deposits as inputs rather than outputs since they are a part of the set of services offered to clients. Accordingly the production approach would seem more appropriate. In a regulated environment one can support the strategy adopted in the paper and basically neglect competition for deposits. However, even then all sources of funds need to be considered. So the neglect of capital market funding is a serious defect of the present analysis. It means that a bank relying on capital market funding performs very highly in the sample while banks relying on deposits perform very poorly. In other words the neglect of capital market funding introduces a bias in favour of the commercial banks, which in Switzerland tend to be the large banks, and against the catonal and savings banks. This concern could be nullified by looking at the efficiency scores of individual banking groups.

Let me summarize. The paper by Sheldon and Haegler has demonstrated the power of methodological advances. Nevertheless the state of the analysis is far from allowing any serious policy advice. Far more research is needed. This research should use and try to combine both the new tools of descriptive data analysis and the theoretical insights, modern industrial economics has to offer.

**Comment on**

**George Sheldon, Urs Haegler: "Economies of Scale and Scope and Inefficiencies in Swiss Banking"**

**Werner Hermann**

Sheldon and Haegler estimate cost functions of Swiss banks. I believe they make a significant contribution towards understanding the impact of technology on the Swiss banking industry. Their merits lie in taking into account the efficiency of production and in applying a promising empirical methodology to the data. To my knowledge Sheldon and Haegler are the first to point out the importance of efficiency differentials in the cost structure of Swiss banks. I would, however, not consider their detailed estimations reliable at this stage and would refrain from deriving conclusions from their empirical findings.

Let me first say in my words what the authors did. They consider four potential cost advantages among banks: Economies of scale and scope, and cost inefficiencies, which is split between technical and allocative inefficiencies. They start with presenting a framework for the measurement of efficiency and economies of scale and scope. Their measure of economies of scale and scope is subadditivity. However, subadditivity is not the only way to define economies of scope. In my own work with Maurer, we focused on transray convexity as a measure of economies of scope. Our definition is more rigorous because subadditivity implies benefits from producing several outputs in a single firm as opposed to producing the same amounts in separate firms. Transray convexity implies that benefits from diversification are bigger than benefits from growth in scale.

The empirical part of the paper consists of estimations of a parametric and a non-parametric model. The estimates of the parametric translog model and the non-parametric model, which uses data envelopment analysis (DEA) find evidence of diseconomies of scale and scope, suggesting room for improving efficiency. A glance at **Figures 3 and 4** of the paper, however, reveals that the evidence concerning efficiency is ambigous. According to the non-parametric model, larger banks seem quite efficient but according to the parametric approach they are highly inefficient. Even if both of the techniques used seem appropriate, such a strong contradiction must raise doubts concerning some elements of the empirical methods. A further source of doubt is the evidence of diseconomies. In practice, it would be quite easy for a bank to avoid diseconomies by breaking up an operation into smaller pieces.

I can imagine three explanations for distorted results: bad quality of data, inappropriate aggregation of products, and difficulties to distinguish between random error and inefficiency.

First, the data stems from the banks' profit and loss accounts and thus might fail to reflect the true costs of production. Sometimes banks like to hide profits. They can do so by padding the costs and building up hidden reserves. Conversely, opportunity costs may be underestimated because inportant elements are omitted. For instance, the use of physical capital that has already been written off.

Second, a major problem of studies on multiproduct firms is the appropriate definition of output. In general it is not possible to consider all the different outputs of a firm separately. The failure to aggregate into appropriate groups of services can lead to false conclusions. Sheldon and Haegler distinguish between seven types of output. Do they pick the right ones? Their choice is lead by the availability of the data. Ideally, one would perhaps also like to include output in payment services, brokerage, and underwriting, speculation activity in gold, foreign exchange and foreign currency as well as private banking.

Third, the parametric approach has to overcome an identification problem. In order to find the production frontier, a standard of efficiency has to be determined. As can be seen from **Figure 4** of the paper only one bank reaches full efficiency and defines the benchmark for all others. The regression of equation (1) is equivalent to a regression without the inefficiency term that has been shifted through the lowest cost bank. This procedure is a safe way to catch any outliers.

It is difficult to solve possible problems stemming from bad data and output aggregation, but it would be easy to mitigate the influence of outliers by considering more data points for the benchmark. One way to do this is to combine the non-parametric and the parametric approaches and to make use of their respective strengths in the following way: let data envelopment analysis find the cost frontier and estimate the translog model using efficient banks as determined by DEA. This would yield more reliable estimations.

# Part II: The Attractiveness of Switzerland for Foreign Banks

## Explaining the Presence of Foreign Financial Intermediaries in Switzerland

**Thomas Helbling**[1]

### 1. Introduction

The presence of a large number of foreign banks (represented either by branches or by subsidiaries) and other financial institutions owned by foreigners has always characterized an international financial center. A large share of the international transactions processed in those centers is carried out by foreign owned financial units. In London, branches and subsidiaries of foreign banks contributed 85 percent to all international bank lending in mid-1991 (BIS (1991), p. 23). In Switzerland, they contributed 73 percent at the same time. They also generate a significant share of the value added created by an international financial center and are part of its reputation. Switzerland is no exception in this respect. A visitor walking through Geneva or Zurich will notice all the advertisements of well known and less well known foreign financial intermediaries. At the end of 1990, the 245 foreign financial intermediaries which were operating in Switzerland owned 33.6 percent of all cross-border assets of all financial intermediaries in Switzerland, earned 20.7 percent of all intermediaries' total income, and had 14.8 percent of all employees in this sector on their payroll.[2] All three shares, as well as the number of financial intermediaries owned by foreigners, have been substantially increasing over the last four decades.

This raises two questions: First, why have all those foreign financial institutions decided to open a branch or a subsidiary in Switzerland? Was it the liberal economic

[1] The author thanks his discussant at the conference, Claudio Generali, as well as Robert Fluri, Hans Genberg, Alexander K. Swoboda, Peter Zweifel and the conference participants for useful suggestions. The author also gratefully appreciates the detailed comments of the editors on the revised version of the manuscript. All remaining errors are mine.

[2] See Swiss National Bank (1991). The difference in the market share of foreign banks in the market of international lending stems from the different concepts used by the BIS and the Swiss National Bank. The National bank takes only cross-border accounts into consideration, whereas the BIS includes lending to domestic residents in foreign currency also.

environment in the country with its tradition of a universal banking system? Or was it the safe haven characteristic of the Swiss Franc with its tradition of being a fully convertible currency with a low inflation variability? Was it perhaps the protection for private investors guaranteed by the banking secrecy which made Switzerland an attractive financial center? Is the attractiveness of Switzerland as a financial center linked to the transactions of the country's exporting and importing sectors as well as to its traditional savings (current account) surplus? Did the restrictions on capital inflows in the 1970s, when the Swiss National Bank tried to limit the appreciation of the Swiss Franc, affect the entry and exit decisions of foreign financial intermediaries? Or should the slow pace of the Swiss economy in the 1970s be considered the origin of the stagnation in the number of subsidiaries and branches of foreign banks during that decade? Second, what factors determine the market share of branches and subsidiaries of foreign financial intermediaries? Were domestic factors such as the evolution of the Swiss economy and Swiss banking regulation more important than external factors such as the evolution of world trading volumes and the banking regulation abroad? At the dawn of the single European Market and the European Economic Area, answers to these questions are needed.

European economic integration might drastically change the international environment for the Swiss financial markets. The attraction of Switzerland as a financial center might fade in view of the deregulation of financial markets and capital account transactions in the neighbouring EC countries. The consequences of the fading attraction might particularly affect the presence of foreign banks which operate mainly in the international banking market, and which have no strong links with the exclusively domestic segments of the Swiss financial markets. This position might make them more sensitive to changes in the neighbouring environment than domestic banks; hence, there is a possibility that they will relocate activities and facilities to their home country or to other larger financial centers in Europe, provided that exit costs are not too large. Of course, much will also depend on the future Swiss reaction to economic integration in Europe, in particular after the rejection of the Swiss participation in the EEA by Swiss voters on December 6, 1992.

In this study, some of the questions above are investigated empirically with respect to financial intermediaries located in Switzerland which are owned by foreign residents or firms (henceforth called foreign financial intermediaries) for the period from 1969 to 1990. The distinction between factors which are related to domestic economic conditions in Switzerland such as export and import activities, and external factors related to regulatory advantages is emphasized as it is seen as being particularly helpful in making projections about the future of Swiss financial markets. This distinction can also be found in the literature on international financial intermediation in which two approaches, the location and the trade approach, are predominant. In the location approach, the advantage of close and local links between financial intermediaries and their clients is the crucial factor explaining the expansion of financial intermediaries abroad. Domestic financial intermediaries enjoy a comparative advantage in dealing with domestic non-bank clients because of lower information and transaction costs. Consequently, when domestic non-bank clients expand abroad, domestic financial intermediaries follow suit and start to set-up a network of branches and subsidiaries in other countries. Local informational advantages must also be present in financial markets in order for this argument to be valid; only under such circumstances will financial intermediaries have an incentive for foreign direct investment abroad, i.e. to build a network of foreign branches and subsidiaries.[3] This approach predicts that the value added created by branches and subsidiaries of foreign financial intermediaries is the greater, the larger the volume of imports and foreign direct investment in that country. With this approach, the positive correlation of financial cross-border activities with the size and the openness of a country can be explained. It is more difficult, however, to explain the relative importance of the financial sector and of financial cross-border activities, given similar country sizes and similar positions in economic development. Some countries such as Great Britain, Luxembourg, and Switzerland simply have a relatively larger financial sector than other countries. The trade approach emphasizes the role of regulatory advantages, economies of scale and of factor endowments. All these factors lead to a

[3] This argument applies readily for export, import and foreign direct investment activities of non-bank clients. A similar argument could be constructed for internationally diversified security portfolios of domestic investors.

specialisation in the production of financial services in a particular country. With this approach and without referring to local information advantages, it is often difficult to explain why the specialisation in the production of financial services is not complete. The two approaches seem to be rather complementary than competing, and the question is to what extent each approach can explain the presence of foreign financial intermediaries in Switzerland.[4]

The importance of these factors for the explanation of the presence of foreign financial intermediaries is empirically investigated by using both a rather informal descriptive approach and a multiple linear time series regression model. The number of foreign financial intermediaries operating in Swiss financial markets and their market share (in total income generated by all banks) are the dependent variables. This approach has been pioneered by Goldberg and Saunders (1981). They examined the determinants explaining the number of offices of foreign banks and their market share in the United States for the period from the fourth quarter of 1972 to the second quarter of 1979. This study is thus an adapted application of their methodology to foreign financial institutions in Switzerland. Choi et al. (1986) were the first to examine the presence of foreign banks in a multi-country study. They used the data entries of a matrix of interconnectedness as the dependent variables. In that matrix, the presence of the world's largest 300 banks in 14 financial centers is recorded for 1970 and 1980. The relevant elements represent the expansion of banks headquartered in one center to another center. They try to detect the determinants of the expansion pattern in a multiple regression model. Jeger et al. (1991) have updated the matrix of interconnectedness for 1989 and have extended the list of explanatory variables with respect to regulatory variables. Zurich and Geneva together formed one of the financial centers in the study. Choi et al. as well as Jeger et al. used only a small subset of all foreign financial intermediaries located in Switzerland (54 of 245 in 1989). This study uses a much larger set of foreign financial intermediaries than Choi et al. (op. cit.) and Jeger et al. (op. cit.), namely all those which report their annual balance sheet and income statement to the Swiss National

[4] Both approaches must assume firm specific advantages as foreign direct investment or, in other words, multinational banks, are implied in both cases.

Bank. It also focuses on the evolution over time rather than on the comparison between countries. This focus, however, is not without problems. The rather short time series for the dependent variables make the results rather tentative, for the specialisation of a country in the production of international financial services is a slow process. The small variability in the regulatory framework of Swiss financial markets makes it hard to test the proposition that Switzerland is an off-shore financial center because of regulatory advantages. Consequently, this study should be considered to be an empirical exploration of the recent history of foreign financial intermediaries in Switzerland rather than an empirical verification of a particular theory.

The study is organized as follows: a descriptive approach is used in section 2 in order to characterize the evolution of foreign financial intermediaries in Switzerland and to establish some stylized facts. In section 3, a survey of theory and empirical studies is provided. A model for Switzerland is then tested in section 4.

## 2. Foreign Financial Intermediaries in Switzerland: Some Stylized Facts

### 2.1. Switzerland as a Financial Center and Foreign Financial Intermediaries[5]

In the international financial markets, financial intermediaries located in Switzerland are specialized in portfolio management, in foreign exchange trading, in gold trading, in medium and long-term financing denominated in Swiss Francs (by bonds and notes), and in international wholesale bank lending and borrowing. The position of banks located in Switzerland in the international financial markets is notoriously difficult to quantify. Euromoney (1991) considers Switzerland to be the fourth largest international financial center after New York, London, and Tokyo (the statistical sources for this judgement, however, are not provided). Switzerland has an old record of being a capital exporter (Iklé (1972)) and having financial links with its neighbour countries (in particular with France and Germany), but only in the aftermath of the political turbulence following the

[5] This section is based on Camen (1992a, 1992b), Christensen (1986), Iklé (1972), and Zimmermann et al. (1991).

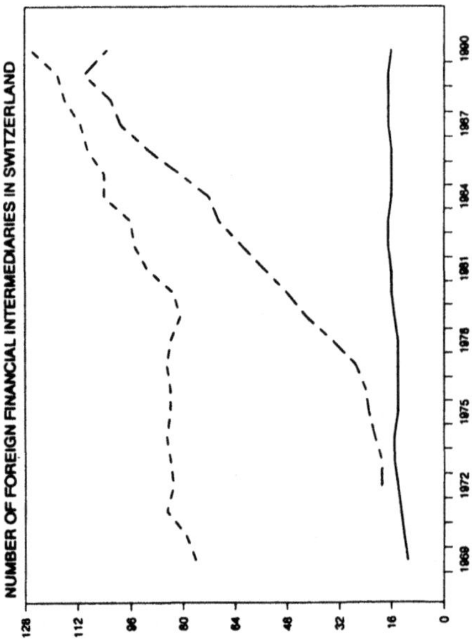

FIGURE 1A

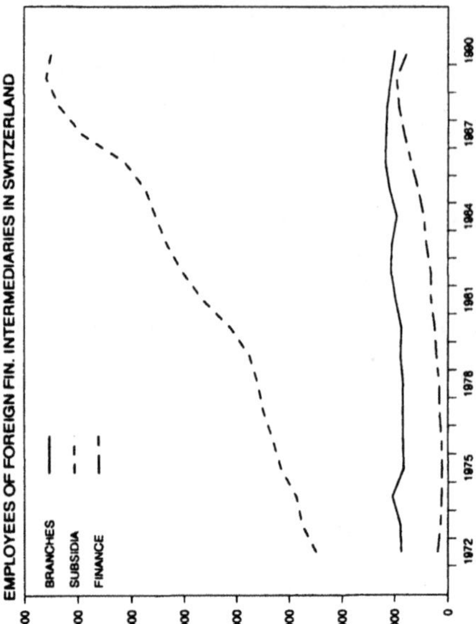

FIGURE 1B

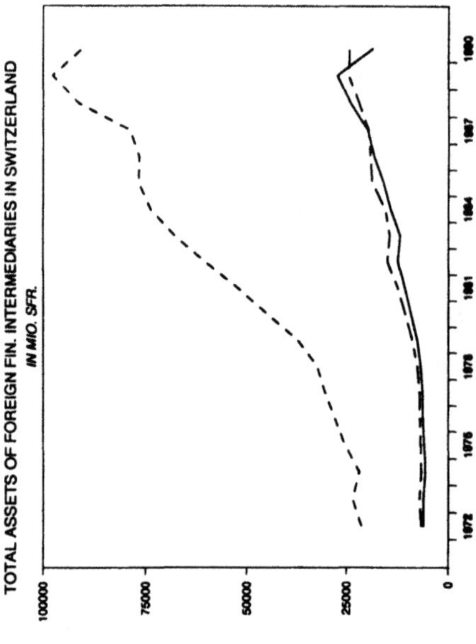

FIGURE 1C

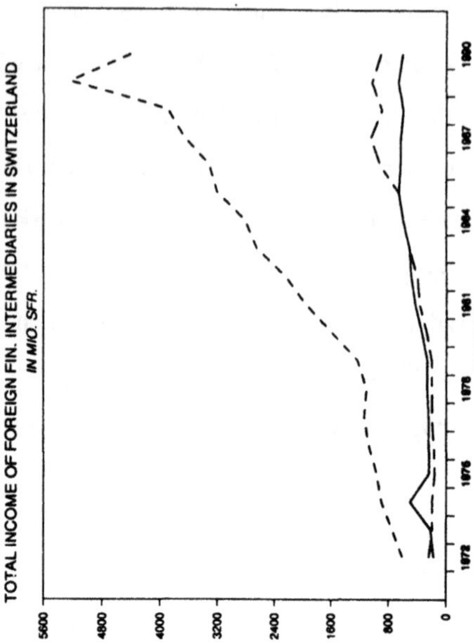

FIGURE 1D

first World War did the Swiss financial markets start to become truly international. Christensen (1986) attributes the successful evolution of Switzerland as an international financial center to the sound framework for financial markets provided by the political stability, the low inflation rates, the strong currency, the solid external position, and the sound government finances. She also recognizes the importance of the banking secrecy, the liberal banking supervision, and the high capital requirements. Iklé (1972) stresses the importance of the tradition of Switzerland being a capital exporter which made the country an attractive place to raise funds.

With the internationalisation of the Swiss financial markets the number of financial intermediaries owned by foreigners was steadily growing. Figures are available since 1969 when the authorization requirement for foreign owned intermediaries was introduced.[6] In that year, 76 subsidiaries and 11 branches owned by foreigners were authorized to operate in Switzerland (See **Figure 1A** and **Table 1** in the appendix). According to Iklé (op. cit.), most of them were established after World War II, although some of the more traditional institutes have a much longer history. The number of foreign subsidiaries stayed rather constant during the 1970s, before it surged by another 43 units to 126 during the 1980s. The number of foreign finance companies is known since 1972. Their number rose from 19 in that year to 103 in 1990 with an almost constant growth rate. The number of branches rose from 11 in 1969 to 16 in 1990. In 1990, 245 foreign financial intermediaries were established in Switzerland.

To characterize the evolution of foreign financial intermediaries only by their number can be misleading as **Figures 1B to 1D** show (cf. also **Table 1** in the appendix). Whereas the number of firms would suggest that the foreign branches and subsidiaries were stagnating while the foreign finance companies were expanding during the 1970s, the figures on total income, total assets, and number of employees yield another interpretation. Foreign subsidiaries and branches were expanding faster than foreign

---

[6] See the discussion in the next subsection.

finance companies. During the 1980s, the number of foreign subsidiaries and foreign finance companies as well as their income, their assets, and their number of employees were growing. It is interesting to notice that all variables peaked in 1989. It also seems that foreign banks have had few incentives to establish themselves in Switzerland in the form of a branch during the last two decades. The number of branches was almost constant, their total income in 1990 was lower than that of 1980, and since 1986 they reduced the number of employees by about 15 percent.

## 2.2. Legal Aspects of Foreign Financial Intermediaries

Foreign financial intermediaries can operate in five different organizational forms in the Swiss financial markets; they either can establish an agency, a representative office, a subsidiary or a branch submitted to Swiss banking regulation, or a so-called finance company. Most foreign intermediaries chose either the organizational form of a subsidiary or a branch submitted to Swiss banking regulation or of a finance company[7]; hence, the study is restricted to these organizational forms. A foreign bank submitted to Swiss law in general and to Swiss banking law in particular is allowed to recommend itself to the public for accepting deposits and savings funds. Until the end of the 1960s, there was no discrimination between foreign and domestic financial intermediaries. Foreign financial intermediaries were allowed to set-up subsidiaries and branches in Switzerland under the same conditions as domestic entrepreneurs (provided they fulfilled the general requirements of Swiss civil law with respect to foreign companies). The rapid increase in foreign subsidiaries and branches during that decade did not remain unobserved by the Federal government, and since July 1, 1969, the establishment of subsidiaries and branches by foreign financial intermediaries is subject to the approval of the Swiss Banking Commission. One of the main requirements for the approval is the reciprocity requirement, which means that Swiss banks must have the possibility of

[7] It is also possible for private non-residents to establish a financial intermediary in Switzerland.

establishing a bank in the country of residence of the founding persons or companies.[8] Until March 1984, branches of foreign bank were also submitted to the Swiss banking supervision.[9] Since then, branches are submitted to home country control; in particular, they are no longer submitted to Swiss capital adequacy requirements. An informal inspection of the number of foreign branches suggests that this fundamental change has not had an impact on the choice of the organizational form in the market entry decision of foreign financial intermediaries.

Subsidiaries and branches can offer all financial services. The so-called non-public finance companies are not subject to the Swiss banking supervision. They are only obliged to report their balance sheet and income statements as well as their capital exports to the Swiss National bank.[10] They are not allowed to raise funds through deposits, however. But they can participate in all important markets for non-balance sheet activities such as underwriting of securities issues, trade in securities, and management of security portfolios. All those activities have become relatively more important compared with the traditional balance-sheet activities. Thus, it is no surprise that the organizational form of the non-public finance company became the most attractive form for the new entrants in the Swiss financial markets (cf. **Figure 1A**). The fact that the non-public finance companies are not subject to Swiss banking supervision made this organizational form particularly attractive. However, a change in the definition of the banking firm in the Swiss banking law subjected the non-public finance companies which were issuing new securities or which were involved in interbank

---

[8] The other two requirements are that the banks follow the restrictions set by the Swiss National Bank's monetary policy and that the name of the subsidiary does not imply a Swiss character of the subsidiary (see Schelhammer (1986)).

[9] See Christensen (op. cit.). The adoption of the principle of home country control by the Swiss Banking Commission was in line with the recommendations of the Cooke committee. Since the Basel accord on the international convergence of capital measurement and capital standards established by the Cooke committee in July 1988, this distinction has become less significant.

[10] Non-public finance companies are not allowed to recommend themselves for the acceptance of deposits and savings for a general, unrestricted class of clients. There exists also the possibility to establish so-called public finance companies which can recommend themselves for the acceptance of deposits and savings in public. Those finance companies are submitted to the Swiss banking regulation. With one temporary exception, however, foreign financial intermediaries have never chosen this organizational form.

## Foreign Financial Intermediaries in Switzerland: Balance Sheet Composition

| | 1972 | 1975 | 1980 | 1985 | 1988 | 1989 | 1990 |
|---|---|---|---|---|---|---|---|
| **Foreign Assets as Percentage of Total Assets** | | | | | | | |
| 5.2 Foreign Subsidiaries | 76.86 | 74.89 | 74.46 | 71.30 | 70.98 | 69.94 | 67.03 |
| 7.0 Foreign Branches | 68.37 | 68.93 | 64.31 | 69.20 | 75.11 | 75.36 | 70.82 |
| 6.4 Foreign Finance Companies | - | - | - | - | 84.50 | 82.04 | 79.66 |
| 2.0 Big Banks | 52.78 | 53.21 | 50.51 | 51.99 | 50.84 | 47.53 | 48.49 |
| 1.0-5.0 All Banks | 34.22 | 33.56 | 35.90 | 37.83 | 36.85 | 34.68 | 34.36 |
| **Foreign Liabilities as Percentage of Total** | | | | | | | |
| 5.2 Foreign Subsidiaries | 63.47 | 58.39 | 57.98 | 53.44 | 48.75 | 50.54 | 49.87 |
| 7.0 Foreign Branches | 59.09 | 53.72 | 51.71 | 56.86 | 74.97 | 77.91 | 71.19 |
| 6.4 Foreign Finance Companies | - | - | - | - | 60.54 | 61.12 | 57.58 |
| 2.0 Big Banks | 43.81 | 40.77 | 39.86 | 40.70 | 39.93 | 39.53 | 42.13 |
| 1.0-5.0 All Banks | 30.41 | 26.04 | 27.89 | 29.17 | 27.95 | 27.70 | 28.42 |
| **Interbank Assets as Percentage of Total Assets** | | | | | | | |
| 5.2 Foreign Subsidiaries | 43.00 | 38.68 | 38.78 | 44.17 | 42.86 | 38.88 | 40.83 |
| 7.0 Foreign Branches | 56.17 | 51.88 | 49.59 | 50.68 | 59.60 | 64.20 | 50.05 |
| 6.4 Foreign Finance Companies | - | - | - | - | 40.58 | 49.00 | 45.53 |
| 2.0 Big Banks | 43.01 | 39.95 | 26.67 | 28.47 | 29.52 | 23.02 | 21.16 |
| 1.0-5.0 All Banks | 29.72 | 28.27 | 22.05 | 24.50 | 24.68 | 20.17 | 19.04 |
| **Foreign Interbank Assets as Percentage of Total Assets** | | | | | | | |
| 5.2 Foreign Subsidiaries | 36.90 | 34.45 | 33.09 | 35.75 | 34.70 | 30.65 | 31.05 |
| 7.0 Foreign Branches | 41.84 | 45.56 | 38.50 | 41.66 | 51.51 | 53.70 | 42.58 |
| 6.4 Foreign Finance Companies | - | - | - | - | 37.06 | 44.98 | 41.90 |
| 2.0 Big Banks | 38.59 | 37.15 | 24.36 | 25.68 | 26.52 | 20.18 | 18.93 |
| 1.0-5.0 All Banks | 23.78 | 21.64 | 16.96 | 18.58 | 18.84 | 14.85 | 14.05 |
| **Fiduciary Accounts as Percentage of Foreign Assets** | | | | | | | |
| 5.2 Foreign Subsidiaries | 7.65 | 88.93 | 103.10 | 141.00 | 125.12 | 158.20 | 180.71 |
| 7.0 Foreign Branches | 0.04 | 148.94 | 227.46 | 191.08 | 110.52 | 103.50 | 169.39 |
| 6.4 Foreign Finance Companies | - | - | - | - | 14.46 | 16.93 | 24.21 |
| 2.0 Big Banks | 18.52 | 24.09 | 39.23 | 37.49 | 31.99 | 42.84 | 38.91 |

Note and source: see Table 1 in the appendix.

**Table 1**

activities on a large scale to the Swiss banking law by the beginning of 1990.[11] Nine foreign finance companies were affected by these changes. Four of them changed their organizational form to that of a subsidiary, while another one merged with another foreign subsidiary. The other four firms left the country.

## 2.3. Principal Activities and Characteristics of Foreign Financial Intermediaries

Foreign financial intermediaries are specialized in cross-border balance sheet activities and in off-balance sheet activities. This proposition is established in this subsection by comparing the composition of their balance sheet and their income statement with that of the big banks, their main competitors, and that of Swiss banks in general. From 1972 to 1990, foreign financial intermediaries reported that foreign assets and liabilities reached on average a share of about 70 percent (See **Table 1**). Foreign assets were more important for foreign branches and foreign finance companies than for foreign subsidiaries. There was a remarkable shift in the relative importance of foreign liabilities for both foreign subsidiaries and branches. Foreign sources became more important in refinancing for branches, whereas domestic sources became more important for subsidiaries.[12] The five big banks, their main domestic competitors in the international financial markets, hold only about 50 percent of their balance sheet as foreign assets (foreign liabilities about 40 percent). The item 'all banks' which includes also cantonal and regional banks has even a smaller share of cross-border items in the balance sheet. Evaluating the activities of foreign financial intermediaries on the base of these figures shows that the transit function of channelling funds through a subsidiary or a branch is an important aspect of the location choice. This proposition is confirmed by the fact that

---

[11] See Swiss National Bank (1991). I am grateful to Robert Fluri for pointing this out to me.

[12] Detailed disaggregated data which allows one to isolate foreign financial intermediaries in the Swiss banking statistics is only available since 1972. In the banking statistics, the distinction between finance companies owned by foreigners and domestic finance companies is made only since 1987. But as foreign finance companies account for more than 80 percent of the assets of non-public finance companies, the items for non-public finance companies in all figures and tables are considered to be representative for foreign finance companies (cf. also the discussion in section 4.1).

**Foreign Financial Intermediaries in Switzerland: Income Statement and its Composition**

| | 1972 | 1975 | 1980 | 1985 | 1988 | 1989 | 1990 |
|---|---|---|---|---|---|---|---|
| Net Interest Income as Percentage of Total Income | | | | | | | |
| 5.2 Foreign Subsidiaries | 23.37 | 25.53 | 18.19 | 17.02 | 11.56 | 5.82 | 14.85 |
| 7.0 Foreign Branches | 32.10 | 35.54 | 31.27 | 13.01 | 8.88 | 3.42 | 1.48 |
| 6.2 Non-Public Finance Companies | 14.34 | 15.84 | -3.96 | 11.02 | 8.65 | 2.31 | -2.76 |
| 2.0 Big Banks | 29.84 | 28.51 | 17.00 | 17.14 | 23.07 | 20.63 | 18.85 |
| 1.0-5.0 All Banks | 32.37 | 32.03 | 25.68 | 24.16 | 26.63 | 23.93 | 26.04 |
| Commissions as Percentage of Total Income | | | | | | | |
| 5.2 Foreign Subsidiaries | 37.05 | 33.67 | 33.47 | 43.19 | 42.10 | 37.50 | 38.00 |
| 7.0 Foreign Branches | 30.06 | 22.19 | 33.33 | 31.34 | 35.59 | 32.09 | 33.35 |
| 6.2 Non-Public Finance Companies | 9.78 | 10.29 | 20.13 | 35.44 | 25.92 | 23.90 | 18.73 |
| 2.0 Big Banks | 32.45 | 30.12 | 29.86 | 34.64 | 33.33 | 35.58 | 34.45 |
| 1.0-5.0 All Banks | 30.70 | 28.77 | 28.11 | 34.31 | 32.89 | 33.76 | 31.89 |
| Foreign Exchange as Percentage of Total Income | | | | | | | |
| 5.2 Foreign Subsidiaries | 12.38 | 13.00 | 17.77 | 10.12 | 10.59 | 8.69 | 9.62 |
| 7.0 Foreign Branches | 25.73 | 17.00 | 18.56 | 21.63 | 17.94 | 17.22 | 16.92 |
| 6.2 Non-Public Finance Companies | 1.01 | 9.41 | 12.63 | 6.78 | 6.43 | 7.79 | 7.37 |
| All Foreign Intermediaries | 12.02 | 13.28 | 17.26 | 11.30 | 10.71 | 9.38 | 10.02 |
| 2.0 Big Banks | 12.21 | 14.33 | 20.46 | 10.85 | 11.35 | 11.63 | 12.47 |
| 1.0-5.0 All Banks | 9.58 | 11.27 | 16.20 | 9.23 | 9.72 | 9.50 | 9.71 |

Note and source: see Table 1 in the appendix.

**Table 2**

interbank transactions are one of their principal external balance-sheet-activities as the large share of interbank assets and liabilities in those external assets and liabilities demonstrates. It is interesting to note that the foreign subsidiaries and the big banks had almost the same share of interbank assets in their balance sheets in 1972. Since then, however, the big banks had significantly reduced the share of interbank assets in their balance sheet, while the foreign intermediaries have kept the share rather constant. Branches put always more weight on the interbank business than subsidiaries. The share of interbank deposits in the balance sheet of finance companies is surprisingly high. Fiduciary accounts, which are not included in the balance sheet, are another domain of specialisation of foreign subsidiaries and branches; the amount of fiduciary accounts

CAPITAL RATIOS OF FINANCIAL INTERMEDIARIES IN SWITZERLAND

*TOTAL CAPITAL IN PERCENT OF TOTAL ASSETS*

FIGURE 2A

RATE OF RETURN OF FINANCIAL INTERMEDIARIES IN SWITZERLAND

*NET PROFITS IN PERCENT OF TOTAL CAPITAL*

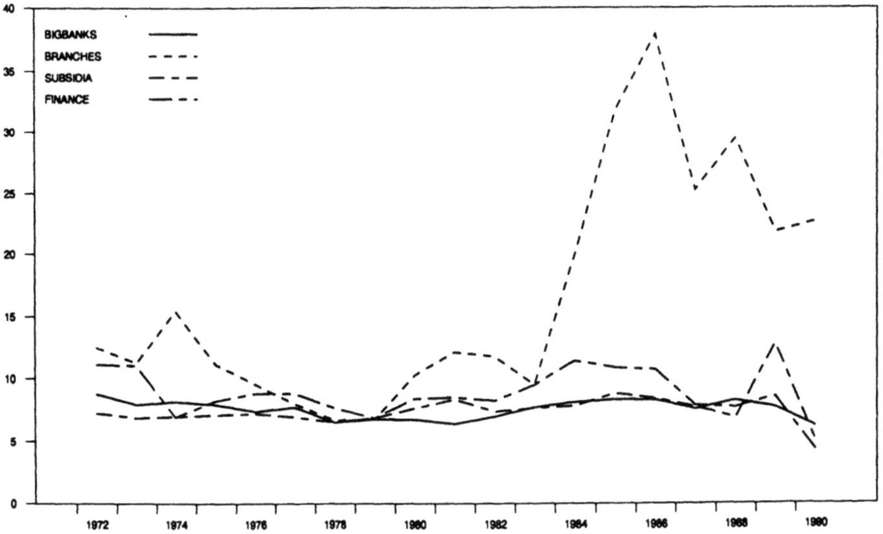


FIGURE 2 B

which they channel to other countries is significantly larger than the foreign assets they hold in the balance sheet (cf. the column 'fiduciary accounts as percentage of external assets' in **Table 1**). Fiduciary account transactions are not among the main activities of finance companies; they account only for a small fraction of their foreign assets. Taking into account that fiduciary accounts are owned mainly by foreign residents and reinvested in the Euromarkets adds another piece of evidence to the proposition that the transit function of Switzerland is the most important function for the balance sheet activities.

The analysis of the foreign intermediaries' income statement reveals that the income from commissions generated by activities such as securities trading, securities underwriting, portfolio management etc., and the income generated by foreign exchange trading are far more important than the net interest income from lending and borrowing activities. Unfortunately, the residence of clients in the market segment of off-balance sheet activities cannot be established. In **Table 2**, the three items are listed as a percentage of total income reported. Foreign subsidiaries were always more oriented towards foreign exchange trading and other commission income generating activities. The general trend towards off-balance sheet activities in international financial markets can be seen in the relative share of net interest income in total income for all financial intermediaries in Switzerland. The development, however, has been more pronounced for foreign subsidiaries and foreign branches than for other banks. It can also been seen that, compared with the other Swiss banks, the foreign subsidiaries have always pursued a strategy that emphasized investment banking and asset management activities more than traditional balance sheet activities.

An interesting characteristic of the foreign financial intermediaries is their high capital ratio. In **Figure 2A**, total capital is shown in percentage of total assets. Foreign subsidiaries and foreign finance companies have a significantly higher capital endowment than the big banks (as well as all banks together).[13] The implications of the

---

[13] I am grateful to Claudio Generali for guiding my attention to this point.

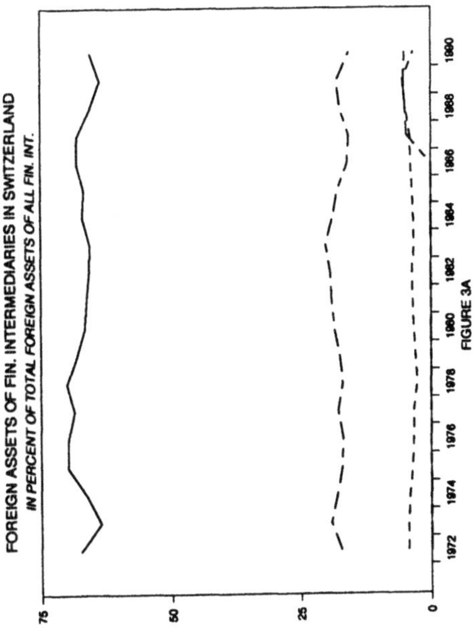


FIGURE 3A

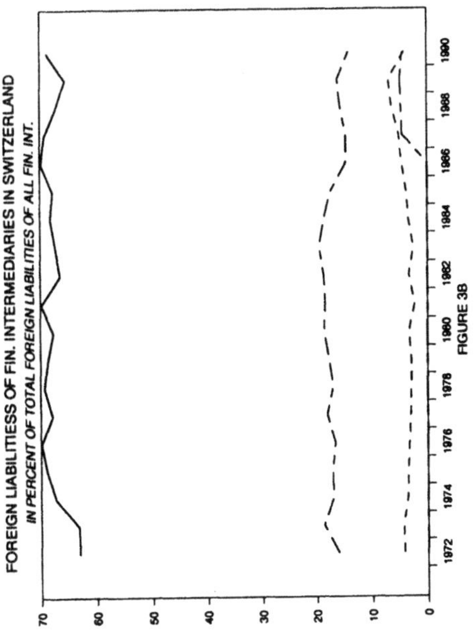


FIGURE 3B

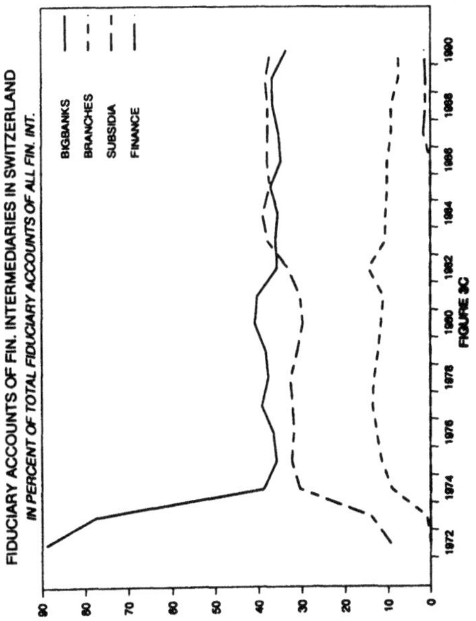


FIGURE 3C

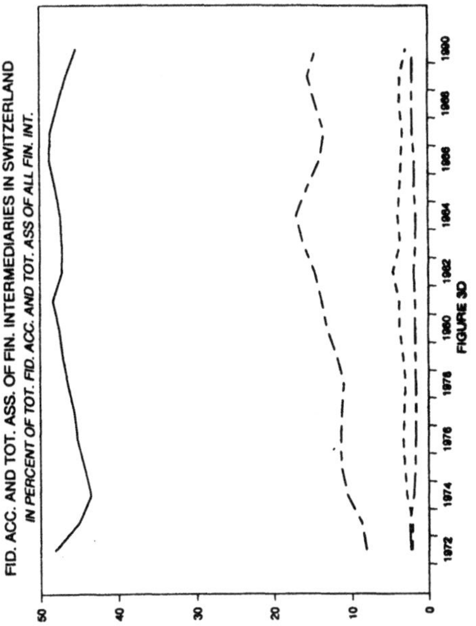


FIGURE 3D

Cooke committee recommendations concerning home country control of branches for the capital ratios of foreign branches in Switzerland can be seen clearly: they dropped immediately to a value below that of the big banks. This is an indication for the difference in motivation for the establishment of a representation in Switzerland by a foreign financial intermediary. Branches are involved in activities segments in which the specific advantages of being incorporated in Switzerland such as the banking secrecy or the stability of the banking system are not particularly relevant. Consequently, branches took the advantages to reduce their costs offered by the introduction of the principle of home country control. Keeping the high capital ratios in mind, it can be seen that the foreign financial intermediaries are profitable: the rate of return on capital is very close to that of the big banks which hold less capital for each unit of assets created by them (**Figure 2B**). Another noticeable feature of the same figure is the almost constant rate of return generated by the included groups of financial intermediaries in Switzerland (with the exception of foreign branches).

## 2.4. Market Shares of Foreign Financial Intermediaries

The foreign financial intermediaries in Switzerland are important players in the markets for cross-border credits and deposits, fiduciary accounts, investment banking, portfolio management and foreign exchange trading. As those fields became generally more important than some rather domestically oriented balance sheet activities, the market share of foreign financial intermediaries in total income of banks has been growing over the last decade. In **Figures 3A to 4D** (and in **Table 2** in the appendix), the market shares of foreign financial intermediaries, the big banks, and all banks in those market segments are reported.[14] Both foreign subsidiaries and foreign branches lost about 1 to 2 percent of their market share in foreign assets and foreign liabilities in the years

---

[14] The Swiss banking statistics distinguishes eight groups of banks: a) cantonal banks; b) big banks; c) regional banks; d) mutual savings banks, e) other banks (including bank subsidiaries of foreign financial intermediaries); f) finance companies; g) branches of foreign banks; and h) private banks. The items for "all banks" include banks listed under a) to e). The total market volume which has been used for all market share calculations does not include the values generated by private banks because the latter do not report all variables used in Table 2.

COMMISSION INCOME OF FIN. INTERMEDIARIES IN SWITZERLAND

*IN PERCENT OF TOTAL COMMISSION INCOME OF ALL FIN. INT.*

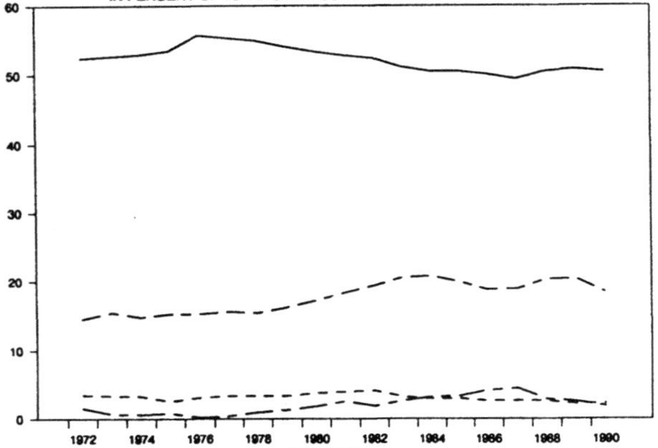


FIGURE 4A

NET PROFITS OF FIN. INTERMEDIARIES IN SWITZERLAND

*IN PERCENT OF NET PROFITS OF ALL FIN. INT.*

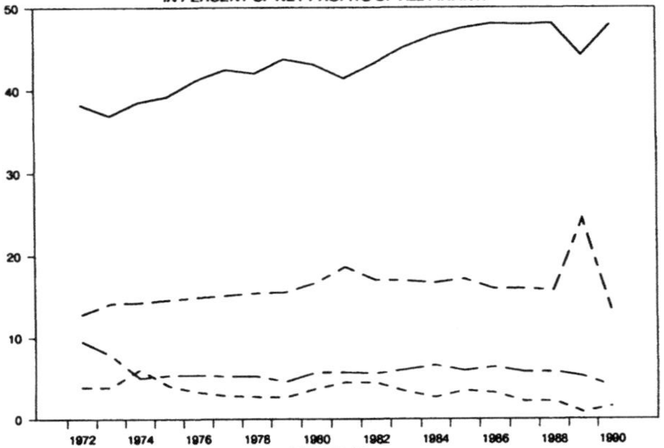


FIGURE 4B

TOTAL INCOME OF FIN. INTERMEDIARIES IN SWITZERLAND

*IN PERCENT OF TOTAL INCOME OF ALL FIN. INT.*

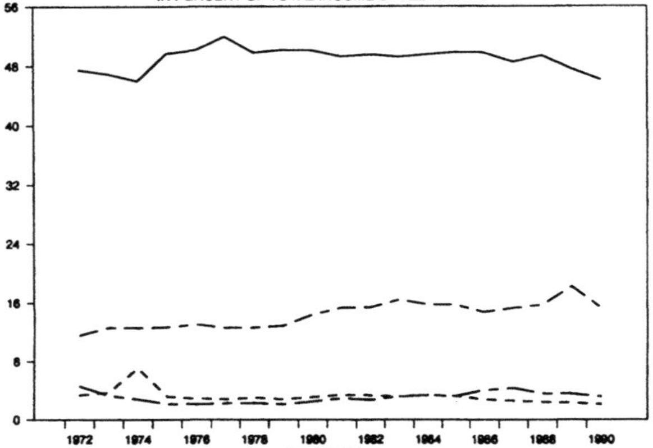


FIGURE 4C

EMPLOYMENT OF FIN. INTERMEDIARIES IN SWITZERLAND

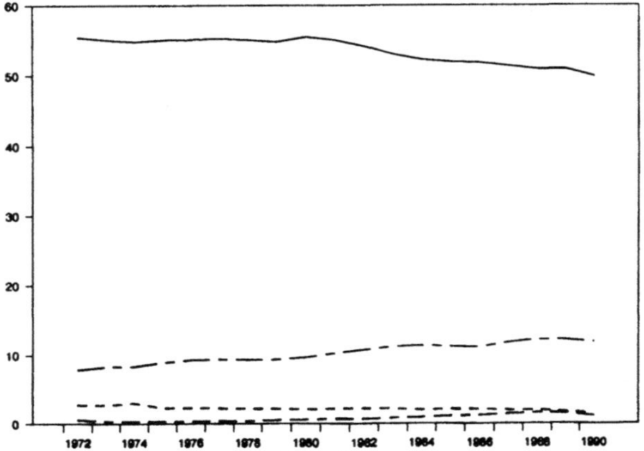


FIGURE 4D

between 1972 and the end of 1990 (**Figures 3A** and **3B**). However, they became the most important players in the market for fiduciary accounts. At the end of 1990, almost half of all those accounts were administered by foreign financial intermediaries. Foreign subsidiaries had a larger market share than the big banks (**Figure 3C**). Measuring international bank lending by the sum of foreign assets and fiduciary accounts shows that foreign financial intermediaries have managed to raise their market share from probably about 22 percent in 1972 to 33.6 percent in 1990. Thus, after the five big banks, they are the most important suppliers in that market segment. In the markets for investment banking, asset management, and foreign exchange trading, the foreign financial intermediaries had a rather constant market share, which has been fluctuating between 20 and 27 percent (**Figure 4A**). Towards the end of the 1980s, it seems that the foreign financial intermediaries have been losing ground in all the three market segments. If their share in the value added created by Swiss financial intermediaries is measured by total income reported to the Swiss National bank, the foreign financial intermediaries have became more important market participants in Switzerland (except for 1990) over time (**Figure 4C**). The increasing share of their staff in total employment confirms this statement (**Figure 4D**). Within the segment of foreign financial intermediaries, subsidiaries and finance companies were gaining at the expense of branches. An interesting aspect of the market shares of finance companies is their seemingly close correlation with the stock market development.

## 2.5. Banking Regulation in Switzerland

In executing the supervision duties as specified in the Swiss banking law, the Swiss banking commission uses three traditional instruments to ensure the stability of the banking system: a) minimum reserve requirements, b) capital adequacy requirements, and c) restrictions on the size and the geographical distribution of credits. Traditionally, the capital adequacy requirements in Switzerland have been the most stringent of all industrialized countries. Another characteristic of the Swiss banking law is the permission of universal banks and the few restrictions on the stock holdings of banks and other financial intermediaries in non-bank companies. Banking operations are not only regulated by the Swiss Banking Commission, but also by the Swiss National Bank which disposes of a set of instruments to pursue its monetary policy. In its attempt to control the monetary base and the exchange rate, the National Bank had used several discretionary measures to limit the appreciation of the Swiss Franc during the 1970s. All measures were designed to discourage capital inflows by either affecting the rate of return on Swiss Franc assets of non-residents held in Switzerland or by restricting foreign exchange operations in Swiss Francs[15]; interest rate bans and negative interest rate taxes were the main instruments from 1971 to 1980. Furthermore, from 1971 to 1977, special minimum reserve requirements limited the banks' holding of foreign deposits (both on Swiss Franc and foreign currency deposits), and banks were forced to cover all open net foreign exchange positions at the end of a business day. By the end of 1980, all those measures have been removed. The Swiss National bank also controls capital exports. The most significant restrictions on capital exports is the requirement that foreign bonds denominated in Swiss Francs are underwritten and issued by financial intermediaries located in Switzerland (location requirements allows branches of foreign banks to participate). This requirement has given banks located in Switzerland a de facto monopoly in bond issues in Swiss Francs. Several other regulations targeted at capital outflows have been removed or liberalized in the beginning of the 1980s, so that capital exports are now more or less unrestricted.[16]

## 3. The Theory of Trade and Foreign Direct Investment in Banking Services and Its Application to Switzerland[17]

### 3.1. Local Informational Advantages

The growth of international transactions in banking services and the growth of foreign banking in many countries after World War II has stimulated considerable research into

[15] See Camen (op. cit.) and Christensen (op. cit.) for a discussion of those policy measures.

[16] See Christensen (op. cit.) on restrictions on capital outflows.

[17] See Helbling (1992) for a broader survey.

their determinants, both on a theoretical and an empirical level. Aliber (1984) provided a recent survey on the topic, summarizing both theoretical and empirical studies. He emphasized the importance of domestic conditions for the evolution of a financial center along the line of argumentation of the 'follow-the-business approach' (which can also be found as 'follow-the-leader approach' in the literature). The core argument of this approach is the cost advantage that domestic banks have in dealing with non-bank clients incorporated in the same country. Lower information and transaction costs are the origin of the cost advantage. The closer a bank is located to their customers, the lower are the monitoring costs, and the more information is available.[18] Non-bank clients which are operating in the export or import sector or which are holding a internationally diversified portfolio have a demand for banking services produced in other countries (or in other currencies or both). Banks can provide those services by establishing subsidiaries of branches abroad; they offer their non-bank clients an integrated package of banking services including international transactions. The literature on trade in services states this informational advantage in more general terms: banking services require physical proximity between buyer and seller. Both buyer and seller are thus considered to be immobile. International expansion of a financial intermediary then implies foreign direct investment. Consequently, we can expect the number of foreign financial intermediaries to be positively correlated with both imports and foreign direct investment. Both variables increase with the degree of market penetration of foreign non-banks.

Goldberg and Saunders (1981) have examined the importance of these factors for foreign banking in the United States from 1972 to 1978 by using a multiple linear regression model. The presence was measured by both the number of foreign bank offices and their share in total bank assets. Only foreign direct investment turned out to have a significant impact on the share of assets of foreign financial intermediaries and on the number of foreign bank offices in the United States. A similar study by Hultham

[18] It is implicitly assumed that information dissemination is costly and increasing with the distance between the financial intermediary and the client. Advances in information technology might be a reason for this argument to lose some of its relevance.

and McGee (1989) confirmed the importance of foreign direct investment as an explanatory variable for the asset share of foreign banks in total assets of all banks in the United States for a larger sample size (from 1973-1986). Jeger et al. (op. cit.) have studied the determinants of the expansion of the world's 300 largest banks in 14 financial centers between 1970 and 1989. Their work is an extension of the study by Choi et al. (1986). They used a matrix of interconnectedness between the 14 centers which shows the number of branches, subsidiaries and representative offices in every center as well as the location of the headquarters (the matrix was established for 1970, 1980, and 1989). They found that both exports and foreign direct investment of companies located in the country with financial center A to the country with financial center B are important determinants explaining the foreign direct investment in financial center B of banks located in center A. They note, however, that both variables are highly correlated, so that they used only one of them in each regression. Both variables in the Goldberg and Saunders study, imports and foreign direct investment, can be expected to have potential importance for the present study. This proposition is also supported by Iklé (op. cit., p. 30) who wrote: "In the postwar period, foreign firms and financial groups decided to establish holding companies in Switzerland in order to control their European affiliated companies from there. The central location of the country, the convertibility of its currency, the fact that several languages were spoken there, all favoured the development described. Similar considerations induced foreign financial groups to set up financial companies and banks in Switzerland". The traditional openness of the Swiss economy and the implied large export and import volumes should also attract foreign financial intermediaries.

Locational information advantages do not only imply that the activities of foreign financial intermediaries are correlated with trade in goods and services, but also with trade in assets. If local financial intermediaries can disseminate information to local residents and other intermediaries at lower costs, merchant banking, investment banking and asset management activities are also characterized by a local advantage (this information dissemination problem might also be the origin of the home country bias in the portfolio composition in the industrialized countries).[19] This suggests that a country with a long-run current account surplus might attract foreign direct investment by financial intermediaries: because of lower information costs, domestic intermediaries might have a comparative advantage in channelling the funds abroad. Consequently, the larger the long-run current account surplus, the more foreign financial intermediaries can be expected to be represented with a subsidiary or a branch. From this point of view, net capital flows (or the current account balance) would be the relevant variable to be included in a regression model. However, it can also be argued that gross flows rather than net flows are relevant.[20] Although it can be observed that a long-run current account surplus leads to the emergence of an international financial center, it can also be noticed that an established center does not cease to exist because of a reversed trend in the long-run current account balance. Once an international financial center is established, then its competitive advantage is 'locked in' because of external effects (large stock of accumulated specific factors of production and knowledge) and sunk costs. It is therefore appropriate to distinguish at least two phases in the historical development of an international financial center. In the second (or the latter) stage(s), the existing stock of assets held or managed in a financial center matters. Hence, gross capital flows rather than net capital flows are the relevant concept for the determination of the relative position of a financial center.

### 3.2. Regulation of Financial Markets

Regulatory differentials are another traditional factor determining the location of foreign banks and trade patterns in banking services.[21] Niehans (1984) argued that liberal banking regulation is the main reason for the emergence of off-shore financial markets

---

[19] Various legal restrictions and differences in securities law also sustain this home country bias.

[20] I am grateful to Alexander K. Swoboda for a clarifying discussion on this point.

[21] Arndt (1988) and Ryan (1990) proposed that a "distorted comparative advantage" because of regulatory differentials is the origin for a large share of trade in banking services, and that a general liberalization and harmonization of regulatory systems would lead to reduction in trade in financial services.

and Euromarkets. The classic examples are the Eurointerbank market and the Eurobond market in London. These markets serve mainly to channel net balances in loanable funds from one regional financial center to another. Regulatory advantages in one country induce banks from other countries with stricter regulations to locate all or parts of their activities (with vertically separable banking technology) in such centers. The establishment of branches and subsidiaries or, in other words, the foreign direct investment by foreign banks implies that the center becomes a net exporter of banking services. The regulatory advantage leads not only to foreign direct investment, it can also be expected that the domestic banks become net exporters of banking services. All activities of the foreign parent bank which are very sensitive to the cost components affected by banking regulation are transferred to the branches and subsidiaries incorporated in that country. Since 1984, when the Cooke Committee on banking regulation recommended to submit branches to home country rather than host country regulation, it can be expected that favourable conditions with respect to banking regulations lead to an expansion of subsidiaries rather than branches. The liberal banking regulation certainly has its importance for the interbank activities of foreign financial intermediaries. According to the BIS, Switzerland was the third largest banking center measured by the volume of cross-border interbank lending in mid-1991.[22] About 80 percent of this volume stems from foreign financial intermediaries.

For further discussion, it is useful to distinguish between five kinds of regulatory measures which have an impact on the location of foreign financial intermediaries: a) restrictions on cross-border capital outflows and inflows, b) measures affecting production costs of banks (such as capital adequacy requirements and minimum reserve requirements), c) measures restricting entry and exit of foreign financial intermediaries, d) restrictions on the range of financial instruments that can be generated by financial intermediaries, and e) taxes. Grilli (1989), in a cross-country study with a pooled cross-section time series multiple regression model, found restrictions on capital inflows, but not on capital outflows, to have a significant negative influence on the amount of cross-

[22] See BIS (op. cit.).

border non-bank deposits in 10 industrialized countries. This is not surprising, inflow restrictions are typically not symmetric with outflow restrictions in to their impact on non-residents. On the contrary, only inflow restrcitons tend to affect non-residents. Restrictions on capital movements did not seem to have had an influence on interbank deposits. Sheldon (1992), who distinguished not only between non-bank and interbank cross-border deposits but also between different currencies of denomination in his empirical investigation on determinants of cross-border deposit holdings, shed some doubt on Grilli's result. According to his findings, not only capital inflow restrictions, but also capital outflow restrictions have a negative impact on cross-border non-bank deposit holdings. With respect to interbank cross-border deposits, Sheldon's results confirm the weak effect of capital flow restrictions detected by Grilli. Jeger et al. (op. cit.) could not detect a significant influence of either restrictions on capital outflows and inflows on the expansion pattern (via establishment of subsidiaries and branches) of the world's 300 largest banks in 14 financial centers. However, the focus on the 300 largest banks in the world probably implies an underestimation of the impact of the capital flow restrictions. The largest bank might have a bigger incentive to be represented in every financial center in order to make a global network available to their clients than smaller intermediaries. In this respect, it is interesting to remember that the subsidiaries and branches of the largest banks constituted only about one fourth of all foreign financial intermediaries in Switzerland in 1989. Furthermore, the fact of being represented with a subsidiary, branch or a representative office in a certain financial center does not yield much information about the transaction volume undertaken in that center. Capital flow restrictions are of interest for the present study: the Swiss attempt to limit the appreciation of the Swiss currency by restricting capital inflows in the 1970s took place at the same time when the number of foreign subsidiaries in Switzerland was almost a constant.[23] It is not clear, however, whether these restrictions were very important for the entry decisions of foreign financial intermediaries. The National Bank tried to achieve its policy goals mainly by preventing the internationalization of the Swiss Franc

---

[23] The stagnation in the number of foreign subsidiaries in Switzerland contrasts with the rapid increase in the number of foreign subsidiaries in other countries such as Luxembourg, the United Kingdom and the United States. See Pecchioli (1983).

and by limiting the purchases of assets denominated in Swiss Francs by foreigners. Assets denominated in other currencies were not affected by most measures. Given the presumption that one reason why foreign financial intermediaries were set up in Switzerland is the possibility to undertake transactions in Swiss Franc assets on behalf of foreign clients, the measures should have had at least some influence nevertheless.

Banking regulation may also affect the production costs of banking services. Capital adequacy requirements and minimum reserve requirements are examples for such measures. Baltensperger and Milde (1987) showed that minimum reserve requirements increase the spread between borrowing and lending rates. Helbling (1992) also demonstrated this for capital adequacy requirements. The pure cost effect of solvency and minimum reserve requirements can only be derived in models with risk neutral investors. If investors were risk averse, the effects of an increase in both a solvency requirement rate and a reserve requirement rate would be less clear-cut. There might be a trade-off between low production costs and the probability of bank failures. The Swiss experience seems to confirm this presumption. The country has always been known to have the strictest solvency requirements in the industrialized countries.[24] Furthermore, the annual Swiss banking statistics of the Swiss National Bank shows that banks always hold more capital than required. The diversity of approaches with which banking supervising authorities in the industrialized countries regulate capital adequacy and liquidity requirements is probably the reason why there does not exist any comprehensive empirical study about the effects of solvency requirements and minimum reserve requirements on the market position of financial centers. Nevertheless, following the Basel accord on capital adequacy requirements in July 1988, these variables became less relevant for the comparative advantage a country has in the production of banking services. For a specific country, this policy instrument still matters, however. Suppose, for example, that a foreign financial intermediary decides to specialize only in off-balance sheet investment banking and portfolio management activities. Then, the restrictions implied by solvency and minimum reserve requirements (and other prudential

[24] See Braillard (1987).

regulatory measures) might have an impact upon the choice of the organizational form within a country. The surge in the number of foreign finance companies in Switzerland during the late 1970s and the 1980s might be case in point.

Restrictions with respect to market entry and exit are another important determinant for the evolution of financial center. If it is true that banking services require frequent interaction between buyer and seller, then entry restrictions are important impediments for the evolution of a country's financial markets. In most European countries, there seem to be few binding entry restrictions provided that the reciprocity requirements are fulfilled.[25]

Taxes are another determinant for trade and location pattern in banking services. Taxes increase the spread between effective borrowing and lending rates (from the point of view of the non-bank client). Tax differentials might induce cross-border trade in banking services if they are imposed upon the producer and not the consumer. Grilli (op. cit.) found interest taxes to have a significant influence of a country's market share in cross-border non-bank deposits and dividend taxes on the market share in cross-border interbank deposits. The empirical evidence reported by Sheldon (op. cit.) confirms Grilli's result by and large, although it is noteworthy that they do not hold for the Swiss case. Jeger et al. (op. cit.) found stamp tax on securities transaction to have a significant negative influence on the expansion of subsidiaries and branches of foreign banks. In Switzerland, both a withholding tax and a stamp tax exists.[26] The withholding tax rate is one of the highest in the world. However, it can be circumvented if the foreign investors choose foreign bonds in Swiss Francs or fiduciary accounts as assets in their portfolio.

---

[25] See Pecchioli (1983), p. 71 f.

[26] Recently, stamp taxation in Switzerland was reformed. Some primary and secondary securities market transactions have ceased to be subject of stamp taxation. However, in the market segments which are particularly sensitive with respect to foreign competition such as transactions in foreign shares and bonds the tax remains.

### 3.3. Economies of Scale, Thick Markets, and Market Size

Grilli (op. cit.) argued convincingly that financial centers are characterized by external economies of scale.[27] He identifies thick market externalities as the origin of decreasing average costs at the industry level. They might stem from better matching processes in the markets for the final goods, financial services, and in the factor markets. The externality is correlated with the market volume as well as the number of firms operating in the center. Once a financial center emerges, there might be a "gravitation pull" effect that leads more and more financial intermediaries to establish themselves with a branch or a subsidiary in that center. Closely related with this argument is that of the external effects resulting from the total knowledge accumulated in a financial center or, in other words, from the stock of human capital. An interesting implication of such external economies of scale is a location hysteresis: once a large financial center is established, smaller regulatory disadvantages do not lead to a reduction in its size. With the thick market externality, it is still competitive. The external economies of scale argument is appealing in theory, but the question is how it should be implemented empirically. The number of financial intermediaries in Switzerland of previous periods is probably a rather problematic variable to detect external economies of scale because the decision to establish a new firm is often motivated by legal reasons rather than economic reasons. The following two variables have been chosen for this paper: the number of employees of financial intermediaries and the secondary market trading volume. The number of employees is a proxy for the human capital stock accumulated in Switzerland. It is a rather crude measure because it does not differentiate between different categories of employees (different education etc.). However, the total stock of human capital should at least be correlated with the total number of employees. The trading volume on secondary securities markets seems to be an important market volume variable as those markets are an area where thick market externalities are particularly important[28]. The liquidity of a market is increasing with the number of investors

[27] See Kindleberger (1974) for a thorough discussion of the geographic implications and historical patterns.

[28] See Pagano (1989) for an elaboration of this argument.

executing their orders. This variable also has the advantage that it includes liquidity enhancing changes in the set-up of secondary securities market. The introduction of permanent trading in the largest Swiss stocks in 1986 or the liberalization of trade in notes in 1982 could serve as examples for such changes.

The market size might also be important if there are "transport costs" between countries and if the financial intermediaries use a production technology with increasing returns to scale.[29] Transport costs are not as easy to define for financial services as they are for goods. For the argument to be valid, it is required that the cost of exchanging financial services is increasing either in the distance from the financial center or in crossing a border. Rising communication costs might be an example. Given increasing returns and two countries, transport costs will induce financial intermediaries to locate in the country with the larger market size. Goldberg and Saunders (op. cit.) tested the market size argument by the difference in GNP growth between the United States and the other OECD countries. The coefficient turned out to have the right sign, but not to be significant. They hypothesize that the group of OECD countries might be too small to be relevant for the market size argument. However, it might also be the case that the GNP as measure of the market size for financial services is too crude because it is based on similar elasticities of the demand for financial services with respect to GNP in the United States as well as in the other OECD countries. Including a market size variable is also of interest for Switzerland. As a small country, its position as an international financial center is particularly dependent on the relative insignificance of transport costs (or on a comparative advantage in producing transport services).

### 3.4. Inflation, Exchange Rates, and Interest Rates

Goldberg and Saunders (op. cit.) also included the US dollar exchange rate and the interest differential between on and off-shore US dollar liabilities in their model. They argued that an undervalued US dollar leads to an undervaluation of United States bank

---

[29] See Helbling (op. cit.) for further discussion.

assets for foreign firms, so that they find a market entry worthwhile. The interest differential between on and off-shore United States Dollar markets (3-month US Federal funds rate minus 3-month Eurodollar rate) indicates the incentives that foreign banks have to refinance their US Dollar assets in the domestic United States asset and credit markets through a subsidiary or a branch. Both variables turned out to have had a significant impact on the expansion of foreign banks in the United States during the sample period. The study by Hultham and McGee (op. cit.) confirmed the importance of the exchange rate for the explanation of foreign banks' presence in this country. The exchange rate might be a relevant variable for the Swiss case also. The overvaluation of the Swiss Franc during the 1970s might have been another reason for the stagnation in the number of foreign subsidiaries in Switzerland during that time.

Valuation effects might be another reason for a negative impact of exchange rates on the number of foreign financial intermediaries and their market share. With a large share of assets denominated in foreign currency in their balance sheet, an appreciation of the Swiss Franc leads to a reduction of asset values and the corresponding income items when those variables are stated in Swiss Francs (as this is the case in the Swiss banking statistics). The interest differential between on and off-shore Swiss markets, however, seems to be less relevant for two reasons. First, only a small fraction of foreign assets and liabilities of banks located in Switzerland are denominated in Swiss Francs.[30] Second, the interest differential between on and off-shore 3-month Swiss Franc (for interbank deposits and large non-bank deposits) has been negligible since 1975.[31]

### 3.5. Banking Secrecy, Stability and Other Factors

Many authors have stressed the importance of factors like banking secrecy, economic and political stability, effective law enforcement and the abundance of human capital.

---

[30] See Camen (1992b) for a detailed analysis of the currency denomination of Swiss banks' assets and liabilities.

[31] See Genberg et al. (1991).

Arndt (1988) considers these "man-made" conditions and resources to be more important for a country's comparative advantage in trade in financial services than other factors. Grilli (op. cit.) found the degree to which the banking secrecy is guaranteed to be an important determinant for a country's market share in cross-border deposits. This result was confirmed by Jeger et al. (op. cit.) who detected banking secrecy to have a significant influence on the cross-border expansion of the 300 largest banks in the world. Both banking secrecy and stability are, of course, traditionally evoked as reasons for Switzerland's status as an international banking center. Empirically, the banking secrecy argument seems to be easier to tackle in a cross-country study than in a study dealing with only one country. In a cross-country comparison one can at least detect a qualitative difference between countries that can be expressed in a dummy or a scale variable. In the study by Jeger et al. (op. cit.), the banking secrecy dummy used by Grilli (op. cit) turned out to have indeed a significant influence on the pattern of expansion of multinational banks. To evaluate the evolution of the banking secrecy over time for a single country, however, is a more difficult task. It seems to be the case that the banking secrecy in Switzerland lost somewhat of its character of being an iron fortress for some cases such as insider trading or money laundering in the 1980s, but the change in the degree of effective protection is hard to measure.[32] Hence, in the present study the banking secrecy is considered to be a constant. The stability argument is even harder to express in a quantitative variable, and it has not been used in any empirical study in the area of international banking known to the author.

### 3.6. A Model for Switzerland

The determinants of the presence of foreign financial intermediaries in Switzerland shall be empirically investigated in the next section. The previous discussion suggests the estimation of the following equations (a definition of the variables can be found in the appendix):

(1) FFI = f(OP, FDI, CAP, EFI lagged, GDP, SEC, EX, REG),

(2) MSFFI = f(OP, FDI, CAP, GDP, SEC, REG, EX).

[32] See Iklé (1972) Braillard (1987) on the evolution of the Swiss banking secrecy.

Two different variables will be used to measure the presence of foreign financial intermediaries in Switzerland. FFI denotes the number of foreign financial intermediaries in Switzerland, MSFFI their market share. The first of these should reflect the market entry decision. It is likely that this variable is somewhat distorted because the decision to set up a firm can also be motivated by legal reasons. However, because the establishment of a financial intermediary involves a special procedure (obtaining the permission of the Swiss Banking Commission), this variable should at least indicate that the foreign owner is interested in using the framework of the Swiss financial markets for his firm. The second variable, the market share, should reveal the degree of market penetration by foreign intermediaries in Switzerland.[33] The market share has been calculated as the share of the total income of all foreign financial intermediaries in the total income of all financial intermediaries in Switzerland.[34] A priori, it is not clear whether an increased presence of foreign financial intermediaries will have an effect on their market share. There are, however, reasons to assume that this should be the case given the experience that the pure domestic balance sheet activities were among the market segment with the slowest expansion over the last two decades. If there were regulatory advantages, foreign financial intermediaries would use Switzerland as a transit station, and the market share should at least stay constant, unless they are severely discriminated against in the factor markets. Furthermore, if locational informational advantages are important, an increased presence of foreign financial intermediaries will raise their market share. As non-public finance companies are not subject to banking supervision, and as the supervision of branches underwent important changes, both equations will be estimated for all foreign financial intermediaries together, and for branches, subsidiaries of foreign banks, and foreign non-public finance companies separately.

---

[33] The profitability of foreign financial intermediaries would also seem to be a variable which reflects the attractiveness of Switzerland as a location. Given the almost constant rate of return of foreign subsidiaries and foreign finance companies though (see Figure 2B), the market share is a more suitable variable for our task.

[34] The market share in total income rather than in the balance sheet volume has been used in order to take into account the very significant off-balance sheet activities. Goldberg and Saunders (1981) used the balance sheet volume as well as the volume of commercial credits as dependent variables.

The local informational advantage argument is tested by the variables OP, FDI, and CAP (openness, foreign direct investment, and capital flows, respectively). All of them should turn out to have a positive coefficient. The exchange rate EX (foreign currency units per Swiss Franc) is expected to have a negative impact on both dependent variables. The regulation variable REG, which is assumed to be increasing in the tightness of regulation, should turn out to have a negative sign. The more stringent the regulatory environment, the less foreign financial intermediaries should want to enter the Swiss market, ceteris paribus. The lagged number of all employees of financial intermediaries in Switzerland, EFI, is intended to capture external economies of scale because of the accumulated knowledge. If they influenced the entry decisions of foreign financial intermediaries, the variable would have a significant positive sign. For the market share of foreign financial intermediaries in a financial center, however, this variable should have no impact. External economies of scale should influence the Swiss market share in the world market for financial services rather than the division between the different market participants in Switzerland. The degree of liquidity in the securities markets is introduced by the variable SEC, the secondary markets turnover. The variable GDP (difference in real GDP growth rates between European OECD countries and Switzerland) is supposed to capture the "transport costs" market size effect. Its coefficient should be negative since this variable decreases when the Swiss market grows relatively faster than the other markets.

## 4. The Data and the Empirical Investigation

### 4.1 The Data

For most time series, the usual data provided by the Federal Office of Statistics or the Swiss National Bank has been used. A comprehensive data description can be found in the appendix. Only annual data are available for the dependent variables. Unfortunately, the time span covered by these time series is rather short. The data for the number of foreign subsidiaries and branches run from 1969 to 1990. The series for the number of foreign non-public finance companies and for the market shares are even shorter, the

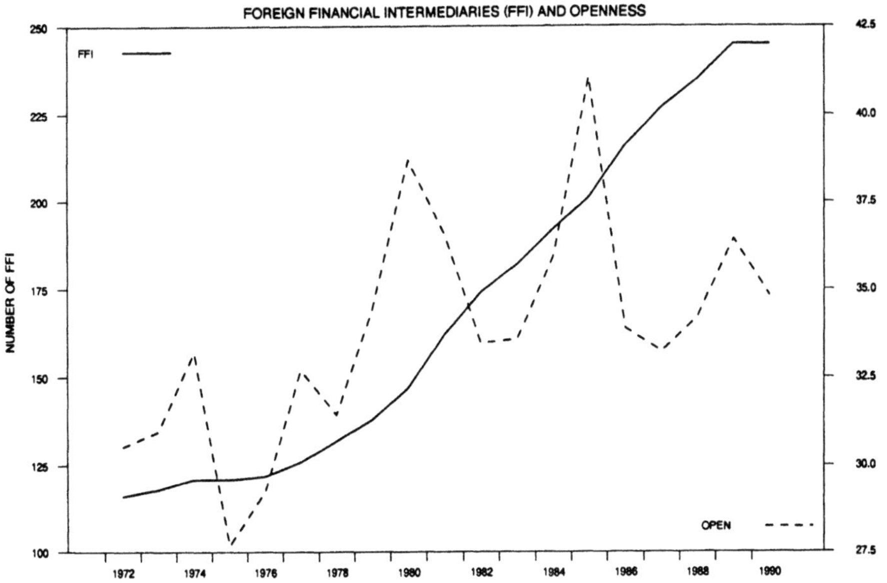


FIGURE 5A

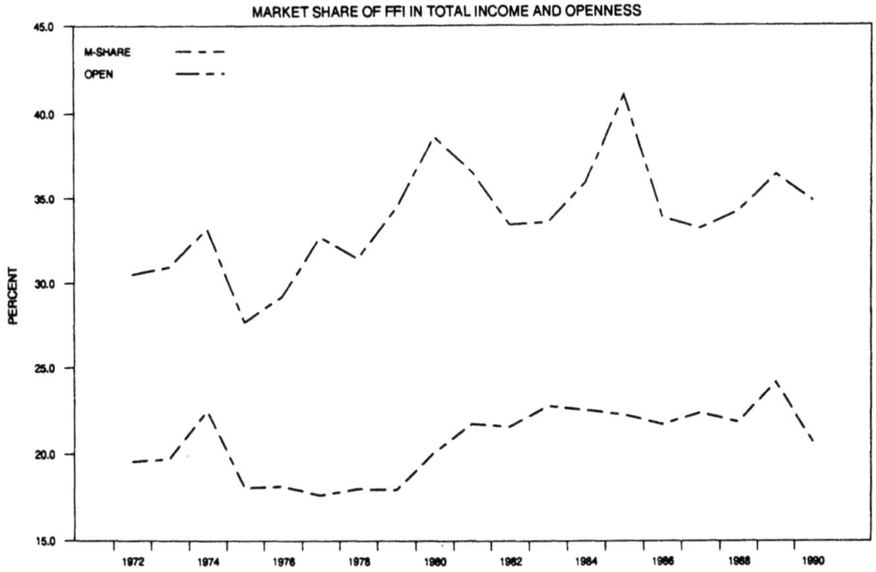


FIGURE 5B

figures are available since 1972.

There were four data problems that had to be solved. First, data on the market share (in total income) of foreign non-public finance companies is not available. Instead, the market share of all non-public finance companies has been used. This approximation is based on the observation that foreign non-public finance companies own about 80 to 85 percent of the assets of all non-public finance companies. Second, there exists no time series for direct investment of foreign firms in Switzerland for the period from 1969 to 1990 as the first complete balance of payments statistics for Switzerland was recorded for 1983 only. Since it is likely that foreign direct investment is highly correlated with imports, this variable was left out of the empirical analysis. For the same reason, there exists no time series on gross capital flows for the whole period from 1972 to 1990. As a proxy, the sum of capital income by non-residents and by residents as recorded in the current account statistics was used. Fourth, the regulation variables were difficult to quantify and the limited number of observations implied a restrictive use of them. The origin of the first difficulty is that the regulatory measures have only an indirect effect on the dependent variables because most of them have only an impact on some specific activities or markets. For example, the negative interest rate on Swiss Franc deposits of non-residents during the 1970s affected only one very specific market segment. In most cases, regulatory measures can only be captured with zero-one dummy variables. The few observations for the dependent variables that were available put a limit on the number of dummy variables to be used. This was the principal reason to restrict the scope of the study on the impact of regulatory measures by the domestic authorities in Switzerland. Otherwise, significant changes in the banking regulation in Switzerland and abroad could have been captured by dummy variables.[35]

One dummy variable, REG, was created in order to include regulatory effects. Its purpose is to capture the capital inflow restrictions imposed by the Swiss National

---

[35] This restriction seems to be rather severe. However, as changes in banking regulations abroad probably have a rather diffuse and indirect influence, one can guess that a significant foreign influence could not be detected anyway.

FIGURE 6A

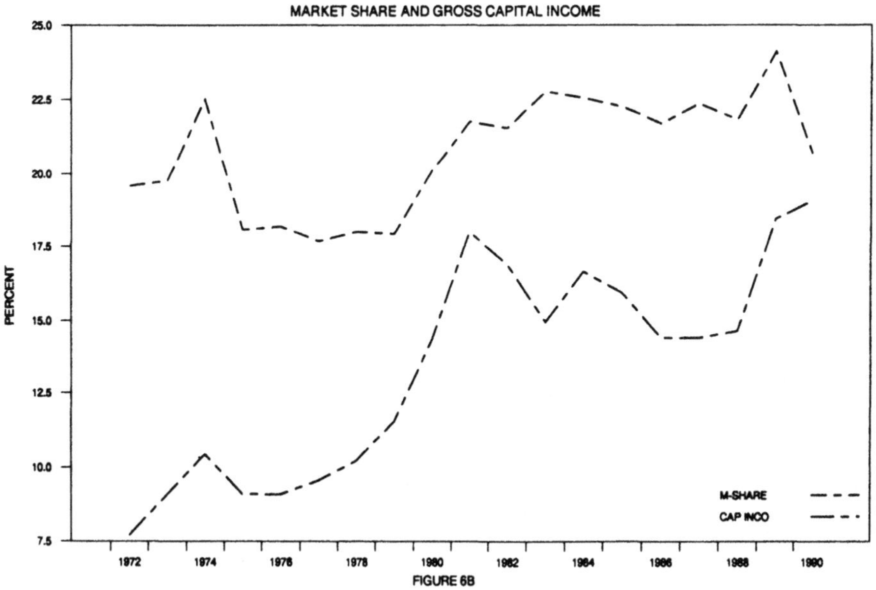


FIGURE 6B

Bank. This variable was set equal to two during the years 1971 to 1977. In that period, there was an interest ban on Swiss Franc deposits and Swiss Franc fiduciary accounts, a negative interest rate on those accounts, and minimum reserve requirements on all deposits of non-residents. The minimum reserve requirements were abolished by the end of 1977. The interest rate ban and the negative interest rate were annulled in the beginning of 1980. Hence, the dummy variable takes the value 1 from 1978 to 1980. From 1981 to 1990, REG is set equal to zero. It can be expected to have a negative impact on both the number of foreign financial intermediaries and their market share.[36]

## 4.2. A Descriptive Empirical Approach

In Figures 5A to 10B, the relation between the number of all foreign financial intermediaries as well as between their market share and various explanatory variables is explored by means of a graphical analysis. The number of foreign financial intermediaries is correlated only with the trend component of the openness variable (**Figure 5A**). The market share is also related rather with the trend component than with the cyclical component of the same variable (**Figure 5B**). It seems that the openness variables shifted upwards to a higher trend plafond in the 1980s, and this shift had the expected implications on the market share. Hence, the increasing economic integration in the industrialized countries seems to be a factor explaining the presence of foreign financial intermediaries. The weak impact of the cyclical component might be a consequence of countercyclical interest rate behaviour. Increasing interest rates in periods of a slow pace of the economy might offset the losses banks experience from the decrease in transaction volumes. The phenomenon that the number of foreign financial intermediaries is only correlated with the trend component of the explanatory variables can also be seen in **Figures 6A** to **10A**. The signs of the correlations between the trend development in the explanatory variables and the number of intermediaries, though, follow the expected pattern in all cases. The sharp increase in gross capital

[36] The variable should also have a negative impact on non-public finance companies because some of the measures like the ceiling on forward operations in the exchange market or limits on securities purchases by non-residents also affected their activities.

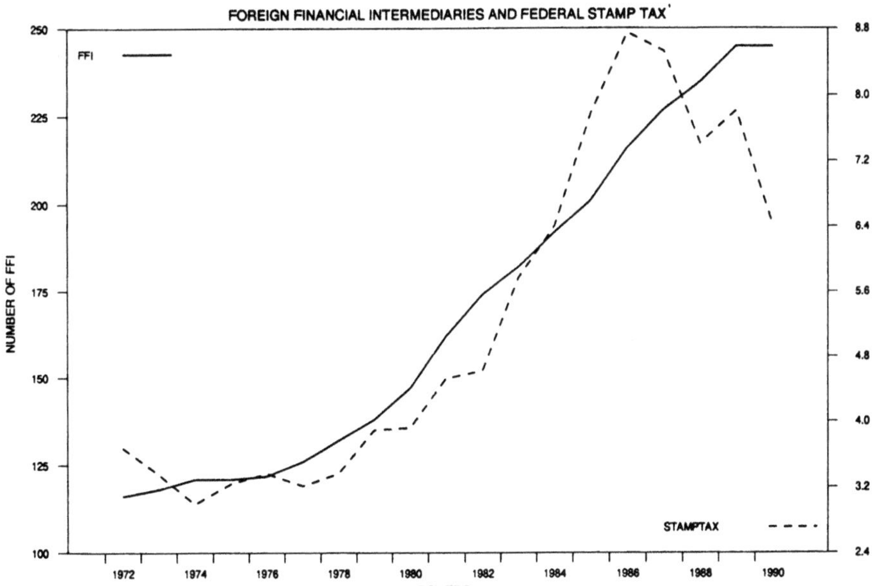


FIGURE 7A

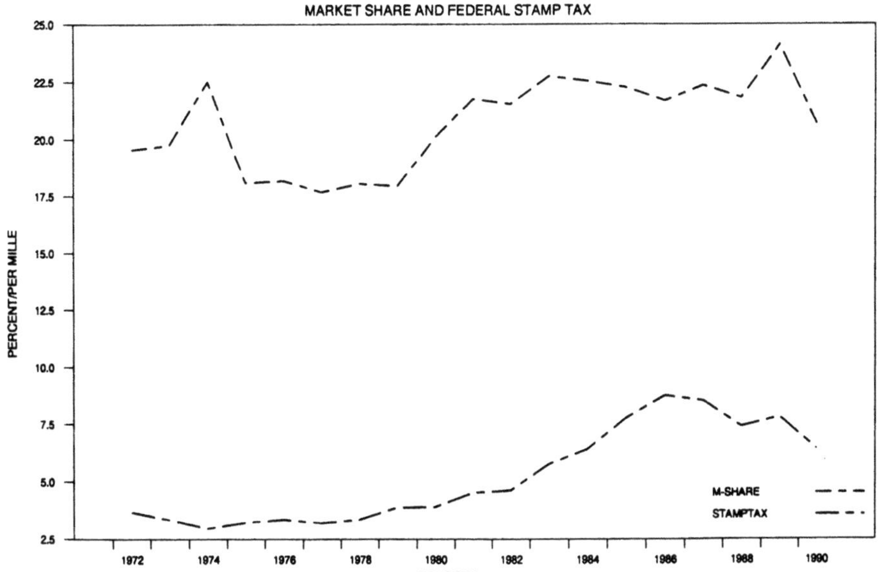


FIGURE 7B

**Explaining the Number of Foreign Financial Intermediaries in Switzerland**

Correlation Coefficients

| | FFIB | FFIS | FFIFC | FFITOT |
|---|---|---|---|---|
| OP | .58964 | .40098 | .55178 | .51595 |
| CAP | .83369 | .75364 | .83397 | .82326 |
| SEC | .74373 | .87492 | .93030 | .92415 |
| REG | -.86346 | -.76384 | -.89317 | -.86781 |
| EX | -.32319 | .76082 | .89583 | .86629 |
| GDP | -.50033 | -.27255 | -.41720 | -.38214 |
| EFI | .79623 | .96001 | .98552 | .98930 |

Note: Definitions of variables in the appendix.

**Table 3**

related in any particular way with the dependent variables. Hence, the changes in the presence of foreign financial intermediaries seems to be triggered by sharp changes in some underlying determinants. There is considerable hysteresis in the presence of foreign financial intermediaries. Consequently, sunk costs and/or externalities must be resent.

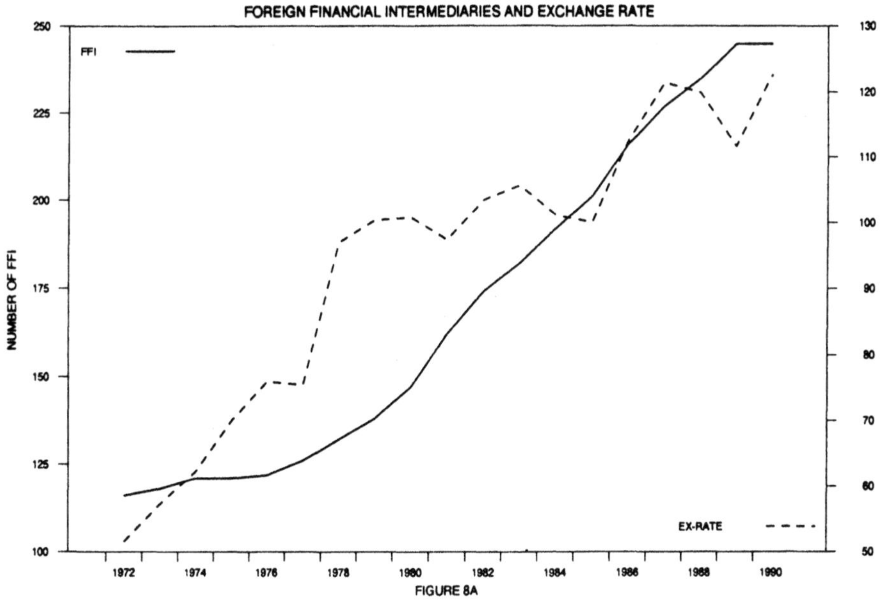


FIGURE 8A

FIGURE 8B

income between 1972 and 1974, between 1979 and 1981, and in 1989 did not fail to have a positive impact on the market share of foreign financial intermediaries (**Figure 6B**). There seems to be a ratchet effect: the market share is related to the last peak in the gross capital income. The fact that the market share did not respond to the fall and the following stagnation of gross capital income in the mid-1980s might be a consequence of the fact that this variable is only an approximation of the underlying stocks of foreign assets held by Swiss residents and of the domestic assets held by non-residents. The correlation between the market share and the stamp tax is rather close (**Figure 7B**). The sharp increase in the market share of foreign financial intermediaries in 1980 and 1981 does not seem to be closely related to the overall developments in the Swiss securities markets. However, it might be related to the safe haven characteristic of Swiss Franc assets. Not all assets are suitable for non-residents, and hence, the stamp tax revenues which originate from transactions in primary and secondary markets of all Swiss assets have only weak explanatory power in times when non-residents change the currency composition of their portfolio. The sharp appreciation of the Swiss Franc between 1972 and 1978 had the expected negative impact on the market share as well as the number of foreign intermediaries (**Figure 8B**). The expected negative correlation between GDP growth differentials and the dependent variables seems also to be confirmed by the data (**Figure 9B**). The growing market share of foreign intermediaries in 1980 and 1981 took place at a time when the Swiss economy grew faster than all European OECD countries together. It can also be seen in the same figure that the market share was almost constant in the mid-1980s when the GDP growth differential was small. Finally, the easing of capital flow restrictions in the end of the 1970s also had its expected impact on the market share of foreign banks (Figure 10B). The descriptive graphical approach seems to support the theoretical reasoning of section 3. The main factors which were identified to explain the presence of foreign financial intermediaries seem indeed to be correlated in the expected way. However, it can also be seen that the correlation is strongest between the trend component of the explanatory variable and the dependent variables and that there are, in particular in the market share, very sharp changes in the dependent variables which are followed by longer periods of no almost no changes. Annual variations in the explanatory variables do not seem to be

FOREIGN FINANCIAL INTERMEDIARIES AND GROWTH DIFFERENTIAL

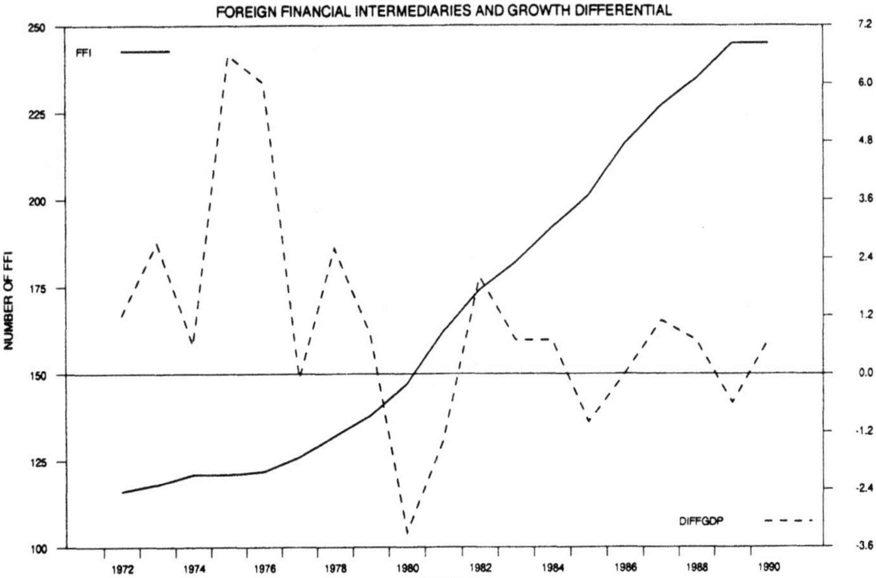


FIGURE 9A

MARKET SHARE AND GROWTH DIFFERENTIAL

FIGURE 9B

### 4.3. Empirical Results for the Different Organizational Forms

The empirical results for equations (1) and (2) are presented in **Tables 3** and **4**. All estimations were run for the period from 1972 to 1990. The estimation of the number of foreign firms turned out to be a rather difficult attempt. Most of the explanatory variables as well as the dependent variable have a strong trend component, so that the problem of multicollinearity and spurious correlation arises. Most coefficients have the right sign, but are statistically insignificant. When the equation is estimated in first differences, the results are rather disappointing as many coefficients have the wrong sign. This is not surprising as the market entry decision is not correlated with the cyclical component of the explanatory variables as **Figures 5A** to **9A** demonstrated. Thus, only the correlation coefficients between the dependent variable and the explanatory variable are shown in **Table 3**.[37] With the exception of the exchange rate, all coefficients have the right sign. The correlation between the number of firms and the security trading volume and the gross capital flows is stronger than between the number of firms and the share of imports in GNP. This suggests that fund raising and securities trading activities were more important than the trading activities in goods and other services. It can also be seen that there is a strong negative correlation between the restrictions on capital inflows and the number of financial intermediaries. The correlation coefficient for the exchange rate does not have the right sign. This should not be surprising: there was a rather large nominal appreciation of the Swiss Franc during the sample period while at the same time there was a sizeable increase in the number of foreign financial intermediaries located in Switzerland. It is interesting to notice that the correlation between the number of foreign branches (FFIB) and the openness variable as well as the GDP variable is stronger than for the other two organizational forms. This might be an indication for the stronger involvement of branches in trade related banking activities. The correlation between the "thick market" variable EFI and the number of foreign subsidiaries (FFIS) and foreign finance companies (FFIFC) is stronger than for the foreign branches. This is another sign for the fact that the presence of branches is

[37] The limited number of observations made the application of more sophisticated econometric techniques impossible.

### 4.3. Empirical Results for the Different Organizational Forms

The empirical results for equations (1) and (2) are presented in **Tables 3** and **4**. All estimations were run for the period from 1972 to 1990. The estimation of the number of foreign firms turned out to be a rather difficult attempt. Most of the explanatory variables as well as the dependent variable have a strong trend component, so that the problem of multicollinearity and spurious correlation arises. Most coefficients have the right sign, but are statistically insignificant. When the equation is estimated in first differences, the results are rather disappointing as many coefficients have the wrong sign. This is not surprising as the market entry decision is not correlated with the cyclical component of the explanatory variables as **Figures 5A** to **9A** demonstrated. Thus, only the correlation coefficients between the dependent variable and the explanatory variable are shown in **Table 3**.[37] With the exception of the exchange rate, all coefficients have the right sign. The correlation between the number of firms and the security trading volume and the gross capital flows is stronger than between the number of firms and the share of imports in GNP. This suggests that fund raising and securities trading activities were more important than the trading activities in goods and other services. It can also be seen that there is a strong negative correlation between the restrictions on capital inflows and the number of financial intermediaries. The correlation coefficient for the exchange rate does not have the right sign. This should not be surprising: there was a rather large nominal appreciation of the Swiss Franc during the sample period while at the same time there was a sizeable increase in the number of foreign financial intermediaries located in Switzerland. It is interesting to notice that the correlation between the number of foreign branches (FFIB) and the openness variable as well as the GDP variable is stronger than for the other two organizational forms. This might be an indication for the stronger involvement of branches in trade related banking activities. The correlation between the "thick market" variable EFI and the number of foreign subsidiaries (FFIS) and foreign finance companies (FFIFC) is stronger than for the foreign branches. This is another sign for the fact that the presence of branches is

[37] The limited number of observations made the application of more sophisticated econometric techniques impossible.

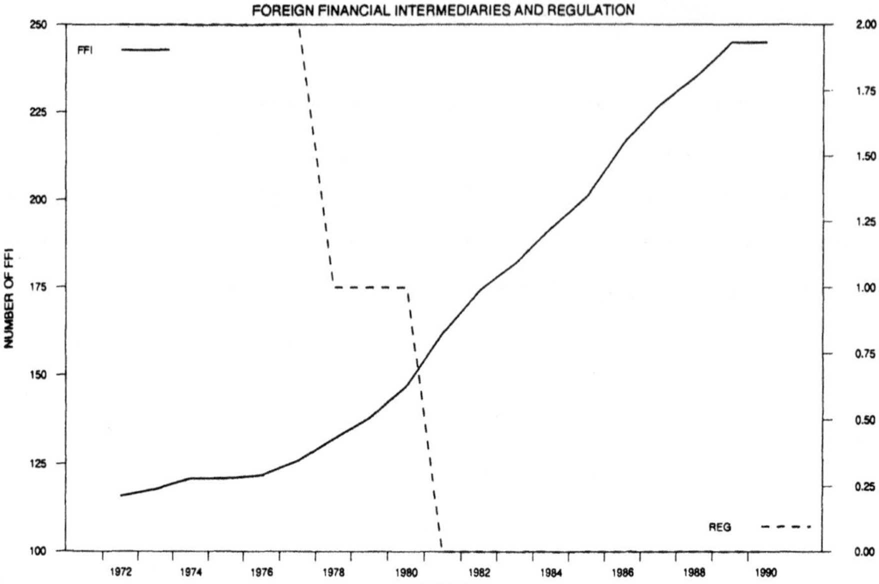


FIGURE 10A

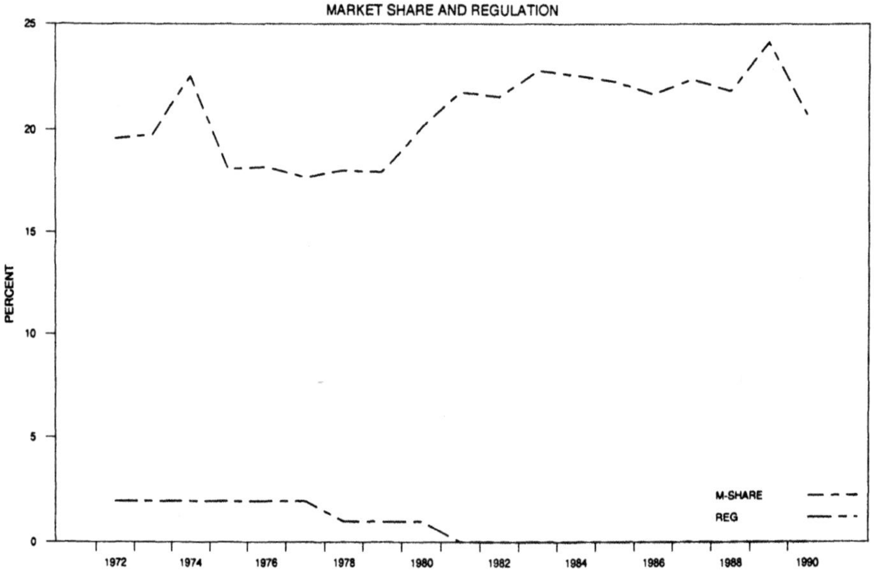


FIGURE 10B

## Explaining the Market Share of Foreign Financial Intermediaries in Switzerland

| | MSFFIB | MSFFIS | MSFFIFC | MSFFITOT |
|---|---|---|---|---|
| CONSTANT | 6.119 | 7.586 | 12.305 | 26.010 |
| | (0.906) | (1.386)* | (5.053)** | (3.265)** |
| OP | 3.926 | 3.388 | -21.568 | -14.254 |
| | (0.230) | (.245) | (-3.505)** | (-0.708) |
| CAP | 2.372 | 35.760 | -1.004 | 37.128 |
| | (0.137) | (2.545)** | (-.1606) | (1.815)** |
| SEC | -80.794 | 272.466 | 408.906 | 600.579 |
| | (-0.396) | (1.649)* | (5.562)** | (2.4967)** |
| REG | -.323 | -.0596 | -.529 | -.9113 |
| | (-0.345) | (-.079) | (-1.565)* | (-0.825) |
| EX | -.0406 | -.06277 | -.0345 | -.0814 |
| | (-1.669)* | (-.318) | (-3.930)** | (-2.834)** |
| GDP | -.0465 | 1.887 | -.253 | -0.211 |
| | (-0.240 | (.565) | (-3.62)** | (-0.921) |
| R**2 | .094 | .798 | .780 | .667 |
| DW | 2.049 | 2.115 | 1.928 | 2.131 |
| Q(9) | 5.754 | 7.179 | 4.897 | 12.284 |

Note: * means significant at the 10 percent level, ** at the 5 percent level.

**Table 4**

not so much related to the role of Switzerland as an international financial center, but rather to the financial transactions in relation with external trade. It also seems that foreign subsidiaries have more domestic clients than foreign branches and finance companies for the correlation between gross capital income and as well as the REG variable and the number of subsidiaries is weaker than for the other two forms.

The regression results for the market share equation (2) in **Table 4** show the differences between the different organizational forms. For foreign subsidiaries (MSFFIS), the coefficient on both the gross capital flows and the securities trading volume are significant and have the right sign, whereas for the foreign finance companies (MSFFIFC) only the securities trading volume is significant. The coefficient for the securities trading volume for the branches (MSFFIB) has the wrong sign, but is insignificant. A disturbing result is that the ratio of imports to GNP has a negative and significant impact on the market share of foreign finance companies. The exchange rate has the expected negative influence on all four market shares, but the corresponding coefficient is only significant for foreign branches and foreign finance companies. A rather surprising result is the negative impact of the capital inflow restrictions on the market share of foreign finance companies. This result might be because of spurious correlation as finance companies experienced a sharp reduction in their commission and foreign exchange income between 1972 and 1977. A discussion on the impact of the explaining variables on the different organizational forms is not possible because there are so many coefficients with a wrong sign.

## 5. Conclusions

Internal as well as external factors will determine the future of Switzerland as an attractive location for foreign financial intermediaries. A liberal regulation of capital flows turned out to have the expected effect on the presence of foreign financial intermediaries. At least as important are the possibility to raise funds and to trade securities. Thus, the creation and maintenance of liquid secondary securities markets with cheap transaction costs and an extension of the instruments offered seems to be the most important aspect of economic policy with respect to the Swiss position in international financial markets. In this respect it is also important to remember that some of the outstanding factors that determine the attractiveness of the Swiss financial markets remained constant over the sample period. Given the importance of stamp tax revenues, the fact that the Swiss National Bank was able to enforce its requirement that only financial intermediaries located in Switzerland can issue foreign Swiss Franc bonds over the whole sample period should probably not be underestimated.

**Literature**

Aliber, R. Z. (1984), "International Banking," Journal of Money, Credit, and Banking, 16, 661-678.

Arndt, H. (1988), "Comparative Advantage in Trade in Financial Services," Banca Nazionale del Lavoro Quarterly Review, 61-77.

BIS (1991), "The Nationality Structure of International Banking Market Since End-1985," International Banking and Financial Market Developments, Basel: Bank for International Settlement, November 1991.

Blattner, N., Genberg, H., and Swoboda, A., eds., (1992), Competitiveness in Banking, Heidelberg: Physica Verlag.

Braillard, P. (1987), Der Finanzplatz Schweiz, Geneva: Georg Editeur.

Camen, U. (1992a), "The Swiss Position in the International Market for Non-Bank Deposits," in: Blattner et al. (1992), 165-190 .

Camen, U. (1992b), "The Swiss Share in International Markets for Bank Deposits and Bonds," in: this volume.

Christensen, B. V. (1986), Switzerland's Role as an International Financial Center, IMF Occasional Paper No. 45.

Euromoney (1991), The 1991 Guide to Currencies, Supplement to September Issue.

Genberg, H., Helbling, T., and Neftci, S. (1992), "Monopoly Power in Swiss Financial Markets," in Blattner et al. (1992), 283-306.

Goldberg, L. G., and Saunders, A. (1981), "The Determinants of Foreign Banking Activity in the United States, " Journal of Banking and Finance, 5, 17-32.

Grilli, V. (1989), "Financial Markets," Economic Policy, 387-421.

Grubel, H. G. (1977), "A Theory of Multinational Banking," Banca Nazionale del Lavoro Quarterly Review, 123, 349-363.

Helbling, T. (1992), Regulation, International Trade, and Location in Banking Services, IUHEI Geneva, mimeo.

Hultman, C. W., and McGee, L. R. (1989), "Factors affecting the Foreign Banking Presence in the U.S.," Journal of Banking and Finance, 13, 383-396.

Iklé, M. (1972), Switzerland: an International Banking and Finance Center, Stroudburg, Pa.: Dowden, Hutchinson & Ross, Inc.

Jeger, M., Haegler, U., and Theiss, R. (1992), "On the Attractiveness of Financial Centers," in: Blattner et al. (1992), 239-272.

Kindleberger, C. P. (1974), The Formation of Financial Centers: A Study in Comparative Economic History, Princeton Studies in International Finance, No. 36 New Jersey: Princeton University.

Niehans, J. (1984), International Monetary Economics, Oxford: Philip Allan.

Pagano, M. (1989), "Trading Volume and Asset Liquidity," Quarterly Journal of Economics, Vol. 103, No. 2, 255-274.

**Pecchioli, R.M. (1987), Prudential Supervision in Banking, Paris: OECD.**

Pecchioli, R.M. (1983), The Internationalisation of Banking. The Policy Issues, Paris: OECD.

Ryan, C. (1990), "Trade Liberalisation and Financial Services," World Economy, 349-366.

Schelhammer, Carlo (1986), Die Banken in der Schweiz, Zurich: Zürcher Kantonalbank.

Sheldon, G. (1992), "Explaining the Cross-Country Distribution of International Bank Deposits", in: Blattner et al. (1992), 191-220.

Swiss National Bank (1991), Das schweizerische Bankwesen im Jahre 1990, Zurich: Orell Füssli.

Swoboda, A. K. (1990), "Financial Integration and International Monetary Arrangements," in: The Evolution of the International Monetary System, ed. by Suzuki, Y., Miyake, and Okabe, M., Tokyo: University of Tokyo Press, 195-221.

Zimmermann, H., Eberle, A. and Rampini, A. (1992), Europa und die Schweizer Banken, Chur, Zurich: Verlag Rüegger.

# Appendix

## Data Definitions

### Dependent variables

FFIB, FFIS, FFIFC Number of foreign branches, subsidiaries, and foreign owned non-public finance companies, respectively, end-of-year values, source: Swiss National Bank, Das Schweizerische Bankwesen, various issues, Zurich: Orell Füssli.

FFITOT = FFIB + FFIS + FFIFC

MSFFIB, MSFFIS, MSFFIFC Marketshare of foreign branches, foreign subsidiaries and non-public finance companies in total income of all banks and finance companies, source: own calculations, based upon data from Swiss National Bank, Das Schweizerische Bankwesen, various issues, Zurich: Orell Füssli.

MSFFITOT =MSFFIB + MSFFIS + MSFFIFC

### Explanatory variables

OP Openness of the Swiss economy, measured by nominal imports of goods and services as percentage of nominal GNP, source: Bundesamt für Statistik, Die Nationale Buchhaltung der Schweiz, various issues: Bern: EDMZ

CAP Sum of capital income by residents and non-residents as a percentage of GNP, source: Kommission für Konjunkturfragen, Die Zahlungsbilanz der Schweiz, various issues, Supplement of the monthly reports of the Swiss National Bank.

SEC Stamp tax revenues of federal government as per mille of nominal GNP, source: Bundesamt für Statistik, Statistisches Jahrbuch der Schweiz, Bern: EDMZ.

EFI Employment of all financial intermediaries in Switzerland, source: Swiss National Bank, Das Schweizerische Bankwesen, various issues, Zurich: Orell Füssli.

GDP Difference between real GDP growth rates in OECD Europe and Switzerland, source: OECD Economic Outlook (1990), Supplement on Historical Statistics, Paris: OECD.

EX Exchange rate, MERM exchange rate index, IMF International Financial Statistics.

REG Regulation variable, see section 4.1.

## Foreign Financial Intermediaries in Switzerland: Some Key Figures

| | 1969 | 1972 | 1975 | 1980 | 1985 | 1988 | 1989 | 1990 |
|---|---|---|---|---|---|---|---|---|
| **Number of Foreign Financial Intermediaries in Switzerland** | | | | | | | | |
| 5.2 Foreign Subsidiaries | 76 | 83 | 84 | 83 | 104 | 116 | 118 | 126 |
| 7.0 Foreign Branches | 11 | 14 | 14 | 16 | 16 | 17 | 17 | 16 |
| 6.2 Non-public Finance | - | 19 | 23 | 48 | 81 | 102 | 110 | 103 |
| Total | - | 116 | 121 | 147 | 201 | 235 | 245 | 245 |
| **Total Income of Foreign Financial Intermediaries (Mio. Fr.)** | | | | | | | | |
| 5.2 Foreign Subsidiaries | - | 610.813 | 970.227 | 1586.86 | 3212.45 | 3902.4 | 5236.7 | 4356.6 |
| 7.0 Foreign Branches | - | 178.343 | 244.547 | 346.458 | 658.395 | 601.76 | 666.68 | 607.71 |
| 6.2 Non-public Finance | - | 241.882 | 166.63 | 274.198 | 658.395 | 900.6 | 1031.7 | 915.06 |
| Total | - | 1031.04 | 1381.4 | 2207.51 | 4529.24 | 5404.8 | 6935.2 | 5879.4 |
| **Total Assets of Foreign Financial Intermediaries (Mio. Fr.)** | | | | | | | | |
| 5.2 Foreign Subsidiaries | - | 21301.6 | 25484.7 | 45058.5 | 76841 | 91527 | 97756 | 90433 |
| 7.0 Foreign Branches | - | 6164.3 | 5877.9 | 9214.7 | 15985 | 24071 | 27432 | 18479 |
| 6.2 Non-public Finance | - | 6658.8 | 6803.8 | 10669.7 | 18788 | 21940 | 24501 | 24262 |
| Total | - | 34124.7 | 38166.4 | 64942.9 | 111614 | 13753 | 149689 | 133174 |
| **Number of Employees of Foreign Financial Intermediaries** | | | | | | | | |
| 5.2 Foreign Subsidiaries | - | 4977 | 6319 | 8224 | 11481 | 14716 | 15174 | 14978 |
| 7.0 Foreign Branches | - | 1747 | 1659 | 1753 | 2192 | 2291 | 2135 | 1986 |
| 6.2 Non-public Finance | - | 376 | 227 | 506 | 1113 | 1850 | 1914 | 1510 |
| Total | - | 7100 | 8205 | 10483 | 14786 | 18857 | 19223 | 18474 |

Note: Classification of financial intermediaries according to the Swiss banking statistics.

Source: Swiss National Bank, Das schweizerische Bankwesen, various issues, Zurich: Orell Füssli.

**Table 1A**

## Foreign Financial Intermediaries in Switzerland: Market Shares

| | 1972 | 1975 | 1980 | 1985 | 1988 | 1989 | 1990 |
|---|---|---|---|---|---|---|---|
| **Foreign Assets** | | | | | | | |
| 5.2 Foreign Subsidiaries | 17.25 | | 18.47 | | 17.34 | 17.97 | 15.64 |
| 7.0 Foreign Branches | 4.43 | 3.61 | 3.26 | 3.59 | 4.82 | 5.43 | 3.37 |
| 6.2 Non-Public Finance Companies | 0 | 0 | 0 | 0 | 4.94 | 5.28 | 4.98 |
| 2.0 Big Banks | 67.43 | 69.87 | 66.56 | 66.75 | 65.61 | 63.68 | 65.50 |
| 1.0-5.0 All Banks | 89.89 | 92.12 | 92.14 | 90.86 | 90.08 | 89.19 | 91.56 |
| **Foreign Liabilities** | | | | | | | |
| 5.2 Foreign Subsidiaries | 16.05 | 17.12 | 18.54 | 17.32 | 15.52 | 16.07 | 14.06 |
| 7.0 Foreign Branches | 4.32 | 3.63 | 3.38 | 3.83 | 6.27 | 6.95 | 4.10 |
| 6.2 Non-Public Finance Companies | 0 | 0 | 0 | 0 | 4.62 | 4.87 | 4.35 |
| 2.0 Big Banks | 63.06 | 68.97 | 67.75 | 67.75 | 67.18 | 65.55 | 68.77 |
| 1.0-5.0 All Banks | 90.00 | 92.07 | 92.31 | 90.83 | 89.06 | 88.16 | 91.53 |
| **Fiduciary Accounts** | | | | | | | |
| 5.2 Foreign Subsidiaries | 9.40 | 32.27 | 29.74 | 37.25 | 37.77 | 38.29 | 37.11 |
| 7.0 Foreign Branches | 0.01 | 11.47 | 11.59 | 10.19 | 9.28 | 7.57 | 7.51 |
| 6.2 Non-Public Finance Companies | 0 | 0 | 0 | 0 | 1.24 | 1.20 | 1.58 |
| 2.0 Big Banks | 89.01 | 35.83 | 40.80 | 37.09 | 36.54 | 36.74 | 33.46 |
| 1.0-5.0 All Banks | 94.05 | 84.30 | 85.10 | 87.31 | 89.44 | 91.19 | 90.85 |
| **Foreign Assets and Fiduciary Accounts** | | | | | | | |
| 5.2 Foreign Subsidiaries | 16.28 | 21.91 | 22.86 | 25.65 | 24.79 | 26.63 | 24.92 |
| 7.0 Foreign Branches | 3.89 | 6.13 | 6.51 | 6.25 | 6.45 | 6.34 | 5.16 |
| 6.2 Non-Public Finance Companies | 0 | 0 | 0 | 0 | 3.59 | 3.54 | 3.51 |
| 2.0 Big Banks | 70.08 | 58.99 | 56.51 | 54.80 | 55.01 | 52.20 | 51.65 |
| 1.0-5.0 All Banks | 90.40 | 89.62 | 89.39 | 89.43 | 89.84 | 90.04 | 91.25 |

Note and source: see Table 1 in the appendix.

**Table 2A**

Note and source: see Table 1.

**Table 2A (continuation)**

| | 1972 | 1975 | 1980 | 1985 | 1988 | 1989 | 1990 |
|---|---|---|---|---|---|---|---|
| Commission Income | | | | | | | |
| 5.2 Foreign Subsidiaries | 14.59 | 15.29 | 17.25 | 19.93 | 20.33 | 20.49 | 18.50 |
| 7.0 Foreign Branches | 3.45 | 2.53 | 3.75 | 2.96 | 2.65 | 2.23 | 2.26 |
| 6.2 Non-Public Finance Companies | 1.52 | 0.80 | 1.79 | 3.35 | 2.88 | 2.57 | 1.91 |
| 2.0 Big Banks | 52.36 | 53.45 | 53.31 | 50.48 | 50.49 | 50.81 | 50.49 |
| 1.0-5.0 All Banks | 94.95 | 96.44 | 94.41 | 93.66 | 94.44 | 95.17 | 95.79 |
| Foreign Exchange Income | | | | | | | |
| 5.2 Foreign Subsidiaries | 14.89 | 14.58 | 15.88 | 16.75 | 17.07 | 16.48 | 15.08 |
| 7.0 Foreign Branches | 9.03 | 4.80 | 3.62 | 7.34 | 4.45 | 4.16 | 3.70 |
| 6.2 Non-Public Finance Companies | 0.47 | 1.81 | 1.95 | 2.29 | 2.39 | 2.91 | 2.42 |
| 2.0 Big Banks | 60.17 | 62.85 | 63.37 | 56.74 | 57.38 | 57.63 | 58.81 |
| 5.0 All Banks | 90.47 | 93.37 | 94.42 | 90.35 | 93.14 | 92.92 | 93.87 |
| Total Income | | | | | | | |
| 5.2 Foreign Subsidiaries | 11.60 | 12.70 | 14.45 | 15.79 | 15.75 | 18.21 | 15.33 |
| 7.0 Foreign Branches | 3.38 | 3.20 | 3.15 | 3.23 | 2.42 | 2.31 | 2.13 |
| 6.2 Non-Public Finance Companies | 4.59 | 2.18 | 2.49 | 3.23 | 3.63 | 3.58 | 3.21 |
| 2.0 Big Banks | 47.50 | 49.64 | 50.06 | 49.86 | 49.42 | 47.58 | 46.12 |
| 5.0 All Banks | 91.05 | 93.77 | 94.19 | 93.37 | 93.69 | 93.93 | 94.51 |
| Net Income | | | | | | | |
| 5.2 Foreign Subsidiaries | 12.74 | 14.51 | 16.62 | 17.09 | 15.66 | 24.42 | 13.27 |
| 7.0 Foreign Branches | 3.90 | 4.03 | 3.74 | 3.51 | 2.26 | 0.87 | 1.57 |
| 6.2 Non-Public Finance Companies | 9.51 | 5.35 | 5.71 | 5.94 | 5.76 | 5.23 | 3.96 |
| 2.0 Big Banks | 38.28 | 39.23 | 43.06 | 47.47 | 48.06 | 44.16 | 47.93 |
| 5.0 All Banks | 84.98 | 89.05 | 90.21 | 90.26 | 91.45 | 93.82 | 94.25 |
| Staff | | | | | | | |
| 5.2 Foreign Subsidiaries | 7.89 | 8.97 | 9.71 | 11.31 | 12.33 | 12.29 | 11.99 |
| 7.0 Foreign Branches | 2.76 | 2.35 | 2.07 | 2.16 | 1.92 | 1.73 | 1.59 |
| 6.2 Non-Public Finance Companies | 0.59 | 0.32 | 0.59 | 1.09 | 1.55 | 1.55 | 1.20 |
| 2.0 Big Banks | 55.52 | 55.10 | 55.56 | 51.98 | 50.98 | 50.96 | 49.97 |
| 5.0 All Banks | 96.48 | 97.14 | 97.30 | 96.71 | 96.49 | 96.68 | 97.17 |

Note and source: see Table 1.

**Comment on**

**Thomas Helbling: "Explaining the Presence of Foreign Financial Intermediaries in Switzerland"**

**Claudio Generali**

The paper of Thomas Helbling is interesting in many respects since it covers the activity of a single segment of the banking industry which, due to the variety of the operations carried out, has never been studied in-depth and has, at most, merely represented a chapter in the many texts written on the Swiss banking system in general.

One difficulty in analyzing foreign banks is in fact rooted in the variety of the participants: banks with an asset structure similar to those of the big universal banks are found side by side with banks specialized in single activities (portfolio management, foreign exchange trading, gold trading, medium and long-term financing in Swiss francs (by bonds and notes) and international wholesale bank lending and borrowing).

On account of the degree of diversity and given the changes in the economic and institutional environment of the system, it has always been difficult to generalize or to identify unified answers to the questions raised in Helbling' paper. It is certain that the strong presence of foreign financial intermediaries in Switzerland and its development over time, as described by Helbling, is due to a number of factors. Some of them are currently losing importance, while others are still powerful. One of the items threatened is the liberal economic environment, which is negatively affected by cartel agreements and by remaining protectionism still characterizing much of the domestic economy of Switzerland. By the way, this was one of the reasons why those of us who want to foster Swiss competitiveness were so decidedly in favour of Swiss participation in the European Economic Area (EEA). The ratification of the EEA Treaty would have necessarily accelerated the dismantling of Swiss domestic protectionism. In addition, even the traditional protection of the private investors' privacy, guaranteed by bank secrecy, appears increasingly doubtful, at least if one fails to discount the not always benevolent allegations made by some observers mainly from abroad. Furthermore, economic stability, with modest but continuous growth rates and stable prices, which in combination with internationally low interest rates was one of the salient features of the Swiss financial centre's economic environment temporarily, came under pressure. Fortunately, in this respect, conditions are currently improving notably. This improvement also affects the Swiss franc the continued strength of which from the Fifties to the end of the Eighties was a main source of its distinctive 'safe haven' feature making it a much sought-after currency.

In this comment on the paper of Thomas Helbling, it is important for me to point out the trend-break in the growth of foreign banks in Switzerland which took place between 1989 and 1990:

To illustrate this I shall use five criteria: total assets, personnel, shareholders' equity, net profits, and return on equity.

**Total assets**

| | 1985 | 1989 | 1990 | 1990/85 | 1990/89 |
|---|---|---|---|---|---|
| | | (billion francs) | | (% Difference) | |
| All banks | 738 | 978 | 1'034 | + 40.1 | + 5.7 |
| Foreign banks | 76.8 | 97.8 | 90.4 | + 17.7 | - 7.6 |
| % of foreign banks | 10.4 | 10.0 | 8.7 | - 16.3 | - 13.0 |

The above figures show that the percentage of total assets of the banking sector held by foreign banks remained relatively stable between 1985 and 1989 and then declined considerably between 1989 and 1990.

However, since non-credit business, in which foreign banks are particularly active, does not affect balance sheet figures, these observations do not yet confirm that total operations of foreign banks declined over time: in fact, the shift from balance sheet items towards private banking, which most likely continued, could have offset the apparent loss of activity shown in the balance sheet data.

**Personnel**

| | 1985 | 1989 | 1990 | 1990/85 | 1990/89 |
|---|---|---|---|---|---|
| | | (thousand employees) | | (% Difference) | |
| All banks | 98.1 | 119.3 | 121.4 | + 23.7 | + 1.8 |
| Foreign banks | 11.5 | 15.2 | 15.0 | + 30.4 | - 1.3 |
| % of foreign banks | 11.7 | 12.7 | 12.3 | + 5.1 | - 3.1 |

During the period 1985/89 foreign banks expanded more than the banking sector as a whole. On the other hand, since 1989 the reversal of the general trend has been more pronounced for foreign banks, which showed a slight decrease of employment.

**Shareholders' equity**

| | 1985 | 1989 | 1990 | 1990/85 | 1990/89 |
|---|---|---|---|---|---|
| | | (billion francs) | | (% Difference) | |
| All banks | 45.1 | 63.4 | 66.7 | + 47.9 | + 5.2 |
| Foreign banks | 7.9 | 11.0 | 11.3 | + 43.0 | + 2.7 |
| % of foreign banks | 17.5 | 17.4 | 16.9 | - 3.4 | - 2.9 |

A comparison of the shareholders' equity of foreign banks with that of all banks shows that between 1985 and 1989 the share of foreign banks remained more or less constant and that only between 1989 and 1990 was there a slight reduction.

These figures need to qualified, however. In general, foreign banks have larger shareholders' equities than other categories of banks. This is shown by the following figures on actual shareholders' equity compared with shareholders' equity required by law (1990): all banks 126 %, big banks 108 %, foreign banks 192 %.

It follows that the more the on-balance-sheet operations decrease in favour of non-credit business, the more there is an increase of shareholders' equity that is not used as leverage to increase profits by extending credits.

**Net profit**

| | 1985 | 1989 | 1990 | 1990/85 | 1990/89 |
|---|---|---|---|---|---|
| | | (billion francs) | | (% Difference) | |
| All banks | 3'706 | 4'976 | 4'048 | + 9.2 | - 18.6 |
| Foreign banks | 702 | 949 | 570 | - 18.8 | - 39.9 |
| % of foreign banks | 18.9 | 19.0 | 14.1 | - 25.4 | - 25.8 |

The indicator 'net profit' is, like the following one on 'return on equity', of fundamental importance when assessing the development of foreign banks.

The figures show that between 1985 and 1989 the net profit of foreign banks remained constant compared with that of all banks. Between 1989 and 1990 there was even a sharp decline which, in percentage points, is twice the banks' total. The sharp decline of the net profit in 1990 is even more worrisome if one recalls that in that year a new procedure was introduced that permitted a bank not to write off the excess value of bond investments over market prices in case those bonds were held until maturity. This certainly made it possible to avoid large write-offs (the extent of which is unknown) if we consider that at the end of 1990 total bond investments held by foreign banks totaled 10.4 billion francs.

**Return on equity**

| | 1985 | 1989 | 1990 | 1990/85 | 1990/89 |
|---|---|---|---|---|---|
| | | (%) | | (% Difference) | |
| All banks | 8.2 | 7.9 | 6.1 | - 25.6 | - 22.8 |
| Big banks | 8.7 | 7.7 | 6.2 | - 28.7 | - 19.5 |
| Foreign banks | 8.9 | 8.6 | 5.0 | - 43.8 | - 41.9 |

The numbers clearly show that between 1985 and 1989 the return on equity of all banking groups was very similar and decreased only slightly. On the contrary, the return on equity drastically declined between 1989 and 1990 for all groups, but it did so in a particularly marked way in the case of foreign banks.

**Conclusions**

The conclusions which can be drawn from the figures shown above are evident. Beyond the particular events of 1990 (the Gulf War), it cannot be denied that change began to affect foreign banks in Switzerland after 1985, and much is still under way. The loss of attractiveness of Swiss financial markets became apparent in that specific period. It should be added that during the same years an extended repeal of the traditional cartel-like banking conventions took place. Competition in the Swiss financial centre became still keener.

In the past foreign banks showed the tendency to transfer capital to Switzerland so as to create a safety net in a strong currency: in those years the yield of invested funds was of secondary importance. It is expected that such a policy will lose in importance and that foreign banks will not keep excess capital in Switzerland as safety net reserves to the same extent as they did before.

Nevertheless, more than a year and a half after my comment was initially presented at the Geneva conference, I can also point to some change which has taken place in the meantime (e.g., the revision of the law on the stamp duty) that open up more encouraging perspectives for the Swiss market. Even the negative vote on the EEA Treaty, deplorable in itself, was not directly harmful to Swiss financial markets. Developments since point to the markets ability to recover. Admittedly, however, the regained strength was also favoured by the confused situation that emerged in the interim in Europe (both at the monetary and political level).

In spite of this, even in a less apocalyptic scenario the conclusions from the preceding analysis remain valid: foreign banks will more and more tend to concentrate on two sectors: on private banking, with the accent on portfolio management, and on capital market activity. Without a solid base in one or both sectors many foreign banks will be compelled to reconsider the opportunity of maintaining their presence in Switzerland.

# Part III: The Swiss Stock Markets

## The Effects of Foreign Competition on Stock Markets: SEAQ International vs. Switzerland

**Thomas Helbling**[1]

### 1. Introduction

In the aftermath of financial market deregulation, capital flow liberalization, and information technology innovations during the early 1980s, the European secondary securities markets were facing a serious challenge. Most stock exchanges lost a significant part of their market share in the trading volume of domestic equities to London, where the SEAQ International (for short: SEAQ), a quote-driven screen-based market maker system, was introduced in 1985.[2] [3] Authorities and market participants reacted by changing the design and the regulation of European secondary securities markets as domestic brokers and banks wanted to regain the market share lost to London.[4] The Swiss stock exchanges have also experienced this competitive pressure. Today, it is a common guess that about fifteen percent of the trading activities in Swiss Blue Chip shares takes place on SEAQ.[5] In this paper, the impact of the establishment of SEAQ on Swiss stock exchanges is investigated. This system is of particular interest because it is the only trading system outside Switzerland with a significant market share in the secondary markets for Swiss equities. However, it is likely that Swiss stock

[1] The author thanks his discussants at the conference, Peter Aerni and Richard T. Meier, as well as George Sheldon, Alexander K. Swoboda, and Peter Zweifel for helpful comments. The detailed comments of Niklaus Blattner and Hans Genberg on the revised version of the manuscript helped to improve the exposition substantially and are gratefully appreciated. All remaining errors are mine.

[2] A similar process seems to have been happening in the US where the New York Stock Exchange (NYSE) lost parts of their share in the market to other, screen based systems such as NASDAQ (The Economist (1992a)).

[3] This static market-share analysis can be misleading because the creation of a new market might also lead to an expansion of the total market from which also the traditional market place might gain.

[4] See Pagano and Roell (1990) for a survey.

[5] See, for example, Zimmermann et al. (1992).

markets have also been affected by changes in secondary securities markets in other countries because they have influenced the trading activities in foreign securities in Switzerland, which were said to have generated as much brokerage income as those in domestic equities.[6]

The competitive pressures exercised by the SEAQ and other European stock markets have provoked a whole range of reforms on Swiss stock exchanges.[7] In order to analyze the impact of competition, it is helpful to use a definition of securities markets given by Schaefer (1990). He defines a securities market by five elements: a) the set of instruments traded, b) the set of agents to whom information is disseminated, c) the market clearing mechanism, d) the settlement mechanism, and e) the regulatory structure. For all five elements, there were major changes in the second half of the 1980s. With the introduction of the SOFFEX option and futures exchange in 1988, the set of instruments available has been expanded considerably. With the introduction of a computerized information system linking the three most important stock exchanges, - Basel, Geneva and Zurich -, the amount of (price) information disseminated has increased. The clearing system has been changed by introducing of permanent trading in the most important stocks. The cost of using the exchange services of stock exchange member firms, the commissions, has been changed twice: in 1986, the structure of the commissions to be paid for securities transactions was changed in favour of larger transactions.[8] In 1991, the commission structure was changed once more: the fixed brokerage commissions (courtage) set by the Association of Swiss stock exchanges were abolished completely.[9] These important developments notwithstanding, the most

---

[6] See Zimmermann et al. (op. cit.), and The Economist (1992b).

[7] This argument does not imply that all the changes were only the consequence of competition by other securities markets. In this respect the timing is important. It was only in May 1988 that the first Swiss shares were listed as 'firm quote securities' (securities for which at least three market makers are ready to offer mandatory two-way quotes during the trading hours) on SEAQ.

[8] See Braillard (1987). The fixed commissions were set by the member banks of Swiss stock exchanges.

[9] It is not clear whether the complete abolition of fixed commissions was only a consequence of the competitive pressure by other stock markets. The federal government would have forced the stock exchange members to eliminate fixed commissions by the end of 1992. The commission arrangement

fundamental change is still on the way: the introduction of a computerized trading system which would replace the traditional open-outcry system at Swiss stock exchanges. Last, but not least, a new federal stock exchange law which would transfer the legal responsibility for the regulation of securities trading from cantons to the federal government is in preparation.

To redesign the secondary securities markets the competitive challenge initiated by SEAQ has to be understood. Only then, questions such as what set of securities should the electronic trading system cover can be answered. This also makes it possible to analyze the impact of the computerized trading system on the market structure for secondary securities trading which has been characterized by the co-existence of big banks and smaller so-called stock markets banks until now. This coexistence might end soon because some of the stock market banks might not be able to afford the participation in a electronic trading system covering all securities.

Given that Swiss shares are traded at three stock markets in Switzerland and one in London, the questions pertaining to their coexistence, the determinants of market shares, and the implications for welfare and public policy arise.[10] These questions are not trivial provided that there are economies of scale or externalities in the production of exchange services. Pagano and Roell (1990) proposed that transaction costs and market liquidity are the most important determinants for the location of securities trading activities, and hence for the trading volume at a certain stock exchange. Competition among stock exchanges might change transaction costs and market liquidity on one market in two ways:

a) Competition might lower transaction costs for several reasons. First, more broker or

---

which can be interpreted as a cartel was shown to have negative economic consequences by an investigation of the Swiss cartel commission. It is only a presumption that this early abolition was also the result of a loss in the market share in the turnover of Swiss equities.

[10] This paper focuses mainly on trading activities in shares. This restriction serves the purpose of limiting the length of the paper. The situation for bond trading seems to be quite similar, however. In particular, a considerable number of transactions in Swiss franc foreign bonds are now effectuated in London.

dealers might enter the market so that the unit price of exchange services will be lowered. Second, stock exchanges might be forced to adapt to technological innovations faster. Third, more stock exchanges might allow for product differentiation (differentiated exchange services), and thus lower transaction costs for the consumer in terms of utility.

b) Competition might be harmful because the overall market liquidity might be negatively affected by the fragmentation of trading activities.

In this paper, competition between stock exchanges is analyzed theoretically and empirically for the case of Switzerland versus London. A comparison of the differences in the five constituting elements of a stock market between Swiss exchanges and SEAQ is the basis of a discussion for the likely impact of competition on market shares, transaction costs, and market liquidity. Unfortunately, the empirical part is rather sketchy and descriptive. The lack of reliable data on transaction costs and market liquidity was the most serious obstacle. Given the difference in the trading systems on SEAQ and on Swiss stock exchanges, it was not possible to investigate empirically the interesting question of whether one of the two systems can generate the exchange services at lower unit costs. For this reason, the empirical part focuses on the evolution of market liquidity. The specific question of whether the establishment of SEAQ has had an effect on the market liquidity of stocks traded on Swiss stock markets is then analyzed in some detail. A comparison of the bid-ask spread and the average deviation of actual transaction prices from the underlying equilibrium prices for permanently traded Swiss stocks listed both on Swiss stock exchanges and on SEAQ and for those listed in Switzerland only provided insight into the effects of competition among the two stock exchanges. This paper can be considered to be a continuation of Aerni (1991) who investigated the same question with respect to competition among the three Swiss stock exchanges. He was unable to detect any significant competitive effect, but discovered a significant fragmentation effect. In this study, no significant impact of market fragmentation on the market quality could be detected. Taking the strong impact on transaction costs into account, the evidence suggests that the competitive effect of SEAQ on Swiss stock markets was stronger than the fragmentation effect.

The paper is organized as follows: in section 2, a comparison of the Swiss stock markets and SEAQ is used to discuss the main characteristics of the actual competition between the two trading systems. A discussion of theoretical and empirical aspects of competition among stock exchanges follows in section 3. Finally, the empirical investigation of the impact of competition on Swiss stock markets is undertaken in section 4.

## 2. Swiss Stock Markets and SEAQ in London

### 2.1. Main Characteristics

Both stock markets can be characterized by using Schaefer's five elements defining a securities market (cf. Introduction). The set of informed traders is virtually the same. prices of Swiss stock markets and quotes from SEAQ are disseminated by world-wide financial market information systems such as Investdata of Telekurs or Reuters Financial News Network. The set of instruments differs considerably. On the Swiss stock markets, there is a wide set of instruments such as equities, bonds, and options available.[11] It is also possible to undertake spot and forward transactions with equities, the instruments on which this study focuses. On SEAQ, only spot prices for eighteen Swiss securities are quoted as so-called 'firm quote securities'.[12] All of those stocks are so-called permanently traded shares on Swiss stock exchanges. Their annual domestic turnover is usually above 1 billion SFr. (see **Table 1**).[13] Measured by the ratio of the sum of the turnover in Switzerland and in London over the end-of-period stock market capitalization, all of them are very liquid (turnover is 50 percent or more

[11] At the Zurich stock exchange, the exchange with the largest turnover, there were 2492 bonds, 576 shares, and 73 options listed in the end of 1991 (Effektenbörsenverein Zurich (1992)).

[12] This takes into account information until the end of March 1992.

[13] There seems to be a tendency that market makers in London refuse to set quotes for equities with a domestic turnover of less than 1 billion SFr. For example, both the Ciba-Geigy participation certificate and the Georg Fischer bearer shares, which were listed as firm quote securities in 1990 and in the beginning of 1991, were eliminated from the list of this category of securities in 1991 when it was foreseeable that their domestic turnover would not reach the 1 billion SFr. limit.

## Some Key Figures for Permanently Traded Swiss Shares

| 1990 a) | Domestic | London | | Market Share | | Stock Market | |
|---|---|---|---|---|---|---|---|
| In Mio. SFr. | Turnover b) | Turnover 1d) | Turnover 2c) | London 1 | London 2 | Valuation e) | Liquidity g) |
| Adia BR | 971.24 | | | | | 1553.94 | 62.50 |
| Alusuisse BR | 2582.95 | 103.66 | 207.32 | 3.86 | 7.43 | 1193.17 | 233.85 |
| Ascom BR | 275.52 | | | | | 709.54 | 38.83 |
| BBC BR | 5864.85 | 859.45 | 1718.91 | 12.78 | 22.67 | 4245.30 | 178.64 |
| BBC P | 1335.28 | 496.42 | 992.85 | 27.10 | 42.65 | 1399.04 | 166.41 |
| Ciba Geigy BR | 1951.09 | 177.74 | 355.47 | 8.35 | 15.41 | 1857.60 | 124.17 |
| Ciba Geigy REG | 3718.17 | 405.82 | 811.63 | 9.84 | 17.92 | 8854.80 | 51.16 |
| Ciba Geigy P | 1086.02 | 165.59 | 331.18 | 13.23 | 23.37 | 672.60 | 210.70 |
| Credit Suisse BR | 3404.21 | 99.89 | 199.78 | 2.85 | 5.54 | 6015.52 | 59.91 |
| Elektrowatt BR | 909.78 | | | | | 2417.00 | 37.64 |
| Georg Fischer BR | 927.81 | 18.75 | 37.51 | 1.98 | 3.89 | 484.20 | 199.36 |
| Holderbank BR | 962.67 | | | | | 1311.40 | 73.41 |
| Nestlé BR | 3820.68 | 364.96 | 729.92 | 8.72 | 16.04 | 8292.14 | 54.88 |
| Nestlé REG | 5813.96 | 1670.98 | 3341.95 | 22.32 | 36.50 | 17421.53 | 52.56 |
| Nestlé P | 548.44 | 291.50 | 583.01 | 34.71 | 51.53 | 1644.00 | 68.82 |
| Roche G | 9765.81 | 938.61 | 1877.21 | 8.77 | 16.12 | 12554.61 | 92.74 |
| Sandoz BR | 1366.96 | | | | | 1174.18 | 116.42 |
| Sandoz REG | 1127.40 | | | | | 6596.62 | 17.09 |
| Sandoz P | 2777.58 | 438.93 | 877.86 | 13.65 | 24.02 | 2571.24 | 142.17 |
| Swiss Bank C. BR | 3025.02 | 192.43 | 384.87 | 5.98 | 11.29 | 3611.73 | 94.41 |
| Swiss Bank C. REG | 681.32 | | | | | 3181.90 | 21.41 |
| Swiss Bank C. P | 1747.74 | 269.88 | 539.76 | 13.38 | 23.60 | 2064.99 | 110.78 |
| Swiss RE P | 1419.68 | | | | | 1637.44 | 86.70 |
| SVB BR | 572.91 | | | | | 1522.60 | 37.63 |
| Swissair BR | 376.89 | | | | | 510.21 | 73.87 |
| Union Bank BR | 6189.72 | 454.48 | 908.97 | 6.84 | 12.80 | 11672.40 | 60.82 |
| Union Bank REG | 963.92 | | | | | 2581.00 | 37.35 |
| Winthherthur BR | 948.68 | | | | | 1108.69 | 85.57 |
| Winterthur P | 1243.85 | 74.25 | 148.50 | 5.63 | 10.67 | 1372.14 | 101.47 |
| Zurich BR | 1310.56 | 34.82 | 69.64 | 2.59 | 5.05 | 1620.00 | 85.20 |
| Zurich P | 1282.29 | 55.54 | 111.08 | 4.15 | 7.97 | 2062.50 | 67.56 |
| Total | 71773.28 | 7113.71 | 14227.41 | 9.02 | 16.54 | 127265.35 | 67.58 |

BR = bearer share, REG = registered share, P = participation certificate.

Notes: a) only from April to December; b) reported turnover of member banks at the three Swiss stock exchanges;

c) turnover reported by SEAQ; d) turnover reported by SEAQ divided by 2;

e) valued at Zurich closing prices of December 28, 1990; f) valued at Zurich closing prices Zurich of December 30, 1991;

g) sum of domestic turnover and London turnover 2 as percentage of stock market valuation.

**Table 1**

of the stock market capitalization).[14] The listing requirements in Switzerland can be considered to be the same as in London, revealing a remarkable spirit for free trade and competition. London recognizes the Swiss listing requirements and allows to list any Swiss security on the SEAQ system provided it is recognized by a Swiss stock exchange.

The real difference between the two markets is the trading or, in other words, the market clearing mechanism. The Swiss stock exchanges are floor trading systems with an open-outcry auction market clearing mechanism. For most stocks, there are two trading sessions with a sequential auction for each share. The permanently traded shares are also auctioned with the open-outcry system, but the auction is continuous. But even with continuous auctions for those shares, the trading for each share is sequential and does not offer the same immediacy as a market maker system. The SEAQ system was designed as a designed as a market maker system.[15] The basic service provided by the London Stock Exchange (which runs SEAQ) is the market set up with a price quotation and information system with the information being dissipated on screen. The actual dealing takes place on the telephone. Every market maker has to put in two-way quotes during the 'mandatory quote period' which is basically identical with the trading time at the Swiss stock exchanges. Market markers can use their own computer system to put the quotes into the central computer system of SEAQ. At least three market makers are required before an equity is considered to be a 'firm quote security' for which an overview page with all quotes, minimum marketable size, and the best spread are displayed on screen continuously.

Currently, there are eighteen securities companies quoting prices as a market maker for a set from one to eighteen Swiss securities (ten market makers cover all eighteen Swiss securities listed, among them are the London subsidiaries of two out of

---

[14] See Zimmermann et al. (1989) for a discussion of this measure of liquidity and its implication as well as Grossman and Miller (1988) for a critique.

[15] See London Stock Exchange (1991) for a more detailed description of SEAQ.

## Some Key Figures for Permanently Traded Swiss Shares (Continuation)

| 1991 | DDomestic | London | | Market Share | | Stock Market | |
|---|---|---|---|---|---|---|---|
| In Mio. SFr. | Turnover b) | Turnover 1 d) | Turnover 2 c) | London 1 | London 2 | Valuation f) | Liquidity g) |
| Adia BR | 812.02 | | | | | 696.60 | 116.57 |
| Alusuisse BR | 2100.59 | 149.42 | 298.84 | 6.64 | 12.45 | 1216.15 | 197.30 |
| Ascom BR | 423.95 | | | | | 851.40 | 49.79 |
| BBC BR | 5970.69 | 1785.57 | 3571.14 | 23.02 | 37.43 | 3555.99 | 268.33 |
| BBC P | 1501.43 | 634.44 | 1268.87 | 29.70 | 45.80 | 1305.10 | 212.27 |
| Ciba Geigy BR | 2662.50 | 246.93 | 493.85 | 8.49 | 15.65 | 2389.42 | 132.10 |
| Ciba Geigy REG | 6340.83 | 2091.88 | 4183.77 | 24.81 | 39.75 | 13343.49 | 78.87 |
| Ciba Geigy P | 788.99 | | | | | 969.63 | 81.37 |
| Credit Suisse BR | 5581.33 | 1362.46 | 2724.93 | 19.62 | 32.81 | 7000.94 | 118.64 |
| Elektrowatt BR | 626.00 | | | | | 1901.80 | 32.92 |
| Georg Fischer BR | 477.16 | 42.23 | 84.47 | 8.13 | 15.04 | 311.14 | 180.51 |
| Holderbank BR | 1004.92 | | | | | 2322.70 | 43.27 |
| Nestlé BR | 5733.00 | 729.83 | 1459.66 | 11.29 | 49.08 | 9853.60 | 73.00 |
| Nestlé REG | 6965.56 | 2762.53 | 5525.05 | 28.40 | 8.65 | 21586.00 | 57.86 |
| Nestlé P | 710.27 | 329.86 | 659.73 | 31.71 | 48.16 | 2010.00 | 68.16 |
| Roche BR | 1215.76 | | | | | 6528.00 | 18.62 |
| Roche G | 12426.26 | 2149.41 | 4298.83 | 14.75 | 25.70 | 18336.80 | 133.22 |
| Sandoz BR | 3470.38 | | | | | 2005.89 | 173.01 |
| Sandoz REG | 3299.88 | 379.55 | 759.11 | 10.32 | 18.70 | 13200.54 | 30.75 |
| Sandoz P | 4117.41 | 674.70 | 1349.40 | 14.08 | 24.68 | 3581.20 | 152.65 |
| Swiss Bank C. BR | 3036.06 | 604.34 | 1208.68 | 16.60 | 28.47 | 4179.09 | 101.57 |
| Swiss Bank C. REG | 1178.54 | | | | | 3906.30 | 30.17 |
| Swiss Bank C. P | 2184.28 | 563.30 | 1126.60 | 20.50 | 34.03 | 2913.00 | 113.66 |
| Swiss RE P | 1854.37 | 108.43 | 216.87 | 5.52 | 10.47 | 1438.78 | 143.96 |
| SVB BR | 471.37 | | | | | 1310.76 | 35.96 |
| Swissair BR | 311.74 | | | | | 655.98 | 47.52 |
| Union Bank BR | 8661.89 | 1478.19 | 2956.39 | 14.58 | 25.45 | 15378.60 | 75.55 |
| Union Bank REG | 636.20 | | | | | 3426.50 | 18.57 |
| Winthherthur BR | 839.74 | | | | | 244.30 | 343.73 |
| Winterthur P | 1227.73 | 180.74 | 361.48 | 12.83 | 22.75 | 1450.00 | 109.60 |
| Zurich BR | 1440.35 | | | | | 1728.00 | 83.35 |
| Zurich P | 1446.13 | 242.48 | 484.97 | 14.36 | 25.11 | 2090.00 | 92.40 |
| Total | 93085.86 | 16516.31 | 33032.63 | 15.07 | 26.19 | 159121.02 | 79.26 |

Sources: Association Tripartite Bourses; SEAQ; UBS Swiss Stock Guide 1991; Zürcher Effektenbörsenverein, Annual Report 1990, 1991.
Notes: see previous page of same table.

**Table 1 (continuation)**

the five big Swiss banks).[16] The minimal order sizes are very different in the two markets. In London, the minimum order size for most Swiss shares is 100 units.[17] The screen quotes are mandatory for this minimal order size, but larger transactions can be set at any price the parties can agree upon. The minimum order size on Swiss stock exchanges varies inversely with the price of a stock; typically, it lies between one and five units. Hence, the market makers on SEAQ have specialized in large block trades.

The description would not be complete, however, if the off-board trading in Switzerland were not mentioned. Financial intermediaries which are active in this market segment act as virtual market makers. Often they are also members on the one or more of the three Swiss stock exchanges. Zimmermann et al. (1989) estimated that the off-board trading volume in equities is about as large as the volume of the three stock exchanges together.[18] Block trading is also a characteristic of off-board trading in Switzerland. The market makers, however, offer only indicative quotes. The off-board market is probably not as thoroughly organized as the market in London and, in this respect, might be less competitive. The fact that market makers in Switzerland had yet to pay stamp tax duties on their own order book transactions was likely to have reduced the incentives for brokers to take up the role of a market maker. From 1993 onward, this part of the stamp tax will not apply any more, however. On the whole, the Swiss market for secondary stock trading is thus a much more diverse market in the sense that different trading systems coexist. However, this diversity also obstructs transparency. All this suggests that the SEAQ system should viewed as a specialized wholesale trading system whereas the Swiss stock markets offer a full range of secondary trading services.

---

[16] This is based on information of the beginning of May, 1992.

[17] This can be illustrated with an example. The minimum size for an order for BBC bearer share on SEAQ is 100 shares. On December 30, 1991, when the final price paid for one of these shares was 3250 SFr., five shares would have been the minimum order size for one transaction in these shares during the auction in Zurich. Even when one takes into account that the average order size is larger, the number of shares transacted per order is less than half of that in London (Cf. Zimmermann et al. (1989), p. 79).

[18] A large amount of the off-board trading volume is included in the turnover figures of the stock exchanges because these figures are based upon total sales by member banks which do not distinguish between floor sales and off-board sales.

The settlement system, which in practice is an important determination for the location of stock market activities (Pagano and Roell (1990)), does not differ very much with respect to the delay in the settlement period (although the settlement system in London does not have a reputation of being very efficient). For transactions at SEAQ, the location of the settlement can be specified for each order, so the Swiss stamp tax could be avoided even in the old system of stamp taxation . The settlement location by default is Switzerland.

## 2.2. Transaction Costs

Until the end of 1990 the member firms of Swiss stock exchanges used to charge fixed commissions agreed upon in the courtage convention. Typically, the commissions had been low in a European comparison, especially for smaller orders (Zimmermann et al. (1989)). Since then, the courtage convention was rescinded, and large orders of a size of more than 0.5 million Swiss francs tend to be processed at very low commission rates (about 0.1 percent of the transaction value).[19] The transaction costs on SEAQ are hard to evaluate because most market makers put net quotes (including commissions etc.) into the system (Pagano and Roell (op. cit.)). Market observers guess that a commission (including taxes) of about 0.2 percent is internationally competitive for order sizes of one million Swiss francs and more. Since the abolition of fixed commission, it seems that costs for brokerage services in Switzerland are close to those on other markets. The Swiss stamp tax, a federal securities turnover tax, has been a disadvantage for domestic brokers because their competitors in London do not face a transaction tax (there is no stamp tax on trades in foreign equity in London). Currently, transactions in Swiss shares are charged with a 0.075 percent stamp tax rate. Including the cantonal taxes and the Stock exchange charge, the total tax rate on transactions in domestic shares in Switzerland mounts up to 0.09 percent. The stamp tax regime will be reformed, however, in spring 1993. Market makers will not be subjected to the stamp tax when they change their own stocks. All other transactions with Swiss stocks though

[19] See Finanz und Wirtschaft (1991).

will still be subjected to the stamp tax.[20]

### 2.3. Market Shares

The evaluation of the market share of Swiss stock exchanges and of SEAQ is not easy for the reporting rules differ. In Switzerland, all the sales of stock market member firms are reported. The sales of non-member firms with a brokerage license are not included, but the transaction volume of non-member banks with non-member clients is probably relatively small (assuming that most non-member firms are not acting as virtual market makers, so that member banks will most often be involved in the transactions of non-member firms with their non-bank clients). On SEAQ, both sales and purchases are reported for transactions with non-member firms, but sales only for transactions between member firms. As there are no figures about the transactions among member firms, the market share of London in the total turnover can only be calculated approximately. In **Table 1**, the market share was calculated under two assumptions: a) there are no transactions among member firms (market share 1), and b) there are only transactions among member firms (market share 2). Both measures of the market share were increasing between 1990 and 1991; it also turns out that the usual guess of a fifteen percent market share of SEAQ is at the lower limit. Several securities which are listed in **Table 1** were only introduced in 1990. It can be observed that they usually start with a rather small turnover in London. However, for almost all of them the market share of London was increasing between 1990 and 1991. This can be interpreted as being the result of slow information dissemination about trading possibilities, tradition, etc. Once a security is well known and fulfills the prerequisites with respect to liquidity and turnover, its London markets share seems to approach a level of about 20 percent. It can also be seen that shares of companies that do not distinguish between residents and non-residents with respect to their registration policy are more often traded on SEAQ than other shares. This indicates that especially non-residents prefer to place their orders on SEAQ. It also suggests that the distinction between bearer shares and registered shares

[20] See Zimmermann et al. (op. cit.) for a discussion of the stamp tax reform.

as well as the ownership restrictions with respect to registered shares were indeed important obstacles that prevented Swiss shares from becoming traded abroad at a large scale (Zimmermann et al. (1989)). The market share of SEAQ in the trading volume of BBC, Ciba-Geigy, and Nestlé securities is now probably between 30 and 40 percent.

## 3. Competition between Stock Exchanges: Theoretical and Empirical Aspects

Pagano and Roell (op. cit.) consider transaction costs and market liquidity to be the determinants for the location of stock market trading. Transaction costs are defined as the sum of explicit costs paid for brokerage services and taxes plus the implicit costs of the time delay in settlements. Liquidity is measured by the impact of the order size on transaction prices. A market is said to be deep if large orders are processed at prices close to the true underlying market value of the stock. The definition of liquidity also encloses a time dimension: the smaller the amount of time needed to process a large order, the more immediate liquidity is provided by a market. Three aspects of transaction costs and market liquidity are analyzed in this section. They are not independent of each other, but it is analytically more convenient to discuss them separately.

### 3.1. Market Entry, Taxes, and Competition

In this subsection, transaction costs are in the focus of the analysis. They are considered to be the price for the services provided by a stock exchange or a stock market. For this purpose, it is useful to assume that a stock exchange or a stock market is a cartel that acts like a single firm providing services which are used as intermediate input in the production of a final good, i.e. the brokerage services and portfolio management services delivered to investors. Competition among stock markets might have two effects on transaction costs for investors. The first effect is the traditional impact of an increase in the number of competing firms on the price mark-up over marginal costs which is given by the inverse of the perceived price elasticity of demand. The provision of centralized exchange services, such as the central settlement or the price recording system, become cheaper as competition raises the number of firms and, thus, also augments the perceived price elasticity of demand of each firm (Helpman and Krugman (1985)). Lower input prices should also reduce the prices of the final good, the brokerage services. Second, competition among stock markets is likely to lower the rents for exchange member firms. Those rents have their origin in the restrictions on the number of member firms which can be observed in reality. Usually, only member firms have access to the services provided by the stock exchange. Competition among stock exchanges can then be expected to lead to an increase in the number of firms providing brokerage services and, hence, to a smaller degree of monopoly power because of reduced cartel discipline. This increase in the perceived price elasticity can also be expected to improve the services such as information on trading provided by a centralized exchange system because competition will also cover the non-price domain.[21] All these effects can be called the "disciplinary effect" of competition among stock exchanges (Neal (1987)).

Given the tax advantage of London when securities transactions in Switzerland were subject to a stamp tax, the question of how this comparative advantage fits into the analysis arises. Traditional microeconomics shows that the tax differential will be reflected fully in the prices in the long run provided that there is price competition among firms. This suggests that every investor will place his order in London as long as he can escape the tax, provided that the cross-country "transportation costs" are low. Assuming increasing returns to scale in the production of brokerage services (price and order size vary negatively with each other), a proportional tax rate also implies that smaller orders will be less affected than larger orders if transportation costs exist. However, traditional microeconomics does not capture the dynamic impact of transaction taxes. If, as it is assumed here, the establishment of SEAQ should be interpreted as the introduction of a new market place with a different technology, a transaction tax influences also the location choice. A market place with a transaction

[21] Aerni (op. cit.) discusses this point in more detail.

cost advantage due to taxes should turn out to be the location choice of brokers.[22] The dynamic impact of transaction taxes is even more important when thick market externalities are taken into account.[23] Transaction taxes in most European countries made London a particularly attractive location for a wholesale trading system in European securities. This specialization of SEAQ allows the London Stock Exchange to benefit from internal economies of scale in the trading system and from external economies provided by a centralized market. This constitutes a first-mover gain which can be expected to be persistent. In this respect, it is no surprise that the abolition of fixed commissions in Switzerland in the beginning of 1991 did not lead to a reduction in the market share of SEAQ.[24]

### 3.2. Fragmentation Effects and the Conditions for Coexistence of Two Markets

It has been argued in the last paragraphs that the discipline exercised by competition will reduce transaction costs. This so-called competition effect results from extending the choice of consumers, in this particular case investors, and illustrates the positive impact of open and free markets. Another consequence of the competition between two markets is the fragmentation of order flows. Traditional neoclassical microeconomics abstracts from problems arising with the geographical and informational fragmentation of markets. However, when there are transaction and information costs, the fragmentation of order flows might reduce the elasticity of excess demand with respect to prices and thus have a negative impact of the liquidity of a market. In general, the liquidity of any secondary securities market can be expected to be increasing with the number of investors placing their orders in that market. Thus, the decision of an agent to trade at a certain exchange has an effect on the other agents in the market. Pagano

---

[22] See Gehrig (1992) for a more detailed discussion of this point.

[23] Thick market externalities were analyzed by Grilli (1989).

[24] Another example in support of this statement is given by the Dutch secondary markets. The abolition of fixed commissions and equity turnover taxes in the Netherlands in July 1990 did not lead to an increase of the market share of the Amsterdam Stock Exchange either. See Worthington (1991) for a discussion.

(1989) investigated the impact of the number of traders on the market liquidity in more depth. Pagano's analysis is based on a model with N traders whose endowment in a stock with an uncertain dividend differs. A trader can hold riskless bonds and stocks in his portfolio. The return on the bond is given by the rate R, the return on stocks by the dividend d. With risk averse investors, there exists an equilibrium in which all agents can improve their utility by trading their endowment. By calculating the indirect utility of a representative agent, Pagano shows that the number of traders has two opposite effects on the gains from trade:

a) The speculative effect: the number of traders reduces the gains from trade because endowment differences are "flattened out" in a larger market or, in other words, the volatility of average endowment decreases with more traders. This also reduces price volatility, thus more traders imply that the chances of buying low and selling high become smaller.

b) The liquidity effect: the number of traders increases the gains from trade. This effect has its origin in the adverse price impact of large orders. When there are few traders, large deviations from the mean endowment imply a big adjustment in the market clearing price (compared to smaller deviations) which reduces the gains from trade in stocks. This loss is a decreasing function of the number of traders, since more traders make the market price less sensitive with respect to the net demand of a single trader.

In a next step, Pagano analyzes the question why traders trade in different markets. He shows that the existence of two markets depends on the number of agents dealing in each market, the variance of their endowment, the costs (transaction and search costs), and the conjectures about the number of traders on each market. There exists a two-market conjectural equilibrium (TMCE) (in which the agents' conjectures are fulfilled) only for a set of rather tight restrictions on the endowment variances and the number of traders in each market. Two of the cases of a TMCE derived by Pagano are interesting for the present study:

a) Two markets with a different number of traders and fixed transaction costs. The market with more traders must also have the higher endowment variance and higher transaction costs. The large traders enjoy the benefits of a more liquid market (more traders) and of a more speculative market (more cross-sectional diversity in the endowment), and for trading larger quantities they are willing to pay a higher fixed cost to enter the market. Pagano also demonstrates that a concentration of the trading activities on one market (the one with lower fixed costs) raises the welfare of all agents at least on the average.

b) Two markets where the "larger investors" (their endowment deviates from the mean endowment on a large scale) place their orders on a search market (to enter the search process involves higher fixed costs than using the auction market in which smaller investors are operating). The search market offers more liquidity for large investors who are consequently willing to pay higher fixed costs. In such a TMCE, concentration might not lead to a Pareto improvement.

Case b) is probably the most relevant for the analysis of the actual competition between auction markets and dealership markets. This is based on the observation that competition between trading systems is fiercest between stock exchanges at which all possible order sizes can be cleared in an auction market and trading systems only clearing large block orders. In the last few years, large block orders became relatively more important because of the shift from private to institutional investors and modern portfolio management techniques like dynamic portfolio insurance. SEAQ can then be interpreted as being a search market with lower transaction costs than off-board trading in Switzerland.

Four aspects of Pagano's analysis are worth to be emphasized. First, market fragmentation such as in case b) is an equilibrium outcome with transaction cost differentials, the number of traders, and the dispersion of order sizes being the main determinants. An equilibrium constellation with two markets is usually a knife-edge outcome unless transaction costs are specific for every trader. Second, the liquidity in a market being defined as the price impact of a buy or sell order is primarily related to the average order size. It is perfectly possible to imagine a very liquid market when there are only small orders. From those two points, it follows that there is not necessarily a continuous relationship between market liquidity and market fragmentation. If there are two markets, the deviations of the observed market liquidity from the sample mean is not necessarily related with the observed market fragmentation. Third, the time dimension of market liquidity is not explicitly taken into account. In reality, the orders are a flow variable, and the clearing frequency is an important factor. Fourth, the nature and determinants of transaction costs are not discussed in Pagano's analysis. For the competition between trading systems, the differences in transaction and liquidity costs between trading systems can be decisive. The last two aspect are discussed in the next subsection.

### 3.3. Market Clearing Mechanism and the Degree of Immediate Liquidity

The analysis of the preceding subsection focused on investors with an elastic demand or supply of a security and neglected the time dimension of liquidity. Many investors, however, have a rather inelastic demand because of transaction and information costs.[25] They are, in the jargon of the literature, so-called liquidity traders. For them, illiquid or thin markets are even worse than for "normal" traders with an inelastic demand as they derive no utility from the speculative effect of such markets. Liquidity has also a time dimension. This dimension is captured by the concept of the execution risk. It is precisely in this dimension in which the two market clearing systems, i.e. the auction and the broker-dealer markets differ.[26] The key difference between these two markets is the execution risk that investors have to bear. This risk arises for two reasons: a) the time delay between the transmission and the execution of the order, and b) the stochastic nature of the price itself (arrival of new information etc.) which makes the execution price uncertain. The execution risk is different in each of the two market clearing mechanisms. In a dealership market, a market maker is ready to buy and sell at a publicly quoted price. There is no execution risk in such a market for the investor, but he has to pay the spread for this insurance. In an auction market, there is no insurance against this risk; the investor has to bid by quoting a price at which he thinks

[25] Certain modern portfolio management techniques such as program trading are another reason for the demand to be price inelastic.

[26] Pagano and Roell (op. cit.) stress this point.

his order may be executed. Given the uncertainty about the actual execution price and the time needed for the execution of the order the possibility of stochastic deviations from an investor's expected ideal portfolio composition arises. Such deviations form the expected costs of the liquidity risk. An investor facing the choice between a dealership and an auction market will base his choice, of course, on expected costs and benefits. If fixed costs are involved in the production of dealership services (at least from the point of view of the investor) but not in an auction market, then the order size will be an important determinant for this choice. To illustrate this point with a clear-cut example, suppose that there is a liquidity trader who has an inelastic supply of a certain stock. For him, the percentage execution risk per share is given by the length of the expected time delay, the instantaneous variance of the expected (equilibrium) rate of return, and the market liquidity. This constitutes a cost which is more or less proportional to the amount of the stocks he wishes to sell.[27] Suppose furthermore that he has the choice to execute his sale either on an auction market or in a dealership market with market makers. In order to use the auction market, he would have to pay a proportional variable cost. The use of the dealership market would also involve fixed costs. The sale at the dealership market would be executed immediately at a already known price. The execution time and the execution price in the auction market would be uncertain. The investor, however, knows the average execution delay and the average instantaneous variance of the rate of return of the stock. It is immediately obvious that there exists a critical order size above which the investor prefers to use the dealership market. This order size varies inversely with the expected execution delay and the expected instantaneous variance.[28] For a smaller order size, the investor prefers to wait.

Market makers are a socially efficient way of organizing the stock market if they can provide insurance against the execution risk at a sufficiently lower cost, be it

---

[27] This statement depends crucially on the relation between market liquidity and order size.

[28] This argument assumes that the market maker's reaction to higher instantaneous variances is smaller than that of a single investor. It is based on market maker's possibility of diversifying risks (See Grossman and Miller (1988)).

because of risk aversion, favourable tax treatment, or favourable lines of credit. Once the decision for a market maker system is made, the question about the entry and trade regulation for market makers arises. Pagano and Roell (op. cit.) cite evidence from the US which shows that trading systems in which market makers compete with floor traders (non-specialists who place limit orders in the market) are more efficient than pure dealership markets. The competition takes place as a consequence of the fact that orders do not have to be executed by the quotes of the specialist. These results, however, may also be dependent on the technology available. One might guess that screen based systems on which many market makers put in their quotes and on which the investors can detect the best quote, might foster competition among market makers through lowering search costs and increasing the dissemination of price information.

The implications of the two different market clearing mechanisms on market liquidity are not easy to evaluate. Pagano and Roell (op. cit.) tried to provide some evidence by comparing the bid-ask spread of stocks traded at SEAQ and at the stock exchange in Paris (where a continuous auction market was established in 1988). According to their calculations, the Paris stock exchange seems to have lower spreads for actual transactions as well as for the initial orders and thus appears to be more liquid. With this result, however, it was difficult to explain the considerable market share of SEAQ. Three reasons were given by the authors. First, transaction costs are lower in London (no stamp tax on foreign equities, and most deals in foreign equities are done without a commission charge). Second, the order sizes are different. Third, SEAQ offers more immediacy for larger deals. In Paris, large orders are mainly processes as over-the-counter-deals (the official transaction is done at the stock market with a special procedure), but the waiting time for matching orders might be considerable. Their results of a lower spread in Paris probably reflect the problems with the bid-ask spread as a measure of market liquidity rather than the underlying forces.[29]

[29] See Grossman and Miller (op. cit.) for a discussion of the bid-ask-spread as a measure of liquidity.

### 3.4. Empirical Studies

Most empirical studies about competition among stock exchanges and trading places were conducted in the US, where competition among stock exchanges was encouraged in the 1970s. Neal (1987) provides evidence on the importance of the disciplinary effects of multiple listing of equity options on the bid-ask spread. His approach is based on the theory of contestable markets. He shows that despite the concentration of trade on a single market place, the options that are listed on other trading exchanges have spreads that are 10 to 20 percent lower that single listed options. He explains this striking difference by the potential competition exercised by multiple listing. He also shows that this "disciplinary" effect is especially important for options with a small trading volume. The distinction between options with a large and a small trading volume is important because of the organisation of option exchanges. There are specialists who hold an inventory position ready for immediate transactions, and floor brokers who enter the market by placing limit orders. Floor brokers generally do not hold own positions, thus they enter the market only when the volume is large enough to reduce the risk of having an uncovered position to a negligible extent. Consequently, the competition for options with a large trading volume is already strong on a single market place, and the competition effect of multiple listings should be important only for options with a small volume. Neal was unable to reject this hypothesis in his empirical tests.

Hamilton (1979) examined the question whether the net effect of fragmented trade in shares is positive or negative by investigating the impact of off-board trading on the bid-ask spread (he calls this the price of marketability) for share transactions at NYSE. He distinguished two influences on the price of marketability: a) the competition effect - off-board trading increases the number of dealers for the listed stock (at NYSE). This increases competition among dealers and forces them to narrow bid-ask spreads; b) the fragmentation effect - off-board trading fragments markets. This might decrease the efficiency of the exchange if the exchange enjoys economies of scale. His empirical analysis showed that both the total number of dealers and the degree of fragmentation have the expected impact on the bid-ask spread. Hamilton calculated the competition effect to be twice as large as the fragmentation effect, but both effects tend to be rather small (a 1 percent change in the degree of fragmentation (measured by the market share) or in the number of dealers alters the bid-ask spread by less than 0.1 percent).

In a recent study, Aerni (op. cit.) investigated the effects of fragmentation for the Swiss stock markets empirically. He established that the Swiss stock market system can be characterized by a high degree of homogeneity with respect to listed stocks, represented brokers, and services offered. The empirical analysis is based on Roll's implicit bid-ask spread measure which he calculated for a sample 30 stocks listed at all three exchanges for June 1990. A first test showed that the differences between the bid-ask spreads at the three stock markets was significant in most cases. Interesting enough is the observation that the difference was often in favour of Basel or Geneva. In 12 of 18 cases (Aerni calculated daily, two-day, and weekly bid-ask spreads for stocks of small and medium companies as well as for large companies), the difference was significant. A second test showed that the bid-ask spread for stocks which are traded permanently was smaller than for periodically traded stocks. He then examined the relationship between the bid-ask spread and the trading volume. The expected negative correlation between bid-ask spreads and total trading volume could be verified for all small and medium stocks (there was a significant negative correlation, except once in Geneva), but not for the large stocks. Based on these results, he concluded that the fragmentation in share trading between three exchanges has had a negative impact upon the liquidity of the Swiss stock markets.

With respect to Aerni's study, it is interesting to notice that Hamilton (op. cit.) did not detect a significant effect of regional stock markets on competition either, but their effect on the fragmentation seems to be the same. If the fragmentation and the competition effect are examined together, Hamilton finds that the off-board markets tend to decrease the bid-ask spread, whereas the regional exchanges tend to increase the spread. These results, however, are based on insignificant coefficients. One could conclude from Hamilton's results that competition between different trading systems has a stronger disciplinary effect than that between exchanges with the same trading system.

## 4. The Effects of Competition on Swiss Stock Markets

### 4.1 Evaluating the Impact of Competition

In almost all available empirical studies the effects of competition and the implied fragmentation on the market liquidity have been investigated empirically by regressing the bid-ask spread on a competition variable (the number of market makers in all markets, for example) and on a fragmentation variable (the market share of market makers in one market, for example). This approach has to be interpreted carefully when it is applied to the present problem of competition between an auction and a dealership market: The bid-ask spread which is supposed to measure transaction costs as well as the market liquidity in a dealership market is not a well defined measure in an auction market, and an uncritical comparison of spreads generates therefore doubtful information.[30] However, a modification of the standard approach allows an analysis of the impact of competition on an auction market. It is based on the idea that there must be critical order size $X_c$ such that the cost of using the dealership market equals the cost of using the auction market on the one hand (see section 3.3.) and the concept of the pricing error on the other hand. It suffers from the drawback, however, that the transaction costs cannot be analyzed empirically. Given the observation that it were transaction costs that changed drastically over the last few years, the exclusive focus on the pricing error or, in other words, the market liquidity yields somewhat limited results. The central equation of the model is an average cost equality:

$$\frac{1}{2} S = L_C + T_C \tag{1}$$

where S denotes the percentage bid-ask spread per share for the order of size $X_c$ quoted

[30] The bid ask spread as a measure for the liquidity of a market is not without problems even in a dealership market (cf. footnote 28). These problems are not of central concern for this paper and are not discussed further, however.

in the dealership market, $L_c$ the percentage liquidity cost per share and $T_c$ the percentage transaction costs per share for the same order size $X_c$ in the auction market. This condition reflects the idea of market segmentation being the consequence of a very unequal distribution of order sizes for two distinct sets of agents. The auction market is assumed to be the market chosen by agents with smaller orders, the dealership market by agents with large orders. It is also assumed that an investor has no direct access to the auction market, but has to place his orders with a broker. The broker charges percentage transaction costs which vary inversely with the order size X:

$$T_C = T(X), \quad T_X(X) \leq 0. \tag{2}$$

The transaction cost equation could also contain a competition variable, reflecting that the broker behaviour is also dependent on the degree of competition. Given the focus on market liquidity, however, this aspect is not included in the analysis. The liquidity costs include the waiting costs $W_c$ and the pricing error $V_p$. The waiting costs are the product of the instantaneous variance of the rate of change of the share price per time unit $\sigma_p$ and the number of time units needed for the complete processing of the order. This time interval is approximated by the ratio of the order size X over the average size of shares processes by a broker per time unit N, so that the waiting costs are given by

$$W_C = \frac{X}{N}\sigma_P \tag{3}$$

The key concept of the analysis is the pricing error occurring at the auction market. It has its origin in the indivisibilities of shares (and of price intervals in reality). Mendelson (1982) shows that the demand and supply schedules in an auction are step functions with discrete jumps. This can be illustrated as follows: For every price P in an interval $P_{[]}$ $[P_L \leq P \leq P_U]$, there is an agent $i^*$ (i=1,2,...,M) with a buy or sell order of size $O_i$ for which this price represents the limit price, so that the total order size at P is given by $\sum_{i*}O_i$. Between subsequently higher prices, the total order size is growing, but in discrete intervals.[31] As a result, the intersection of demand and supply schedules does not necessarily yield a unique price which would reflect the underlying equilibrium price but an interval - the pricing error interval - which puts a lower and an upper limit to the market clearing price. In a very specific set-up with buy and sell orders distributed as independent, identical Poisson processes, Mendelson (op. cit.) demonstrated that the variance of this interval in a sealed-bid double auction varies positively with the underlying equilibrium price (defining the interval $P_{[]}$) of the share and negatively with the order arrival rate and the frequency of the clearing. In an open outcry market the pricing error interval should also depend on the strategic behaviour of brokers, so that the interval should also be influenced by the degree of competition from other markets. In this sense, the pricing error variable is an overall "market quality" variable rather than a pure liquidity variable. Interpreting Mendelson's results rather casually, the following function for the pricing error standard deviation per share arises:

$$\Psi_P = \Psi(P^*, k_A, Y), \quad \Psi_P(.) \geq 0, \Psi_k(.) \leq 0, \Psi_Y(.) \leq 0, \tag{4}$$

where $P^*$ denotes the expected equilibrium price, Y the order arrival rate and $k_a$ a constant reflecting the degree of competition. The underlying equilibrium price and the instantaneous variance of its rate of change of a share are assumed to be exogenous variables, determined by firm specific characteristics and, may be, general capital market characteristics. The secondary trading activities exert therefore no feedback effects on these "fundamentals".

The determinants of the dealer's bid-ask spread are, of course, essential for the analysis. There exists a substantial literature on the elements explaining a market maker's bid-ask spread. It can be summarized as follows: The spread asked by market makers depends on the instantaneous variance of the rate of change of equilibrium prices $\sigma_p$, the degree of competition $k_d$, the underlying equilibrium price, and the order

[31] Mendelson (op. cit.) treats buy and sell orders symmetrically.

arrival rate.[32] The following functional relationships between the spread and those variables can be established: The riskiness of a market makers' position increases with $\sigma_p$, hence the spread which should compensate the market maker for the risk taken can be expected to vary positively with $\sigma_p$. The share price is linked with the spread through the following mechanism: the amount of capital a market maker needs to finance his positions in a stock augments with the price per stock, consequently, the spread should be an increasing function of the share price. The order arrival rate determines the probability that a market maker ends up having a net position in a stock for a certain time after a deal has been concluded. The spread should therefore be negatively related to the order arrival rate. The degree of competition has the usual effect on the spread. Hence, the following function determining the percentage spread can be established:

$$S = S(\sigma_p, k_D, P, Y), \quad S_\sigma(.) \geq 0,\ S_k(.) \leq 0, S_P(.) \geq 0,\ S_Y(.) \leq 0. \tag{5}$$

In Mendelson's model as well as in the models explain the determinants of a dealer's spread, the order arrival rate is an exogenous variable. However, in a world with two segmented markets, the total order arrival can still be an exogenous variable, but the fragmentation of this total order flow between the two markets has to become an endogenous variable in the model. This can be done as follows: In a first step, equations (4) and (5) have to be interpreted as supply functions. The spread function (5) represents the supply curve of the dealership market, say London in our case. The pricing error function determines the brokerage service supply function in the auction market, say the Swiss stock exchanges in our case. The order arrival rate Y is reinterpreted as being the amount of sell orders cleared in a certain time interval, say a day or so, in a market. The concentration on sell orders can be explained by the assumption of symmetry between buy and sell orders. We can then reinterpret the order arrival rates in both markets as demand functions. The demand functions, where a subscript Z stands for the auction market and the subscript L for the dealership market, are determined by :

[32] See Hamilton (op. cit.), Glosten (1987), and Stoll (1989) for a discussion of the determinants of the spread. Mendelson (1987) discusses competition among market makers in some detail.

$$Y_Z^D = Y_Z(O_Z), \quad Y_O \geq 0,$$
$$Y_L^D = Y_L(O_L), \quad Y_O \geq 0. \tag{6}$$

The concept of the order arrival potential O needs further explanations. The order arrival potential which is measured in nominal units is based on the idea that the order inflow for a certain share is related to certain firm specific variables which are not influenced by the behaviour of broker or dealers or the secondary market design on the one hand and the fragmentation on the other hand. The firm specific aspects are assumed to be captured by the nominal firm size V. Furthermore, it is assumed that the order arrival potential is increasing with the firm size. The crucial assumption closing the model is that the market fragmentation θ (0 < θ < 1) varies positively with the critical order size $X_c$. This implies that when condition (1) holds with a high order size $X_c$, the fragmentation is higher in the auction market. This implies that the order arrival potential can be written as

$$O_Z = \theta V,$$
$$O_L = (1 - \theta)V \tag{7}$$

Imposing market equilibrium with

$$Y_Z^D = Y_Z^S,$$
$$Y_L^D = Y_L^S \tag{8}$$

yields a solution to the model for the equilibrium spread, the equilibrium pricing error standard deviation, and the equilibrium fragmentation. It explains those variable as being the outcome of the reaction of brokers and market makers to firm specific variables such as the firm value and the instantaneous variance of price changes and the institutional set-up such as the degree of competition between exchanges. It is an ad hoc model, however, because the behavioural equations are postulated on the basis of a priori plausible assumptions rather than being derived from explicit optimization analysis. For the present focus on the market liquidity on Swiss stock exchanges, it is sufficient to derive the following semi-reduced form for $\Psi_p$:

$$\Psi_p = \Psi(P, k_A, Y(\theta V)) = \Psi(P, k_A, \theta, V) \tag{9}$$

It can be seen that the equilibrium pricing error standard deviation is reduced by a higher degree of competition and by a higher fragmentation of market shares in the auction market. Total differentiation of (9) yields

$$\Delta\Psi_p = \Psi_P(.)\Delta P + \Psi_k(.)\Delta k + \Psi_Y(.)V\Delta\theta + \Psi_Y(.)\theta\Delta V. \tag{10}$$

Equation (10) will be the basis of the empirical work. It will be used to determine the size of the coefficients empirically. It has the advantage of using only observable variables as an argument, provided that the concept of the pricing error can be implemented empirically, an issue that will be discussed in the next subsection. However, equations (1) to (8) would also allow to solve the model for the degree of fragmentation, the spread and the pricing error.

## 4.2. Implementing the Pricing Error Concept Empirically

Roll (1984) showed that the existence of a bid-ask spread should result in a negative serial covariance in a sequence of price changes on a stock exchange. In an informationally efficient market, a spread can be the only reason why a sequence of price changes is correlated. Therefore, this covariance allows to infer the bid-ask spread. Roll proved that the relation between the percentage spread S and the covariance of daily returns $r_t$ is given by

$$COV(r_{t+1}, r_t) = -\frac{S^2}{4}, \text{ with } r_t = \frac{P_t}{P_{t-1}} - 1. \tag{11}$$

In a dealership market, the spread compensates a dealer for his readiness to buy or sell a security because it implies that he must hold a portfolio which might deviate from the optimal composition. In an auction market, it is not immediately obvious why there should be a bid-ask spread. However, as it was argued in the previous subsection, it can be expected that there is some equilibrium pricing error arising from indivisibilities and broker behaviour. The question then becomes whether the implicit bid-ask spread calculated with prices generated by an auction market can reflect this pricing error rather than the spread. The answer is yes; the mechanics works in a similar way. Between two subsequent order crossings, the price should only move within the price error interval given by the supply and demand step functions provided that no new information arrived. Hence, the covariance between subsequent price changes should also be negative, and Roll's measure should reflect the pricing error range. It was applied to the German (auction) stock markets by Haller and Stoll (op. cit.). They argue not in terms of the pricing error but postulate that Roll's implicit bid-ask spread reflects temporary selling or buying pressures which do not immediately induce traders to submit the offsetting orders when they expect orders to be crossed at a price which deviates from the true equilibrium price. This interpretation is compatible with the pricing error concept if it is assumed that the information processing capacities of brokers and the exchange in general are limited in such a way that they are an obstacle to information flows.

The implementation of Roll's measure, however, has not been successful in most cases.The most flagrant problem with its application is the mass of negative spreads it produces.[33] Roll's seminal paper is only the first in a row of studies that are plagued by that problem.[34] Probably, this is a consequence of the restrictive assumptions which are underlying Roll's derivation. It is not certain that all markets are informationally efficient all the time, and, probably more important, even in informationally efficient markets subsequent price changes can be positively correlated if expected returns are.[35] Nevertheless, the implicit bid-ask spread has become a standard in the literature. This is the reason why it has also been computed in this paper. Computations of the percentage monthly bid-ask spread for permanently traded Swiss stocks for the period

---

[33] The reason why a negative spread arises is not immediately obvious. It reflects Roll's attempt to circumvent a mathematical problem. When the covariance between subsequent price changes is positive, the minus sign within the square root which is implicit in (11) would imply a spread containing imaginary values, a result that is hardly explainable by economic reasoning. Roll thus proposed to move the minus sign out of the square root, acknowledging that the economic meaning of his measure becomes obsolete.

[34] See, for instance, Haller and Stoll (op. cit.), Pagano and Roell (op. cit.), and Aerni (op. cit.).

[35] See Pagano and Roell (op. cit.) for an elaboration on those arguments.

**Hasbrouck's Pricing Error and Roll's Implicit Bid-Ask Spread**

| | Opening Prices | | Closing Prices | | SEAQ c) |
|---|---|---|---|---|---|
| | Pricing a) | Spread b) | Pricing a) | Spread b) | |
| ADIA BR | 0.00134 | 0.008966 | 0.00119 | 0.008164 | 0 |
| ALUSUISSE BR | 0.00423 | 0.011078 | 0.00409 | 0.001520 | 1 |
| ASCOM BR | 0.00598 | 0.008517 | 0.00573 | 0.009745 | 0 |
| BBC BR | 0.00381 | 0.007703 | 0.00355 | 0.006856 | 1 |
| CIBA GEIGY BR | 0.00301 | 0.007423 | 0.00245 | 0.005236 | 1 |
| CIBA GEIGY REG | 0.00231 | 0.008660 | 0.00215 | 0.006850 | 1 |
| CIBA GEIGY P | 0.00507 | 0.002947 | 0.00479 | 0.005485 | 1 |
| CREDIT SUISSE BR | 0.00326 | 0.003063 | 0.00257 | 0.004700 | 1 |
| ELEKTROWATT BR | 0.000185 | 0.003762 | 0.000172 | 0.004156 | 0 |
| FISCHER BR | 0.00649 | 0.006078 | 0.0074 | 0.010515 | 1 |
| HOLDERBANK BR | 0.00367 | 0.005696 | 0.00362 | 0.006392 | 0 |
| NESTLE BR | 0.000364 | 0.003286 | 0.000316 | 0.007837 | 1 |
| NESTLE REG | 0.00255 | 0.003315 | 0.00276 | 0.006870 | 1 |
| NESTLE P | 0.00165 | 0.006118 | 0.00138 | 0.007078 | 1 |
| ROCHE G | 0.00141 | 0.005686 | 0.00127 | 0.006813 | 1 |
| SWISS REINSURANCE P | 0.00429 | 0.007224 | 0.00373 | 0.004148 | 0 |
| SANDOZ REG | 0.00333 | 0.003528 | 0.00314 | 0.004464 | 0 |
| SANDOZ P | 0.00473 | 0.005055 | 0.00411 | 0.004493 | 1 |
| UNION BANK BR | 0.00042 | 0.005992 | 0.000375 | 0.006298 | 1 |
| SWISS BANK BR | 0.00114 | 0.005606 | 0.000937 | 0.004453 | 1 |
| SWISS BANK P | 0.000807 | 0.005145 | 0.000691 | 0.004653 | 1 |
| SVB | 0.00268 | 0.004655 | 0.00337 | 0.007622 | 0 |
| SWISSAIR BR | 0.00291 | 0.007868 | 0.00378 | 0.008548 | 0 |
| WINTERTHUR BR | 0.00285 | 0.009463 | 0.00241 | 0.005794 | 0 |
| WINTERTHUR P | 0.00446 | 0.003776 | 0.00511 | 0.006494 | 1 |
| ZURICH BR | 0.00382 | 0.005346 | 0.00362 | 0.011660 | 1 |
| ZURICH P | 0.00437 | 0.005904 | 0.00321 | 0.003010 | 1 |
| Mean | 0.003005 | 0.005995 | 0.002886 | 0.006798 | |
| Standard deviation | 0.001701 | 0.002173 | 0.001767 | 0.002652 | |

Notes: a) Hasbrouck's pricing error, see section 4.2, b) Roll's implicit bid-ask spread, see section 4.2,
c) 1 indicates that share is listed on SEAQ system, 0 that the share is not traded in London (during sample period).

**Table 2**

of April to July 1990 can be found in **Table 2.**[36] In order to avoid problems with negative spreads, the average of positive monthly bid ask-spreads was used. Because there is a ring information system between the stock exchanges, it was assumed that there are no arbitrage opportunities between the three exchanges for permanently traded stocks. Hence, only price information of the Zurich stock exchange was utilized. As it has become standard in the literature, the spreads were calculated with daily price changes.[37]

Given all the problems with Roll's measure of the bid-ask spread, Hasbrouck (1991) proposed another measure of the pricing error.[38] It is based on the decomposition of a non-stationary time series (in our case transaction prices at the Zurich stock exchange) into a permanent and a transitory component, a procedure which is familiar from the recent macroeconometric literature.[39] The permanent component reflects the underlying unobservable equilibrium share price. The transitory component reflects the pricing error. Formally, the logarithm of the transaction price $p_t$ can be written as the sum of the logarithm of the equilibrium (the efficient) price and the pricing error $\psi_t$ :

$$p_t = p_t^* + \psi_t \tag{12}$$

Any decomposition of a non-stationary time series into a permanent and a transitory component is essentially arbitrary as the two components are not identified.[40] However, there are several benchmark cases in the literature. Most of them are based upon the assumption that the permanent component follows a random walk. Applied to share

---

[36] The implicit bid-ask spread was computed as a percentage of the security price.

[37] At Swiss stock exchanges, there is a sequence of prices for each stock during every daily auction. Therefore, Aerni (op. cit.) also calculated intra-daily spreads. The mean spreads are very similar to those calculated by Aerni for the Zurich stock exchange. Hence, the use of opening and closing prices instead of all intra-daily transaction prices does not seem to bias the results.

[38] To the best of my knowledge, Hasbrouck also created the term "pricing error".

[39] See Stock and Watson (1989) for a survey.

[40] See Stock and Watson (op. cit.), and Quah (1992) for a discussion of this problem.

prices, most economist would probably agree that the approximation of the short-run time series behaviour of this variable by a random walk is appropriate and corresponds to the theory of efficient markets. They differ in the treatment of the correlation between the increments of the permanent and the transitory components. Two polar cases are prominent in the literature: that of no correlation and that of perfect correlation. Hasbrouck (op. cit.) establishes that the variance of the pricing error in the case of a perfect correlation reaches the lower bound of all possible cases from zero to perfect correlation. This result is convenient because it allows a comparison between shares for a well defined case. The model then consists of two equations:

$$p_t^* = p_{t-1}^* + w_t , \quad w_t = i.i.d.\ N(0, \sigma_w), \qquad (13)$$
$$\psi_t = \alpha w_t$$

where $w_t$ denotes the increments of the random walk and $\psi_t$ the pricing error. This implies that the following first-order moving average model

$$\Delta p_t = e_t + \beta e_{t-1} \qquad (14)$$

can be estimated. The variance of the pricing error $\Psi_P$ is then given by $\beta^2\sigma_w$. The MA(1) equation (14) has been estimated with daily transaction prices for the same permanently traded Swiss shares for the period from April to December 1990. The implied pricing error standard deviations are also shown in **Table 2**. The use of lower bound values has the disadvantage that the economic interpretation is somewhat flawed. The perfect correlation means that the band between the limit price of the incoming buy orders and the incoming sell orders is entirely determined by the variance of the increments of the price changes. It rules out any information unrelated effects. In this respect it is interesting to compare the standard deviation of the Hasbrouck pricing error and Roll's implicit bid-ask spread in **Table 2**. It can be seen that the mean of the pricing error standard deviation of the opening prices and both spreads is significantly different from zero at the five percent level. The mean standard deviation of the pricing error calculated with closing prices are significantly different from zero at the ten

**Comparison of Pricing Error and Bid-Ask Spread for Listed and Unlisted Shares**

| | Opening Prices | | Closing Prices | |
|---|---|---|---|---|
| | Pricing Error | Spread | Pricing Error | Spread |
| Shares listed in London (18) | | | | |
| Mean | 0.002994 | 0.005677 | 0.002821 | 0.006917 |
| Standard deviation | 0.001730 | 0.002110 | 0.001730 | 0.002947 |
| Shares unlisted in London (9 ) | | | | |
| Mean | 0.003026 | 0.006631 | 0.003016 | 0.006559 |
| Standard deviation | 0.001414 | 0.002279 | 0.001414 | 0.002074 |
| Test-statistics[a)] | | -4.2340 | | 1.3694 |

Note:
a) Test-statistics for a significant difference in the mean with estimated sample variances, distributed standard normally with a critical value of 1.65 (5 percent level).

**Table 3**

percent level.[41] Second, the presumption that the implicit bid-ask spread should be larger than the standard deviation of the Hasbrouck pricing error because it imposes less structure and allows for effects which are uncorrelated with price information is confirmed by the mean of both measures. The information uncorrelated pricing error seems to be about 50 percent of the size of the total spread. The hypothesis is not confirmed at the level of the individual shares. However, it should be noted that the information uncorrelated effect in the average is smaller than 0.3 percent of a share's value when it is measured by the implicit bid-ask spread. Before drawing conclusions, though, it should be remembered that both measures are rather weak and that the results are therefore tentative.

## 4.3. The Effects of Competition on the Implicit Bid-Ask Spread and the Pricing Error

Based upon the analysis of section 4.1., the following linear regression is analyzed in this section:

$$\begin{gathered}\Psi_P = \Psi_k + \Psi_P \Delta P + \Psi_\theta \theta + \Psi_V V, \\ \Psi_P \geq 0,\ \Psi_V \leq 0.\end{gathered} \tag{15}$$

where the expected sign of the coefficients is indicated on the second line. The task of the actual estimation is to evaluate whether $\Psi_\theta$ is bigger or smaller than zero and whether it is significantly so. However, before proceeding with the estimation, two interesting tests only involving the spreads and the pricing errors are reported.

In **Table 3**, the results are reported on whether the mean spread of the shares traded in London is different from that of those only traded in Switzerland. The mean of the standard deviation of the pricing error is also given, although no tests were conducted for the sample size is small. It can be seen that the mean pricing error for

---

[41] This argument deals very generously with the central limit theorem although the sample size is rather small.

**Decomposition of Rates of Return: Results before and after the Introduction of Share at SEAQ**

| | Ciba Geigy P | Fischer BR | Winterthur P | Zurich BR | Zurich P |
|---|---|---|---|---|---|
| Standard Error Random Walk Opening Prices | | | | | |
| STDVT a) | 0.039077 | 0.05872 | 0.037116 | 0.044006 | 0.05448 |
| STDV1 b) | 0.045768 | 0.061291 | 0.049617 | 0.046421 | 0.074109 |
| STDV2 c) | 0.024113 | 0.055568 | 0.021827 | 0.041317 | 0.030296 |
| F-Statistics d) | | 1.216588992 | 5.167409829 | 1.262325697 | 5.983720811 |
| Standard Error Pricing Error Opening Prices | | | | | |
| STDVT | 0.005071 | 0.006489 | 0.004464 | 0.003817 | 0.004372 |
| STDV1 | 0.007840 | 0.007625 | 0.011474 | 0.003482 | 0.010569 |
| STDV2 | 0.001081 | 0.004669 | 0.001471 | 0.004301 | 0.001798 |
| F-Statistics | | 2.667054855 | 60.84212102 | 0.655418429 | 34.5532117 |
| Standard Error Random Walk Closing Prices | | | | | |
| STDVT | 0.036942 | 0.066975 | 0.042485 | 0.041785 | 0.040027 |
| STDV1 | 0.045585 | 0.076388 | 0.061309 | 0.046581 | 0.003212 |
| STDV2 | 0.020016 | 0.055132 | 0.023183 | 0.035655 | 0.030296 |
| F-Statistics | | 1.919741635 | 6.993735356 | 1.706776812 | 0.011240367 |
| Standard Error Pricing Error Closing Prices | | | | | |
| STDVT | 0.004794 | 0.007401 | 0.005109 | 0.003624 | 0.058864 |
| STDV1 | 0.007809 | 0.009504 | 0.014177 | 0.003494 | 0.008395 |
| STDV2 | 0.000897 | 0.004633 | 0.001562 | 0.003712 | 0.001069 |
| F-Statistics | | 4.208121 | 82.37712 | 0.885992 | 61.67171 |

Notes:

a) Standard deviation for whole sample: April 3 to December 28, 1992,

b) Standard deviation for first subsample: April 3 to August 31, 1992 (to September 28 for Ciba Geigy P),

c) Standard deviation for second subsample: September 3 to December 28, 1992 (October 1 for Ciba Geigy P),

d) Squares of b over c; F distributed with 108 and 82 degrees of freedom (128 and 62 Ciba GeigyP).

**Table 4**

shares which are only traded in Switzerland is only a tiny bit larger than for those traded in London also. For the spreads calculated with opening prices, the hypothesis that the mean spread for both types of shares is the same can be rejected. For spreads based on closing prices, the null-hypothesis of an equal mean cannot be rejected, however. These results suggest that hardly any consistent differences between shares not traded at SEAQ and shares traded there can be detected in the data.

Another interesting perspective about the impact of competition on market liquidity follows from the investigation of the differences in pricing errors and implicit bid-ask spreads before and after a Swiss share was listed on the SEAQ system. In **Table 4** the effects on the pricing error can be found, whereas in **Table 5** the impact on the implicit bid-ask spread is shown. The Ciba Geigy participation certificates and the Zurich bearer shares were only traded at SEAQ from April 1990 to the end of September 1990 and August 1990, respectively. The pattern of the impact is not unique: The abolition of trading activities in London reduced the pricing error for Ciba Geigy participation certificates significantly, but increased the pricing error for Zurich bearer shares, although the change of the latter is not significant. The implicit bid-ask spreads, however, suggest exactly the opposite impact: The spread increased for Ciba Geigy participation certificates, but decreased for Zurich bearer shares. The Fischer bearer shares, the Winterthur and the Zurich participation certificates are listed on the SEAQ system only since the beginning of September 1990. The pricing error measure always suggests that the competitive effect outweighs the fragmentation effect because the pricing error is significantly lower in the period in which the securities are traded in both markets. The results of the bid-ask spread measure are mixed: in some cases, the bid-ask spread is lower whereas in some other cases it is higher. These rather mixed results prevent any strong conclusion from being drawn although it seems that the competitive effect is somewhat stronger than the fragmentation effect.

The last question, of course, is whether the degree of fragmentation has any effect on the pricing error and the implicit bid-ask spread respectively. The choice of the price variable was not easy: although the absolute price gives the theoretical bounds

**Roll's Implicit Bid-Ask Spread: Results Before and After the Introduction of a Share at SEAQ**

| | Ciba Geigy P | Fischer BR | Winterthur P | Zurich BR | Zurich P |
|---|---|---|---|---|---|
| **Bid-Ask Spread Opening Prices** | | | | | |
| Spread a) | 0.002947 | 0.006078 | 0.003776 | 0.005346 | 0.005904 |
| Spread1 b) | 0.002275 | 0.009511 | 0.002980 | 0.006167 | 0.003017 |
| Spread2 c) | 0.004290 | 0.002645 | 0.004970 | 0.004115 | 0.010235 |
| **Bid-Ask Spread Closing Prices** | | | | | |
| Spread | 0.005485 | 0.010515 | 0.006494 | 0.011660 | 0.003014 |
| Spread1 | 0.005385 | 0.012734 | 0.006587 | 0.014960 | 0.003015 |
| Spread2 | 0.005585 | 0.008300 | 0.006355 | 0.008362 | NA |

Notes:

a) Standard deviation for whole sample: April 3 to December 28, 1992.

b) Standard deviation for first subsample: April 3 to August 31, 1992 (to September 28 for Ciba Geigy P).

c) Standard deviation for second subsample: September 3 to December 28, 1992 (October 1 for Ciba Geigy P).

**Table 5**

for price movements and order inflows, it is hardly a good measure for the short run fluctuations around the equilibrium price. For this reason, both the price and the variance of price changes were used as explanatory variables. There was a choice between two measures of price change variances; one being the sample variance of percentage price changes, the other being the estimated variance of the increments of the random walk component in actual transaction prices. Because the pricing error and the increments of the random walk were assumed to be perfectly correlated for the calculation of the pricing errors only the variance of the price change was used with the pricing error as dependent variable. The level of the share price was implemented in the equation with the average price over the sample period. The sample period for each share was chosen such that only the period during which it was traded in London was covered. The fragmentation variable is of course an endogenous variable. For that reason, an instrumental variable procedure using the lagged fragmentation (defined as being the market share 2 of SEAQ discussed in section 2.3. ) and the total current and lagged total market fragmentation as instruments were used to determine the average fragmentation for the same period for which the dependent variable was calculated. The end of 1990 value of the outstanding shares was used for the firm value variable. The regression results are displayed in **Table 6**. Only shares which were listed on the SEAQ system were included in the data set. It can immediately be seen that the variance of the pricing error or the price change seems to be the variable that explains most as its coefficients are of the right sign and, with one exception, always significant. The expected negative relation between market liquidity and firm value is confirmed when the bid-ask spreads calculated with closing prices or the pricing errors are used as dependent variables. However, the coefficients are only significant with the pricing error as dependent variables. The average price variable has the expected sign with the same dependent variables as discussed with respect to the firm value. It is disturbing to note that the average price and the firm value have significant coefficients with a wrong sign when the implicit bid-ask spread calculated with the opening prices was used. The effect of the market fragmentation on market liquidity is negative in five out of six cases. It follows that the competitive effect outweighs the fragmentation effect. However, in none of the six cases is the coefficient significantly different from zero. The fact that the

**Determinants of the Implicit Bid-Ask Spread and the Pricing Error**

| Dependent Variable | Spread | | | | Pricing Error | |
|---|---|---|---|---|---|---|
| | Opening Prices | Opening Prices | Closing Prices | Closing Prices | Opening Prices | Closing Prices |
| Constant | -0.0039<br>(0.0027) | -0.0120**<br>(0.0037) | 0.0026<br>(0.0043) | 0.0052<br>(0.0049) | 0.0040**<br>(0.0019) | 00058**<br>(0.0026) |
| Log Average Price | -0.0012**<br>(0.0003) | -0.0011**<br>(0.0003) | 0.0010<br>(0.0007) | 0.0012*<br>(0.0007) | 0.0005**<br>(0.0002) | 0.0006**<br>(0.0002) |
| Fitted Fragmentation | -0.0016<br>(0.0034) | 0.0001<br>(0.0030) | -0.0102<br>(0.0071) | -0.0104<br>(0.0068) | 0.0034<br>(0.0035) | 0.0035<br>(0.0037) |
| Log Firm Value | 0.0015**<br>(0.0005) | 0.0015**<br>(0.0005) | -0.0004<br>(0.0007) | -0.0008<br>(0.0006) | -0.0012**<br>(0.0002) | -0.0013**<br>(0.0003) |
| Variance Pricing Error | 0.1774**<br>(0.0371) | | 0.0586<br>(0.0536) | | | |
| Variance Price Change | | 0.7506**<br>(0.1393) | | 0.0532<br>(0.2614) | 0.1922**<br>(0.0615) | 0.1392**<br>(0.0725) |
| R-BAR2 | 0.306 | 0.461 | 0.076 | 0.040 | 0.588 | 0.516 |
| SEE | 0.0021 | 0.0018 | 0.0032 | 0.0032 | 0.0011 | 0.00191 |

Notes:
Sample Period: April until December 1990 (exceptions indicated in the text); * significant at the 10 percent level; ** significant at the 5 percent level; standard errors of coefficient were calculated using a consistent estimate of the variance-covariance matrix allowing for heteroskedasticitiy.

**Table 6**

results are not clear and suffer from problems with sign and significance of coefficients suggests that the fragmentation has no direct effect on market liquidity.

## 5. Conclusions

The competitive pressure which the London based SEAQ exercised upon the Swiss stock markets had the expected impact upon transaction costs in Switzerland. The fragmentation of order flows does not seem to have had a significant influence on market liquidity at Swiss stock exchanges. It even seems that the pricing error and the implicit bid-ask spread for shares which are listed both at Swiss stock exchanges and SEAQ in London are somewhat lower than for those listed at Swiss exchanges only. This means that the possible adverse effects on market liquidity are dominated by the competition effects resulting from an increase in the number of brokers and dealers in the market for Swiss stocks.

However, this proposition needs further confirmation. The empirical evidence is suffering from the small data sample and from the quality of the variables which served as an approximation for the market liquidity. It should also be remembered that the competition between SEAQ and the Swiss stock exchanges affects only a small subset of all Swiss stocks, namely the very liquid shares of large, internationally known companies. The result suggests that the stamp tax has been a serious impediment for domestic securities brokers and that the possibility of integrating block trading into a stock exchange system is a serious challenge for the next decade. Assuming that the benefits reaped by investors from lower transaction costs are larger than the losses incurred by producers of stock trading services, the results lead to positive welfare implications of the competition among stock markets. It must be mentioned, however, that the feedback effects of competition on the more domestic market segments have not been investigated yet.

**Literature**

Aerni, P. (1991), "Eine Analyse der impliziten Geld-Briefkursspannen des schweizerischen Börsenplatzes", Schweizerische Zeitschrift für Volkswirtschaft und Statistik, 127, pp. 395-408.

Braillard, P. (1987), Der Finanzplatz Schweiz, Geneva: Georg Editeur.

Copeland, T. E. , and Weston, J. F. (1988), Financial Theory and Corporate Policy, Reading, MA: Addison-Wesley.

The Economist, (1992a), "The Next Hundred Years", Vol. 323, No. 7758, May 9, pp. 101-102.

The Economist, (1992b), "Can the Centre Hold? A Survey of Financial Centres", Supplement to Vol. 323, No. 7765, June 27..

Garbade, K. D., and Silber, W. L. (1976), "Price Dispersion in the Government Securities Market", Journal of Political Economy, Vol. 84, No. 4, 721-740.

Gehrig, T. (1992), Comment, in: Competitiveness in Banking, ed. by Blattner, N., Genberg, H., and Swoboda, A., Heidelberg: Physica Verlag.

Grilli (1989), "Europe 1992: Issues and Prospects for the Financial Markets", Economic Policy, October, pp. 388-421.

Grossman, S. J., and Miller, M. H. (1988), "Liquidity and Market Structure", Journal of Finance, Vol. 43, No. 3, 617-637.

Glosten, L. R. (1987), "Components of the Bid-Ask Spread and the Statistical Properties of Transaction Prices, Journal of Finance, 42, pp. 1293-1307.

Haller, A., and Stoll, H. R. (1989), "Market Structure and Transaction Costs", Journal of Banking and Finance, 13, pp. 697-708.

Hamilton, J. L. (1979), "Marketplace Fragmentation, Competition, and the Efficiency of the Stock Exchange", Journal of Finance, 34, pp. 171-187.

Helpman, E., and Krugman, P. R. (1985), Market Structure and Foreign Trade, Cambridge, MA: MIT Press.

London Stock Exchange (1991), Guide to the International Equity Market 1991-1992, London: London Stock Exchange.

Mendelson, H. (1982), "Market Behaviour in a Clearing House", Econometrica, Vol. 50, No. 6, 1505-1524.

Mendelson, H. (1987), "Consolidation, Fragmentation, and Market Performance", Journal of Financial and Quantitative Analysis, Vol. 22, No. 2, 189-207.

Neal, R. (1987), "Potential Competition and Actual Competition in Equity Options", Journal of Finance, 42, pp. 511-531.

Pagano, M. (1989), "Transaction Volume and Asset Liquidity", Quarterly Journal of Economics, 103, pp. 255-274.

Pagano, M., and Roell, A. (1990), "Stock Markets", Economic Policy, 10, pp. 63-115.

Quah, D. (1992), "The Relative Importance of Permanent and Transitory Components: Identification and Some Theoretical Bounds", Econometrica, Vol. 60, No. 1, 107-118.

Roll, R. (1984), "A Simple Implicit Measure of the Effective Bid-Ask Spread in an Efficient Market", Journal of Finance, 39, pp. 1127-1139.

Stoll, H. R. (1989), "Inferring the Components of the Bid-Ask Spread: Theory and Empirical Tests", Journal of Finance, 44, pp. 115-134.

Stock, J. H., and Watson, M. W. (1988), "Variable Trends in Economic Time Series", Journal of Economic Perspectives, Vol. 2, No. 3, 147-174.

Worthington, P. M. (1991), "Global Equity Turnover: Market Comparisons", Bank of England Quarterly Bulletin, No. 2, pp. 246-249.

Zimmermann, H., Eberle, A., and Rampini, A. (1991), Europa und die Schweizer Banken, Chur, Zurich: Verlag Rüegger.

Zimmermann, H., Bill, M., and Dubacher, R. (1989), Finanzmarkt Schweiz, Zurich: Zürcher Kantonalbank.

**Comment on**

**Thomas Helbling: "The Effect of Foreign Competition on Stock Markets: SEAQ International vs. Switzerland"**

**Richard T. Meier**

It is very positive that academia also in Switzerland starts to think analytically about market organization, about questions like "Why is one market better than another one?" or "What determines market quality?". Until rather recently, such questions were not asked in University class rooms.

The study of Helbling contains a lot of theoretical background and reasoning which I would not like (and not dare) to discuss. Still, a few comments may be of interest from somebody who, for the last 25 years, has been involved in developments of securities markets in Switzerland and who has been a close observer of what happened in the world in this respect.

### Fragmentation vs. concentration of markets

Many stock exchanges - but not the Swiss ones - have vigorously argued against fragmentation for years. No wonder! Concentrating trading on the exchanges is clearly in their interest - as any monopoly is in the interest of the ones it benefits.

Market economists however should not simply adopt this view without asking a few further questions. The 'fragmentation vs. concentration' issue regarding markets has something to do with free competition vs. monopolistic structures. Just look at the arguments against market fragmentation. With roughly the same arguments, one could speak against 'fragmenting' the car production. Theoretically, concentration often looks fine; practically competition grants the best results - and brings about the right degree of fragmentation or concentration.

**Market mechanisms**

Economic theory often looks at markets as 'black boxes' under all sorts of ceteris paribus-assumptions. It deals with aggregate figures for supply and demand and their changes. Such exercises are of considerable value mainly in the macro-economic field. But they deal with something that is remarkably far away from real life in terms of market organization.

A market is a huge and complex interplay of a large number of human interventions. Those interventions always have to do with emotions as much as with pure rational reasoning. This interplay is fundamentally dynamic. Every little change has potential to bring about many more changes, brings in new market players and makes others disappear. From an organizational point of view, the question is: how do you organize this mechanism, this interplay of market forces to come to optimum market quality and efficiency? To this question there is certainly no easy answer - and not one single answer either.

A key issue: it is often taken for granted that a good market is a transparent market. It would however be wrong to conclude that the best market is the most transparent one. Let us look at some of the interests involved.

From a theoretical point of view, the pricing mechanism and hence the economic steering mechanism of the market works best, if market participants (including potential participants) have best and broadest possible information. Politically, equal and fair treatment of small investors and market participants is an important issue. And what is practically the interest of all those market players who ultimately make up for the bulk of the market? - Generally speaking it is fairly simple: every one would like to have best possible transparency about what the others do or intend to do, but without revealing his own intentions.

Obviously this describes a conflict of interest. A conflict between purely practical views and political goals, between big and small, between market professionals and customers and between individual participants. There is no easy way to solve this conflict. Markets need both, market professionals and customers; it is generally believed that they need not only big, but also small players; and they need a reasonably good reputation.

This discussion leads to another aspect, and London again sets an interesting example. The London Stock exchange promotes the 'Professional Whole Sale Market'. This is meant to be an international market with only professional access. As a consequence, it would need only little regulation as it does not have to take care of small investors. This freedom for market players appeals to many big market participants. But the 'Professional Whole Sale Market' concept led to enormous and ongoing discussions at the political level.

While the concept has a lot of practical merits, it raises problems in other financial centers and mainly for their regulators. Markets travel easily around the world and big market players with them. Hence the great interest of market regulators for international coordination and harmonization of market regulation. While the globalisation of markets brought about a competitive atmosphere for regulators, they try to escape it through international harmonization, thus fighting against what they call a competitive regulatory race to the bottom. From the market's point of view this competition is to be warmly welcomed.

There is some evidence that SEAQ offers a good balance between the different attributes of a market: efficiency, transparency, profitability, reputation. It is obvious, that market players, buyers and sellers, appreciate to be among themselves when they trade. One prove of this can be observed on electronic markets where 'prearranging' of trades seems to be a very common habit. In so far the telephone offers quite adequate 'trading technology'. Of course, the privacy at the time of concluding a deal must be balanced by sufficient pre- and after trade transparency. Otherwise a market would most probably loose credibility.

**Judging the competitiveness of a stock exchange**

Of course, one can define certain key-characteristics of stock exchanges and then discuss competitiveness of exchanges based on these criteria (such as trading instruments, member firms, pricing mechanism, regulatory structure, clearing and settlement). I am not sure whether this leads to very useful results. Common wisdom says, that clearing and settlement is a very important ingredient of an efficient market. But London proves that you can be 'third world' in clearing and settlement and still world league as a market place. Perhaps we should rather be aware of the positive effects of competition. Although many London market players suffered after Big Bang, the market place as a whole has gained a lot as a consequence of increased competition.

**The role of computerized trading**

Computerization of stock exchange trading has been a hot issue for at least two decades. Heated discussions almost led to 'religious wars'. With the benefit of hindsight it is easy to say that there were a lot of wrong answers to wrong questions - and they show up also in academic studies.

So far, we haven't seen any clear proof that, as such, electronic trading is superior to traditional trading. Rather, under given circumstances, certain organizational patterns are more suited for trading that others. A few examples:

- SEAQ and the London Stock Exchange do certainly not prove that electronic trading is better. To the contrary, SEAQ has proven how efficient old fashioned telephone trading can be (particularly if supported by an electronic information system). Also, the London Stock Exchange has proved clearly that you don't need a floor anymore with today's communications means. This was very important for Big Bang to be successful. It would have been difficult to accomodate on the floor so many new member organizations; and it would have been difficult and costly for those new market players to set up new floor trading operations.

- Certain exchanges (e.g. the New York Stock Exchange) insist on keeping their floor. This is probably a very good idea for them because the floor allows a strong stock exchange to keep its technical monopoly.

- Globalisation and deregulation have changed some basic facts for many stock exchanges. The advantages of floors can turn into disadvantages when markets become fragmented because an exchange looses market share to other exchanges or markets. In such a situation, members tend to change their priorities and prefer to trade from their own trading room. From there it is easier to have optimum communication facilities to all relevant markets at all times than from a floor (which is public ground).

- Apart from this general aspect there is a specific one for Switzerland (as for other small countries with international outlook). The Swiss market has less than 2 % of the world's capitalisation. For worldwide portfolio managers and market players like our major Swiss members, it doesn't make sense to waste management, trading and research resources for several floors in this rather small country.

- With derivatives we did not only get additional trading instruments and markets. They have added a lot of complexity to the market place. Hence, the demand for expertise of market operators has grown dramatically. This puts considerable pressure on redundant markets.

- Of a complete securities trade (from receiving the order until completion of clearing and settlement, customer confirmation etc.), the pure trading activity is between 10 and 20 % of the total of activities (and cost). All activities except for trading are highly computerized. When cost pressure asks for the streamlining of existing procedures, computerizing trading comes to mind quite naturally.

Finally, the Swiss discussion about electronic trading has a lot to do with doing away with the Swiss federalistic stock exchange system. Once again, political aspects seem to outweigh technical ones.

**Comment on**

**Thomas Helbling: "The Effects of Foreign Competition on Stock Markets: SEAQ International vs. Switzerland"**

**Peter Aerni**

Helbling's analysis of the effects of SEAQ's competition on Swiss stock markets, in particular Zurich, deals with the recently heavily debated issue of competition between stock exchanges. As the author points out in the introduction, the main motivation for the strong interest in this field has been the huge success of SEAQ International in London. Over the last years, SEAQ's market share in internationally traded European stocks has constantly grown causing concern on the Continent how domestic market shares can be preserved. Consequently, most research on competition among stock exchanges revolves round the keyword of competitiveness. What measures need to be taken to increase the competitiveness of a country's securities market system?

Helbling's paper follows this 'tradition' only partially. The goal of the paper is not to uncover the impact of reforms - be they planned or already in effect - on the competitiveness of the Swiss stock exchanges. Helbling instead goes farther back and raises questions about the costs and benefits of different trading systems, about conditions for their coexistence, and about the effects of competition among them. To assess the impact of reformatory strategies, an analysis of these problems is absolutely necessary. It also allows to emphasize an issue that is often lost in research concentrating on the competitiveness of a particular securities market system, namely the issue whether competition between stock exchanges is socially desirable or not. What are the costs and benefits of offering the same intermediation services in more than one marketplace? In this respect, Helbling's analysis of the Swiss open-outcry auction system, known as 'à-la-criée', and SEAQ's dealership market can be seen as a welcome contribution to the growing literature on competition between stock exchanges.

Helbling's analysis is divided into three parts. It starts with a description of the main characteristics of the Swiss stock exchanges and SEAQ International in London, their biggest foreign competitor. The second part of the paper analyzes the pros and cons of competition between Zurich and London from a theoretical viewpoint. Helbling closes with an empirical analysis. My comments focus on questions raised in the theoretical part of the paper. A few remarks on the empirical part close my discussion.

In the theoretical part Helbling discusses factors influencing the location choice of investments in dually-traded stocks, i.e. stocks traded both in Zurich and London. He rightly interprets competition between SEAQ and Zurich in dually-traded shares as competition between an "order-driven" auction and a "quote-driven" dealership market and identifies as key difference between the two trading systems the price of the execution risk that investors have to bear, i.e. the risk of trading at an off-equilibrium price due to temporary imbalances in supply and demand. Along the lines of Pagano and Roell (1993a), one can argue that dealership markets are socially more desirable if market makers as individuals or as a group are less risk averse than their customers and therefore more able to carry execution risks. In this setting, if investors are homogeneous and if there are no intermarket frictions such as information or communication costs, the coexistence of an auction and a dealership market is not possible. One trading system would outperform the other to such an extent that no investors would be willing to trade in the inferior market. What are the reasons that the two trading systems coexist?

Besides intermarket frictions as a reason for the coexistence, Helbling rightly points to the heterogeneity of investors as a possible explanation. If customers differ with respect to risk aversion and/or liquidity needs and therefore with respect to their ability to carry execution risks, we can expect the two trading systems to coexist, attracting different groups of investors. According to Helbling's argument in Sections 3.2 and 3.3, "there exists a critical order size above which the investor prefers to use the dealership market". For orders below this critical size, investors prefer to use the auction market. Helbling's analysis leads to the conclusion that large institutional investors, or more generally professional portfolio managers with a distinct demand for immediacy are expected to prefer to trade in a dealership market. Smaller investors are expected to trade in auction markets.

Helbling's argumentation is confirmed by the following empirical observation on which the paper does not put much emphasis. As Helbling notes, Zimmermann

(1989) estimated that the number of shares transacted per order in Zurich is less than half of that in London. Obviously, SEAQ International has been able to specialize in trading bigger orders. Large institutional investors seeking immediacy evidently prefer the more liquid dealership market in London.

Besides the lack of immediacy another reason for institutional investors to concentrate on dealership markets might stem from the different degree of intra-market transparency offered by the two trading mechanisms (see Harris (1992)). An institutional investor usually places orders that are large enough to significantly move the market due to temporary imbalances of supply and demand. His order therefore contains exclusive information on future transaction prices that stockbrokers can take advantage of by trading on their own account before the customer's order is executed as a whole or in parts.[1] When stockbrokers do so, they 'front-run' clients' orders. If the corresponding front-running profits are made at the expense of the order-placing customers, large institutional investors might prefer to trade with brokers who either have a reputation of not using order book information or are prohibited to front-run.[2]

But even when it is prohibited to front-run the orders of customers, placing large orders can be quite expensive in markets with a trading system that disseminates order flow information to the market. In such an environment, the exposition of large orders to the market can lead to a front-running by competing brokers. If that's the case, and if front-running costs are borne by the order-placing investors themselves, large investors will prefer to trade in the market with the least revelation of order flow information.

The Swiss open-outcry auction market system, known as 'à-la-criée', is likely to reveal more order flow information to competitors than a dealership market. In Zurich, a broker handling a large customer order at the ring must, on the one hand, identify other brokers likely to be interested in trading. On the other hand, he must guess the quantity that potential trading partners are willing to trade. Even an

---

1 In Zurich as well as in London intermediaries are allowed to trade shares on their own account in addition to bringing their clients' orders to the market, a practice known as dual trading or dual-capacity trading.

2 The question, whether front-running costs are borne by the order-placing customers themselves or not, has generated great controversies. For a theoretical treatment of this question see for instance Fishman and Longstaff (1992) and Pagano and Roell (1993b).

experienced ring veteran cannot fulfill this task perfectly. At least part of the order flow information will be exposed to competitors who may front-run on this information.

Large customers could protect themselves against this risk by sequentially submitting only parts of their order. No one in the market can then infer the full size of their orders. But following this strategy is likely to be, on the one hand, very time-consuming and therefore in conflict with the interests of investors seeking immediacy. On the other hand, the investor faces the same problem when managing order exposure as a broker at the ring: How much quantity is the counter-party ready to absorb at what price? If even brokers with their superior information on market conditions cannot solve this problem perfectly, we cannot assume that an investor outside the exchange can do so.

Dealership markets such as SEAQ provide a way out of these problems. In a dealership market, an institutional investor's broker always knows which market maker is ready to buy and sell what quantity at preannounced prices. A broker can therefore trade large orders by sequentially filling parts of the order. By doing so, he reveals the order only to the extent that market makers are willing to trade. In contrast to the Swiss open-outcry system, a broker cannot possibly misjudge the willingness to trade of the contra-side. Depending on the stock exchange's rules about order book transparency, front-running behavior by competitors can more or less be ruled out.

In contrast to large customers, small investors do not run the risk to move the market in any significant manner. Therefore, an exposure of small orders is unlikely to provoke any front-running. One can even expect small investors to like the exposure of their orders as this information might attract other traders. Accordingly, small customers prefer the intra-market transparency offered by auction markets.

The different degree of intra-market transparency offered by the two trading systems might therefore be another reason for large investors to concentrate in dealership markets. If these conclusions are right, the listing of Swiss stocks at SEAQ has led to an investor-specific segmentation of the market. London has specialized in offering intermediation services tailored to the needs of large institutional investors whereas the Swiss open-outcry trading system seems to fit the needs of smaller investors.

If the installation of SEAQ in 1985 has segmented the market, the listing of a Swiss share in London might not lead to lower transaction costs in Switzerland by increasing competition among stockbrokers as Helbling argues in Section 3.1. On the one hand, investor-specific market segmentation creates possibilities to price-discriminate between different groups of customers. On the other hand, market segmentation based on trading systems can have positive effects too by bringing those investors together that share higher gains from trade. Therefore, market segmentation is likely to lower implicit transaction costs by lowering the search costs of finding the best possible trading partner. This effect might overcompensate possible negative effects due to the higher price-discriminatory power of brokers. The overall effect remains ambiguous.

Let me now turn to the empirical part of the paper. To analyze the implications of his theoretical arguments empirically, Helbling identifies transaction costs and market liquidity as main factors influencing the location choice of traders. He argues along the lines of Pagano and Roell (1990) that market shares depend negatively on transaction costs and positively on market liquidity. Stock exchange competition should influence both. One would expect a positive competitive effect due to the disciplinary pressure of competition causing explicit and implicit transaction costs to decrease and a negative liquidity effect caused by the fragmentation of the order flow that may worsen market liquidity. Depending on whether the positive effect outweighs the negative one, competition among stock markets is socially desirable or not. But empirical verification of the two effects is not easy. Evidence put forward in favor of one or the other effect may lead to different conclusions if one alters the assumptions regarding the competition among stock exchanges.

As a measure of market liquidity, respectively implicit transaction costs, Helbling uses measures proposed by Roll and Hasbrouck. The crucial assumption in Roll's model is the semi-strong information efficiency of transaction prices. To assess the impact of London's SEAQ on Zurich using Roll's bid-ask spread Helbling therefore has to assume that London and Zurich are informationally integrated markets which is a very strong assumption.

The transparency of the Zurich stock exchange is too low to uphold the assumption of perfect integration. Market makers in London certainly do have information regarding the transaction prices in Zurich but they have no information concerning the volumes that go with those prices. Not even a broker in Basel or Geneva has this information. Since prices only form one argument of the corresponding excess demand schedules the assumption of informationally integrated marketplaces is too strong. Informational asymmetries, if they exist, do influence the pricing in both Zurich and London. Therefore, the results of Helbling's empirical analysis of Roll's measure might well be mixed with informational effects making an interpretation very hard.

Consider the empirical evidence Pagano and Roell (1990) found concerning the 'fourchette' in Paris and the bid-ask in London. The spread at SEAQ tends to get narrower when the Paris stock exchange is open at the same time. As Pagano and Roell state, on the one hand, this observation can be due to the disciplinary effect of competition among stock exchanges, but on the other hand, it can also be ascribed to an information effect. When Paris is open at the same time as SEAQ, the dealers in London can take the Paris transaction prices as a guideline for their quoting strategy and vice versa. The risk premium to be charged as insurance against information-motivated trades falls. If this information effect exists, the assumption that the implicit bid-ask spread can be measured by computing Roll's measure is no longer valid. Similar problems arise with Hasbrouck's pricing error.

To test the impact of SEAQ's competition on Swiss stock markets, Helbling compares the differences in pricing errors and implicit bid-ask spreads before and after a Swiss share was listed on the SEAQ system. The mixed results Helbling gets might be due to the problem of comparing two different time periods. Implicit transaction costs do depend on market conditions that change over time. A decrease in implicit transaction costs might therefore be the result of more favorable market conditions in the particular time period and not the result of increased competition. In this respect, an interpretation of the results is not possible.

Briefly concluding, Helbling's paper is a welcome contribution towards understanding the impact of competition among stock exchanges. But many problems are as yet unsettled. Helbling's restriction of the analysis on the influence of liquidity needs of investors might capture the main factors influencing the location choice in the short run. In the long run however, other factors and therefore other questions might gain importance. An important issue is whether full-service banks as the predominant bank type in Switzerland have a competitive advantage or disadvantage compared to the specialized firms operating in London? Another issue not addressed by Helbling concerns the implications of stock exchange competition on the regulatory structure of Swiss stock markets. The discussion in Switzerland on the necessity of a new federal stock exchange law seems to manifest that stock exchange competition does not only take place at the level of brokerage services but also at a more global level concerning the market microstructure as a whole. In this respect, Helbling's paper can be seen as an important contribution to an area of research that is still largely unexplored.

**Literature**

Fishman, M.J. and Longstaff, L.A. (1992), "Dual Trading in Futures Markets", in: Journal of Finance, 47, 2, pp. 643-671.

Harris, Lawrence (1992), Consolidation, Fragmentation, Segmentation and Regulation, mimeo, University of Southern California.

Pagano, M., and Roell, A. (1990), "Trading Systems in European Stock Exchanges: Current Performance and Policy Options", in: Economic Policy, 10, pp. 63-115.

Pagano, M., and Roell, A. (1993a), "Auction Markets, Dealership Markets and Execution Risk", in: Conti, V. and Hamaui, R., (eds.) Financial Markets' Liberalisation and the Role of Banks, Cambridge University Press, Cambridge.

Pagano, M., and Roell, A. (1993b), "Front-Running and Stock Market Liquidity", in: Conti, V. and Hamaui, R., (eds.) Financial Markets' Liberalisation and the Role of Banks, Cambridge University Press, Cambridge.

Zimmermann, H., Bill, M., and Dubacher, R. (1989), Finanzmarkt Schweiz, Zürcher Kantonalbank, Zürich.

# Part IV: The International Market for Bank Deposits and Bonds

# The Swiss Share in International Markets for Bank Deposits and Bonds

**Ulrich Camen**[1]

## 1. Introduction

Independently of the rejection of Swiss EEA membership in the recent popular vote, deregulation of financial markets will be an important concern of banks located in Switzerland in the foreseeable future. This paper assesses the position of banks located in Switzerland in international financial markets and attempts to identify the key factors that will affect their position. The focus will be on two main international activities: on-balance-sheet activities including fiduciary transactions, and activities in the international bond markets. In both activities Swiss banks had traditionally a strong position internationally.

The first two sections of the paper analyze the position of banks located in Switzerland in the markets for external deposits and international bonds respectively. The analysis of these two markets will identify the factors that have determined the position of Switzerland in international financial markets. Against this background the final section identifies the main regulatory and economic factors that are likely to influence the position of Swiss banks in these two financial markets in the medium term.

---

[1] I would like to thank Pascal Bridel, Hans Genberg and members of the research teams in Basel and Geneva for helpful comments and suggestions. This research was financially supported by a grant of the Swiss National Science Foundations.

## 2. The International Markets for Bank Deposits and Credits[2]

### 2.1 The position of Swiss banks in the international markets for deposits and credits

Since the early seventies the position of Swiss banks in the international markets for deposits and credits has deteriorated significantly. Whereas Swiss banks held the second largest market shares in the two markets in 1971, they occupied only the sixth position the end of the eighties (**Figure 1**)[3] . The Swiss market shares declined substantially in the early 1970's when total liabilities to non-residents fell from about 12 percent in 1971 to 6.8 percent in 1974 and total credits fell from 16.4 percent in 1971 to 9 percent in 1974. This sizeable reduction is generally seen as a result of the capital control measures of the Swiss National Bank (SNB) in July 1972. Since 1975 the fraction of Swiss deposits in the world total showed only a slightly declining trend from 6.4 percent to 5.1 percent in 1989.

In contrast to the market shares of banks in Switzerland and the UK, those of the other main financial centers increased over the last twenty years. Important gains were made by the off-shore centers, Hong Kong and Singapore, and Japan, although increases differed in size and timing. Whereas the shares of Hong Kong and Singapore increased tenfold since the early seventies, the Japanese shares increased by a factor of three within the second half of the 1980's. Presently, the off-shore centers rank highest in the market for deposits and credits with shares of about 20 and 21 percent, respectively.

Instead of using data prepared by the International Monetary Fund (IMF) for

---

[2] This section is based on material that was presented in Camen (1990) and Camen (1992).

[3] The market shares are measured as the ratio of total deposits (credits) by non-resider with Swiss banks to the worlds total external assets. The IMF data is used here which takes into account fiduciary accounts. Non-residents are all non-banks and banks which are not located in the reporting country. For more details on the data used see Annex.

**FIGURE 1**

A) TOTAL LIABILITIES, IN % OF WORLD TOTAL

B) TOTAL CREDITS, IN % OF WORLD TOTAL

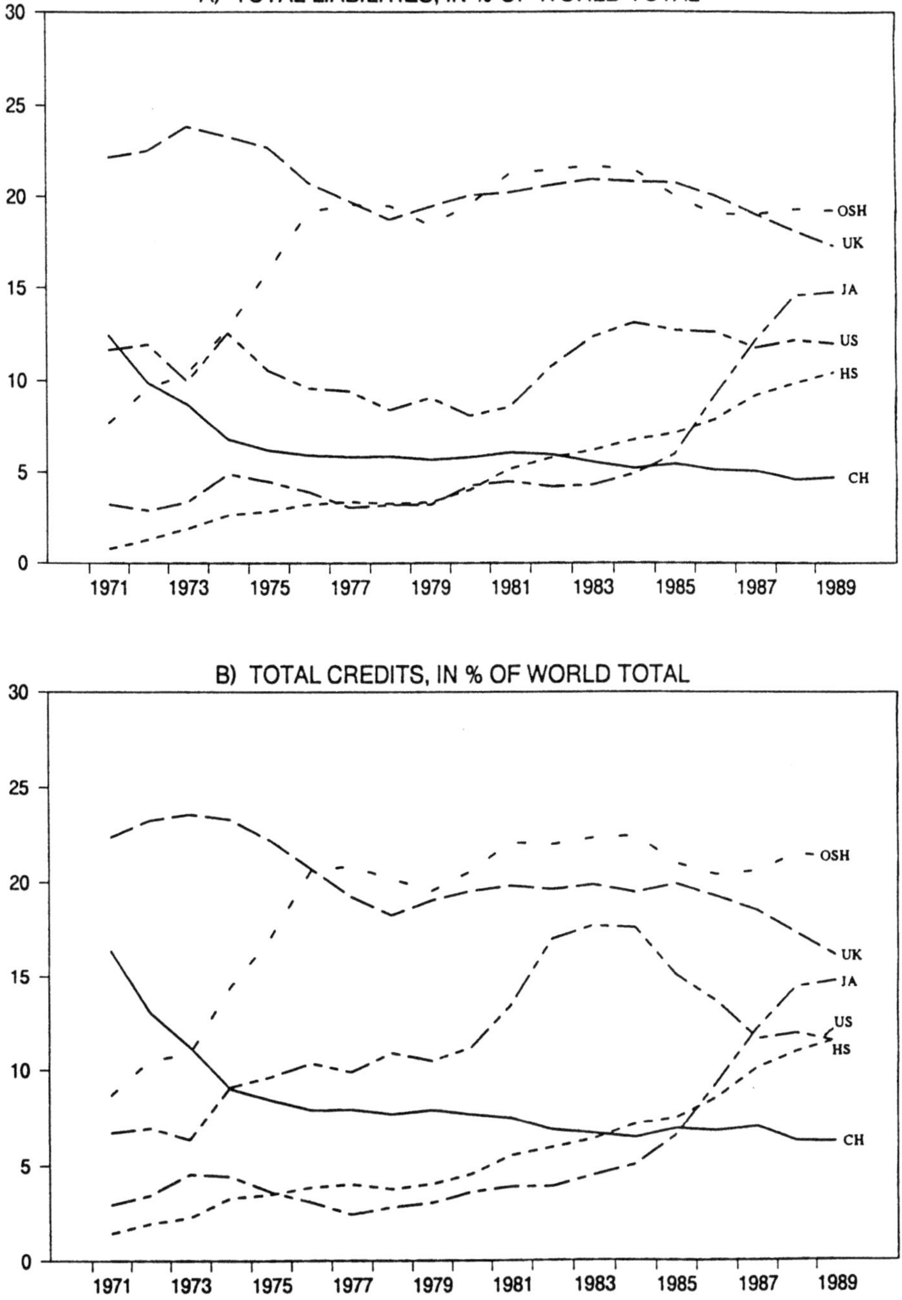

calculating market shares, one can follow Bridel (1974)[4] and compute market shares by using data that is published by the Bank for International Settlement (BIS). **Table 1** presents market shares for comparison based on data from both sources. Since 1974, the first year for which BIS data are available, both measures indicate a decline in the Swiss market share although the size of the reduction differs between the two measures.

**Figures 2 and 3** show market shares separately for non-bank and inter-bank deposits and credits. As can be seen from these graphs, Swiss banks had traditionally a very strong position in the market for non-bank deposits (**Figure 2A**) but played a less pronounced role in the market for non-bank credits (**Figure 2B**). With about 30 percent in 1971, Swiss banks had the largest market share in the market for non-bank deposits compared to below 15 percent in the market for non-bank credits. In the inter-bank market the Swiss market share has been larger in credit (**Figure 3B**) than in deposits (**Figure 3A**). This asymmetry between the non-bank and inter-bank market is a reflection of the well-known specialization of Swiss banks in collecting external deposits which then are partly reinvested in inter-bank credits.

The Swiss market share of non-bank deposits declined drastically in the early seventies from close to 30 percent in 1971 to 17 per cent in 1974 placing Swiss banks in a middle position with respect to the other industrialized countries. This strong decline underlies the reduction in the share of overall deposits. Since the mid-1970's the share of foreign non-bank deposits in Switzerland stayed rather stable varying between 14 and 18 percent.

In contrast to Switzerland, the off-shore centers (OSH) massively increased their shares in the market for non-bank deposits and credits between 1973 and 1978 which resulted in a substantial increase also in their share in overall deposits. This increase made them together with the UK, the centers with the highest shares in non-bank deposits, a position they already had in the inter-bank market. Presently, the off-shore

---

[4] For differences between the banking statistics of the IMF and the BIS see annex.

**Table 1**

**Swiss Banks' Market Share**
**(%)**

| | *IMF Data* | | *BIS Data* | |
|---|---|---|---|---|
| *Year* | *Liabilities* | *Credits* | *Liabilities* | *Credits*[1] |
| *1971* | 12.4 | 16.4 | | |
| *1972* | 9.9 | 13.0 | | |
| *1973* | 8.7 | 11.2 | | |
| *1974* | 6.8 | 9.0 | | 14.7 |
| *1975* | 6.1 | 8.4 | | 12.4 |
| *1976* | 5.9 | 7.9 | | 11.2 |
| *1977* | 5.8 | 7.9 | | 10.9 |
| *1978* | 5.8 | 7.7 | | 10.5 |
| *1979* | 5.6 | 7.9 | | 10.6 |
| *1980* | 5.8 | 7.7 | | 11.0 |
| *1981* | 6.1 | 7.5 | | 10.5 |
| *1982* | 5.9 | 6.9 | | 9.6 |
| *1983* | 5.5 | 6.6 | | 9.5 |
| *1984* | 5.2 | 6.4 | | 8.5 |
| *1985* | 5.4 | 6.9 | | 8.7 |
| *1986* | 5.1 | 6.8 | | 7.9 |
| *1987* | 5.1 | 7.0 | | 8.0 |
| *1988* | 4.6 | 6.3 | | 7.5 |
| *1989* | 4.7 | 6.2 | | 7.6 |

1 BIS reporting banks' liabilities to Switzerland as share of total external assets of BIS reporting banks. This is the same definition as the one used by Bridel (1974) as method A and Christensen (1986) Table 13.

## FIGURE 2

A) SHARES IN MARKET FOR NON-BANK DEPOSITS, IN % OF WORLD TOTAL

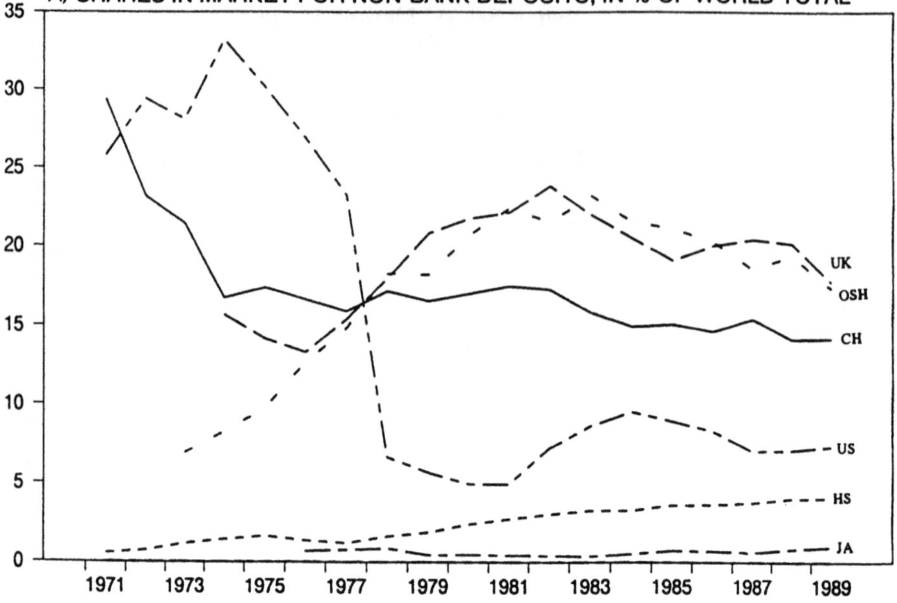


B) SHARES IN MARKET FOR NON-BANK CREDITS, IN % OF WORLD TOTAL

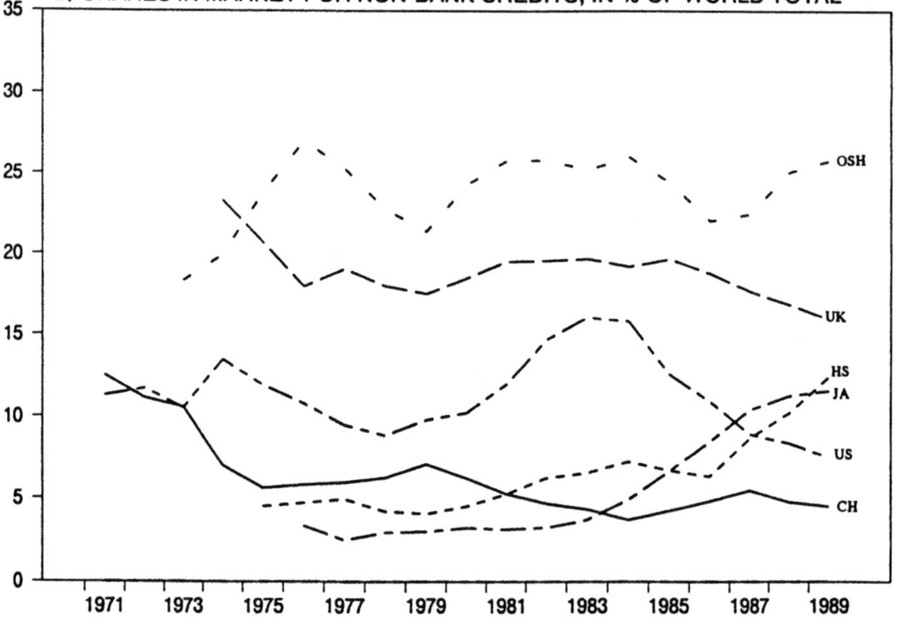

## FIGURE 3

A) SHARES IN MARKET FOR BANK DEPOSITS, IN % OF WORLD TOTAL

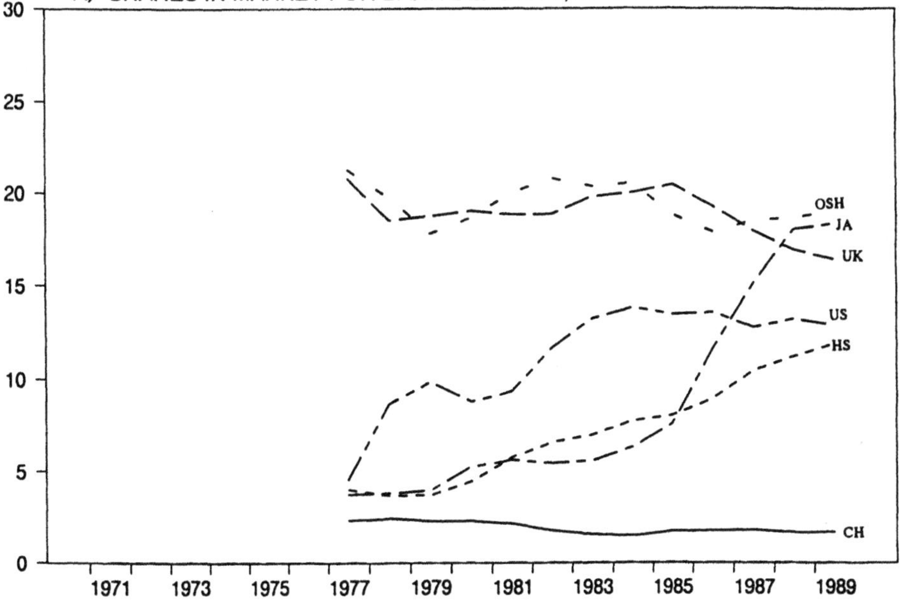


B) SHARES IN MARKET FOR BANK CREDITS, IN % OF WORLD TOTAL

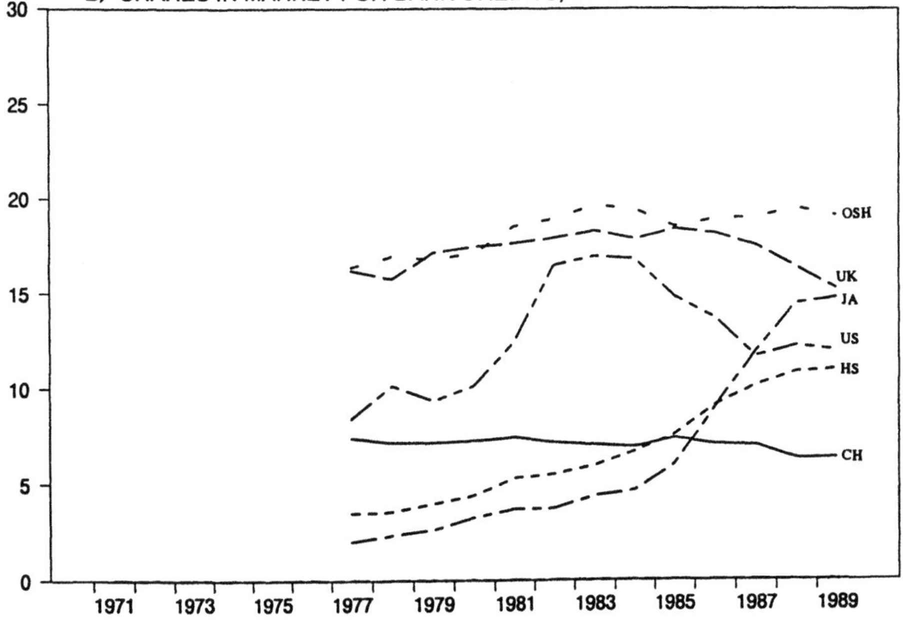

financial centers have the highest market shares in the non-bank as well as in the bank markets.

The increase in the overall market shares of financial centers in Asia which took place in the eighties appears to have been primarily due to an expanding position in the inter-bank markets. The Japanese share in the inter-bank markets for deposits increased from about 5 percent in 1980 to 18 percent in 1989 and the share of Hong Kong and Singapore increased from 4.5 percent to about 14 percent. The share of the Asian countries in non-bank deposits has been, in contrast, comparatively low.

## 2.2 Main characteristics and determinants of the activities of Swiss banks in the market for external non-bank deposits

External non-bank deposits with Swiss banks show two important characteristics. A large portion of non-bank deposits are fiduciary accounts and a high percentage of deposits is denominated in foreign currencies especially in U.S. dollars.[5] The main changes with respect to the structure of external deposits of Swiss banks over the last twenty years have been (i) a drastic decline of the share of Swiss banks in the market for non-bank deposits in the first half of the seventies followed by a slight decline in the following years till 1990, (ii) a continuous shift towards fiduciary accounts since 1971, and (iii) an increase in the fraction of deposits denominated in foreign currencies in the early 1970's. Various economic, institutional and regulatory determinants can explain these structural changes.[6]

Economic factors include interest rate differentials, exchange rate expectations and generally the economic stability of the country in which the bank is located in. In the

---

[5] See Camen (1992) for more details.

[6] For a more detailed discussion and econometric tests of some of the hypothesis presented here , see Camen (1992).

case of Switzerland it can be questioned whether these economic determinants have played an important role. The fact that between 70 to 90 percent of external deposits were constantly denominated in foreign currencies suggests that non-residents do not deposit their money with Swiss banks to invest in Swiss francs. It appears, instead, that investors appreciate characteristics of the Swiss banking system that are not directly related to the Swiss franc.

Although economic determinants do not seem to have played a predominant role in the determination of the Swiss share in the market for external non-bank deposits, this does not imply that they did not play some role. Depending on the type of external deposit, between 10 to 30 percent of deposits are denominated in Swiss francs, and for this fraction of deposits economic factors are likely to be important determinants. Since the fraction of deposits denominated in Swiss franc decreased over the last twenty years, the importance of economic factors that determine the Swiss market share can be assumed to have diminished over time. Also, the policy of the SNB during large parts of the seventies was to limit investments in Swiss francs by non-residents by imposing capital control measures (see below). Consequently, the low share of external non-bank deposits in Swiss francs is at least partly the result of capital control measures.

Institutional and regulatory factors constitute another important group of variables that determine why non-residents deposit their funds with banks in a foreign country. According to findings by Grilli (1989), institutional determinants of the level of non-bank deposits are the level of the interest tax, the existence of controls on capital inflows and the extent of banking secrecy. Variables that determine the level of inter-bank deposits are the rate of dividend taxes, the existence of capital controls and the size of the economy.

The absence of the withholding tax for fiduciary accounts in the case of Switzerland appears to be an important incentive for non-banks to deposit money with Swiss banks, judging by the fact that the share of fiduciary accounts grew rapidly over the last twenty years and currently account for about 65 percent of non-bank deposits.[7] Other institutional and regulatory factors that appear to have been important for determining the market share of Swiss banks include the safe haven characteristics of Switzerland and Swiss banks (no capital controls, stability of the banking system, and economic and political stability) as well as the existence of bank secrecy. Using data on external deposits in Switzerland disaggregated by origin, Christensen (1986) found evidence for the safe haven role of Switzerland.

Empirical evidence that banking secrecy plays a role in determining a country's market share in the international market for non-bank deposits was reported in Grilli (1989). In contrast to Grilli, Sheldon (1992), found no evidence for such effects but Camen (1992) argues that the loosening of banking secrecy in Switzerland since 1983 explains part of the reduction of the Swiss share in the market for external non-bank deposits.

Factors that appear to be of specific importance for explaining the decline in the Swiss market share since the early seventies include the capital control measures by the Swiss National Bank (SNB), and the deregulation of capital market in the eighties. To limit investments in Swiss francs by non-residents the SNB implemented three main measures in the seventies: a ban on interest payments, a commission charge (the so-called negative interest rate), and minimum reserve requirements. The drastic drop in the Swiss share in the market for non-bank deposits in the period 1971 to 1975 was largely the result of the implementation of these capital control measures in the years 1971 and 1972. The slight trend decline in the Swiss market share between 1975 and 1990 appears to be explained in part by from domestic factors such as the loosening of banking secrecy and in part by external developments. The external factors include the general deregulation of capital markets in industrial countries, especially the reduction of capital controls in several European countries.

---

[7] This conclusion is consistent with the finding by Grilli (1989) that the tax regime is important for explaining non-bank deposits.

## 3. International Bond Markets

### 3.1 The share of the Swiss bond market for foreign issues in the market for international bonds

The Swiss franc has been traditionally one of the most important currencies of denomination for bond issues in the international bond market. After the U.S. dollar, which had market shares that fluctuated between 40 percent and 60 percent, the Swiss franc held the second position in most years during the seventies and early eighties (**Figure 4A**)[8]. The share of Swiss franc bond issues peaked in 1979 when it reached 25 percent of total international bond issues.

During the eighties, however, the Swiss franc share declined strongly. In 1989 and 1990, it was less then 10 percent of bond issues in the international market. As a result, the shares of several currencies, including the Swiss franc, the Japanese yen, the Deutschmark and the Pound sterling, converged in the second half of the eighties so that neither one of them can be clearly identified as the second most important currency after the U.S. dollar. Another feature of the eighties is that the group of 'other' currencies gained an important market share which was largely due to the increased role of the ECU.

**Table 2** shows that outstanding Swiss franc international bonds consist exclusively of foreign bonds.[9] Euro-bonds denominated in Swiss franc have not been issued with the exception of one issue in 1963. The reason for this characteristic is that the SNB only approves foreign bond issues in Swiss francs if the financial institutions that underwrite an issue are located in Switzerland (Syndizierungsregel). This requirement in

---

[8] The data for figures 4 to 6 has been provided by the BIS.

[9] International bonds are generally disaggregated into Euro-bonds and foreign bonds. As a general rule bonds belong to the Euro-sector if they are issued through an international (in respect of ownership of the financial institution) syndicate of security houses. Foreign bonds are such if the issuer's country of residence does not correspond to the bond's currency of denomination. See Benzie (1992).

**FIGURE 4**

A) INTERNATIONAL BOND ISSUES BY CURRENCIES, IN % OF WORLD TOTAL

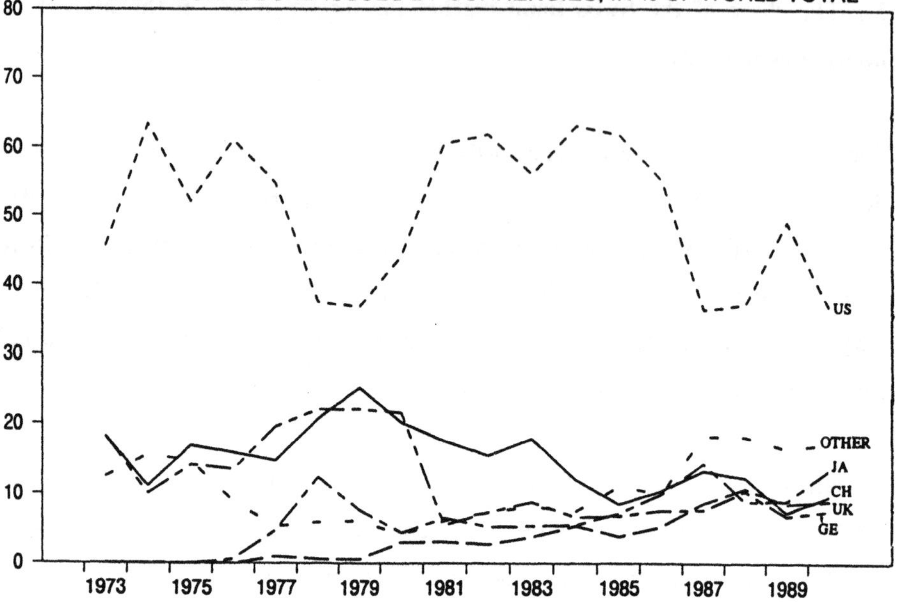


B) SFR INTERN. BONDS BY TYPE, IN %

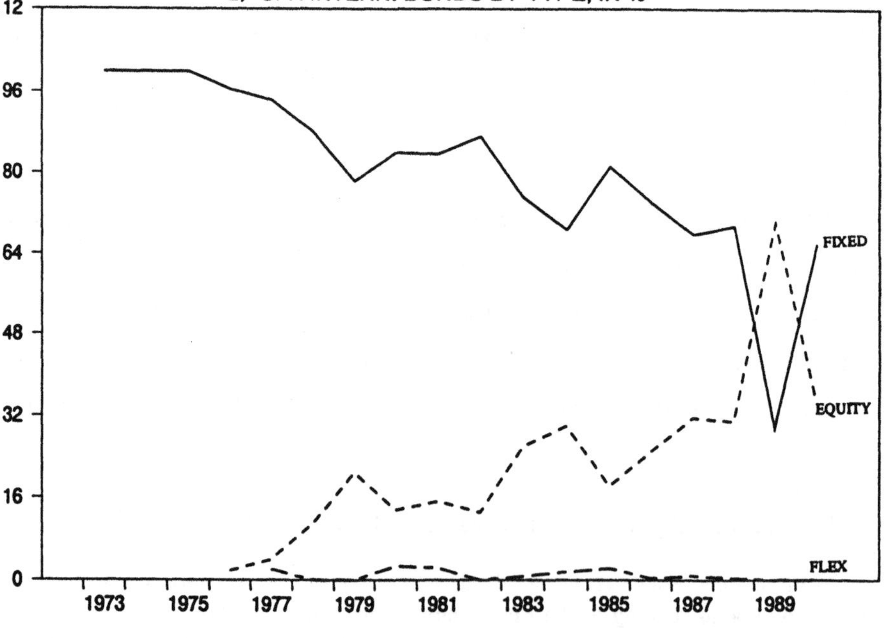

## Table 2

**The largest twenty-one currency sectors of the global bond market, end-1990**

Nominal value outstanding, billions of US dollars equivalent[1]

| Bond market | Total publicly issued | Domestic sector | | | | | | International sector | |
|---|---|---|---|---|---|---|---|---|---|
| | | Public sector | | | Private sector | | | | |
| | | Central govern-ment | Agency | State and local | Non-financial | Bank | Non-bank financial | Foreign | Euro |
| US dollar | 5,984.9 | 1,653.4 | 1,413.5 | 596.0 | 1,187.6 | 109.2 | 417.6 | 81.7 | 525.9 |
| Japanese yen | 2,576.9 | 1,163.6 | 387.2 | 143.3 | 212.0[2] | 502.8 | - | 52.1 | 115.9 |
| Deutsche Mark | 1,123.8 | 295.3 | 49.3 | 27.0 | 1.7 | 603.1 | - | 147.4 | |
| Italian lira | 759.4 | 594.0 | 23.1 | - | 4.3 | - | 123.5 | 0.5 | 14.0 |
| French franc | 487.3 | 152.5 | 213.6 | 4.4 | 87.8[2] | - | - | 1.5 | 27.5 |
| Pound sterling | 370.3 | 225.7 | - | 0.5 | 28.0[2] | - | - | 9.5 | 106.6 |
| Canadian dollar | 361.7 | 119.5 | - | 145.4 | 48.9[2] | - | - | 1.1 | 46.8 |
| Swiss franc | 271.1 | 8.8 | - | 11.4 | 28.3[2] | 30.9 | 16.4 | 175.3 | - |
| Belgian franc | 250.1 | 140.9 | 52.0 | 5.0 | 10.4 | 39.5 | - | 1.9 | 0.4 |
| Danish krone | 212.6 | 66.5 | - | - | 9.6 | - | 131.3 | 0.2 | 5.0 |
| Dutch guilder | 190.4 | 121.6 | - | 0.4 | 25.9[2] | 13.7 | 3.5 | 10.1 | 15.2 |
| Swedish krona | 174.7 | 40.9 | - | 0.9 | 10.4 | 4.6 | 115.8 | 0.1 | 2.0 |
| Australian dollar | 122.6 | 25.8 | - | 59.5 | 7.3 | - | 4.0 | 0.2 | 25.8 |
| Spanish peseta | 100.0 | 53.0 | 5.3 | 3.6 | 15.8 | 3.4 | 13.3 | 5.2 | 0.4 |
| Austrian schilling | 87.7 | 30.6 | 2.3 | 0.6 | 2.9 | 44.6 | - | 2.6 | 4.1 |
| Norwegian krone | 49.7 | 13.1 | 4.0 | 5.9 | 1.7 | 1.1 | 23.2 | 0.2 | 0.5 |
| Finnish markka | 33.3 | 7.9 | - | 0.5 | 6.5 | - | 16.5 | 0.2 | 1.7 |
| Irish pound | 23.5 | 23.3 | - | - | - | - | - | - | 0.2 |
| Luxembourg franc | 12.6 | - | - | - | - | - | - | 4.3 | 8.3 |
| New Zealand dollar | 11.3 | 7.8 | 1.1 | - | - | - | - | 0.1 | 2.3 |
| Ecu | 117.4 | 42.8[3] | - | - | - | - | - | - | 74.6 |
| Total | 13,321.3 | 4,787.0 | 2,151.4 | 1,004.4 | 1,689.1 | 1,352.9 | 865.1 | 1,471.4 | |

[1] All local currency figures are converted at end-1990 exchange rates. [2] Includes some issues made by financial sector entities. [3] Includes ecu-denominated CTEs, OATs and Bonos del Estado issued by the Italian, French and Spanish governments respectively.

Source: BIS (1991)

combination with a gentleman agreement between the SNB and other Central Banks has up till now effectively prevented financial institution that are not located in Switzerland from underwriting Swiss franc bond issues.[10] The requirement has been introduced by the SNB in order to control capital exports and in this way to prevent an internalization of the Swiss franc.

Considering only foreign bonds instead of overall international bonds the position of the share of Swiss franc issues even outperforms that of the U.S. dollar. Since the late seventies to the mid-eighties the share of the Swiss franc foreign bonds was larger than the U.S. dollar share making it to the most important currency of denomination for foreign bond issues. The Swiss franc share of foreign bond issues varied between 40 percent and 50 percent while the U.S. dollar share declined from about 50 percent in 1977 to 15 percent in 1985.[11]

The importance of Swiss franc foreign bonds in comparison to the market in domestic bonds can also be seen in **Table 2**. The value of outstanding foreign bonds in Swiss francs was almost double the value of domestic bonds at the end of 1990. Apart from Luxembourg, Switzerland is the only country where the value of outstanding foreign bonds is larger than the corresponding value of domestic bonds.

While the Swiss franc plays an important role in the international bond market issues of bonds in currencies other than Swiss francs by banks located in Switzerland are very few.[12] Consequently, the Swiss bond market for foreign issues is confined largely to Swiss franc issues.

---

[10] Benzie (1992), p.20, explains how a central bank can exert such a decisive influence over markets outside its jurisdiction.

[11] Christensen (1986).

[12] Christensen (1986).

### 3.2 The main characteristics of the Swiss franc foreign bond market

Two principle features can be noted with respect to the types of Swiss franc foreign bonds that are issued. A first feature is that most of the Swiss franc foreign bonds issues were straight fixed rate issues and that floating rate note issues played only a very minor role over the whole period under consideration (**Figure 4B**). Whereas the share of straight fixed rate issues was above 80 per cent in most years till the early eighties the share of floating issues was below 1 per cent. Currently, the share of straight fixed rate issues accounts for about 60 percent of Swiss franc foreign bond issues. The very minor role that floating rate notes have played in the Swiss franc market for bond issues is also reflected by the low market share of the Swiss franc in the market for floating rate notes (**Figure 6A**).

A second main feature is that the share of equity-related Swiss franc issues, which consists of convertible bonds and bond issues with equity warrants, increased substantially from about 2 per cent in 1975 to 34 per cent in 1990 while the share of straight fixed issues decreased (**Figure 4A**). The year 1989 was an exceptional year since the share of equity-related issues accounted for about 70 per cent of all business in the market for Swiss franc bond issues. This drastic shift in shares was brought about by a drastic decline (70 per cent) of new fixed rate issues and a massive increase (63 per cent) in the volume of equity related business.

The two features just noted are reflected also in the shares of fixed-rate and equity-related Swiss franc denominated issues in the international bond market. In fixed-rate issues the Swiss share declined from around 20 per cent (second place after the US dollar) in the seventies less then 10 per cent in recent years (fourth place). In equity related issues (**Figure 5b**) there has also been a decline but the Swiss franc still ranks second after the US dollar with a share fluctuating between 15 and 25 per cent.

The national origin of issuers of foreign bond issues in Switzerland has been rather stable with respect to the split up between OECD countries, developing countries and

## FIGURE 5

A) INTERN. FIXED RATE BOND ISSUES BY CURRENCIES, IN % OF WORLD TOTAL

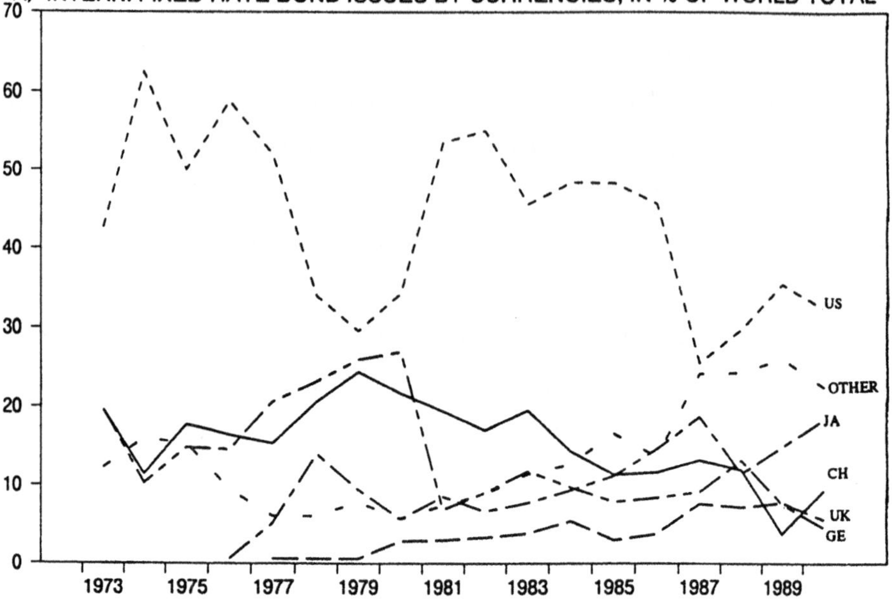


B) INTERN. EQUITITY-RELATED BOND ISSUES BY CURRENCIES, IN % OF WORLD TOTAL

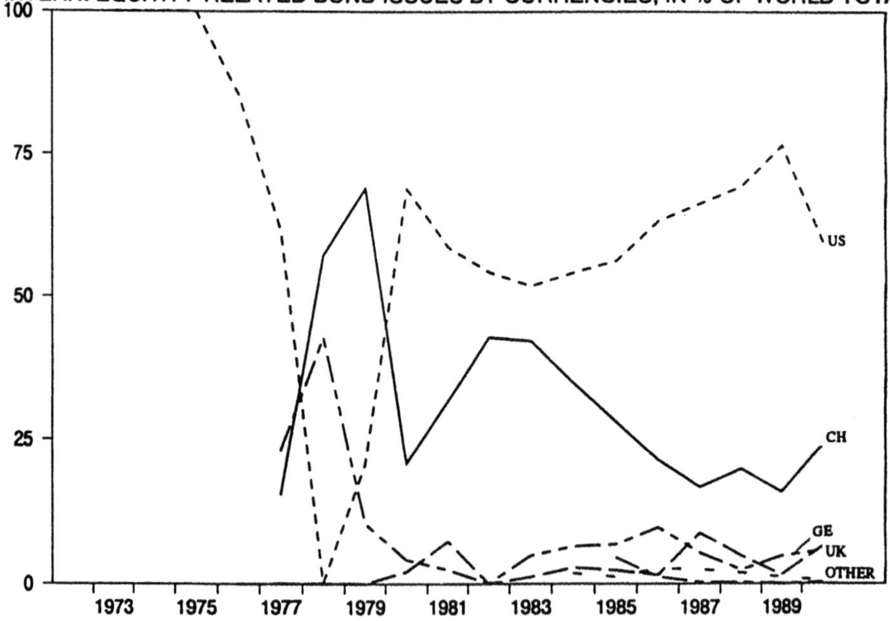

**FIGURE 6**

A) INTERN. FLEXIBLE RATE BOND ISSUES BY CURRENCIES, IN % OF WORLD TOTAL

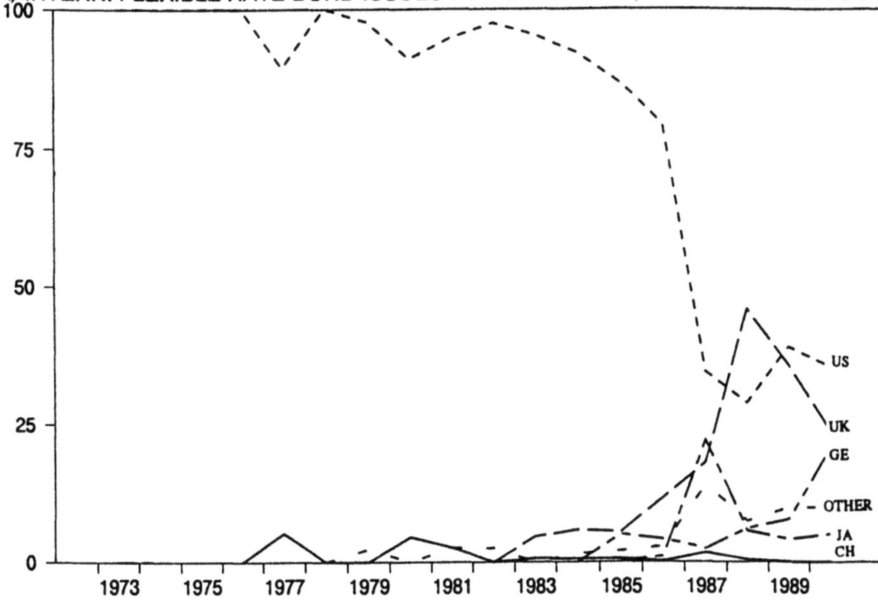

international organizations. While above 90 percent of the bonds are issued by borrowers from OECD countries only very few foreign bonds are issued in the Swiss bond market by borrowers from developing countries (**Table 3**). Borrowers from Japan are the issuers of the largest share in the Swiss foreign bond market with 42.5 percent in 1990 and even 69 percent in 1989. Even though the share of issuers from developing countries has been low, it has been suggested that the quality of foreign issues in the bond market has declined in recent years. This view seems to be confirmed by the increasing differential between the yield for foreign Swiss franc issues and the yield for domestic confederation bonds which can be taken as an indicator for the quality of foreign bond issues. Comparing the two rates it can be noted that since about 1988 the rate for foreign bonds increased more strongly creating a yield differential between the yields of the foreign and domestic bonds which reached 2.5 percent in 1990 and 2 percent in 1991 (**Figure 6A**).

### 3.3 Determinants of the share of Swiss franc foreign issues

The main features of the position of the Swiss franc in the international bond market that are to be explained include the historically large Swiss franc share in the international bond market and the trend decline of the Swiss market share throughout the eighties.

The sizeable market share of Swiss franc denominated foreign bond issues is generally mainly explained by the high placing power of Swiss financial institutions in Swiss francs. The high placing power is the result of the internationally high saving ratio in Switzerland and the sizeable foreign funds that Swiss financial institutions manage and which are partly reinvested in foreign bonds. A comparison of saving ratios for the main industrialized countries confirms that the Swiss ratio is one of the highest of the main OECD countries (**Figure 8**). In the seventies and eighties the Swiss saving ratio varied between 25 and 32 percent compared to the US ratio which fluctuated between 14.5 and 21 percent. Japan is one of the few countries whose saving ratio has been higher than the Swiss ratio.

## Table 3

## Foreign Bond Issues in Switzerland

*SF billion*

| *Borrowers:* | *1988* | *1989* | *1990* | *January-August 1990* | *January-August 1991* |
|---|---|---|---|---|---|
| *O E C D* | *36.5* | *29.1* | *30.0* | *21.3* | *20.0* |
| Australia | 1.3 | 0.3 | -- | -- | -- |
| Austria | 2.1 | 0.6 | 1.5 | 1.4 | 1.3 |
| Belgium | 0.7 | 0.1 | 0.1 | 0.1 | 0.3 |
| Canada | 1.8 | 0.1 | 2.1 | 1.7 | 1.0 |
| Denmark | 1.1 | 0.3 | 0.2 | 0.2 | 0.1 |
| Finland | 0.3 | 0.3 | 0.3 | 0.1 | 0.5 |
| France | 2.5 | 1.8 | 1.9 | 1.3 | 1.9 |
| Germany | -- | -- | 0.5 | -- | 1.4 |
| West Germany | 1.1 | 0.7 | 2.2 | 2.2 | -- |
| Ireland | 0.3 | -- | 0.2 | 0.2 | 0.3 |
| Italy | 1.2 | -- | 0.3 | 0.3 | 0.2 |
| Japan | 14.9 | 21.1 | 13.7 | 8.9 | 9.3 |
| Netherlands | 1.3 | 1.0 | 0.8 | 0.7 | 0.2 |
| New Zealand | 0.2 | 0.3 | 0.2 | -- | -- |
| Norway | 1.0 | 0.1 | -- | -- | -- |
| Portugal | 0.1 | -- | -- | -- | -- |
| Spain | 0.9 | -- | -- | -- | -- |
| Sweden | 1.0 | 0.3 | 0.6 | 0.5 | 0.5 |
| United Kingdom | 1.8 | 1.0 | 0.7 | 0.5 | 0.6 |
| United States | 1.1 | 0.3 | 2.6 | 1.6 | 1.6 |
| EEC institutions | 1.0 | 0.5 | 1.5 | 1.2 | 0.8 |
| Other OECD | 0.8 | 0.3 | 0.6 | 0.4 | -- |
| *DEVELOPING COUNTRIES* | *0.5* | *0.1* | -- | -- | *0.1* |
| *INT. DEV. ORGANISATIONS* | *0.8* | *1.3* | *2.2* | *1.4* | *0.9* |
| *OTHER* | *0.3* | *0.1* | -- | -- | *0.1* |
| TOTAL | 38.1 | 30.6 | 32.2 | 22.7 | 21.1 |
| *Quarterly data:* | | | | | |
| *Q1* | 12.7 | 7.2 | 12.0 | | 7.6 |
| *Q2* | 10.1 | 8.4 | 5.3 | | 7.7 |
| *Q3* | 8.2 | 7.2 | 7.5 | | |
| *Q4* | 7.1 | 7.8 | 7.4 | | |

Source: OECD (1991)

## FIGURE 7

A) SFR DOMESTIC AND FOREIGN BOND RATES

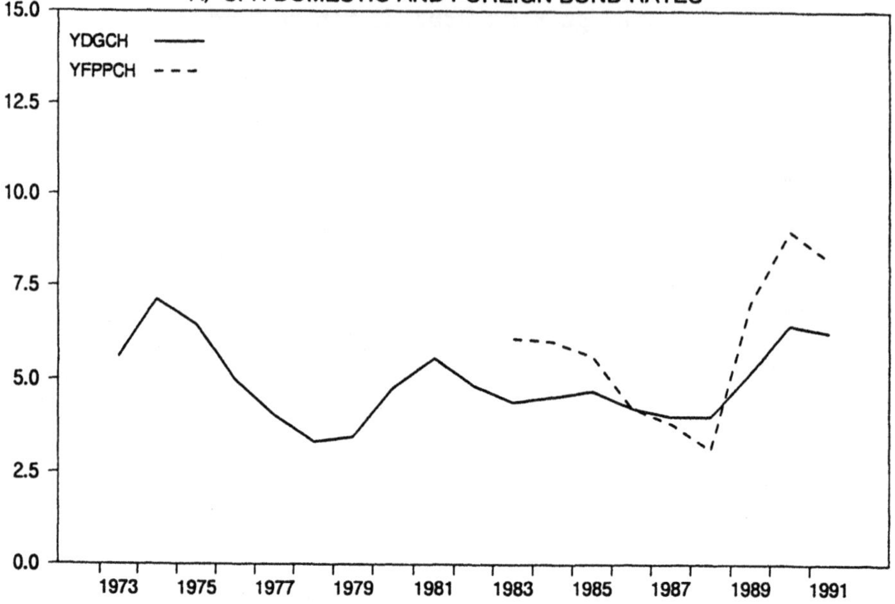


B) DOMESTIC GOVERNMENT BOND RATES, INDUSTRIALIZED COUNTRIES

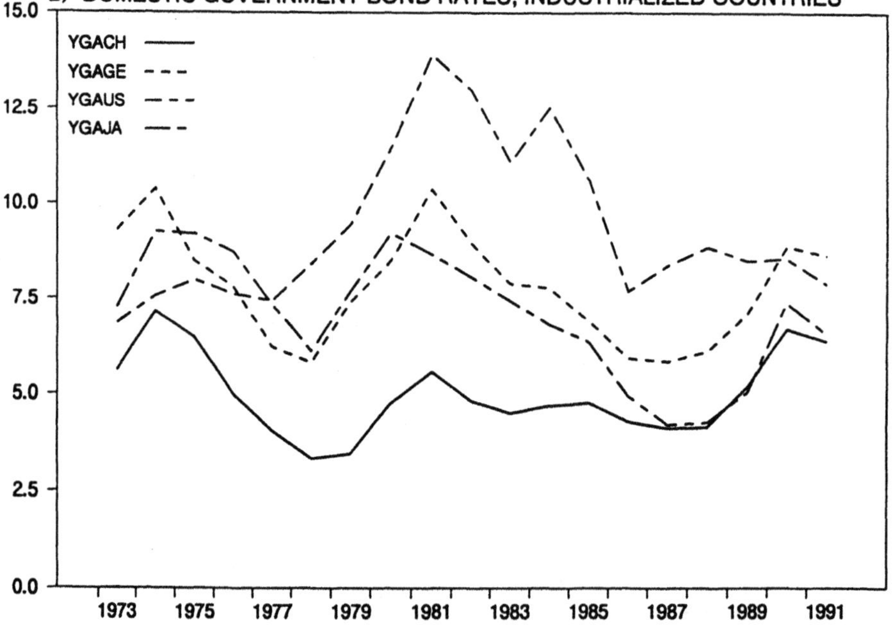

**FIGURE 8**

A) 3 MONTH EURO-SFR RATE AND SWISS GOVERNMENT BOND RATE

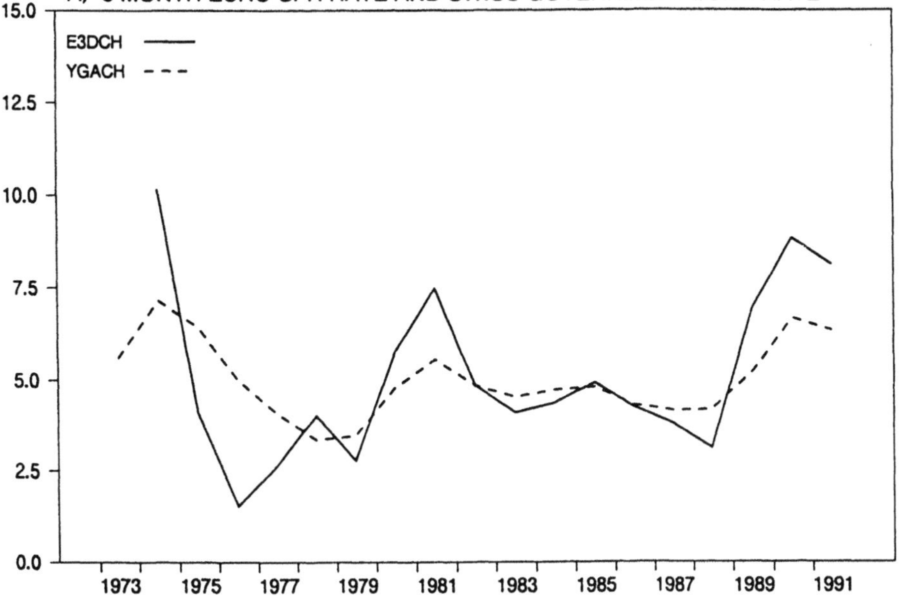


B) SAVINGS RATIO, IN % OF GNP/GDP

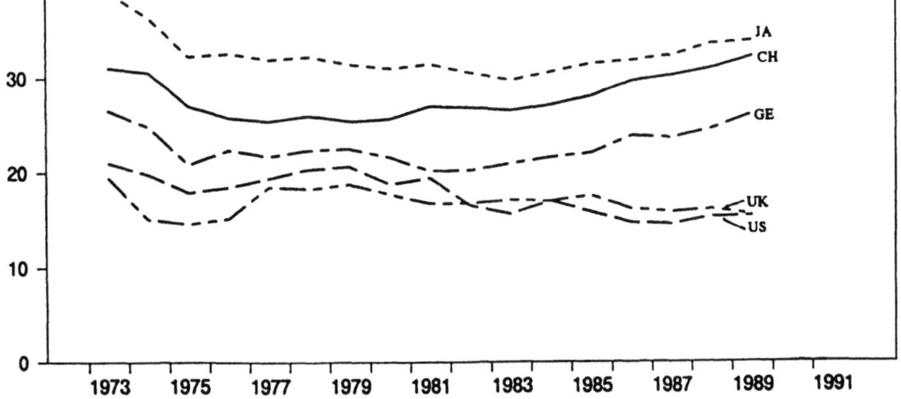

The second determinant that is important for explaining the high market share of Swiss franc foreign bonds in the international bond market is the traditionally low level of Swiss interest rates in comparison to interest rates in other industrialized countries as can be seen from **Figure 7B**. The interest advantage for foreign borrowers in Swiss franc was highest at the end of the seventies and early eighties when rates in the U.S. Japan and Germany increased more strongly then rates in Switzerland. In 1981 for example the rate for Swiss government bonds was about 6 percent compared to about 14 percent for U.S. government bonds. The widening of the interest differential between Swiss franc and U.S. dollar rates between 1977 and 1981 which made borrowing in Swiss franc cheaper is likely to be the most important factor that explains the increase in the share of the Swiss franc foreign bond issues over the same period.

Of course, the interest differential measures only the gross cost advantage of borrowing in Swiss francs. To get a measure of the net gains that arise with borrowing in Swiss francs several costs that a foreign borrower incurs by borrowing in Swiss franc have to be taken into account. One cost that turned out to be of importance for foreign borrowers in the seventies and eighties was the appreciation of the Swiss franc. The cost from an appreciation of the Swiss franc arises for the borrower when he repays the debt at the maturity of the bond. An estimate of the cost at the time of borrowing is given by the borrowers exchange rate expectations which are likely to differ depending on the borrowers domestic currency.

Issuer of Swiss franc foreign bonds can cover themselves against exchange risks by hedging the exchange rate risk through an exchange rate swap. Therefore many bond issues in Swiss francs have been combined with an exchange rate swap and in these cases swap rates in combination with bond yields become an important determinant of the supply of Swiss franc issues. But even when an exchange rate swap is used in combination with a bond issue the borrower incurs additional transaction costs which lower the interest advantage.

An other factor that increased the cost of borrowing in Swiss francs for foreign movements.[13] One of these measures required that issue proceeds had to be converted into foreign currency at the time of issue while repayment of the debt took place at current, generally appreciated, rate of exchange. This implied that the borrower ran the full exchange risk on Swiss franc denominated bonds from the very first day of issue. Although these capital control measures increased the real cost of borrowing by foreigners in Swiss francs they do not seem to have prevent a strong increase of the Swiss market share in the second half of the seventies.

In addition to the cost mentioned, foreigners who borrowed in Swiss francs incurred higher cost of issuance than in other currencies and they had to pay a stamp duty which is not required in most industrialized countries. The commission costs incurred by a borrower at the time of a Swiss franc issue varried according to the type of placement (private placement or public offering), the amount per issue, and the maturity. In 1987, the commission on a Sfr 100 million foreign straight bond issue with a maturity of 8 years was 2.75 percent excluding out-of-pocket expenses which could reach a maximum of Sfr 125,000.[14] In addition, the foreign borrower had to pay a stamp duty of .6 percent on the issue price.[15] The cost for issuing a Swiss franc foreign bond amounted to 3.05 percent compared to a cost of 2 to 2.5 percent in the Euro-bond markets.[16] An important part of this cost difference was due to the stamp duty which was either not used at all (New York and Luxembourg) or not applied to foreign securities (London).

Although these cost factors made it less advantageous to borrow in Swiss francs the interest advantage of borrowing in Swiss franc was large enough to more then offset these costs in the late seventies and early eighties. Later, however, the interest

---

[13] For an overview of policy measures by the Swiss National Bank in the seventies see OECD (1979).

[14] Binder (1989), p. 495.

[15] The investor has to pay in addition a stamp duty of .3 percent when the issue is placed.

[16] Gilbert and Fluri (1990).

advantage of borrowing in Swiss francs diminished substantially. In 1991, the yield differential between U.S. and Swiss government bonds diminished to 1.5 percent compared to 8.3 in 1981 and the difference between yields for Japanese and Swiss government bonds was reduced from 3.1 percent in 1981 to .2 percent in 1991. This reduction of the interest differential which increased the relative importance of the cost disadvantages of borrowing in Swiss francs is one potential explanation for the trend decline of the market share of Swiss franc foreign bonds in the eighties (Section 2.1).[17] The parallel movement of the market share of Swiss franc foreign bonds and interest differentials is consistent with the hypothesis that interest rate differentials are an important factor for explaining the share of Swiss franc foreign bonds.

The attractiveness of Swiss franc foreign bonds for investors is explained by factors such as economic and political stability of Switzerland, the strength of the Swiss franc, and the lack of the withholding tax on investments in foreign bonds. A factor that has been important in reducing the demand for Swiss franc bonds in recent years is the inversion of the Swiss yield curve. Since 1989 short-term Swiss interest rates have been higher than long-term rates favoring short-term investments (**Figure 8A**). Although the inverted yield curve likely had a negative impact on the demand for Swiss franc foreign bonds its impact is difficult to assess since little information is available on the demand side for Swiss franc foreign bonds. Factors that also contributed to reducing the demand for Swiss franc bonds are that Swiss savers became more sophisticated about the return on their placements and foreign investors no longer see an investment into the Swiss franc as sure hedge against exchange rate risk.[18]

The fact that bond issues denominated in Swiss francs are almost exclusively confined to issues of foreign bonds can be largely explained by the higher cost of issuance and the existence of the stamp duty in Switzerland. The higher costs give Swiss banks a

---

[17] According to information from Credit Suisse cost of issuance stayed constant since at least 1987. Only cost of issuance on Swiss franc issues by international development banks decreased slightly.

[18] Financial Times, December 17 1991.

disadvantage in comparison to other banks in the Euro-bond market. A comparison of the position of Swiss banks in the market for Swiss franc foreign issues and their position in the market for foreign issues denominated in currencies other than Swiss francs suggests that the position of Swiss banks in the former market is primarily explained by their monopoly in this market that arises from the requirement that only banks located in Switzerland can underwrite foreign issues denominated in Swiss francs.

### 3.4 The secondary market for bonds in Switzerland

The secondary market for bonds in Switzerland is known to be small and illiquid. Whereas data on transactions of Swiss franc bonds in Switzerland are not available, market makers report that transactions especially of bulk positions take place in London or in private trading.[19]

The illiquidity of the Swiss bond market can largely be attributed to the fact that Swiss investors generally keep top rated bonds in their portfolio until maturity and to the existence of the stamp duty. The stamp duty is levied on all capital transactions in which one of the parties is a securities dealer resident in Switzerland or Liechtenstein, and it is charged at the rate of 0.3 percent on foreign securities, and 0.15 percent on domestic securities if the period to maturity is longer than three months.[20] Since stamp duties are not at all levied on large transaction of over Sfr 1 million in other industrialized countries the existence of the stamp duty penalizes trading of securities in Switzerland. A recent comparison of brokerage fees for transactions in securities in main financial centers showed that fees charged in Switzerland are competitive to that of other financial centers.[21] This comparison confirms that the main cost disadvantage for trading securities in Switzerland arises from the existence of the stamp duty.

---

[19] Financial Times, December 17 1991,

[20] Witschi (1987).

[21] UBS (1991).

## 4. Concluding remarks: market shares of Swiss banks and changes in the regulatory and economic environment

A key difference of the positions of banks located in Switzerland in external non-bank deposits and international bond issues is due to the role of the Swiss franc in the respective markets. The position of Swiss banks in the market for external non-bank deposits is largely independent of the role of the Swiss francs in this market, whereas their position in the market for international bond issues is directly linked to the role of Swiss franc foreign issues in this market since banks located in Switzerland have a monopoly in issuing Swiss franc foreign bonds.

Mainly due to this difference, the determinants of the market shares of Swiss banks in the two markets are not the same. While institutional and regulatory factors play a role in both markets, they do so in different ways. The decisive factors in attracting external non-bank deposits to Switzerland have been the lack of the withholding tax on fiduciary accounts, bank secrecy, and the stability of the Swiss banking system. In the case of bond issues, higher commission fees and the stamp duty lower the attractiveness of bond issues and trading in Switzerland, whereas the requirement by the Swiss National Bank that only financial institutions located in Switzerland can underwrite Swiss franc foreign bonds has created an effective monopoly for banks in Switzerland. Tax advantages on foreign bonds also play a role in attracting investors.

As was shown in the previous sections of this paper, economic factors that determine the allocation of funds across currencies such as interest differentials and exchange rate expectations have not played an important role in determining the share of Swiss banks in the market for external non-bank deposits. In contrast they are crucial in determining the share of Swiss franc foreign bond issues in the market for international bonds. Specifically, interest differentials, yield curves, and exchange rate expectations that determine the value of the Swiss franc have been important.

How are changes in the regulatory and economic environment are going to influence the position of Swiss banks in the foreseeable future? Although Swiss EEA membership has been rejected in a popular vote in December 1992, the impact which it would have had on the position of Swiss banks in the two markets considered is still of interest since the deregulation process which is likely to take place in Switzerland in the future will be largely modelled according to the practice in EC countries.

Since Switzerland has had a liberalized system with respect to external deposits and credits, the regulatory changes required for the EEA membership would not have influenced the regulatory environment with respect to activities of Swiss banks in the international markets for external deposits.[22] Swiss EEA membership would, however, have required changes in regulations governing foreign bond issues in Swiss francs. One important regulation has recently been made compatible with the practice in EC countries although Switzerland does not participate in the EEA. Before April 1, 1993 the approval of a foreign bond issue in Swiss francs required that the financial institutions underwriting an issue were located in Switzerland (Syndizierungsregel). This requirement was not compatible with the liberalized system of capital flows in the EEA.[23] Since April 1, 1993 the 'Syndizierungsregel' has been replaced by the requirement that only the lead manager of an issue has to be a bank that is located in Switzerland ('Verankerungsprinzip').[24] With this change the SNB follows the practice in Germany and England. The change was made possible since the Bundesrat decided that a stamp duty is not anymore levied on foreign bond issues in Swiss franc after April 1.

Other measures related to Swiss franc foreign bond issues had already been implemented in recent years. At the end of 1990, several conventions agreed between

[22] EEA membership would have modified the procedures required to implement emergency measures to control capital imports; see Breining-Kaufmann and Merz (1992).

[23] Zwahlen (1992); Breining-Kaufmann and Merz (1992). The required approval was not compatible with the practice in EC countries since control of capital exports is only applicable in situations of emergencies.

[24] See revised Article 8 of the Bankengesetz.

members of the Swiss Bankers Associations have been abolished or modified. Although competition between the main Swiss banks in the Swiss bond market seems to have been little affected up till now by these changes, there are increased signs that the competitive environment in this market has changed.[25]

The abolition of the 'Syndizierungsregel' and the stamp duty on foreign bond issues will further change the competitive environment in the Swiss franc foreign bond market. While the abolition of the 'Syndizierungsregel' exposes financial institutions located in Switzerland to more competition by eliminating their monopoly in the Swiss franc foreign bond market the parallel abolition of the stamp duty helps these institutions to gain competitiveness. The role of the Swiss franc in the international bond markets will largely depend on whether Swiss interest rates remain lower than interest rates in other industrialized countries to conserve the interest advantage of borrowing in Swiss francs. According to a recent study even a Swiss membership in the EEA would not have affected the interest differential of Switzerland vis-à-vis other European countries.[26] Further research is required, however, before conclusions can be drawn whether the Swiss interest advantage will be conserved in the medium term. Such research would have to explain the lower cost of borrowing in Swiss franc and specifically analyze the question whether saving behavior has changed in Switzerland over the last years.

---

[25] Euromoney, May 1992.

[26] Arbeitskreis Kapital und Wirtschaft (1992).

**Literature**

Andrist, F. and Schlup, Th. (1990), Das Auslandsgeschäft der Banken 1975 - 1989, Volkswirtschaft, Mai 1990.

Arbeitskreis Kapital und Wirtschaft (1992), Bedroht der EWR die Zinsinsel Schweiz? Sriftenreihe Rahmenbedingungen, Zürich.

Benzie, R. (1992), The Development of the International Bond Market, Bank for International Settlement Economic Paper No. 32, January, Basel.

Binder, E. (1989), The Swiss Franc Bond Market, in: The European Bond Commission, The European Bond Markets. An Overview and Analysis for Issuers and Investors, Chicago, Ill.: Probus Publishing Company.

BIS (1991), International Banking and Financial Market Developments, May, Basel.

Breining-Kaufmann, Ch. and Merz, P. (1992), Auswirkungen des freien Kapitalverkehrs im EWR-Vertrag, Aktuelle Juristische Praxis, 10.

Bridel, P. (1984), Essai d'estimation de la part suisse à l'activité financière internationale 1975-1983, Geld, Währung, und Konjunktur.

Camen, U. (1992), The Swiss Position in the International Market for Non-Bank Deposits, in: Blattner, N., Genberg, H., and Swoboda, A. (Eds.), Competitiveness in Banking, Heidelberg: Physica-Verlag.

Christensen, B. V. (1986), Switzerland's Role as an International Financial Center, IMF, Occasional Paper 45, July, Washington.

The Economist, September 15, 1990.

Euromoney, May 1992.

Financial Times, various issues, London.

Gilbert, A. R. and Fluri, R. (1990), The International Bond Market: Why is the Market in Switzerland so large? unpublished paper.

Grilli, V. (1989), Financial Markets, Economic Policy, October.

OECD (1991), Financial Market Trends No. 50, October, Paris.

OECD (1979), Financial Market Trends No. 10, June, Paris.

Sheldon, G. (1992), Explaining the Cross-Country Distribution of International Bank

Deposits, in: Blattner, N., Genberg, H. and Swoboda, A. (Eds.), Competitiveness in Banking, Heidelberg: Physica-Verlag.

SNB (1990), Statistische Erhebungen and Informationen, Zürich.

UBS (1991), UBS International Finance, Winter 1991.

Witschi, D. (1987), Swiss Money Market in Transition, in: Swiss Bank Corporation, Economic and Financial Prospects no. 6.

Zwahlen, J. (1992), La place financière suisse et la politique monètaire face au processus d'intégration européenne, conférence publique organisée par le Centre International d'Etudes Monétaires et Bancaires à l'Institut Universitaire de Hautes Etudes Internationales (HEI), Genève le 26 novembre 1992.

## 5. Annex: Main sources for statistics on bank deposits and credits and their differences.

Three main sources for data on banking activities exist in Switzerland[27]: the end-of-year statistic (Jahresendstatistik), the monthly account (Monatsbilanz), and the euro-currency statistic (Eurodevisenstatistik)[28]. Since these three banking statistics differ in important ways the data provided by each of these statistics is not directly comparable.

One main difference between these statistics is that they are either based on balance sheets of banks located in Switzerland and Liechtenstein or on consolidated balance sheets taking into account foreign branches of Swiss banks[29]. Other important differences are the number of banks and financial institutions which are included in the sample, the frequency with which data are collected, and whether the statistic includes fiduciary accounts. The distinction between domestic and foreign bank activities is generally made according to the domiciliary principle. A bank activity is classified as domestic or foreign depending on the domicile of the bank's creditor or debtor.

The end-of-year statistic is the most comprehensive banking statistic that is available for Switzerland in terms of the number of banks and financial institutions included and

---

[27] For detailed information see SNB (1990).

[28] The end-of-year banking statistic is published in the annual publication 'Das schweizerische Bankwesen im Jahre ...' by the Swiss National Bank. The monthly account is presented in the Swiss National Bank's Monthly Report. The Euro-currency statistics have been until now only be published in an aggregated form by the BIS. Starting in September 1990 parts of the Euro-currency statistic will be published by the Swiss National Bank in a supplement to the Monthly Report.

[29] Swiss banking statistics are either based (i) on balance sheets of domestic and foreign banks and financial institutions located in Switzerland and Liechtenstein (inländische Bankstellen), (ii) on balance sheets of banks as under (i) that, however, have been consolidated to include legally dependent branches abroad (Unternehmung), or (iii) on consolidated balance sheets that take into account in addition to branches abroad also subsidiaries abroad (Konzern). Banking institutions in Liechtenstein are considered domestic institutions since the end of 1984 in accordance with the treaty between the Swiss Confederation and Liechtenstein of June 19, 1980.

the depth of information. Its statistics summarize the banking activities of all banks and financial institutions in Switzerland (626 institutions). The main characteristics of the end-of-year statistic are that it is based on the consolidated balance sheets of banks in Switzerland, i.e. activities of branches of Swiss banks abroad are included, and that it reports information on fiduciary accounts.

Monthly accounts are based since 1984 on the reporting of all banks with a balance sheet total of 100 million Swiss francs and more which amounts currently to 353 banks. Financial institutions are not taken into account in the monthly accounts. In contrast to the end-of-year statistic the monthly account is not only compiled on the basis of banks' consolidated balance sheets including branches but also on the basis of balance sheets of banks located in Switzerland. A separate monthly statistic is published for fiduciary accounts.

The Euro-currency statistic is compiled quarterly and based on the reporting of currently 146 banks. The statistics are compiled using the balance sheets of banks located in Switzerland and Liechtenstein. In contrast to the end-of-year statistic and the monthly accounts this statistic does not report data on fiduciary accounts. Data on deposits and credits for the euro-currency statistic is collected disaggregated by country of origin but the data is only published in an aggregated form.

How does the data published in Swiss banking statistics form the basis of the data reported by the International Monetary Fund (IMF) and the Bank for International Settlement (BIS). The assets and liabilities of Swiss banks' reported by the IMF are the statistics compiled by the SNB in the monthly accounts on the basis of the balance sheets of banks located in Switzerland. Fiduciary transactions are included in the Fund's statistics. The banking statistics of the BIS are based on the euro-currency statistics collected by the SNB. The difference between the banking statistics of the IMF and that of the BIS are therefore similar to those between the monthly account and the euro-currency statistic. An important difference between the two statistic until the 3rd quarter of 1989 was that the BIS statistics did not take into account fiduciary transactions. In December 1989 this has been changed and BIS statistics now also include fiduciary accounts.

**Comment on**

**Ulrich Camen: "The Swiss Share in International Markets for Bank Deposits and Bonds"**

**Pascal Bridel**

Eight years ago, when I produced what I think was the first paper making an estimate of the Swiss share in international banking, I solemnly promised myself never, ever, to grapple with this topic again.

At that particular time, however, I was benefiting from nearly five years of regular meetings of the BIS Euro-currency standing committee: clearly, one of the best observation posts for monitoring international banking and financial market developments.

Despite, and maybe because of, my comparative advantage over academic researchers, I encountered nightmarish problems in searching for decent statistical series and, above all, trying to solve frustrating analytical problems linked with the idea of market share left me with very bad memories. It was thus not without some trepidation that I agreed to make a few comments on Ulrich Camen's paper.

Coming back to the scene of the crime, I find things pretty much unchanged. Camen reaches conclusions not very dissimilar to mine but, of course, very much updated. I completely agree with his many notes of caution on the data and his broad conclusions:

- the crucial importance of the non-bank deposits (held mainly in foreign currencies[1]);

- the shift towards fiduciary accounts (though these series can be extremely erratic, notably on a monthly basis);

---

1 This peculiarity raises some awkward valuation problems; exchange rate fluctuations (particularly vis-à-vis the dollar) can send very misleading signals in terms of market shares of non-bank deposits in Switzerland relative to those in other financial centres.

- the fact that economic 'fundamentals' play second fiddle to international and regulatory factors in the determination of the Swiss market share for non-bank deposits. In the light of the recent jumpiness of the Swiss Franc, this should be very good news, particularly for private bankers;

- the (decreasing) importance of the Swiss share in the international bond market and the fact that the bond market for foreign issues in Switzerland is for all practical purposes confined to Swiss Franc issues;

- these features are the result of the existence of the stamp duty and the higher transaction costs besides, of course, the Swiss National Bank requirements.

My appetite was very much whetted by Camen's subtitle 3.4 on the secondary market for bonds in Switzerland. I was however disappointed by its content. Aren't there any other reasons than the stamp duty to explain the smallness and the illiquidity of this market?

At this juncture, I would like to make two very general comments on Camen's broad methodology followed by two factual remarks on the possible evolution of the market for Swiss Franc foreign issues.

1. Consider first the very idea of market share. Camen's paper strengthens my conviction that this idea - to use Aloys Schwieter's own words - "is very old fashioned and is hardly suitable to appreciate the international competitiveness of a financial/banking system". Even if we accept Haegler and Jeger's argument that there is a simple causal relationship running from size to cost efficiency in the banking industry, it is clearly too simple industrial economics to judge the international importance and competitiveness of the Swiss banking system by the size of its shares in very broadly defined types of business. What is the point of being big if, for example, the return on assets, the return on equity and/or the value added are miserable. Clearly, my understanding of Haegler and Jeger's contribution on the performance of Swiss banks should encourage us to stop simply watching the vagaries of a rather non-descript aggregate (the market-share) and to start afresh with a more market-segmented approach. Market shares and market power are obviously very different in traditional international banking deposits as opposed to off-balance sheet fiduciary activities.

A connection between these different types of international activities and the proportion of foreign operations within the total balance sheets of various institutions should also go some way towards explaining the growth-trend of the share of Swiss banks relative to the overall international market (or, better, relative to some of its segments). The evolution of the Swiss market shares in parts of international banking is clearly not independent from what is going on at home.

2. My second comment is also linked to this necessity to disaggregate, to segment, this market-share approach. It is more a query than a comment. In a recent special report[2] on Derivative Financial Instruments, the Bank for International Settlements sent a shiver down my spine by drawing our attention (for the first time in print) to the size of a problem I was only dimly aware of:

> "As a proportion of the international assets of BIS reporting banks, the identified outstanding notional volume of derivative contracts on interest rates and currencies rose from around 25 % at end-1986 to nearly 75 % at end-1990 ...
>
> Activity in the futures markets has also complemented or displaced more traditional forms of banking activity. The ratio of open positions in Euro-dollar contracts to the outstanding dollar-denominated interbank assets of BIS reporting banks rose from less than 15 % at end-1987 to 40 % at end-1991.
>
> ... The increasingly important role of derivatives in banks' business is reflected, for example, in the ratio of the notional value of off-balance-sheet activity (including non-derivative products) to on-balance-sheet assets, which a few US banks reported in their published financial accounts as exceeding 700 % last year." (pp. 15-16)

This type of growth rate is certainly worth watching; and I wonder if, in view of such an evolution, a basic analysis in terms of shares of international inter-bank market as an aggregate should not undergo some drastic revision.

---

2 Bank for International Settlements (BIS), International Banking and Financial Market Developments, Basle, May 1992, pp. 15-27.

We return now to two factual remarks on the foreign bonds market.

1. On two occasions, Camen mentions what Blattner has nicely dubbed in his address "the pretty old fashioned requirement that only banks located in Switzerland are allowed to underwrite foreign bonds denominated in Swiss francs". Blattner goes even as far as to consider these requirements a sort of monopoly. Camen is also puzzled by this regulation that he, quite rightly, sees as having been introduced to avoid during the Seventies an excessive internationalisation of the Swiss franc. This rather quaint regulation is in fact technically no monopoly. The SNB, though powerful some people wish it to be, is powerless to forbid bonds in Swiss francs being floated outside its jurisdiction. This requirement is simply the result of a gentlemen's agreement passed in the early Seventies between the major Central Banks (the Fed excepted). Basically, these Banks agreed to use 'moral suasion' to "discourage" foreign bonds in currencies others than theirs to be underwritten within their jurisdiction. Switzerland is thus no particular exception. Discussions and 'exchanges of views' are currently going on between European Central Banks to assess if this gentlemen's agreement is still compatible with EEC free circulation of capital rules. Were it not, and should the European Central Banks be forced to drop this long standing agreement, the so-called monopoly of Swiss banks for foreign bonds in Swiss francs would be seriously dented; and Camen's time series would undergo some very sharp jolts.

2. In section 3.3 (including in particular **Figure 7B**), Camen discusses inter alia the role of nominal interest rate differentials as determinants of the share of Swiss franc foreign issues. In view of recent developments with inflation differentials, and despite the well-known high Swiss saving ratio and low level of interest, I wonder if the results obtained by Camen would not be altered more than marginally if real interest rates were considered.

I am clearly no specialist in banking economics but these two last remarks - though of a highly speculative nature - might well prove to be of some relevance soon. The interpretation of Camen's main results could thus undergo some very radical changes.

Finally, coming back to my main comments on the very idea of market share, Camen's paper confirms the prejudices I have entertained against that idea ever since my own 1984 paper. Prejudices can, of course, always be revised but it will take some very strong arguments to convince me that this notion can be used as a performance index to assess the international competitiveness of Swiss banks in various types of business.

The micro, industrial economics approach has, in my opinion, to come to the rescue[3] here. In particular, the Pagano criteria frequently mentioned during this conference could well be brought into Camen's picture. I am, however, glad not to have been asked to reconcile these two approaches. It will have to be done and the sooner the better.

3 Recent ventures into banking economics by some of the leading theorists in industrial economics are, of course, very promising. See in particular Tirole's 1992 Walras-Pareto Lectures.

# Part V: The Swiss Financial Sector at the Turn of the Century

# Banking Policy and Regulation in Switzerland: Summary and Implications of Two Years of Research

Niklaus Blattner, Hans Genberg, Alexander Swoboda

## 1. Introduction

The issues that are dealt with in the contributions to this volume can be aptly illustrated by two headlines: the most recent publication of the OECD Committee on Financial Markets carries the title 'Banks under Stress' (OECD, 1992), and The Economist's 'A Survey of World Banking' (May 2, 1992) is summarised on its cover by a dark painting of lost bankers on their way out through a revolving door, the whole piece of art entitled 'Time to Leave'.

Both publications deal with banking in general and only rarely refer to Switzerland. If Swiss banks are mentioned at all, the comparisons are usually favourable. This ought not reassure us too much, however. Economic history teaches that there is no such thing as an unassailable market position. This applies to every business, banking clearly included. Consider **Table 1** of the world's top ten banks (in terms of capital). In 1990 one finds five Japanese banks, none of which was listed in 1980. In 1990 one also finds a Swiss bank among the top ten, which was not the case a decade earlier. (The Economist, op. cit.) Those banks that dropped out probably did not envisage that possibility while they were still at the top. Similarly, a number of factors may cause banks that are considered strong today to look weaker tomorrow.

Some of these factors are linked to the reactions of the banks themselves to the current pervasive trend to keener competition in markets everywhere, as well as to the prevailing rapid technological change in the industry. Another set of factors relates to the regulatory environment which determines the options open to a given country's banks. A third set of factors, finally, encompasses the many influences which determine the competitiveness of a financial center and thus indirectly the banks which operate out of this center.

In the OECD report mentioned before, five strategic choices are identified that have to be made by banks and which are likely to affect their competitive position significantly:

- "diversification ('multipurpose banking') versus specialisation ('niche playing');
- consolidating home market positions versus further expansion abroad;
- product-orientation versus distribution or client-orientation;
- own establishment versus merger or acquisition, joint venture, or cooperation agreements;
- large versus medium or small-scale operations."(OECD, 1992, p. 16)

The same source lists several types of financial regulations, ranging from the restriction of market forces and prudential regulation (with the aim of preventing systemic risks), to the prevention of individual risks (in the sense of depositor and investor protection), and ending with the promotion of systemic efficiency (meaning competition policy including the regulation of mergers and acquisitions). (OECD, 1992, p. 33) Additionally, it is important to mention tax policies such as stamp taxes on financial transactions, legal issues like bank secrecy, and "structural" issues like the existence of a qualified work force which in principle also affect the attractiveness of a financial centre to banks.

Starting in the spring of 1990, research on these themes was carried out by teams at Basel (FAI) and Geneva (ICMB) as part of a project financed by the Fonds National Suisse de la Recherche Scientifique (FNRS) within the National Research Programme No. 28. The discussion that follows is based primarily on the output of this research. The first part was published earlier in a volume entitled 'Competitiveness in Banking' (Blattner, Genberg, Swoboda, 1992), and the remainder is contained in the present volume.

In what follows the above mentioned three groups of reasons for changes in the competitive position of banks and financial centres, namely the firms' own strategic choices, the regulatory environment, and other structural factors, will be used as an organising framework for an assessment of what can be learned from recent research about some of the crucial banking policy issues and about the strengths and weaknesses of banking and finance in Switzerland.

## 2. Performance of the Swiss Banking Sector

### 2.1. Profitability

During the 1980s, the Swiss banking sector as a whole performed very well in comparison with those of the USA, Japan, and Germany. Bossard, Wirth, and Blattner (1992, pp. 85-8) found that Swiss banks fared well with respect to return on assets, excelled in financial intermediation, provided their services at highly competitive interest margins, outperformed the competition in terms of unit costs, and offered safety to their customers by maintaining the highest capital ratio. Several of these findings were recently confirmed by the OECD (1992, pp. 128-37) for a wider sample including France and the United Kingdom. (**Table 2**)

This satisfactory picture is based on aggregate data which are not always exactly comparable across countries. The results should therefore be interpreted with caution and not be a source of complacency. An adequate performance in the aggregate can for example hide variations both across individual banks as well as across time. To get a more complete picture it is thus necessary to investigate disaggregated data for individual banks. Wirth (1993) uses information from balance sheets and profit and loss accounts for some 450 Swiss banks to compute various measures of performance such as the traditional return on equity, return on assets and productivity as well as the more recently developed indicator Added Value/Input Costs. (**Table 3**) From the point of view of making comparisons between banks with different specialisation and, especially, between banks and non-bank establishments, it can be argued that the last measure is the most adequate. In principle, a positive value of this measure indicates super-normal profits, i.e. economic rents. This is due the substraction of the opportunity costs of the own capital from profits, where the opportunity costs are measured by the interest rate for Federal Government bonds. A negative value, on the other hand, suggests that it would have been preferable to invest the capital of the bank elsewhere: in another bank, in a different industry, or simply in government bonds. Against this interpretation it is noteworthy that Wirth's data indicate that the number of banks with negative Added Value/Input Costs increased from slightly over ten percent in 1987 to just under forty percent in 1990. (**Table 4**)

Before these results rouse alarmist conclusions about the health of the Swiss banking industry, a number of caveats should be kept in mind. First, the usual reservations about the quality of the data apply. Secondly, entry or exit decisions cannot reasonably be taken on the basis of one indicator only and with a horizon of only five years. Finally, more should be known about the underlying causes of the measured performance differences among firms and over time.

Haegler, Jeger (1993) address the last of these issues. Their objective is to explain the variation across time and across individual banking establishments in the performance measures calculated by Wirth. Basing their work on the economic theory of industrial organisation, they derive an equation in which performance is explained by balance-sheet variables (intended to capture the structure of the bank's business) on the one hand, and industrial variables ( e.g. market share, size) on the other. Using conventional regression analysis they were able to uncover significant and relevant distinctions between banks. For example, banks more active in the traditional business of financial intermediation must be distinguished from those more actively engaged in off-balance-sheet activities. Furthermore, stock exchange membership, which implies even more pronounced specialisation, makes a difference for profitability.

On the basis of their findings, the authors argue that there is considerable evidence of positive effects of specialisation. Specialisation seems to breed specific returns. In relative terms, off-balance-sheet banks are outperforming more traditional institutions in off-balance-sheet activities. Banks more heavily engaged in financial intermediation are more successful in this activity than their competitors specialised in the off-balance-sheet business. In addition, stock exchange membership leads to even higher returns from off-balance-sheet activities.

The lesson from the Haegler-Jeger study appears to be that specialisation leads to improved profitability, confirming the basic message of standard trade theory which teaches us the benefits of specialization according to comparative advantage. But, as argued by for instance Porter (1990, pp. 16-21), the problem is not only more complex but also more interesting than it appears at first sight because comparative advantage is not exogenous, neither for nations as a whole nor for individual banks. The management of any bank first has to answer the following question: where and in what respect can it develop comparative advantages most efficiently? From this follows the location chosen, i.e. the financial centre selected, the amount and kind of investment in human capital, the products supplied and the production technology installed, the size of operations envisaged, realised either through internal growth or through mergers and acquisitions, the marketing strategy deemed necessary, etc. Looked at it in this way, a given specialisation is the logical consequence of the shaping of a bank's comparative advantages by its own management. In the light of this, the proper prescription is not: specialise, and you will prosper! but rather: develop your comparative advantages efficiently in order to make specialisation succeed! Interpreting the results of Haegler, Jeger in this way we find that banks in Switzerland in general prepare their strategies well, since estimates show that specialisation leads to above average performance.

## 2.2. Cost efficiency

Successful cost control is widely accepted as one of the urgent requirements for a reduction of what the OECD (1992, p. 127) calls the 'financial fragility' in banking, meaning "a deterioration of banks' balance sheets as a result of lower asset quality and lower net earnings." Swiss banks are not those most affected by this phenomenon. In an international comparison, they are even considered to be among the best at managing costs. Nevertheless, the Swiss banks' operating expenses still fluctuate just below 60 % of gross income. Or, put otherwise, a reduction of costs by 10 percent would, cet. par., increase the share of profits before tax by almost 6 percentage points, which would mean a considerable improvement. (For the data, see OECD, 1992, p. 132)

The OECD study also points out that aggregate data might mask quite important differences in cost efficiency among banks. The OECD refers to Berger, Humphrey (1990) who "show that, in the United States, these differences are substantial and conclude that inadequate cost control has been an important cause of the financial strains presently experienced by a number of US banks." (OECD, 1992, p. 129)

What can be said about differences in cost efficiency among banks in Switzerland? A bank is cost inefficient either if it utilises more factors of production than technologically required - a case of 'technical inefficiency' - or if it uses production factors in a proportion unwarranted by relative factor prices - 'allocative inefficiency'. A reduction in cost inefficiency permits either an increase of production without an increase in costs, or a reduction of costs at a constant level of a bank's output.

Sheldon, Haegler (1993) apply these concepts to the data for banks in Switzerland. Their findings are similar to those for the USA. Although technical efficiency is rather high, allocative efficiency is much lower. On the whole, estimated cost efficiency is at 57 percent. This means that banks in Switzerland could reduce noticeably the costs of producing the given output, or, under conditions of constant returns to scale, considerably expand output at given costs.

A further result of the Sheldon, Haegler study is that cost efficiency varies considerably among banks. The larger the bank, the more cost efficient it is. The threat of inefficiency is strongest for the smaller banks, therefore. Note the difficulty in determining the causality in the relationship between size and cost efficiency implied by these results. One way of interpreting the results would consist of saying that a bank can increase cost efficiency simply by growing. It is, however, not clear what mechanism would be responsible for such an association. An alternative, perhaps more convincing, explanation for the empirical finding is that only those banks that have their costs under control can grow.

Economies of scale and scope do not appear to be important when estimated with data for Switzerland, again a result similar to those obtained with US data. Sheldon and Haegler found that scale advantages are exhausted at relatively low levels of output, and estimates of economies of scope do not show a clear pattern.

One of the intriguing issues raised by the results in the aforementioned studies is whether a banking industry like the Swiss one, consisting of very heterogenous members of all size-classes can be stable despite considerable differences among different establishments in cost efficiency. A possible answer to this puzzle suggested by Sheldon and Haegler is that inefficiency and scale-related cost advantages tend to offset each other. An alternative explanation is that the market structure of the Swiss banking industry did not represent a sustainable equilibrium during the years covered by the empirical work, i.e. 1987-90. Recall that, apart from 1990, these years were comparatively good years for the Swiss banking sector. Perhaps this generally favourable environment allowed inefficient firms to maintain operations while efficient firms enjoyed above-normal returns. If so, the observed deterioration of the performance of banks from 1987 to 1990 might be a harbinger of difficult years to come for certain segments of the sector provoked by steeply increasing competitive pressures originating both at home and abroad.

Earlier research findings had already suggested that competition might be increasing in the Swiss financial sector. Genberg, Helbling, Neftci (1992) argued that market conditions in Switzerland have evolved such that there is less and less scope for monopolistic competition in setting local interest rates. As a consequence, they predicted that the differential between foreign and domestic interest rates will continue to erode. Similarly, Sheldon's explanation of the cross-country distribution of international bank deposits also induced him to write that "consistently below-average interest rates could increasingly become a thing of the past in Switzerland." (Sheldon, 1992, p. 217)

## 3. Switzerland as a Financial Center

The success or failure of the Swiss banking and financial industry, like any other domestic industry for that matter, does not depend only on how cost efficient the industry is or how effective it is in attracting customers. As already noted, the options offered by the regulatory environment and a number of factors that influence the attractiveness of Switzerland as a country in which to conduct business also affect the health of the industry. Our research has dealt with these issues under three broad headings each of which is discussed in turn below: locational choice and trade in banking services, the market share of Swiss institutions in international deposit taking and bond issuance, and the attractiveness of Swiss stock markets in an international comparison.

### 3.1. Locational Choice and Trade in Banking Services

Building on the modern theory of international trade in general and on the concept of 'attractiveness' of a country to internationally mobile factors of production (Jones, 1980) in particular, Helbling (1992) studied the formation of financial centres and the determinants of trade in financial services. In Helbling (1993 a) he continues this work with the objective of uncovering the main reasons why foreign financial firms establish branches and subsidiaries in Switzerland. A number of factors are identified as being potentially important. From the traditional theory of foreign direct investment emerges the concept of local informational advantages according to which a bank incurs certain cost advantages, such as lower monitoring costs, by being close to its customers. Active commercial relationships between countries would thus encourage foreign direct investment by banks.

Regulatory differences between countries constitute a second important set of factors influencing the location of financial intermediaries. At least five different types of regulatory measures can be distinguished: (i) restrictions on cross-border capital flows, (ii) measures affecting the cost of intermediation (for instance, capital adequacy and minimum reserve requirements), (iii) direct controls on entry and exit by intermediaries, (iv) restrictions on the type of business a foreign intermediary may engage in, and (v) taxes.

A third group of reasons for foreign investment by financial intermediaries and hence for the emergence of financial centres is the existence of various types of external economies of scale. These may be the result of so called 'thick markets' (Grilli, 1989) associated with a clustering of intermediaries in one location or they may be due to the existence of human capital particularly suited for financial institutions. Finally one might point to considerations such as a stable political environment, a strong currency, and a generally business-friendly atmosphere.

Empirical implementations of these ideas were carried out by Jeger, Haegler, and Theiss (1992) and by Helbling (1993 a). Jeger, Haegler, and Theiss attempted to explain the attractiveness of Switzerland as an international financial centre in competition with other major financial centres. Their empirical results confirmed the importance both of variables related to banking regulation and of macro factors like liberalised trade and direct investment in general. Among the regulatory variables, bank secrecy appeared to be particularly important as an explanation for the presence of foreign banks. Based on their findings, the authors conclude that the attractiveness of Switzerland to foreign banks might suffer should the country fail to enter the European Economic Area (EEA) or, later, the European Community (EC). However, the benefits of the European integration for Switzerland's position as a financial centre could be reduced if this integration would imply sacrificing important elements of the existing bank secrecy provisions.

Helbling (1993 a) focused on the reasons why foreign financial intermediaries have entered the Swiss market and on the evolution of the market share of these foreign firms during the 1970s and the 1980s. He found that a liberal regulatory framework for capital flows had the expected stimulatory effect on the presence of foreign financial intermediaries and that the maintenance of liquid secondary markets with low transactions costs was an important condition for maintaining the Swiss position in international financial markets.

### 3.2. Share of Switzerland in the International Market for Deposits and Bonds

Another measure of the success of a financial center is its market share in internationally contestable lines of businesses such as the market for bank deposits and international bond issues. Camen (1992) and Sheldon (1992) analysed the determinants of the first of these market shares. Focusing exclusively on Switzerland and using time-series data from the Seventies and Eighties, Camen found that both institutional and regulatory factors were important for the decision of investors to hold deposits with banks located in Switzerland. The lack of a withholding tax on fiduciary accounts, bank secrecy, and the safety of the Swiss banking system were shown to be particularly decisive variables. Sheldon, using cross-country estimations found less evidence for the importance of bank secrecy, and only little support for the effects of international tax competition. Grilli, who earlier had found significant effects of these variables in his own empirical explanation of countries' market shares for bank deposits, challenged Sheldon's findings. (Grilli, 1992) On balance, and recalling that Sheldon concentrated on short-term deposits (three months), it seems safe to conclude that differential taxes and regulations, as well as other variables that influence the expected return, at least in part do have an impact on the decision of depositors as to the location of their investments. But the precise size of the impact requires further study.

Camen (1993) confirms his earlier findings that variables identified by economic theory as being important for investment decisions do help explain the evolution of market shares although it appears that a different set of variables is important in the case of international bond issues compared to the case of bank deposits. In bond issues interest rate differentials play an important role whereas this was not the case for deposits. Similarly, tax advantages favoured certain types of deposits in Swiss banks while stamp duties constitute a handicap for bond issues in Switzerland. But in spite of these differences, the basic conclusions remain, namely that regulatory and tax policies can have significant effects on financial markets in Switzerland and therefore on the health of the financial industry.

### 3.3. Competition among stock markets

A final aspect of the competitiveness of the Swiss financial system concerns the stock markets. Helbling (1993 b) analyses the impact of external competitive pressures on Swiss Stock exchanges. A measure of this external pressure is the fact that some fifteen percent of the trading activities in Swiss Blue Chip stocks takes place on the SEAQ International in London.

By studying the evolution of implicit bid-ask spreads for shares that are listed both at Swiss exchanges and in London, and by calculating and analyzing so-called pricing errors, Helbling is able to establish that the external competition has had the impact of lowering transactions costs on the domestic exchanges. Apart from the presumably beneficial effects that domestic investors can reap from this type of development, an implication of Helbling's findings is that financial institutions in Switzerland are under constant pressure from international competition, and that to survive this pressure they must continue to adapt and upgrade their know-how and market position.

## 4. Conclusions

The research project, the results of which are summarised in this final chapter of the present volume, carries the title 'The Swiss Financial Sector at the Turn of the Century'. When at the end some conclusions are taken up again, this does not happen in the sense of one of those forecasts which always tend to stimulate our phantasy, only to become obsolete pretty rapidly afterwards. Our perspective rather is: What are the insights that can be identified on the basis of the analysis of the authors as well as on that of the research results described above? In answering this question the authors address themselves to those responsible for banking policy, economic policy, international trade policy, and to those in charge of the regulation of banking and of financial markets.

Let us remember where we started: Banks and financial markets are internationally under stress. Overcapacity is frequent. In numerous countries the banking system is subject to extended restructuring. Switzerland is no exception. Also in this country the banking industry's structure is changing rapidly. The research showed that the performance of the banks in Switzerland is quite strong if compared internationally. But the industrial landscape is not stable. The discrepancies in terms of performance and costs are pronounced. Market pressure within the country and from abroad will continue to grow. A further accentuation of the selection process must be expected. This implies that we do not think that in the future the banking sector will continue to contribute to the economic prosperity of Switzerland in the same problem-free, doubtless and self-evident way we became accustomed to in the past, e.g. producing a growing proportion of gross value added, based on a rapidly growing labour productivity, and all the same increasing its share in the employment total.

Under today's circumstances bank managements will foremost have to control costs even more. Cost control appears to be a decisive precondition for any further growth. Specialisation is another, and without doubt a well-known catch-word. The advantages of specialisation might lead to a dimishing superiority of the universal bank. But the research results show that specialisation is not a general recipe for success. Specialisation is particularly promising when it is shaped according to a bank's specific strengths with respect to its existing activity profile and its location. The management must identify the strongholds of its bank and develop them further. The same is true for those responsible for economic policy at large, for trade policy and for regulation. Their policies decide on the attractiveness of the Swiss financial centre, which affects the bank managements' decisions as an exogenous variable. In this way, the success of a strategy to specialise depends not only on the ability of management but also on the success of politics in improving the business environment.

During the controversy about the advantages and disadvantages of the participation of Switzerland in the EEA the significance of the competition between economic systems was rightly stressed. Since the negative outcome of the referendum on the EEA Treaty on December 6, 1992, the dice is cast. Switzerland will not quickly enter the EEA. A quick direct entry into the EC is even less likely. Now, Switzerland has the opportunity to become even more active in the field of systems competition. Our research points to the value of the protection of the clients' private sphere (bank secrecy). Outside the EEA, this asset needs to be preserved even more. This is no pleading for a primitive off-shore strategy. Switzerland is a European country. In addition, the country's weight in the financial markets is much to great to allow for a permanent success of regulatory niche playing as the only instrument to control competitors. The international rules of the game will continue to require to be observed by Switzerland, even if this country is not formally integrated in the EC or the EEA. On the other hand it would appear equally absurd to sacrify existing advantages in terms of a more liberal regulation and supervision for the benefit of Eurocompatibility, if this would not lead to further concrete economic or political gains. Similarly, it would also be a mistake not to dismantle evident disadvantages still existing e.g. in the area of transaction and witholding taxes. Also, it would seem out of question to seek to protect the financial sector of Switzerland against competition from abroad by trade policy measures. The rôle of trade policy on the contrary is to secure the non-discriminatory access of Swiss firms to foreign markets. In this way, and not by protectionist and anti-competitive policies, trade policy can contribute to the strengthening of the competitiveness of the Swiss financial centre.

Further recommendations apply to competition policy. This policy also ought to be developed further autonomously after the negative vote on the EEA Treaty. Structural change must not be obstructed. Obstacles, motivated by distributional or regional policy considerations, must not be introduced. All the same, it appears to be justified that simultaneously measures are taken to prevent disruption caused by bankruptcies, a possibility never to be excluded in the field of banking. Consequently, the corresponding measures taken by banking associations and government institutions are welcomed in principle.

A special problem arises in relation to concentration. In general, it appears to be true, that "cost efficiency is better served by adequate cost control than by mergers." (OECD, 1992, p. 131) But in the area of banking, depositor as well as systemic risks very often can be better controlled through a merger or an acquisition than by individually attempts to control costs in order to preserve a bank's independence. In the light of this it is difficult to accept without reservation the request for the introduction of merger control also in the banking sector. (Vontobel, 1992)

Let us end with a note of caution: The research results summarised in this chapter are not readily exploited for the purpose of policy recommendations. This was neither the aim of the numerous authors of the contributions to the project nor of ourselves.

What we hope to have shown, however, is, that empirical work, which is based on economic theory, can contribute to the solution of problems that are important for the Swiss economy, its policy makers, regulators and managers.

Table 1

## Top Ten
Biggest banks, by capital

| Then (1980) | $bn | Now (1990) | $bn |
|---|---|---|---|
| 1. Crédit agricole | 6.2 | 1. Sumitomo | 15.7 |
| 2. National Westminster | 5.1 | 2. Dai-Ichi Kangyo | 14.8 |
| 3. Barclays | 4.8 | 3. Fuji | 13.8 |
| 4. Bank America | 3.9 | 4. Sanwa | 13.4 |
| 5. Citicorp | 3.9 | 5. Union Bank of Switzerland | 13.2 |
| 6. Banco do Brasil | 3.6 | 6. Crédit Agricole | 13.2 |
| 7. Lloyds | 3.3 | 7. Mitsui Taiyo Kobe | 12.2 |
| 8. Midland | 3.2 | 8. Barclays | 11.9 |
| 9. Paribas | 3.0 | 9. Mitsubishi | 11.9 |
| 10. Allgemene Spaar-en Lijfrenteras | 3.0 | 10. National Westminster | 10.7 |

Source: *The Banker*

Table 2

## Performance of banking systems in comparison: Estimates for the period 1981-1990

(Average values, all figures in %)

| | USA | JAP | UK* | GER | FRA | SWI |
|---|---|---|---|---|---|---|
| Return on assets | 0.82 | 0.50 | 0.80 | 0.64 | 0.37 | 0.71 |
| Return on equity | 13.49 | 20.48 | 16.85 | 17.90 | 14.16 | 11.20 |
| Interest margin | 3.33 | 1.26 | 3.15 | 2.30 | 2.47 | 1.38 |
| Unit costs | 67.62 | 65.73 | 65.75 | 62.57 | 67.31 | 58.55 |
| Provisions | 0.69 | 0.04 | 0.92 | 0.45 | 0.59 | 0.50 |
| Own capital ratio | 6.12 | 2.53 | 4.93 | 3.57 | 2.64 | 6.35 |

* Average values 1984-1990

Sources: OECD, Swiss National Bank

Table 3

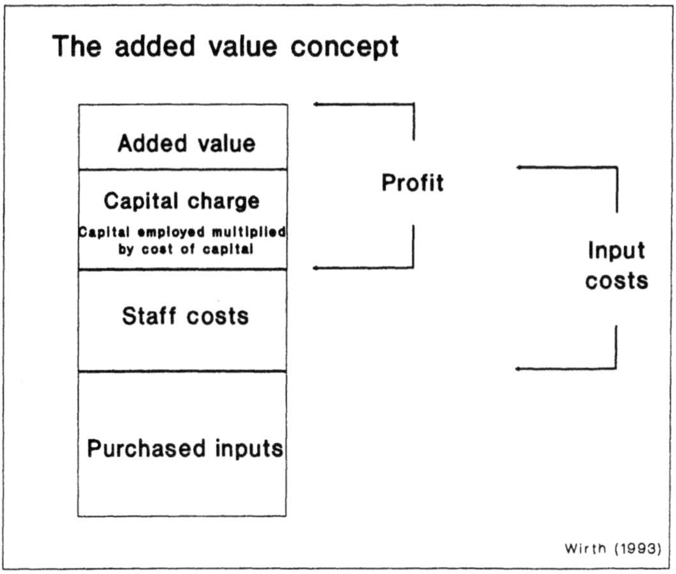


Table 4

Added value over input costs AV/IC
(cumulative frequency function for 455 banks, 1990)

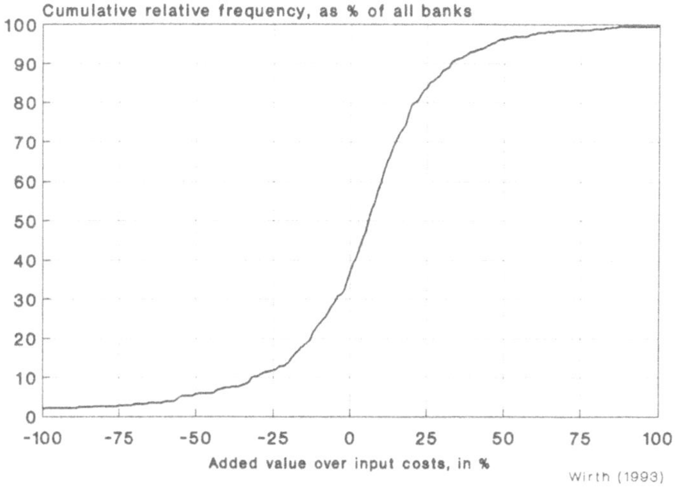

**Literature**

Berger, A., Humphrey, D. (1990), 'The Dominance of Inefficiencies over Scale and Product Mix Economies in Banking', Finance and Economics Discussion Series, Nr. 107, Federal Reserve Board, Washington D.C.

Blattner, N., Genberg, H., Swoboda, A. (eds.) (1992), Competitiveness in Banking, Heidelberg.

Bossard, A., Wirth, M., Blattner, N. (1992), 'The Swiss Banking Sector: Development and Outlook', in: Blattner et al. (1992)

Camen, U. (1992), 'The Swiss Position in the International Market for Non-Bank Deposits', in: Blattner et al. (1992).

Camen, U. (1993), 'The Swiss Share in International Deposit and Bond Markets', in this volume.

Genberg, H., Helbling, Th., Neftci, S. (1992), 'Monopoly Power in Swiss Financial Markets', in: Blattner et al. (1992).

Grilli, V. (1989), 'Financial Markets', in: Economic Policy Vol. 4, No. 2.

Grilli, V. (1992), 'Comment', in: Blattner et al. (1992).

Haegler, U., Jeger, M. (1993), 'Explaining the Performance of Swiss Banks from 1987 - 1990', in this volume.

Helbling, Th. (1992), 'Regulation and Technology as Determinants of International Trade in Banking Services', in: Blattner et al. (1992).

Helbling, Th. (1993 a), 'Explaining the Presence of Foreign Banks in Switzerland', in this volume.

Helbling, Th. (1993 b), 'The Effect of Foreign Competition on Swiss Stock Markets', in this volume.

Jeger, M., Haegler, U., Theiss, R. (1992), 'On the Attractiveness of International Financial Centres', in: Blattner et al. (1992).

Jones, R.W. (1980), 'Comparative and Absolute Advantage', in: Schweiz. Zeitschrift für Volkswirtschaft und Statistik, 116, 3.

OECD (1992), Banks under Stress, Paris.

Porter, M. E. (1990), The Competitive Advantage of Nations, London.

Sheldon, G. (1992), 'Explaining the Cross-Country Distribution of International Bank Deposits', in: Blattner et al. (1992).

Sheldon, G., Haegler, U. (1993), 'Economies of Scale and Scope and Inefficiencies in Swiss Banking', in this volume.

Vontobel, H.-D. (1992), 'Gedanken zur Reform des Finanzplatzes Schweiz', in: Vontobel, H.-D., and Morscher, L. (1992), Wettbewerb als Chance, Zürich.

Wirth, M. (1993), 'Measuring the Performance of Banks: Conceptual Problems and Results for Switzerland (1987 - 1990)', in this volume.

**Comment on**

**Niklaus Blattner, Hans Genberg, Alexander Swoboda: "Banking Policy and Regulation in Switzerland: Summary and Implications of Two Years of Research"**

**Aloys Schwietert**

## 1. Introduction

Let me first say that I am not going to comment on Blattner et al. paper as a peer from the academic research sphere. Having left university back in the Fifties and having worked for years now within a large universal bank, I prefer to offer some remarks more from the outside or, perhaps I should say, from the point of view of a 'consumer'. For after all, as I am sure you will agree, one of the purposes of this research is to provide the banks themselves - as well as the regulatory authorities - with useful input on which to base their actions.

Well, to start with, there is one fundamental question I want to deal with right away. Does the kind of literature discussed at this seminar find a receptive audience with banks in the first place? I am pleased to be able to answer with an unequivocal "yes". Not only on behalf of my own bank, but certainly for many other banks as well. That, of course, doesn't necessarily mean that the type of paper produced here is part of every bank executive's bed-time reading! But in modern organizational structures based on the division of labour, virtually any bank beyond a certain size has a unit or department whose job it is to keep itself - and the bank - up to date on current research into the financial markets and draw the relevant conclusions for steering corporate policy. We very much appreciate therefore the highly topical applied research programme of the two Institutes involved as well as the support it got from the Swiss National Science Foundation.

## 2. The optimal size of a bank

A good example of the interest aroused within the bank by this research is the question of the optimal size we should be aiming for. Not all that long ago, 'size' was an issue the big Swiss banks approached with very mixed feelings. The first wave of deregulation in the early 1980's and the strong inroads made by the Japanese into international lending supplied the arguments for those pundits who saw ongoing concentration combined with a series of mega-mergers as being the inevitable consequence. Concrete figures on the pattern of the overall average cost curve were not available. Even if they had been, they wouldn't have played much of a role. At that time, the talk was only of market share and market influence.

Those days are very definitely gone. And I know of scarcely any bank which has not thought twice about the issue of growth and optimum size. From our internal discussions at Swiss Bank Corporation I can report that, in addition to our own insights and practical experience, the numerous academic studies which show little evidence of 'economies of scale and scope' beyond certain relatively low benchmarks have been attentively digested. We ourselves - based on ongoing comparisons of the earnings performance of around 30 internationally active banks which we have defined as our 'peer group' - have reached the conclusion that even for an international, universal bank-style player a headcount of 20 - 25 000 represents a size beyond which certain relative performance ratios evidently cannot be improved on and beyond which purely organizational risks take on an added dimension.

Within our self-defined international peer group of 25 banks, Swiss Bank Corporation last year held place no. 9 based on a wide range of criteria. Looking into Wirth's paper, which was summarized by Blattner et al., I learned that among the 50 banks with the absolute highest profits in 1990 Swiss Bank Corporation (and for that matter our big Swiss competitors, too) fare rather badly. In terms of productivity, ROE and ROA we belong to the third quartile only. Depending on the bank and the criterion applied, the rankings range from 25 to 41. And remember, that's out of 50! These results make me wonder if, in this sort of analysis, we are not comparing apples and oranges. The best performers are small private banks or the subsidiaries of foreign institutes which can bank on their parent's name in Switzerland. If I draw on our internal data relating to private banking only, the results change remarkably in favour of Swiss Bank Corporation. So what is the conclusion we should draw from the comparison of measured performance of almost all the banks working in Switzerland? Should we leave? Should we slim down and become a niche player? Who bears the cost of slimming down? How long can you benefit from playing the niche in an open and highly competitive, constantly changing market?

### 3. Risk adjusted returns and cyclical aspects

Blattner et al. say themselves that we have to be careful in interpreting the results of the research which is based on data for 5 years only, i.e. 1987 - 1991. I could not agree more. The main argument I have concerning interbank performance comparisons, especially if the institutions involved offer different financial services, relates to the cyclical pattern which has to be factored out. There is the overall business cycle as well as the cyclical nature of certain financial activities, and the take-off and maturing phases on markets for special financial products. Think of the bond market euphoria in the early 1980's the subsequent slowdown, the revival in 1988/89 and the renewed slowdown in 1990. Or think of the rapidly growing market for derivates, which hardly existed 10 years ago.

Furthermore, and quite apart from the cyclical movements, it is to be expected that the more volatile the business, the more volatile the return on equity or on assets. Interbank comparisons therefore should refer to risk adjusted return figures. If they are not available, the only solution is to base those comparisons at least on figures covering more than one cycle, and that means covering at least a decade.

### 4. Strengthen your stengths

Specialisation leads to superior performance. This is another conclusion drawn from the empirical research work discussed by Blattner et al. Probably based on the experiences Blattner was able to collect in his position as economic advisor to the Swiss Bankers Association the authors modify the conclusion quite a bit in order ro arrive at a proper prescription. The prescription is not: "Specialise, and you will prosper! but rather develop your comparative advantages efficiently in order to make specialisation succeed!" Strengthen your strengths would be another way we could formulate this recipe and once again our experience at Swiss Bank Corporation during the 1980's confirms precisely this. And it can be confirmed not only for certain professional capabilities in the more narrow sense. It is equally true in relation to business culture and managerial skills.

For universal banks in the traditional continental sense, the question is not how to be all things to all men but rather to define the special profile which best fits their individual tradition, culture and comparative advantages. Within almost every market segment, universal banks have to compete with strong specialized institutions which focus on that particular business (not to say 'niche'). The profit differentials Haegler and Jeger found between specialising in traditional banking on the one side and off balance sheet activities on the other highlight the critical decisions a universal bank is confronted with today. Fortunately, the term 'off balance sheet business' is so vague that a good part of it can readily be found in traditional good old prudent banking!

## 5. The hidden potential for cost reductions

Based on the paper produced by Sheldon and Haegler, Blattner et al. write that the technical efficiency of Swiss banks is rather high while allocative efficiency is much lower. If this distinction means that we are producing certain services not at the most feasible cost but with rather perfect and advanced systems, my comment is 100 % affirmative. Whether more than 40 % of our costs could be saved I don't know. But that we can and will improve our allocative efficiency remarkably in the years to come I am sure. And, if we achieve only a part of this rationalisation potential, I would not be worried at all about our international competitiveness.

This - by the way - is one of the points we missed in Moody's recent study on Swiss Banks. The big banks in particular stand to gain from this expected change. More efficient cost management has become not only a popular slogan but also a concrete strategic target at all big banks.

## List of Authors

**Peter Aerni,** Basel Centre for Economics and Business, University of Basel, P.O. Box, CH-4003 Basel

**Prof. Dr. Niklaus Blattner,** Labour and Industrial Economics Research Unit (FAI), University of Basel, Missionsstrasse 64 A, CH-4055 Basel, and Swiss Bankers Association, P.O. Box 4182, CH-4002 Basel

**Prof. Dr. Pascal Bridel,** University of Lausanne, CH-1015 Lausanne-Dorigny

**Dr. Ulrich Camen,** The Graduate Institute of International Studies (IUHEI), University of Geneva, P.O. Box 36, CH-1211 Geneva 21

**Prof. Dr. Günter Franke,** University of Konstanz, P.O. Box 5560, D-7750 Konstanz 1

**Dr. Thomas Gehrig,** Banking Research Center, Kellogg Graduate School of Management, Northwestern University, Leverone Hall, 2001 Sheridan Road, Evanston, Illinois 60208, USA

**Prof. Dr. Hans Genberg,** The Graduate Institute of International Studies (IUHEI), University of Geneva, P.O. Box 36, CH-1211 Geneva 21

**Claudio Generali,** Banca del Gottardo, P.O. Box, CH-6901 Lugano

**Urs Haegler,** London School of Economics and Political Science, Houghton Street, London WC 2AE, U.K.

**Thomas Helbling,** The Graduate Institute of International Studies (IUHEI), University of Geneva, P.O. Box 36, CH-1211 Geneva 21

**Dr. Werner Hermann,** Swiss National Bank, P.O. Box, CH-8022 Zurich

**Dr. Matthias Jeger,** Société Fiduciaire Suisse - Coopers & Lybrand SA, P.O. Box, CH-4002 Basel

**Prof. Dr. Oliver Landmann,** Programme Director, Swiss National Science Foundation, National Research Programme 28, Möndenweg 77, D-7854 Inzlingen

**Dr. Richard T. Meier,** Zurich Stock Exchange, P.O. Box, CH-8021 Zurich

**Beat C. Philipp,** Bank J. Vontobel & Co. Ltd., P.O. Box, CH-8022 Zurich

**Dr. Aloys Schwietert,** Swiss Bank Corporation, P.O. Box, CH-4002 Basel

**PD Dr. George Sheldon,** Labour and Industrial Economics Research Unit (FAI), University of Basle, Missionsstrasse 64 A, CH-4055 Basel

**Prof. Dr. Klaus Spremann,** University of Hong Kong Business School, Hong Kong, and Swiss Institute of Banking and Finance, University of St. Gallen, Merkurstrasse 1, CH-9000 St. Gallen

**Prof. Dr. Alexander K. Swoboda,** The Graduate Institute of International Studies (IUHEI), University of Geneva, P.O. Box 36, CH-1211 Geneva 21

**Matthias Wirth,** Swiss Bankers Association, P.O. Box 4182, CH-4002 Basel

**Prof. Dr. Peter Zweifel,** Institute for Empirical Research in Economics, University of Zurich, Blümlisalpstrasse 10, CH-8006 Zurich

**List of Participants**

Peter Aerni, Basel
Dr. Svein Andresen, Basel
Jan Atteslander, Bern
Andrea Behrends, Bern
Prof. Dr. Niklaus Blattner, Basel
Dr. Andreas Bossard, Basel
Prof. Dr. Pascal Bridel, Lausanne-Dorigny
Dr. Ulrich Camen, Geneva
Dr. Pierre-Alexis Cosandier, Geneva
Dr. Christian Etter, Bern
Robert Fluri, Zurich
Prof. Dr. Günter Franke, Konstanz
Dr. Thomas Gehrig, Evanston
Prof. Dr. Hans Genberg, Geneva
Claudio Generali, Lugano
Dr. Urs Graf, Basel
Prof. Dr. Olivier de la Grandville, Geneva
Urs Haegler, London
Thomas Helbling, Geneva
Dr. Werner Hermann, Zurich
Prof. Dr. Gérard Hertig, Geneva
Dr. Matthias Jeger, Basel
Prof. Dr. Jacques l'Huillier, Geneva
Prof. Dr. Jean-Christian Lambelet, Lausanne-Dorigny
Prof. Dr. Oliver Landmann, Inzlingen
Jean-Luc Lederrey, Geneva
Prof. Dr. Henri Loubergé, Geneva
Sylvain Matthey, Basel
Dr. Richard T. Meier, Zurich
Prof. Dr. Salih Neftci, Geneva
Aidan O'Connor, Lausanne-Dorigny
Zsolt Papp, Zurich
Debra Perry, Geneva
Beat C. Philipp, Zurich
Dr. Markus Ruffner, Zurich
Dr. Gary Sampson, Geneva
Dr. Claude de Saussure, Geneva
Urs Schneider, Carouge/Geneva
Dr. Aloys Schwietert, Basel
PD Dr. George Sheldon, Basel
Raju Jan Singh, Geneva
Prof. Dr. Klaus Spremann, St. Gallen
Marian Stepczynski, Geneva
Prof. Dr. Alexander K. Swoboda, Geneva
Roland Theiss, Basel
Robert Trachsel, Zurich
Andrew Walo, Zurich
Remigi Winzap, Bern
Matthias Wirth, Basel
Stefan Wolter, Zurich
Prof. Dr. Peter Zweifel, Zurich

# Studies in Contemporary Economics

B. Hamminga, Neoclassical Theory Structure and Theory Development. IX, 174 pages. 1983.

J. Dermine, Pricing Policies of Financial Intermediaries. VII, 174 pages. 1984.

Economic Consequences of Population Change in Industrialized Countries. Proceedings. 1983. Edited by G. Steinmann. X, 415 pages. 1984.

Problems of Advanced Economies. Proceedings, 1982. Edited by N. Miyawaki. VI, 319 pages. 1984.

Studies in Labor Market Dynamics. Proceedings, 1982. Edited by G. R. Neumann and N. C. Westergard-Nielsen. X, 285 pages. 1985.

A. Pfingsten, The Measurement of Tax Progression. VI, 131 pages. 1986.

Causes of Contemporary Stagnation. Proceedings, 1984. Edited by H. Frisch and B. Gahlen. IX, 216 pages. 1986.

O. Flaaten, The Economics of Multispecies Harvesting. VII, 162 pages. 1988.

D. Laussel, W. Marois, A. Soubeyran, (Eds.), Monetary Theory and Policy. Proceedings, 1987. XVIII, 383 pages. 1988.

G. Rubel, Factors Determining External Debt. VI, 264 pages. 1988.

B. C. J. van Velthoven, The Endogenization of Government Behaviour in Macroeconomic Models. XI, 367 pages. 1989.

A. Wenig, K. F. Zimmermann (Eds.) 3, Demographic Change and Economic Development. XII, 325 pages. 1989.

J. K. Brunner, Theory of Equitable Taxation. VIII, 217 pages. 1989.

E. van Imhoff, Optimal Economic Growth and Non-Stable Population. IX, 218 pages. 1989.

P. S. A. Renaud, Applied Political Economic Modelling. XII, 242 pages. 1989.

H. König (Ed.), Economics of Wage Determination. XI, 373 pages. 1990.

C. Dagum, M. Zenga (Eds.) Income and Wealth Distribution, Inequality and Poverty. Proceedings, XIII, 415 pages. 1990.

A. J. H. C. Schram, Voter Behavior in Economic Perspective. X, 274 pages. 1991.

J. B. Woittiez, Modelling and Empirical Evaluation of Labour Supply Behaviour. VI, 232 pages. 1991.

R. Arnason, T. Bjorndal (Eds.), Essays on the Economics of Migratory Fish Stocks. VIII, 197 pages. 1991.

Ch. Czerkawski, Theoretical and Policy-Oriented Aspects of the External Debt Economics. VII, 150 pages. 1991.

D. Stern, J. M. M. Ritzen (Eds.), Market Failure in Training? VII, 233 pages. 1991.

M. Savioz, New Issues in the Theory of Investment. XVI, 216 pages. 1992.

W. Franz (Ed.) Structural Unemployment. X, 132 pages. 1992.

N. Blattner, H. Genberg, A. Swoboda, (Eds.), Competitiveness in Banking. VIII, 315 pages. 1992.

M. Carlberg, Monctary and Fiscal Dynamics. VIII, 194 pages. 1992.

H.-J. Wagener, On the Theory and Policy of Systemic Change. VIII, 234 pages. 1993.

E. Wurzel, An Econometric Analysis of Individual Unemployment Duration in West Germany. V, 244 pages. 1993.

W. Gebauer, Foundations of European Central Bank Policy. VI, 258 pages. 1993.

G. de Wit, Determinants of Self-employment. XII, 194 pages. 1993.

W. Smolny, Dynamic Factor Demand in a Rationing Context. VIII, 242 pages. 1993.

A. Haufler, Commodity Tax Harmonization in the European Community. XIV, 216 pages. 1993.

N. Blattner, H. Genberg, A. Swoboda (Eds.), Banking in Switzerland. VIII, 330 pages. 1993.